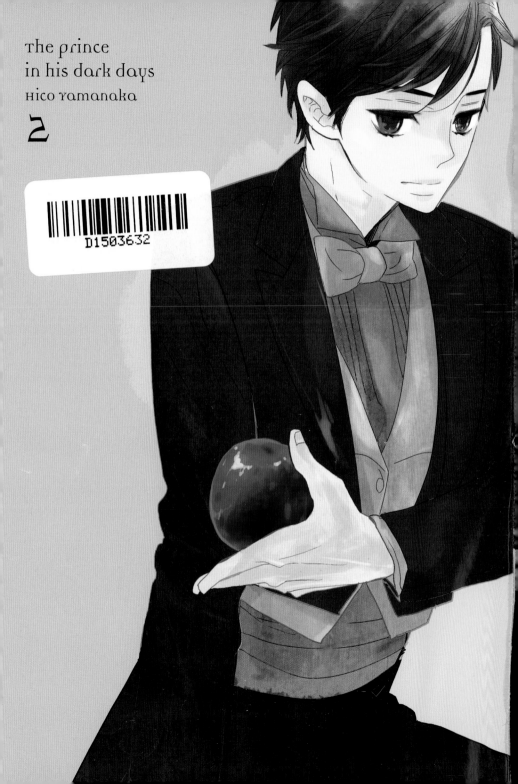

The prince in his dark days

Hico Yamanaka

2

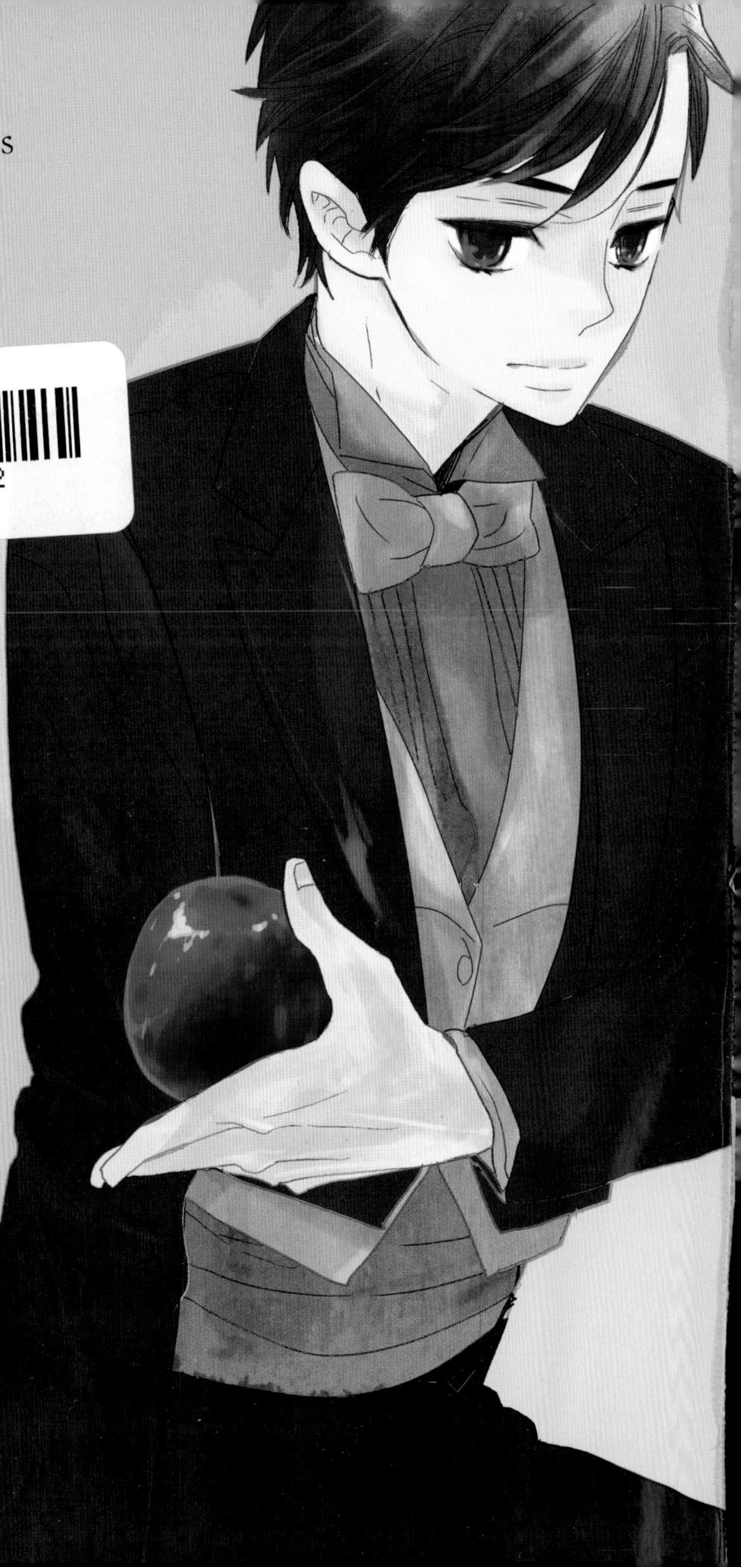

contents

The prince in his Dark Days

Hico Yamanaka

character

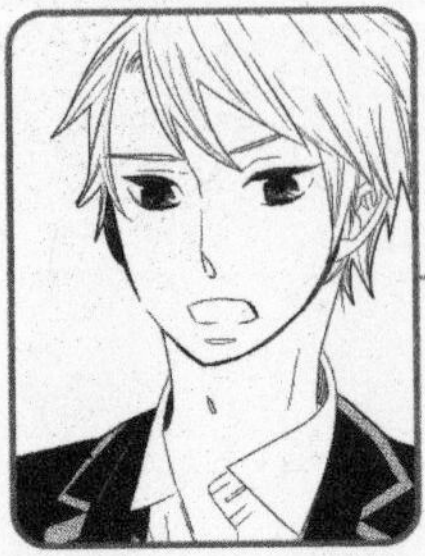

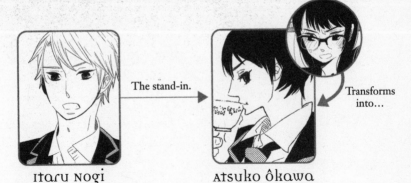

The stand-in.

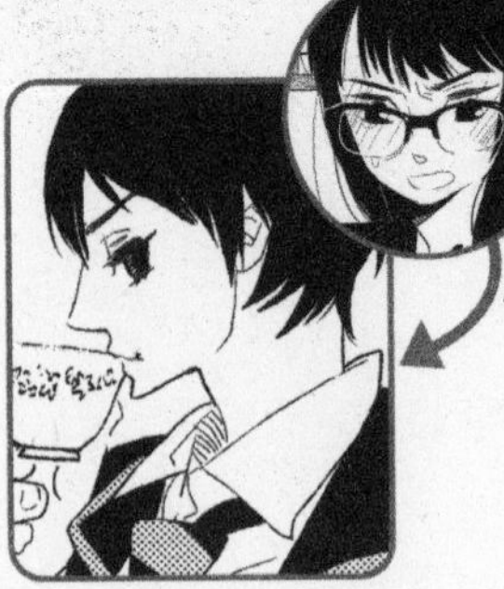

Transforms into...

Itaru Nogi

Heir to a wealthy family.
His hobby of dressing in women's clothing is a dire secret. Fed up with the restraints of his princely lifestyle, he runs away.

Atsuko Ôkawa

A high school girl born into a poor household. She looks just like Itaru, so she is dressing as a man and acting as his double.

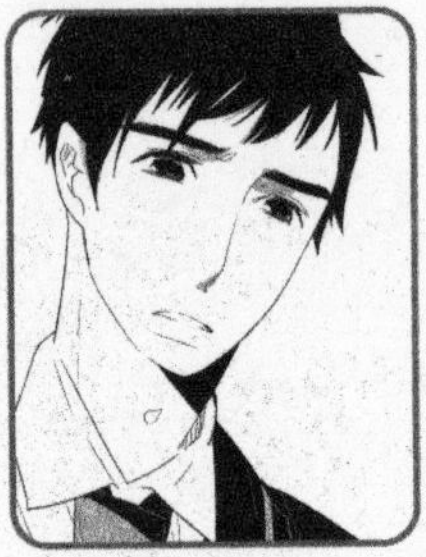

Nobunari Mukai

A longtime friend of Itaru and Ryô.
He is in love with Itaru.

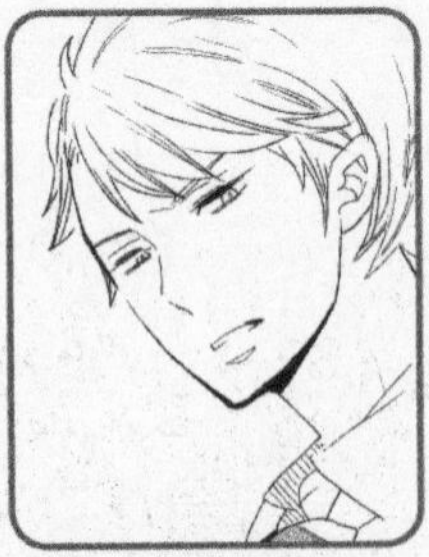

Ryô Sekiuchi

Itaru's half-brother.
After Itaru's disappearance, he trains Atsuko and accompanies her everywhere.

story

Atsuko is a high school girl living a miserable life of poverty. One day, she meets Itaru—the heir to the Nogi Group—and his right-hand men, Ryô and Nobunari. Atsuko's fate changes when Itaru, the wealthy heir who looks just like her, suddenly disappears. She begins to dress as a man and live in a palatial estate as Itaru's double. Despite her rigorous training and her heartbreak over Nobunari, the joy of being needed inspires Atsuko to continue her efforts to be the perfect prince. But palace life isn't as charmed as she had believed—she discovers complicated relationships between the prince and his associates, and the suffering that comes with them...

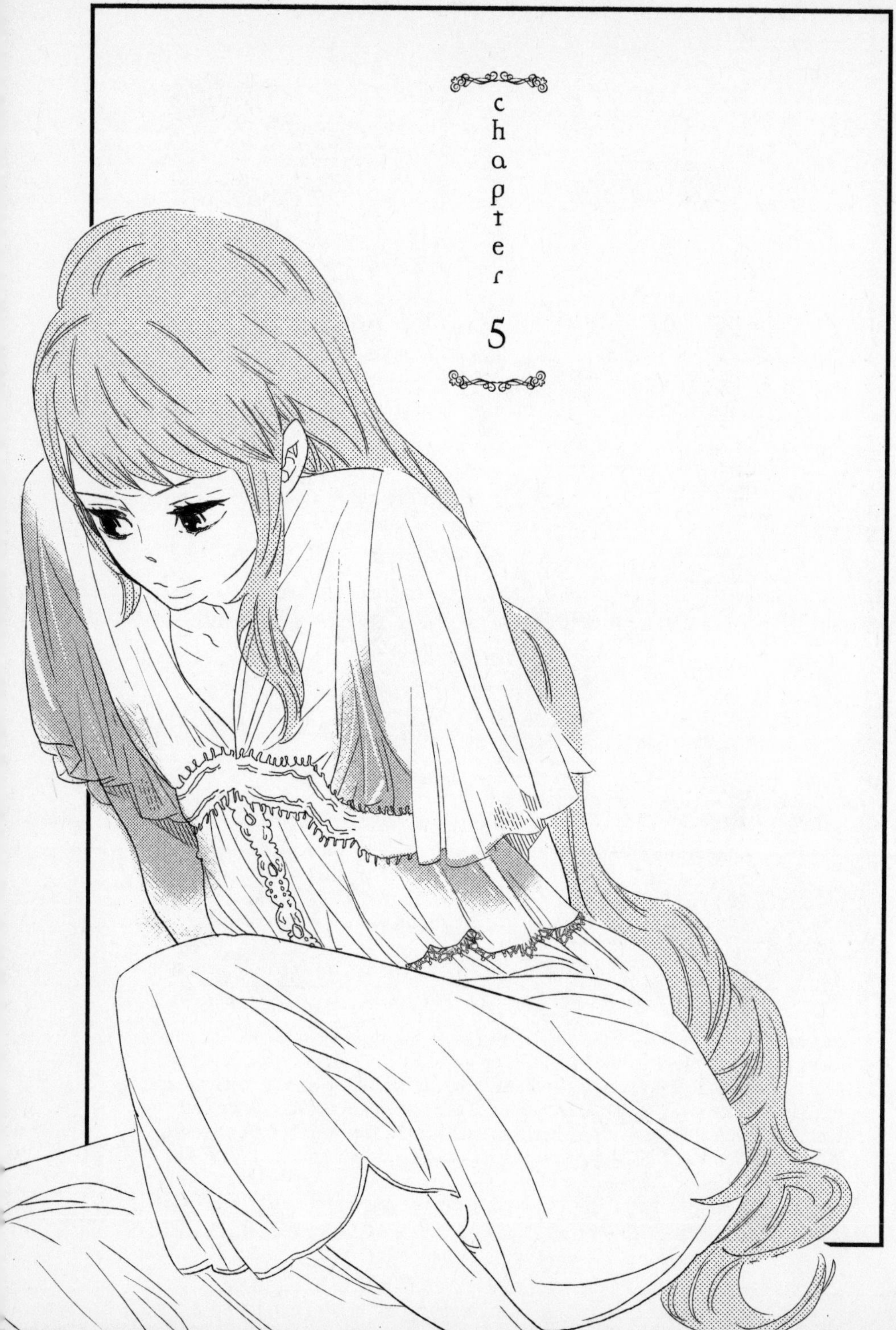
chapter
5

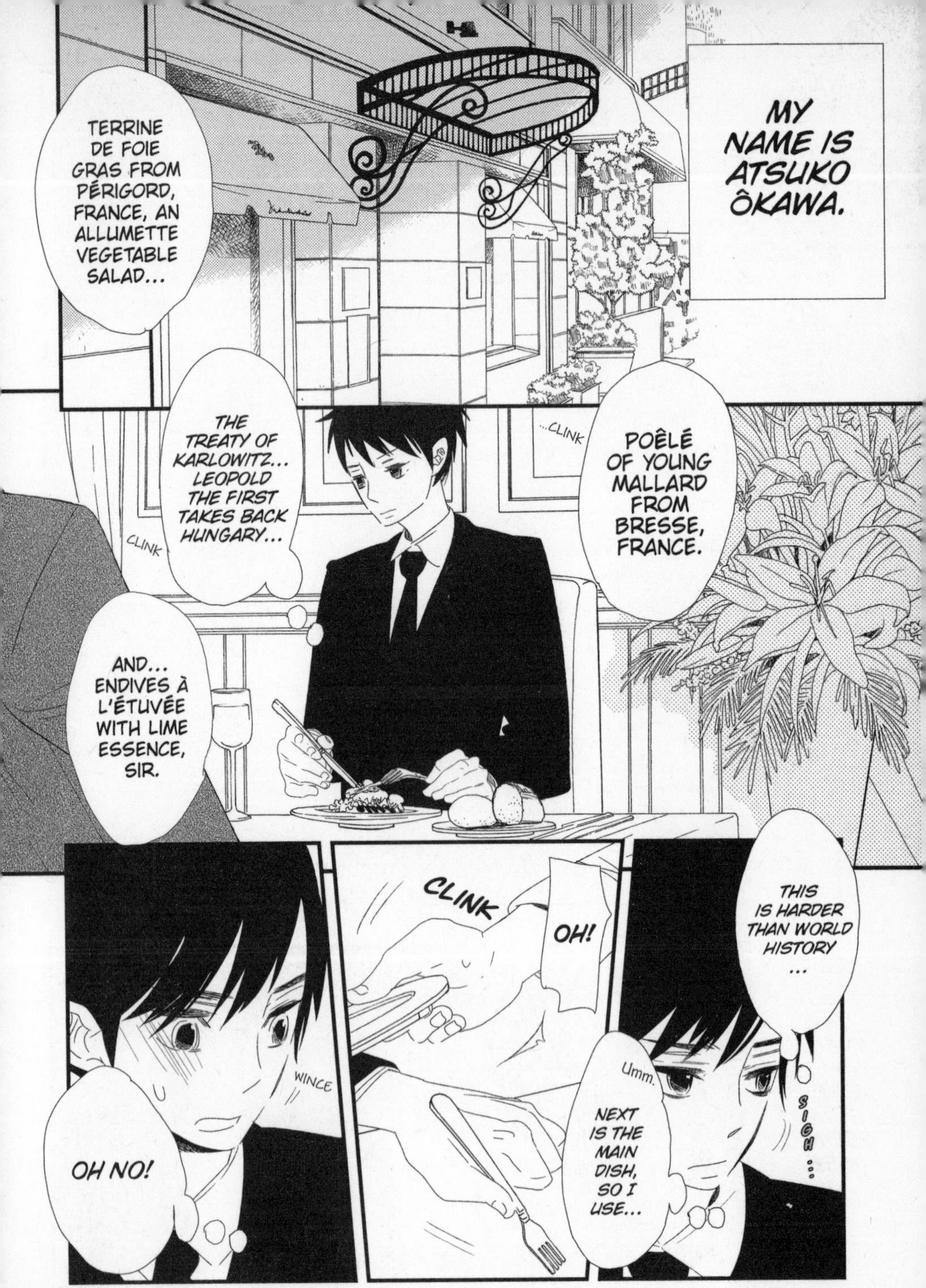
MY NAME IS ATSUKO ÔKAWA.
TERRINE DE FOIE GRAS FROM PÉRIGORD, FRANCE, AN ALLUMETTE VEGETABLE SALAD...
...CLINK
POÊLÉ OF YOUNG MALLARD FROM BRESSE, FRANCE.
THE TREATY OF KARLOWITZ... LEOPOLD THE FIRST TAKES BACK HUNGARY...
CLINK
AND... ENDIVES À L'ÉTUVÉE WITH LIME ESSENCE, SIR.
THIS IS HARDER THAN WORLD HISTORY ...
Umm.
NEXT IS THE MAIN DISH, SO I USE...
SIGH...
CLINK
OH!
WINCE
OH NO!

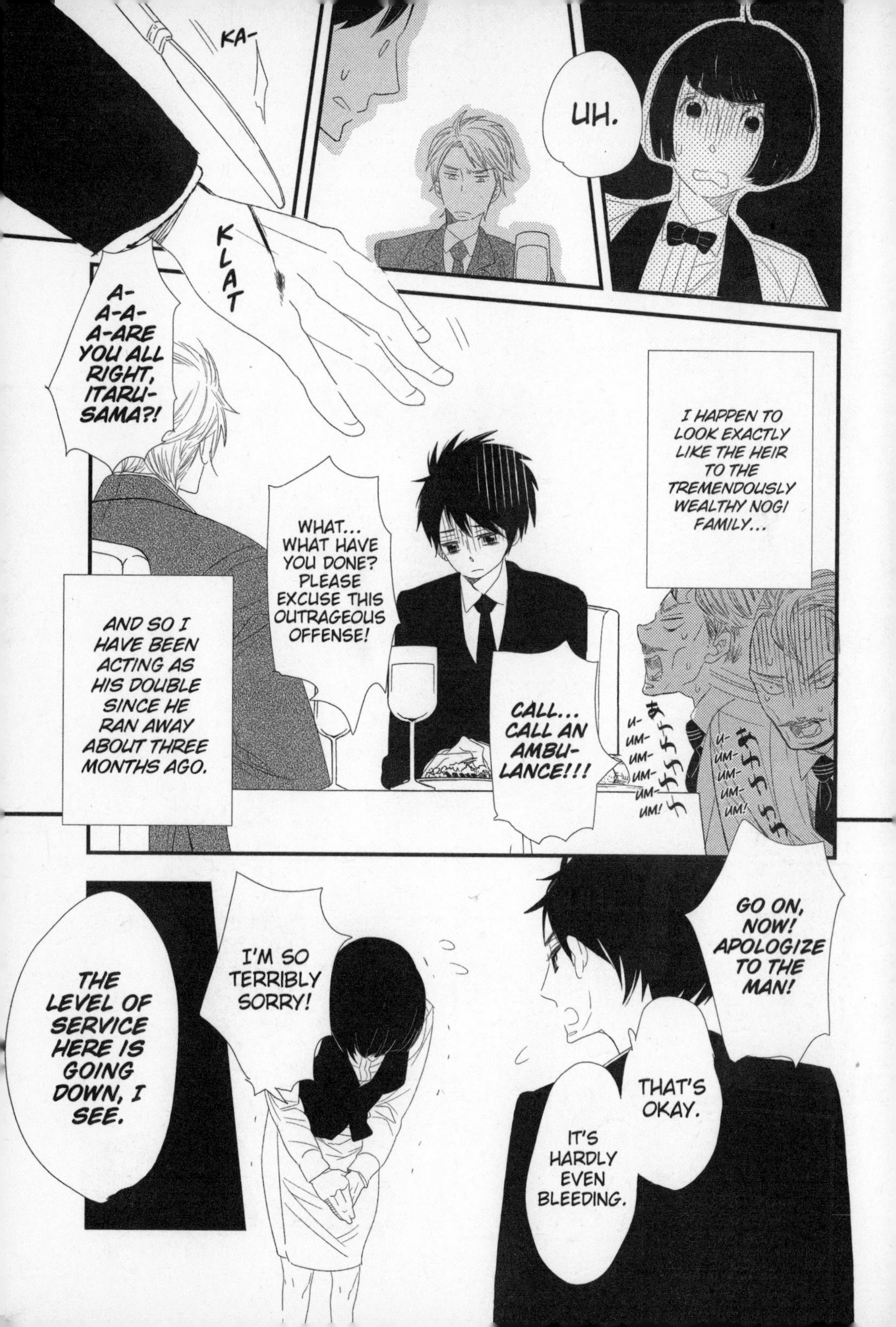
UH.
KA-
KLAT
A-A-A-A-ARE YOU ALL RIGHT, ITARU-SAMA?!
I HAPPEN TO LOOK EXACTLY LIKE THE HEIR TO THE TREMENDOUSLY WEALTHY NOGI FAMILY...
U-UM-UM-UM-UM-UM!
U-UM-UM-UM-UM-UM!
CALL... CALL AN AMBULANCE!!!
WHAT... WHAT HAVE YOU DONE? PLEASE EXCUSE THIS OUTRAGEOUS OFFENSE!
AND SO I HAVE BEEN ACTING AS HIS DOUBLE SINCE HE RAN AWAY ABOUT THREE MONTHS AGO.
GO ON, NOW! APOLOGIZE TO THE MAN!
THAT'S OKAY.
IT'S HARDLY EVEN BLEEDING.
I'M SO TERRIBLY SORRY!
THE LEVEL OF SERVICE HERE IS GOING DOWN, I SEE.

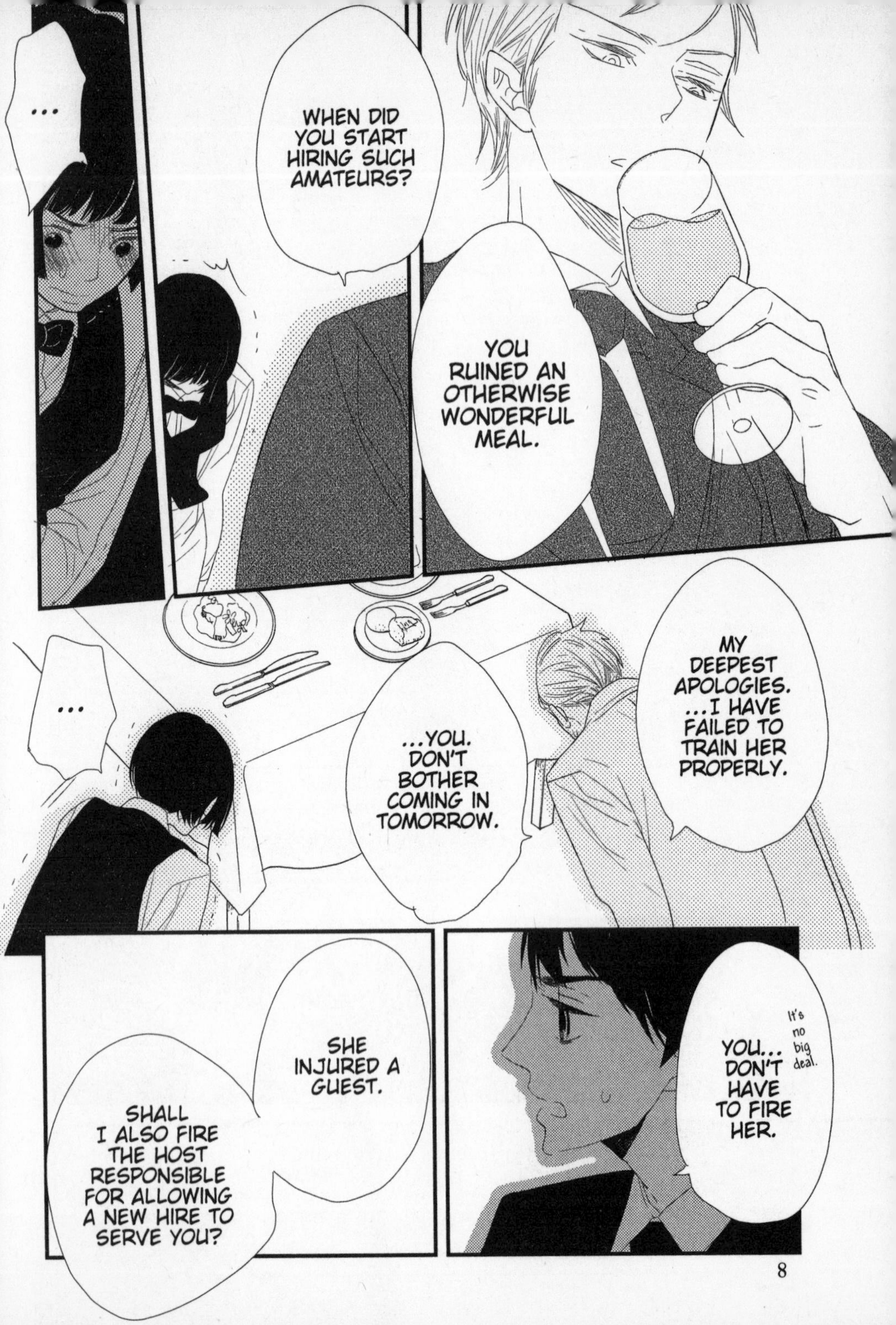
WHEN DID YOU START HIRING SUCH AMATEURS?
YOU RUINED AN OTHERWISE WONDERFUL MEAL.
...
MY DEEPEST APOLOGIES. ...I HAVE FAILED TO TRAIN HER PROPERLY.
...YOU. DON'T BOTHER COMING IN TOMORROW.
...
YOU... DON'T HAVE TO FIRE HER.
It's no big deal.
SHE INJURED A GUEST.
SHALL I ALSO FIRE THE HOST RESPONSIBLE FOR ALLOWING A NEW HIRE TO SERVE YOU?

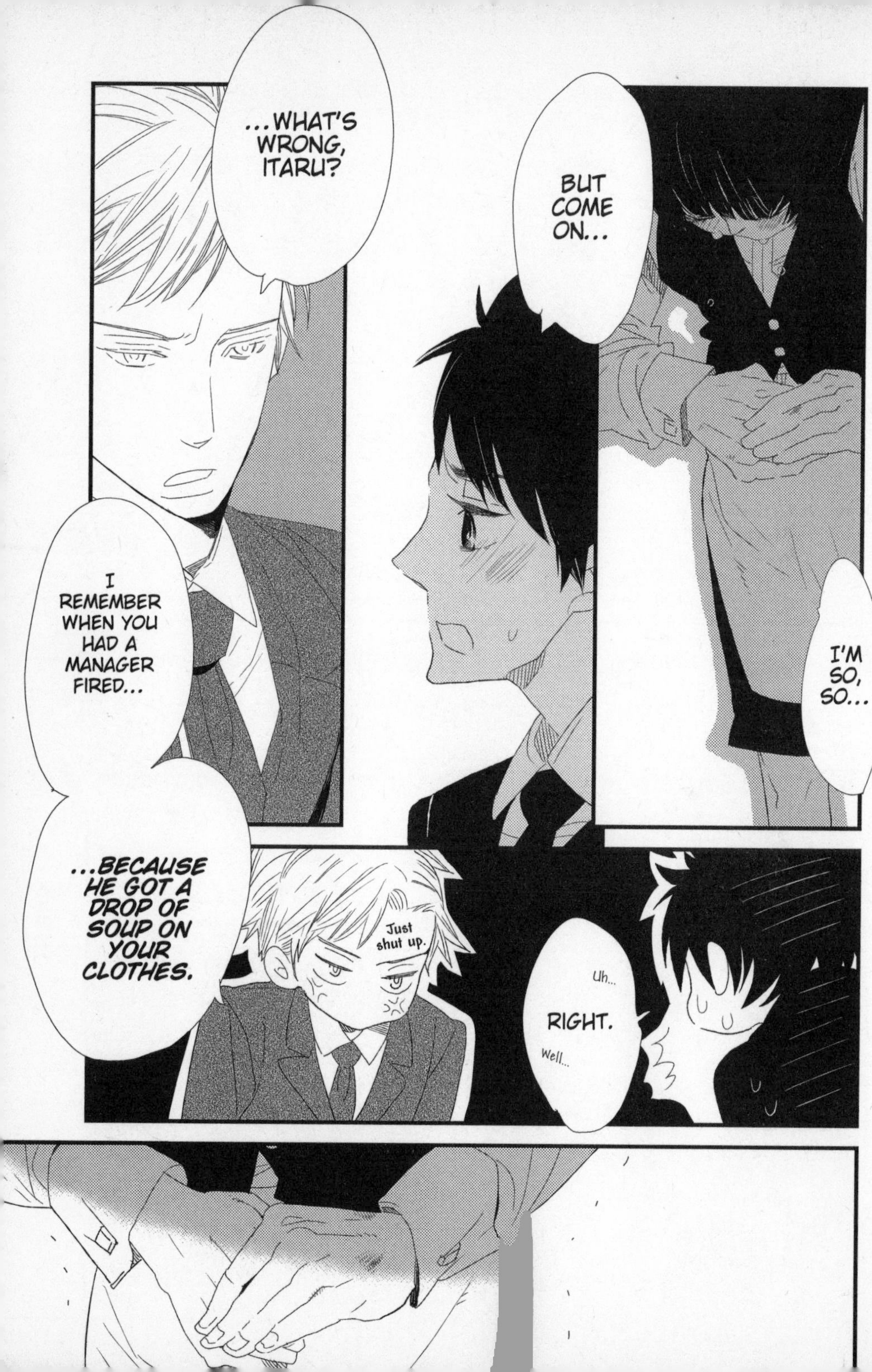
I'M SO, SO...
BUT COME ON...
...WHAT'S WRONG, ITARU?
I REMEMBER WHEN YOU HAD A MANAGER FIRED...
...BECAUSE HE GOT A DROP OF SOUP ON YOUR CLOTHES.
Uh...
RIGHT.
Well...
Just shut up.

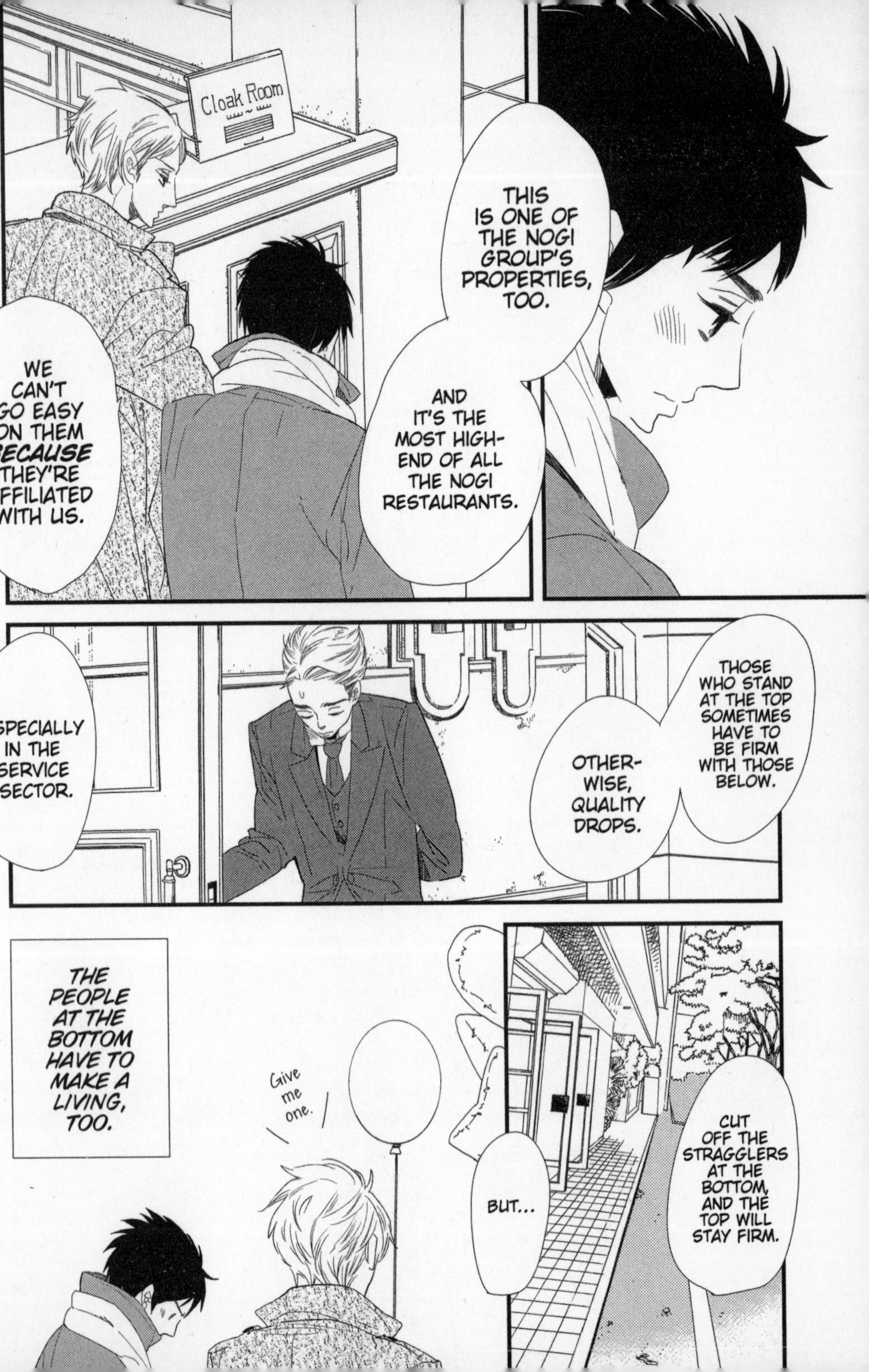
THIS IS ONE OF THE NOGI GROUP'S PROPERTIES, TOO.
AND IT'S THE MOST HIGH-END OF ALL THE NOGI RESTAURANTS.
WE CAN'T GO EASY ON THEM *BECAUSE* THEY'RE AFFILIATED WITH US.
THOSE WHO STAND AT THE TOP SOMETIMES HAVE TO BE FIRM WITH THOSE BELOW.
OTHER-WISE, QUALITY DROPS.
ESPECIALLY IN THE SERVICE SECTOR.
CUT OFF THE STRAGGLERS AT THE BOTTOM, AND THE TOP WILL STAY FIRM.
BUT...
THE PEOPLE AT THE BOTTOM HAVE TO MAKE A LIVING, TOO.
Give me one.
Cloak Room

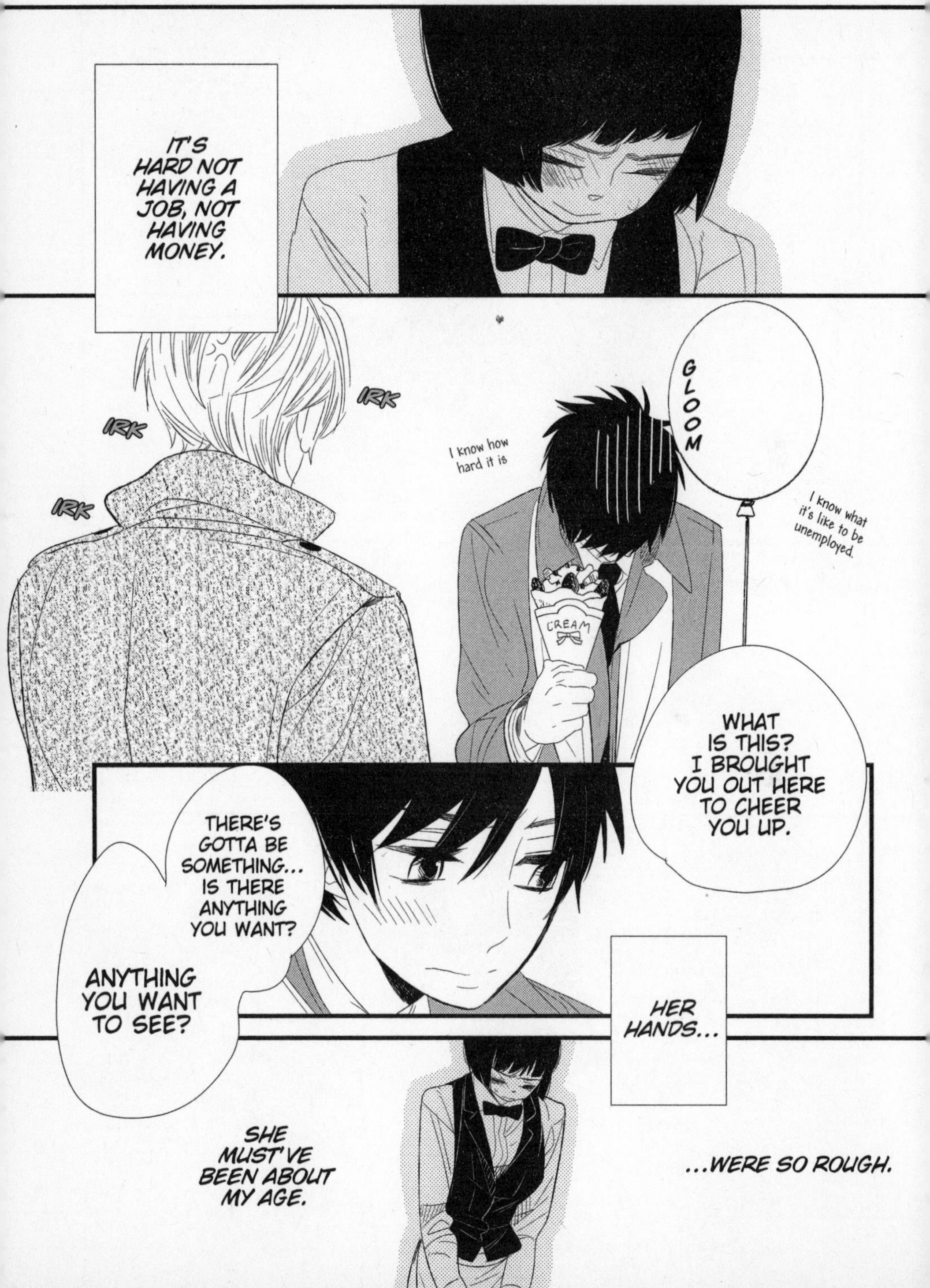
IT'S HARD NOT HAVING A JOB, NOT HAVING MONEY.
GLOOM
I know what it's like to be unemployed.
I know how hard it is
IRK
IRK
IRK
WHAT IS THIS? I BROUGHT YOU OUT HERE TO CHEER YOU UP.
THERE'S GOTTA BE SOMETHING... IS THERE ANYTHING YOU WANT?
ANYTHING YOU WANT TO SEE?
HER HANDS...
...WERE SO ROUGH.
SHE MUST'VE BEEN ABOUT MY AGE.

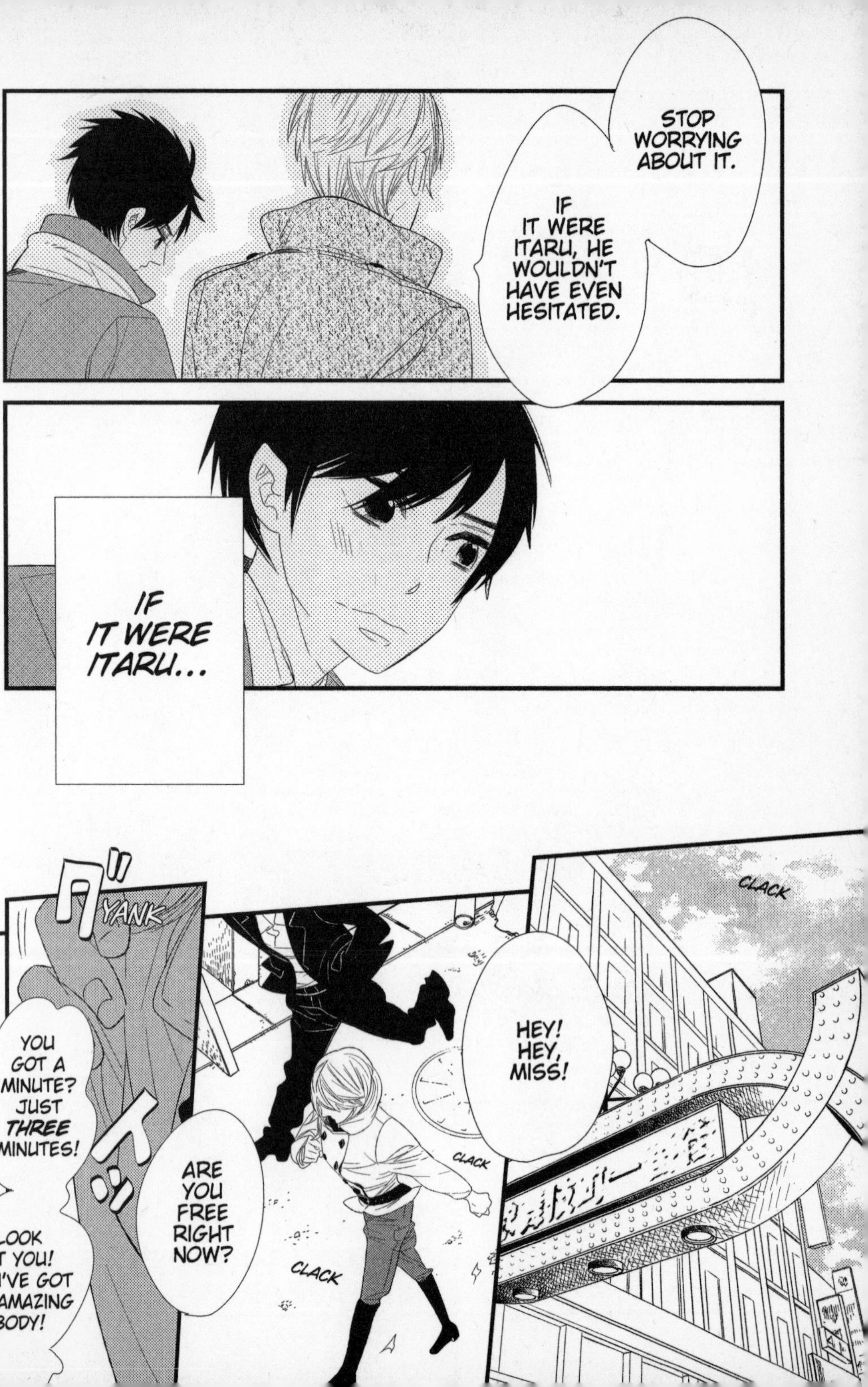
STOP WORRYING ABOUT IT.
IF IT WERE ITARU, HE WOULDN'T HAVE EVEN HESITATED.
IF IT WERE ITARU...
CLACK
HEY! HEY, MISS!
CLACK
ARE YOU FREE RIGHT NOW?
CLACK
YANK
YOU GOT A MINUTE? JUST *THREE* MINUTES!
LOOK AT YOU! YOU'VE GOT AN AMAZING BODY!

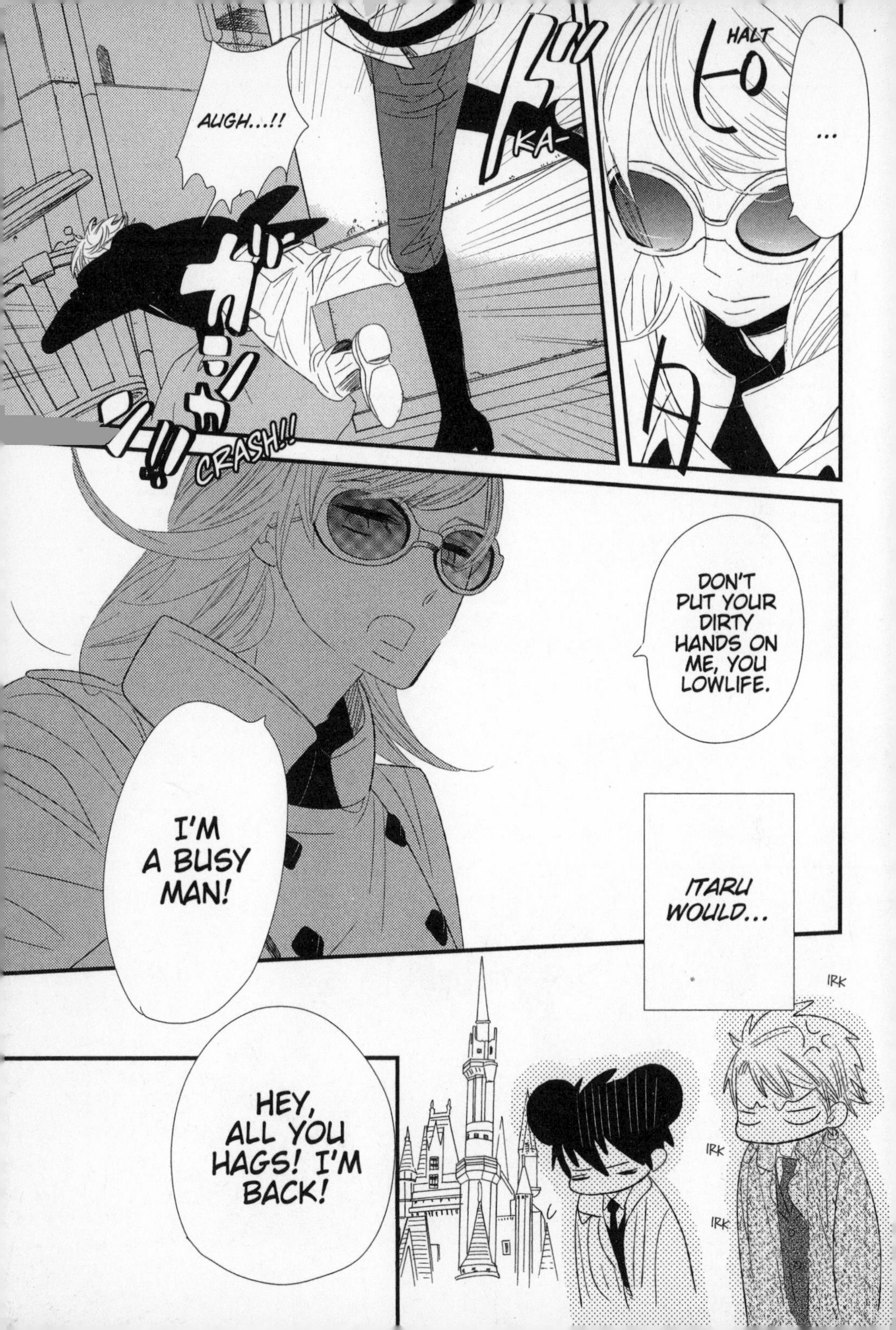
HALT
...
KA-
AUGH...!!
CRASH!!
DON'T PUT YOUR DIRTY HANDS ON ME, YOU LOWLIFE.
I'M A BUSY MAN!
ITARU WOULD...
IRK
IRK
IRK
HEY, ALL YOU HAGS! I'M BACK!

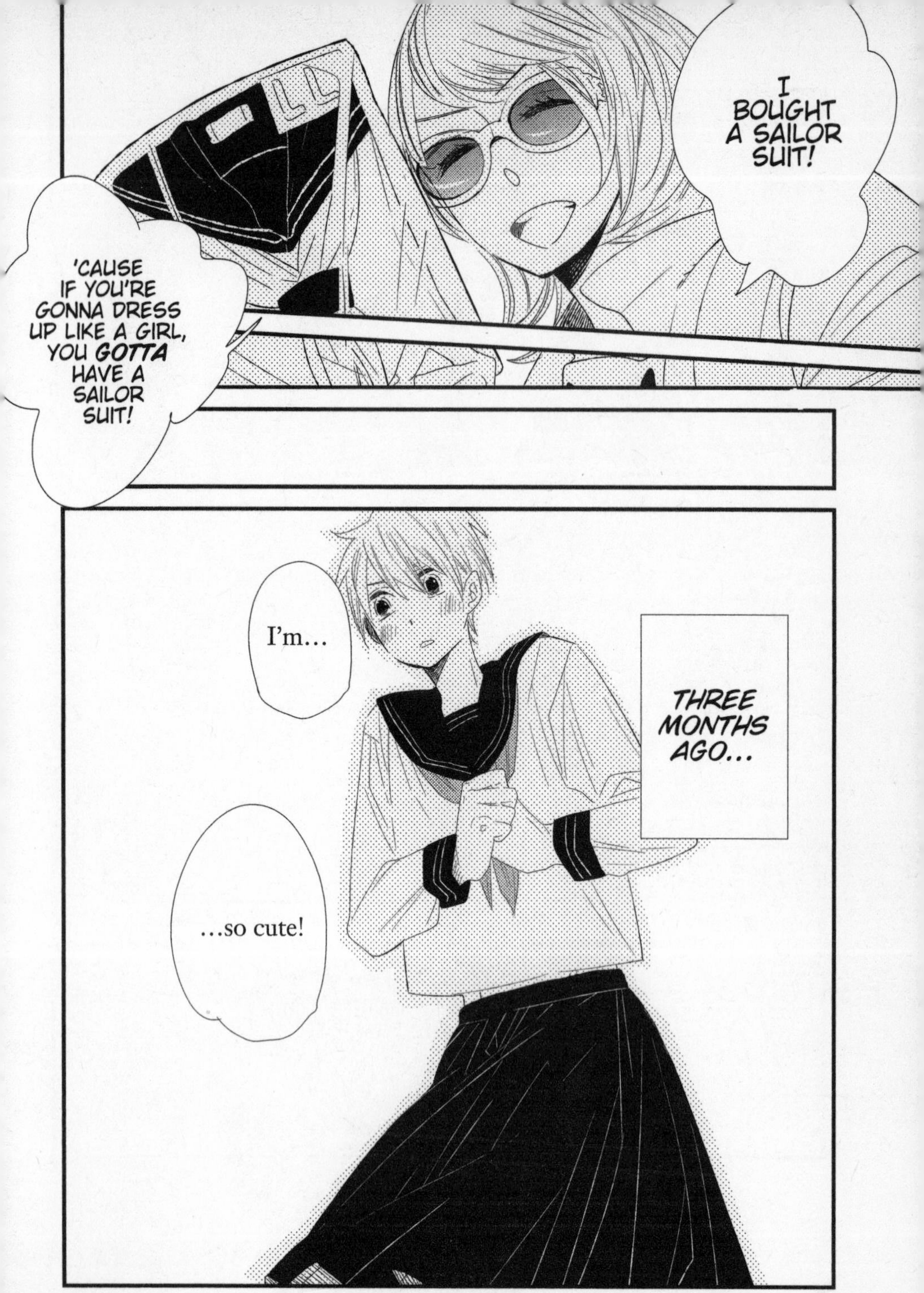
I BOUGHT A SAILOR SUIT!
'CAUSE IF YOU'RE GONNA DRESS UP LIKE A GIRL, YOU GOTTA HAVE A SAILOR SUIT!
THREE MONTHS AGO...
I'm…
…so cute!

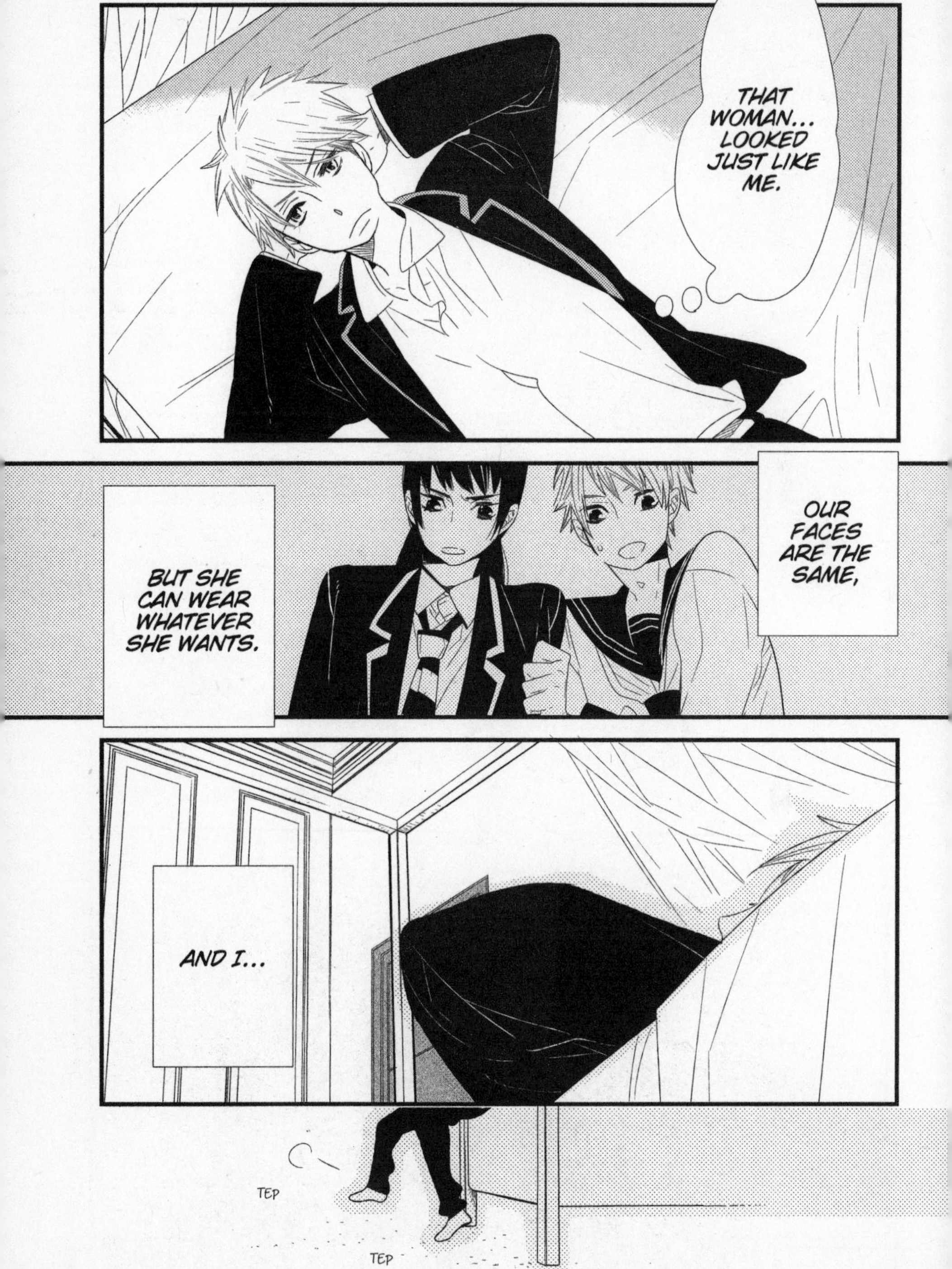
THAT WOMAN... LOOKED JUST LIKE ME.
OUR FACES ARE THE SAME,
BUT SHE CAN WEAR WHATEVER SHE WANTS.
AND I...
TEP
TEP

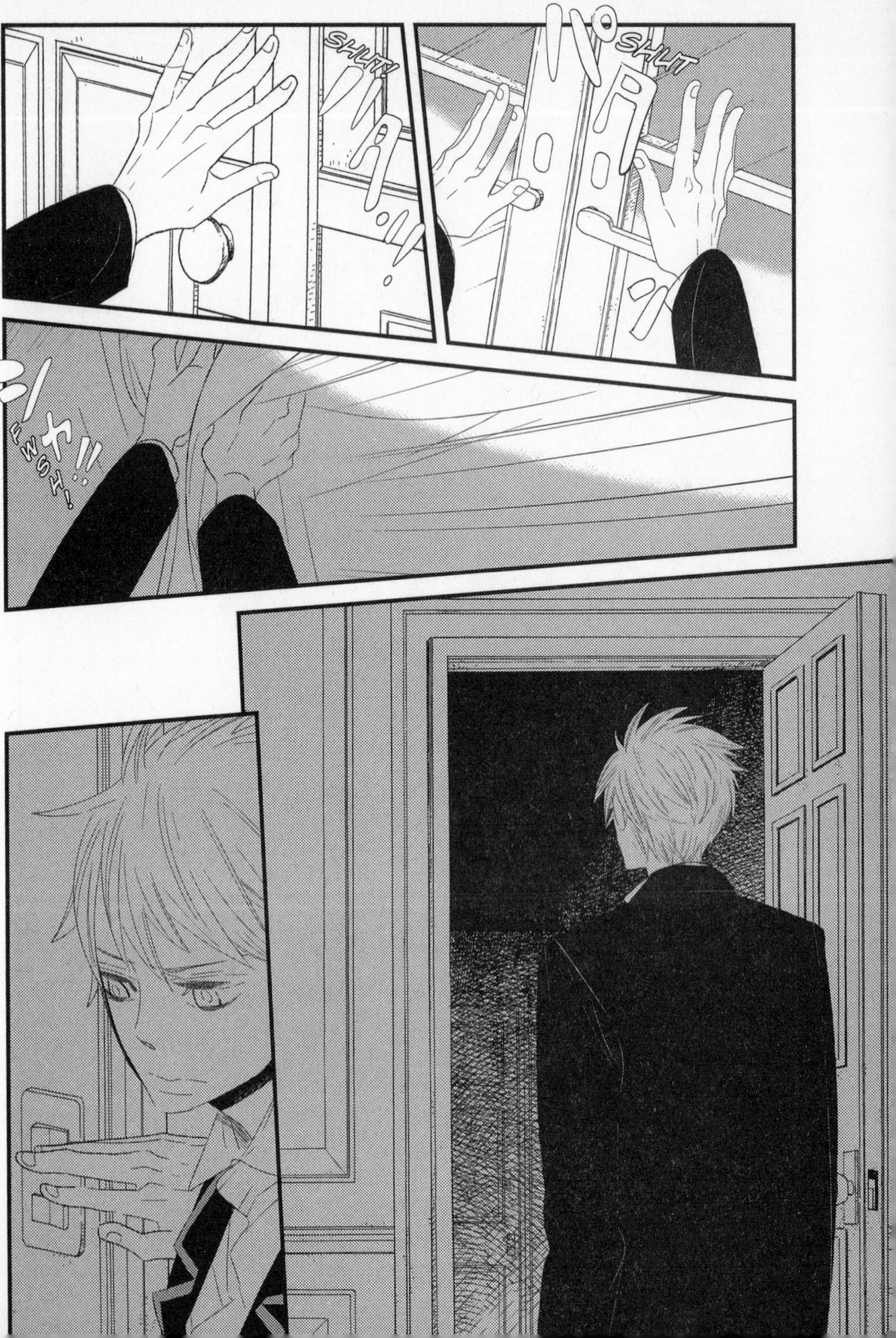
SHUT
SHUT!
FWSH!

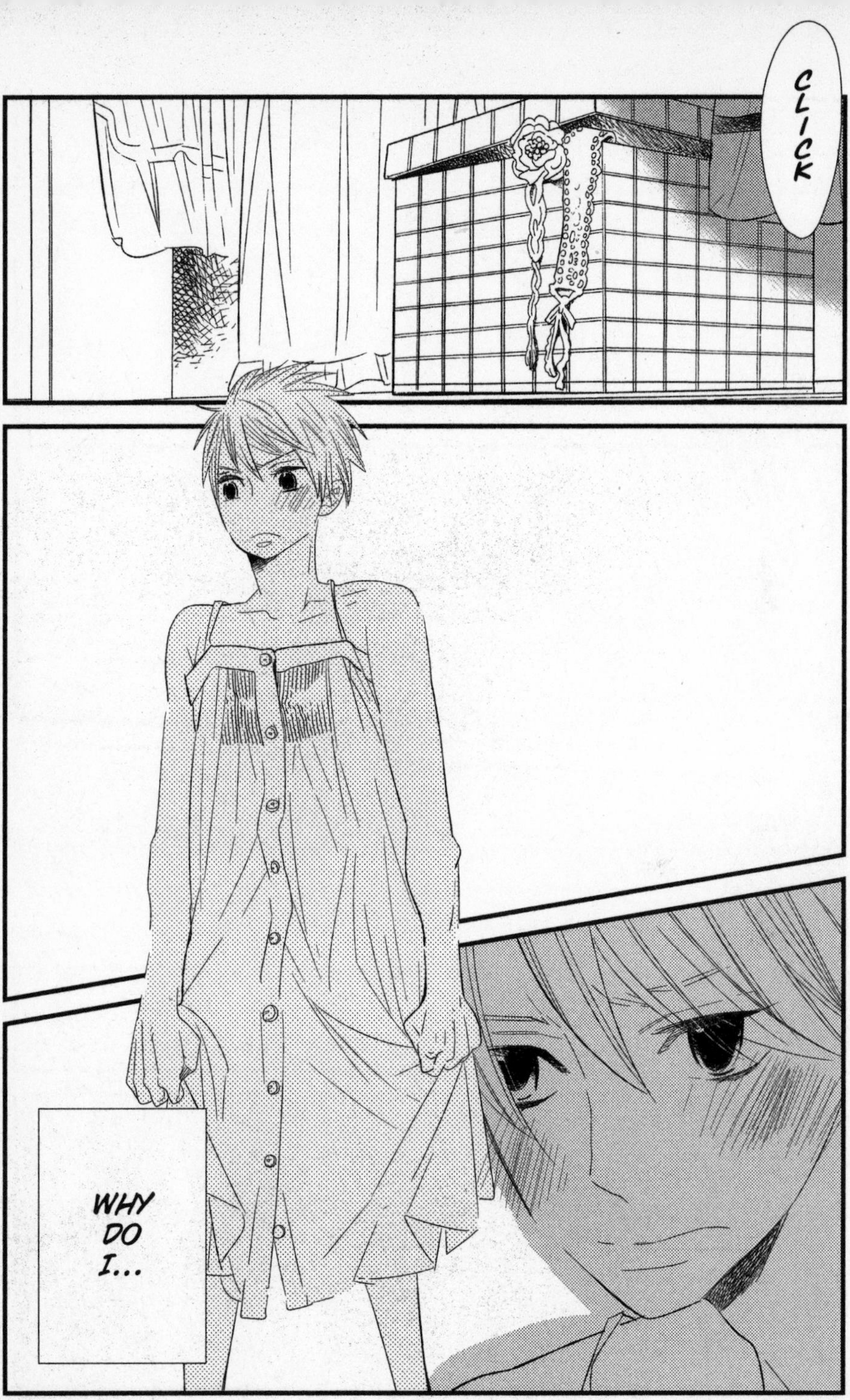
CLICK
WHY DO I...

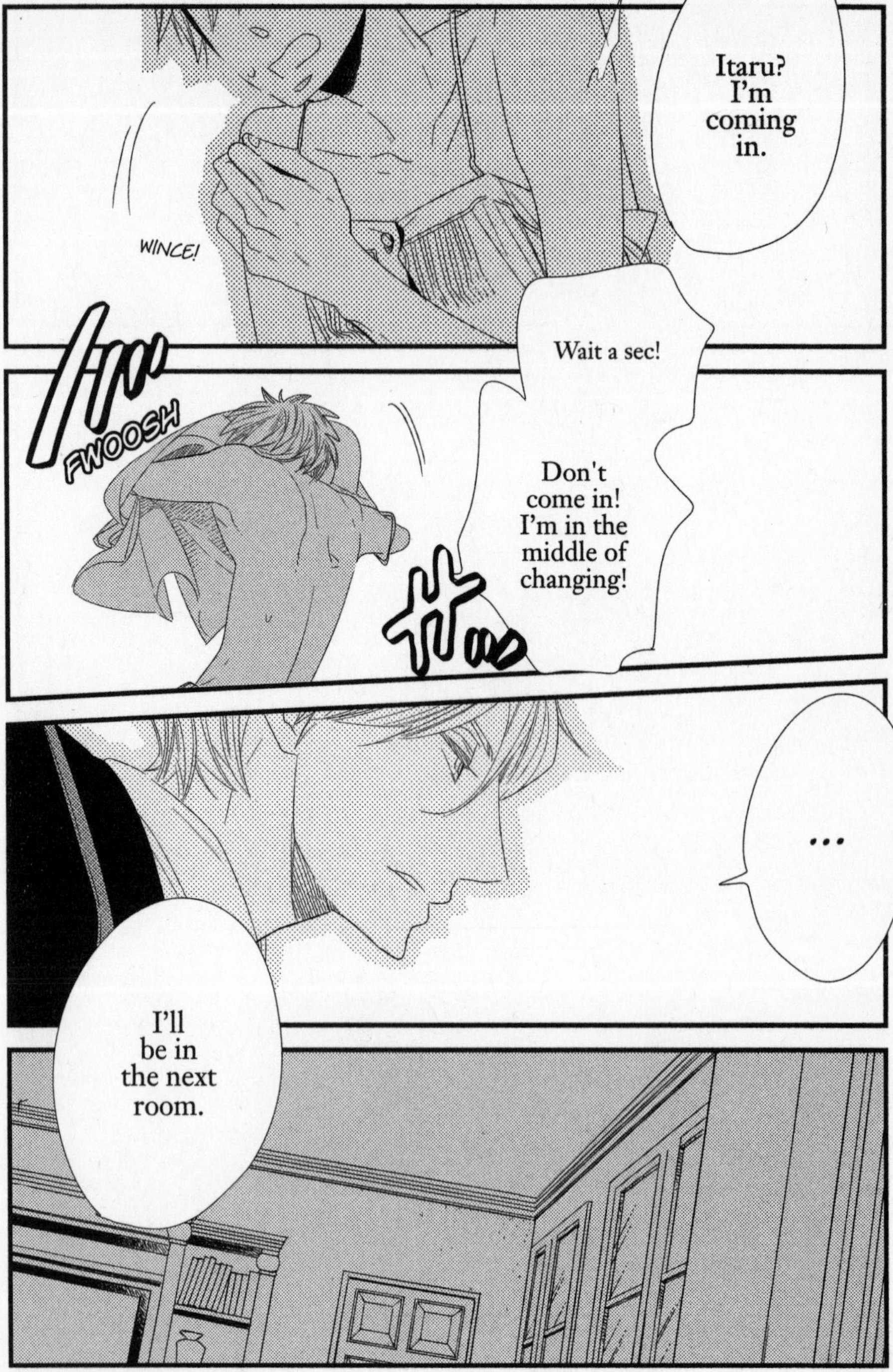
Itaru? I'm coming in.
WINCE!
Wait a sec!
FWOOSH
Don't come in! I'm in the middle of changing!
...
I'll be in the next room.

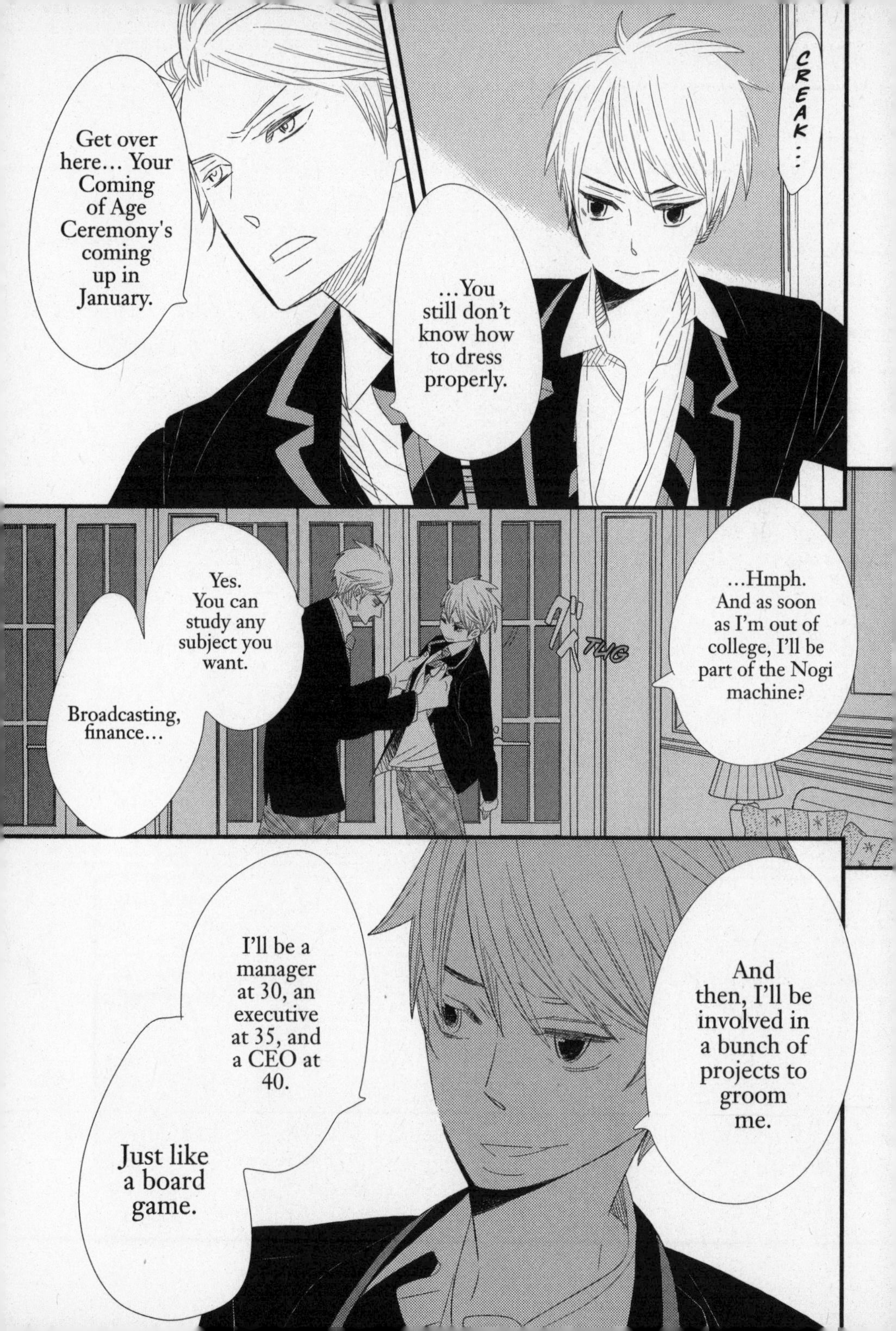
CREAK...
...You still don't know how to dress properly.
Get over here... Your Coming of Age Ceremony's coming up in January.
...Hmph. And as soon as I'm out of college, I'll be part of the Nogi machine?
TUG
Yes. You can study any subject you want.
Broadcasting, finance...
And then, I'll be involved in a bunch of projects to groom me.
I'll be a manager at 30, an executive at 35, and a CEO at 40.
Just like a board game.

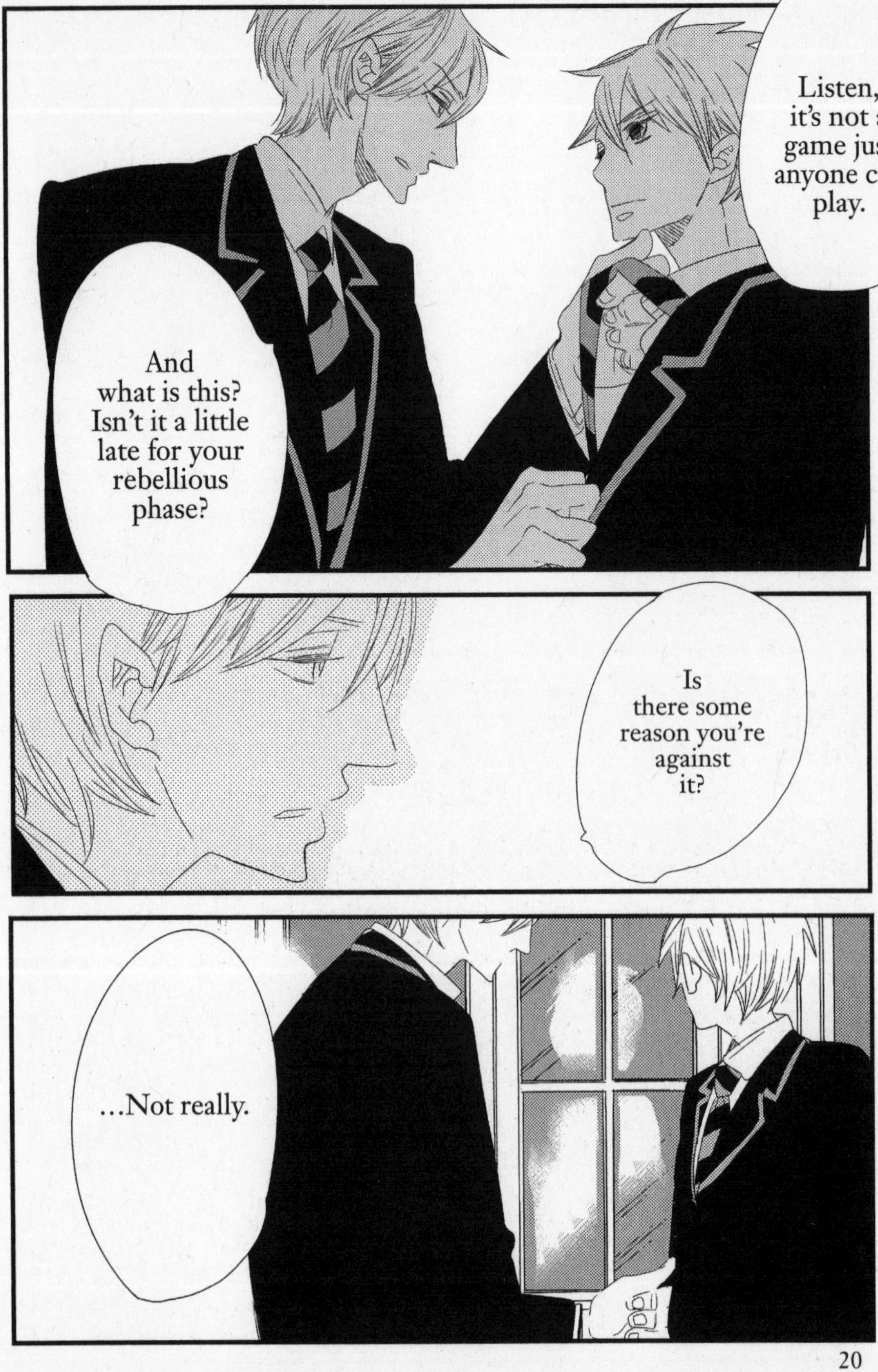
Listen, it's not a game just anyone can play.
And what is this? Isn't it a little late for your rebellious phase?
Is there some reason you're against it?
...Not really.

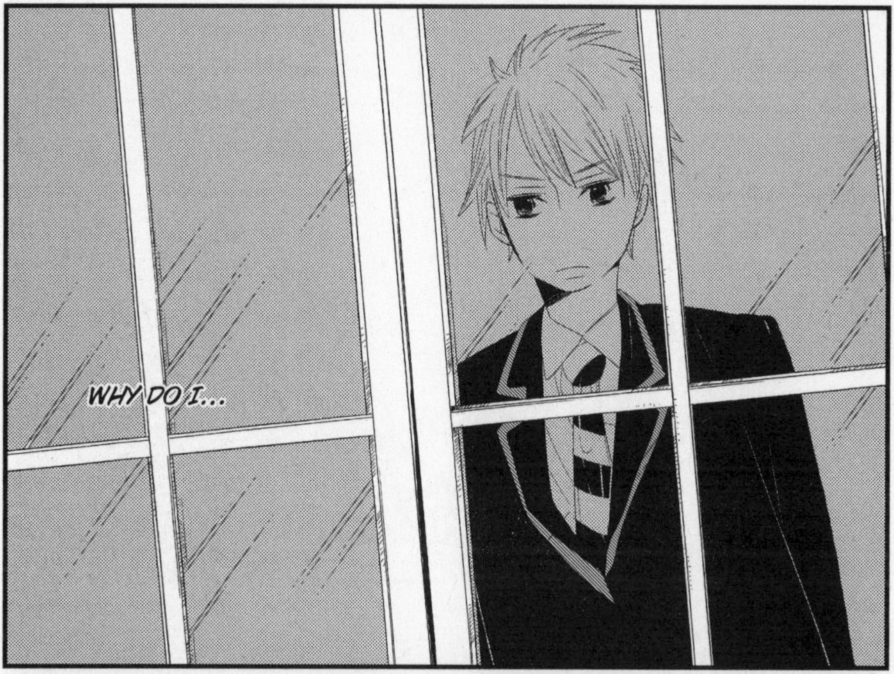
WHY DO I...
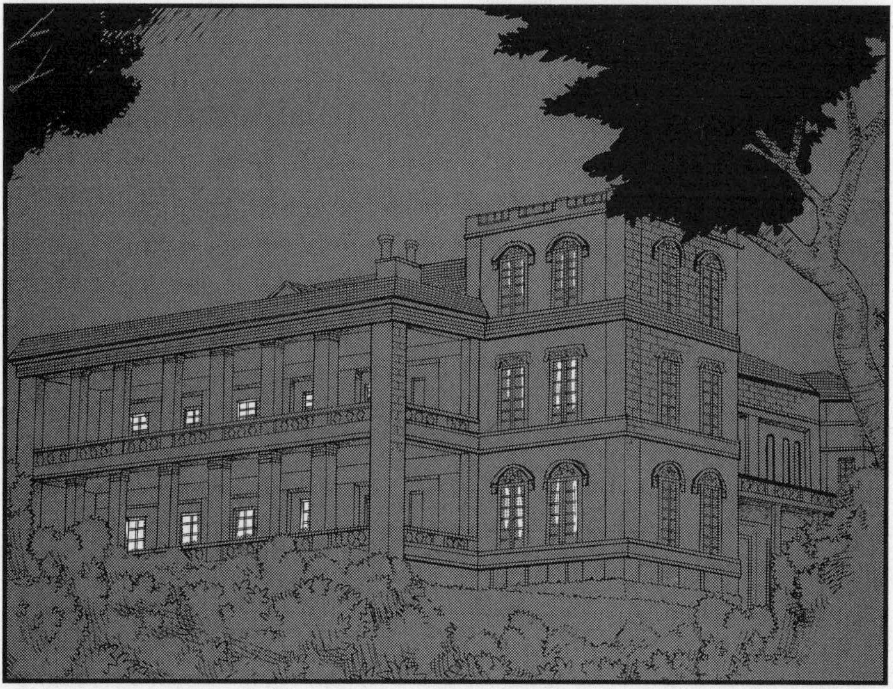

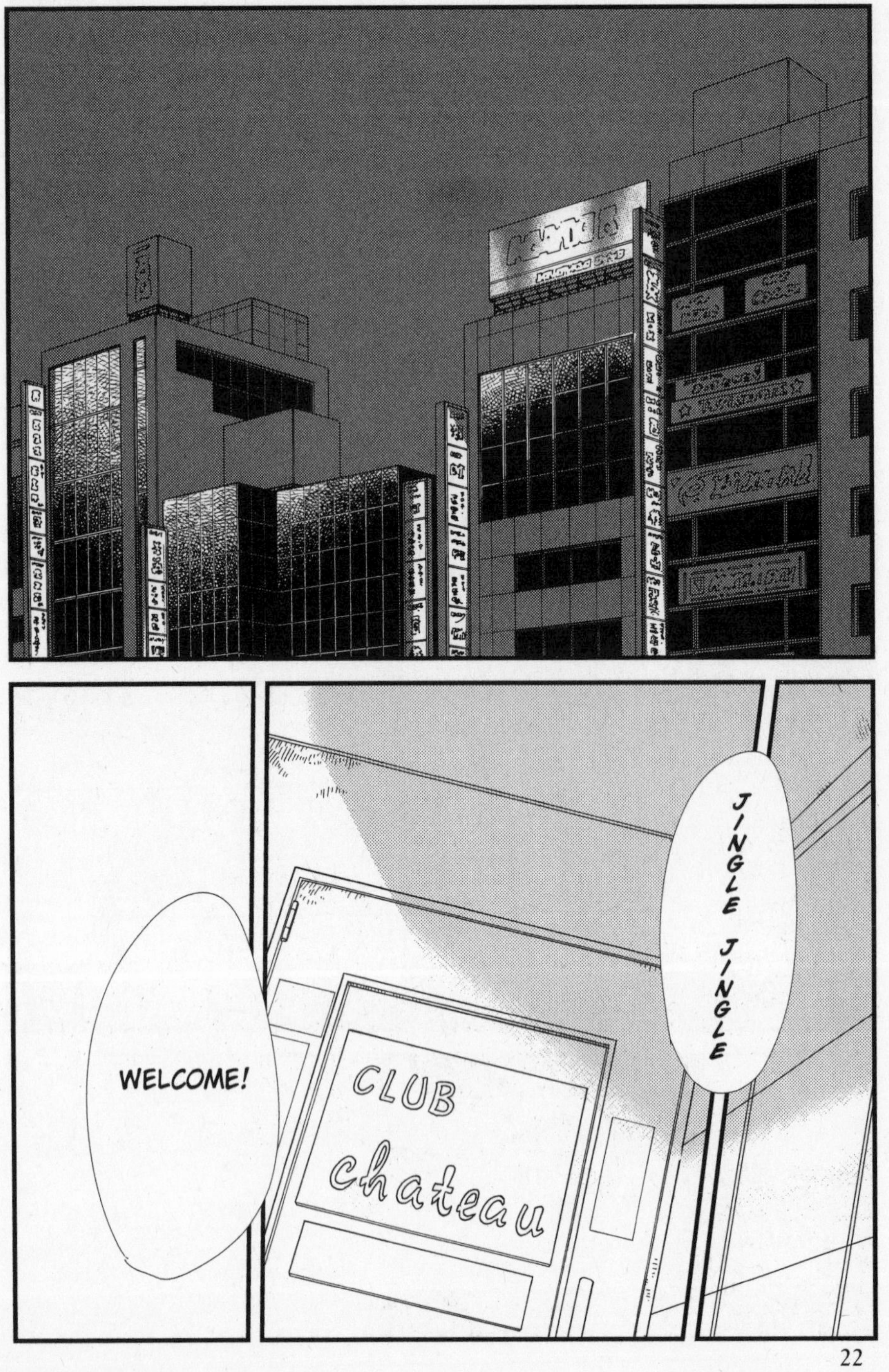
JINGLE JINGLE
CLUB chateau
WELCOME!

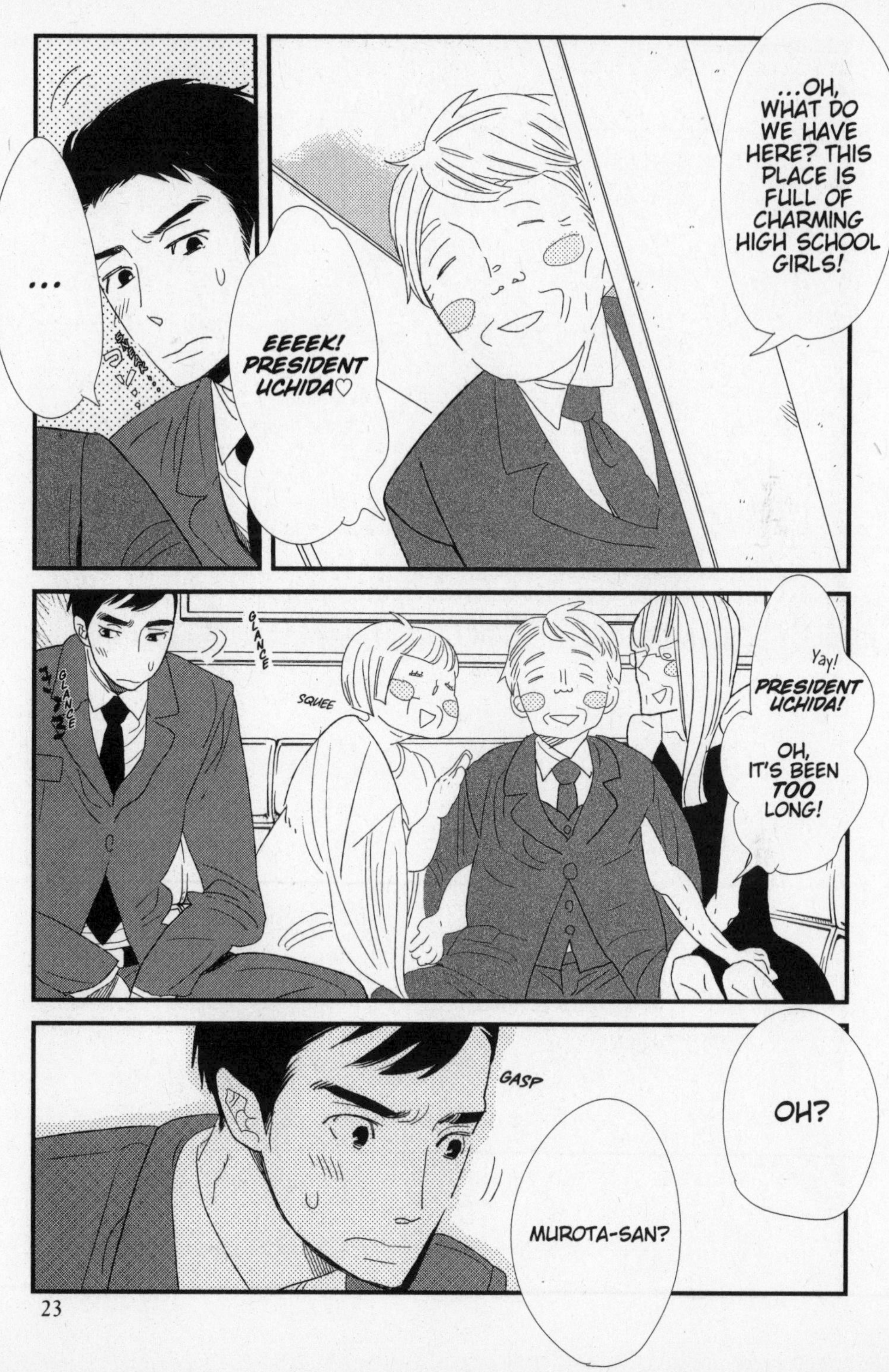
...OH, WHAT DO WE HAVE HERE? THIS PLACE IS FULL OF CHARMING HIGH SCHOOL GIRLS!
EEEEK! PRESIDENT UCHIDA♡
...
Yay!
PRESIDENT UCHIDA!
OH, IT'S BEEN TOO LONG!
SQUEE
GLANCE
GLANCE
OH?
MUROTA-SAN?
GASP

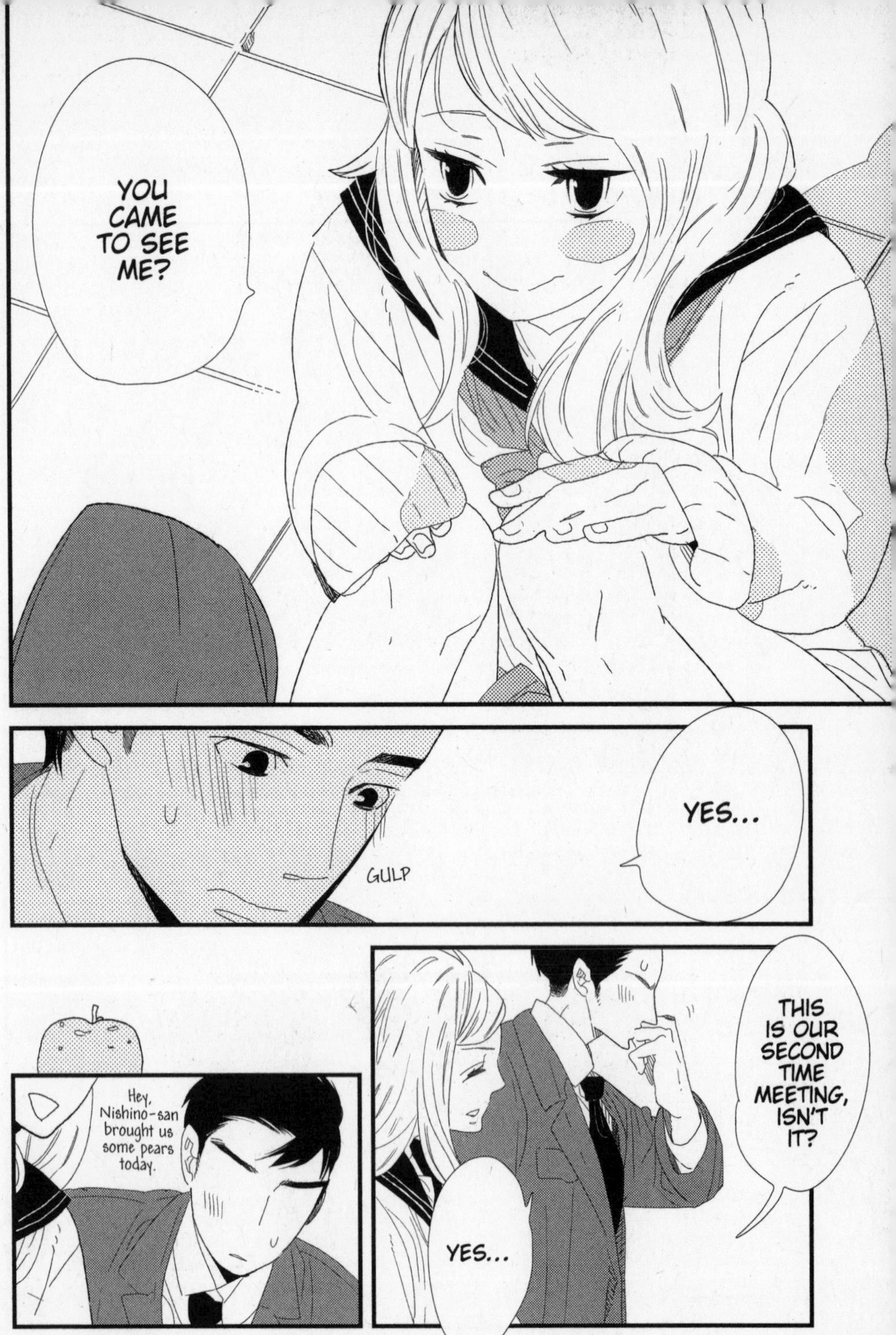
YOU CAME TO SEE ME?
YES...
GULP
THIS IS OUR SECOND TIME MEETING, ISN'T IT?
YES...
Hey, Nishino-san brought us some pears today.

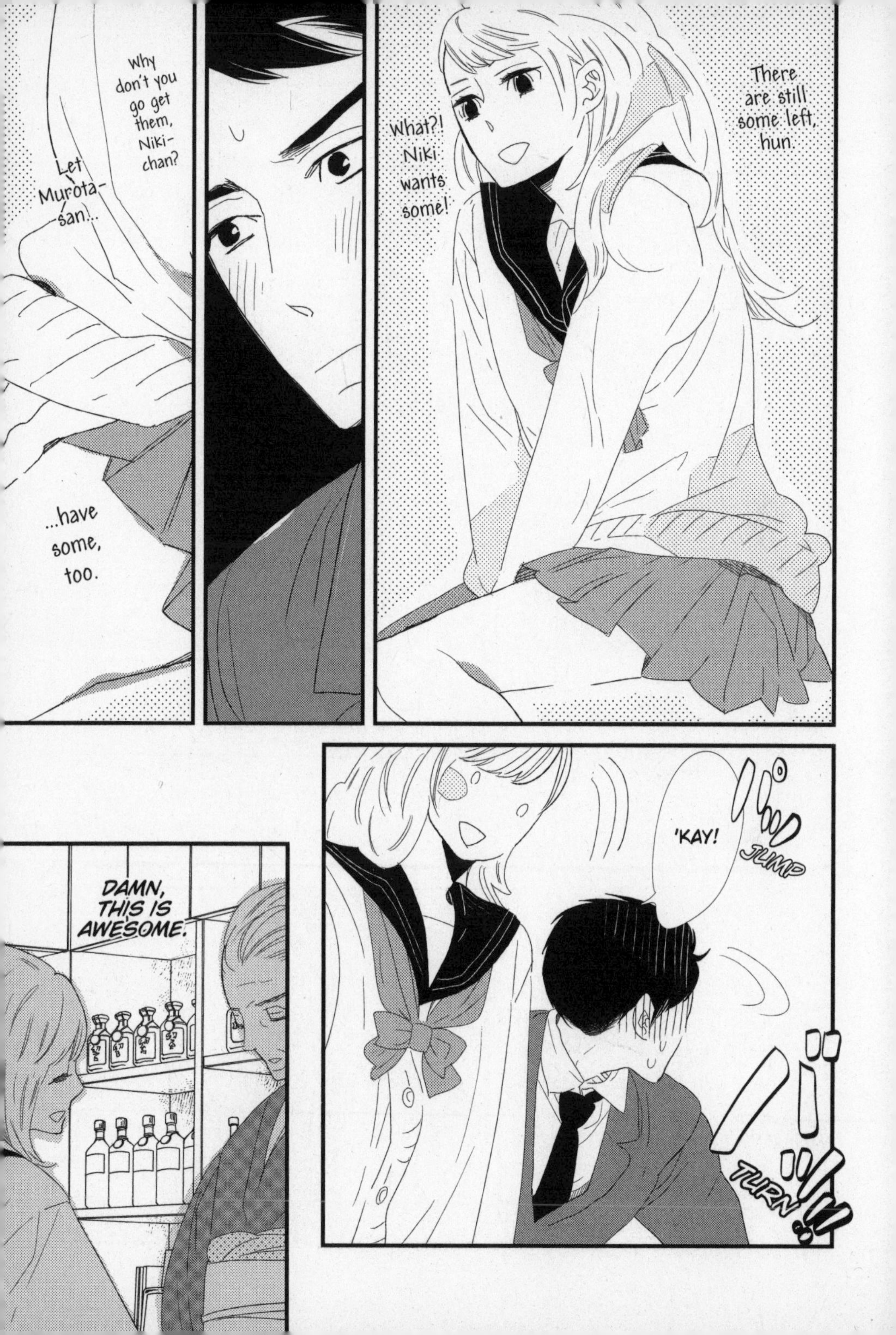
There are still some left, hun.
What?! Niki wants some!
Why don't you go get them, Niki-chan?
Let Murota-san...
...have some, too.
'KAY!
JUMP
TURN
DAMN, THIS IS AWESOME.

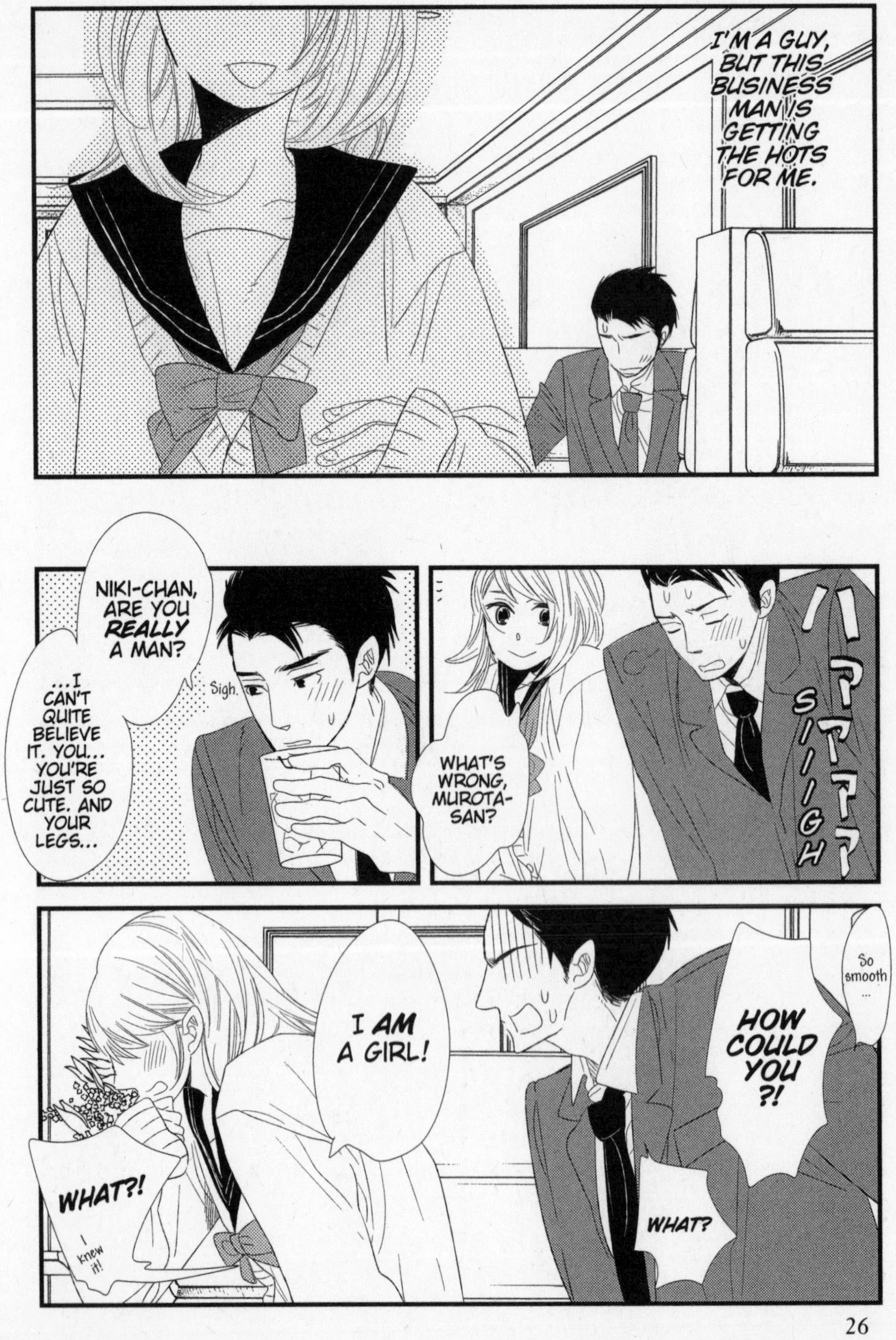
I'M A GUY, BUT THIS BUSINESS MAN IS GETTING THE HOTS FOR ME.
ハアアア
SIIIGH
WHAT'S WRONG, MUROTA-SAN?
NIKI-CHAN, ARE YOU REALLY A MAN?
Sigh.
...I CAN'T QUITE BELIEVE IT. YOU... YOU'RE JUST SO CUTE. AND YOUR LEGS...
So smooth ...
HOW COULD YOU ?!
WHAT?
I AM A GIRL!
WHAT?!
I knew it!

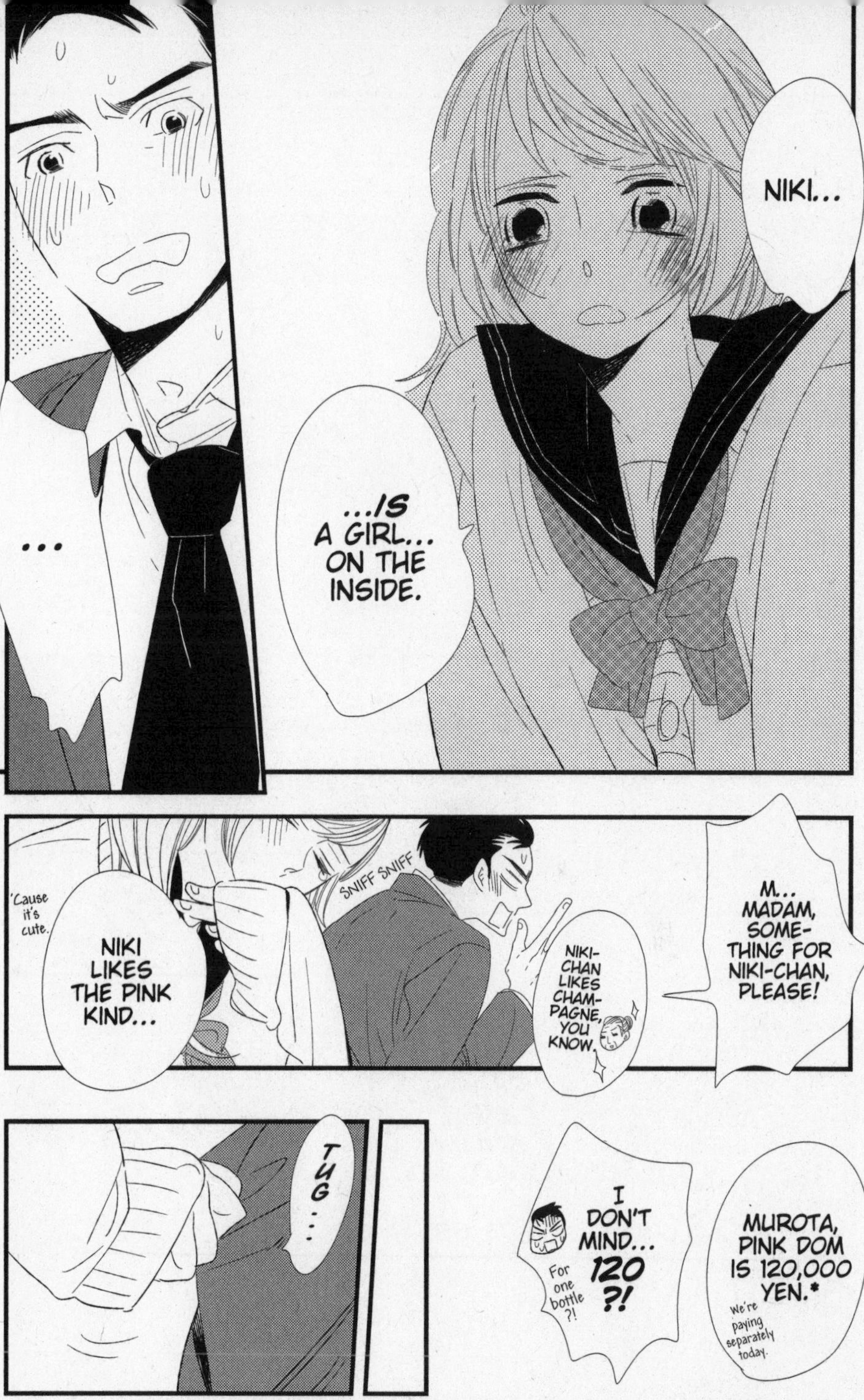
NIKI...
...IS A GIRL... ON THE INSIDE.
...
M... MADAM, SOME-THING FOR NIKI-CHAN, PLEASE!
NIKI-CHAN LIKES CHAM-PAGNE, YOU KNOW.
SNIFF SNIFF
NIKI LIKES THE PINK KIND...
'Cause it's cute.
MUROTA, PINK DOM IS 120,000 YEN.*
We're paying separately today.
I DON'T MIND... 120?!
For one bottle?!
TUG...

*Dom Perignon Rosé, about $1,200 USD.

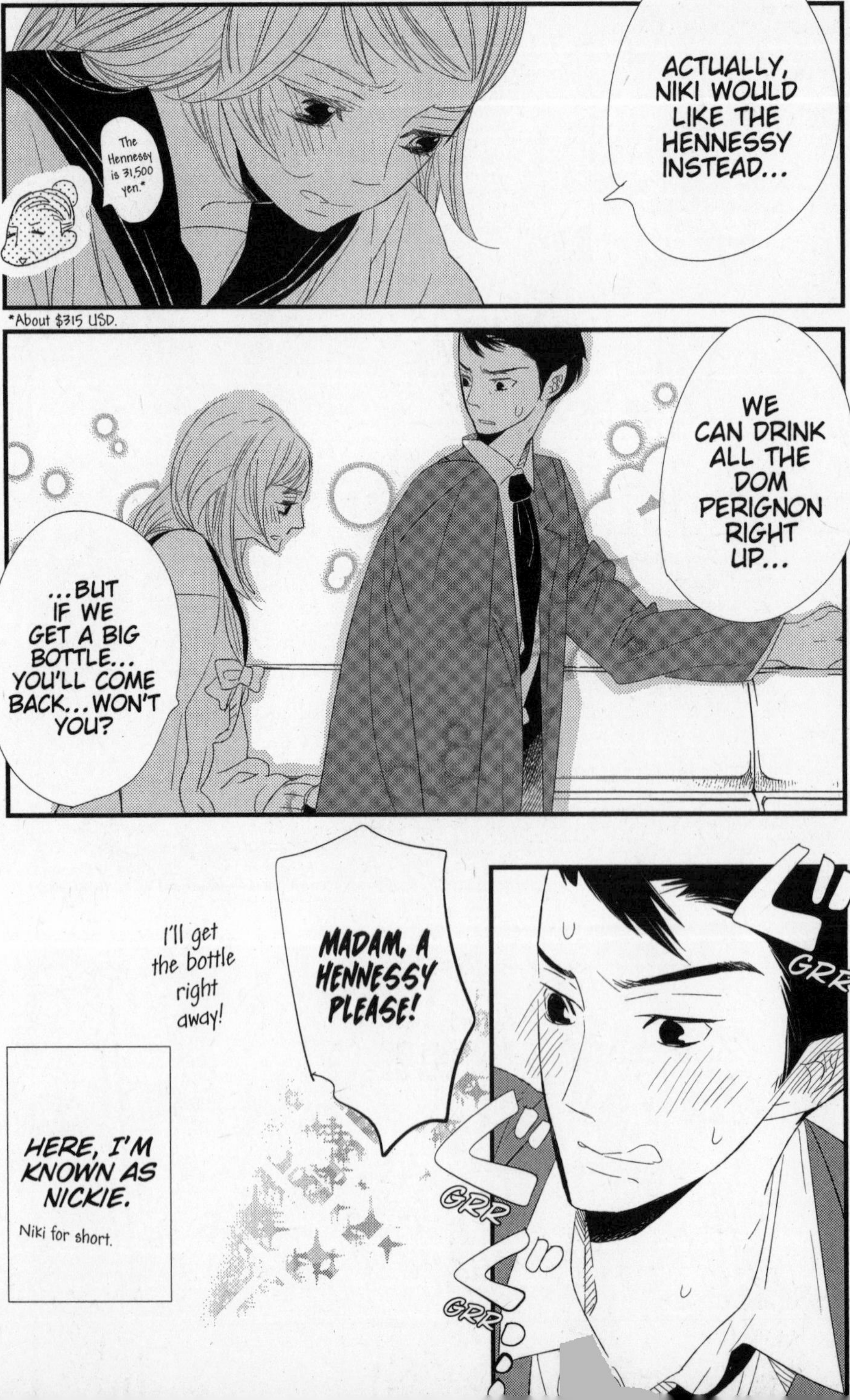
ACTUALLY, NIKI WOULD LIKE THE HENNESSY INSTEAD...
The Hennessy is 31,500 yen.*
WE CAN DRINK ALL THE DOM PERIGNON RIGHT UP...
...BUT IF WE GET A BIG BOTTLE... YOU'LL COME BACK...WON'T YOU?
GRR
GRR
GRR
MADAM, A HENNESSY PLEASE!
I'll get the bottle right away!
HERE, I'M KNOWN AS NICKIE.
Niki for short.

*About $315 USD.

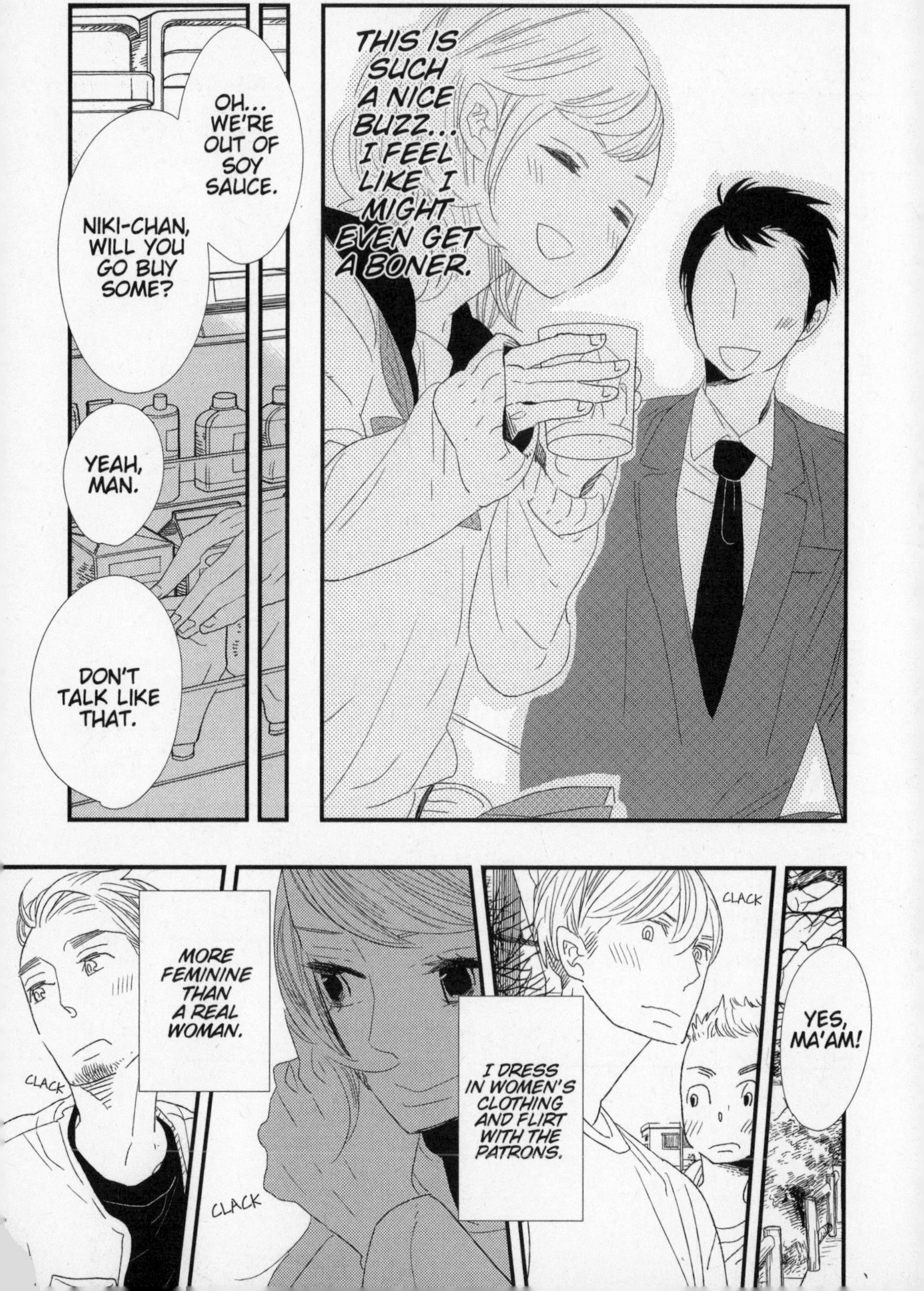
THIS IS SUCH A NICE BUZZ... I FEEL LIKE I MIGHT EVEN GET A BONER.
OH... WE'RE OUT OF SOY SAUCE.
NIKI-CHAN, WILL YOU GO BUY SOME?
YEAH, MAN.
DON'T TALK LIKE THAT.
YES, MA'AM!
CLACK
I DRESS IN WOMEN'S CLOTHING AND FLIRT WITH THE PATRONS.
MORE FEMININE THAN A REAL WOMAN.
CLACK
CLACK

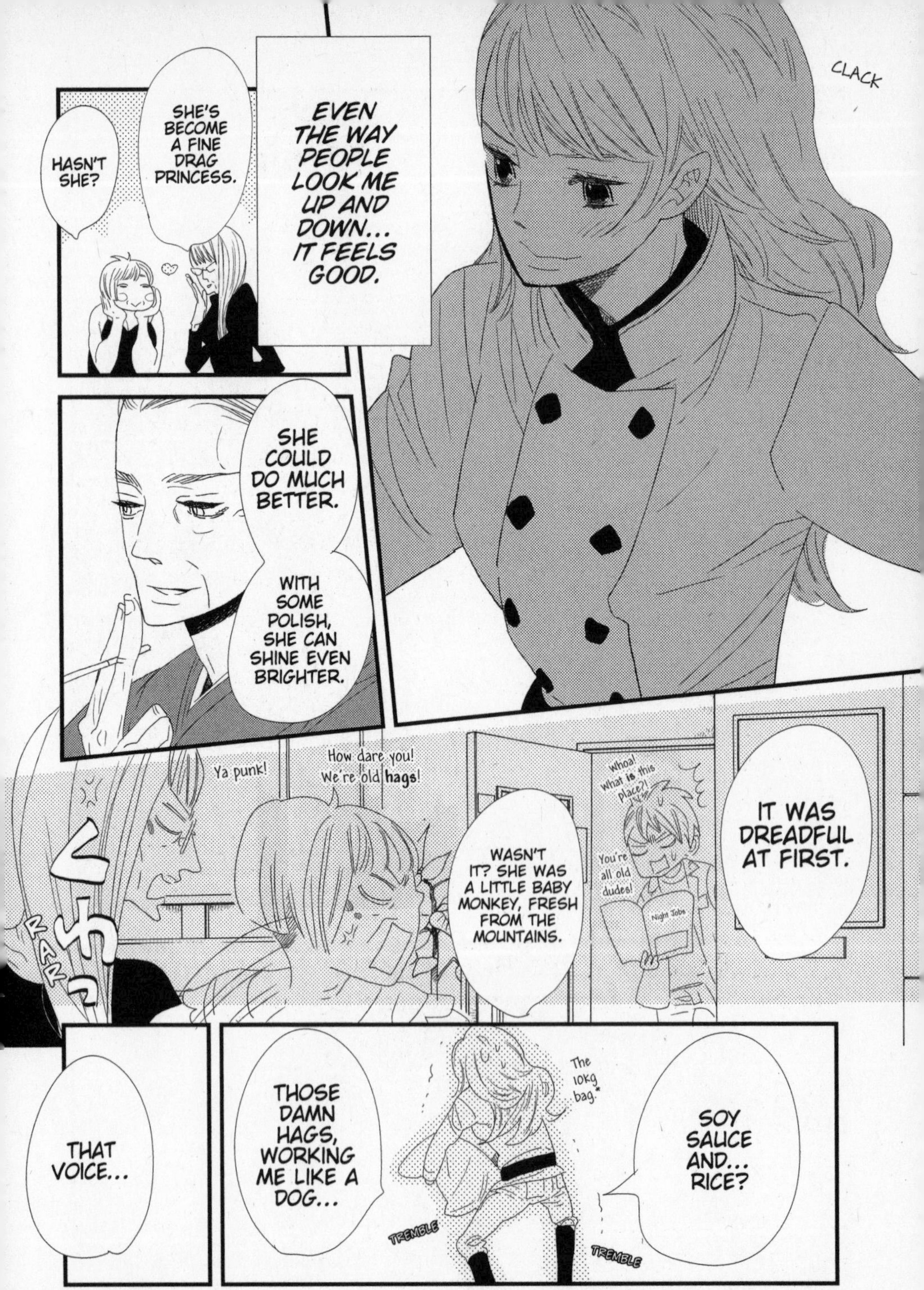
CLACK
EVEN THE WAY PEOPLE LOOK ME UP AND DOWN... IT FEELS GOOD.
SHE'S BECOME A FINE DRAG PRINCESS.
HASN'T SHE?
SHE COULD DO MUCH BETTER.
WITH SOME POLISH, SHE CAN SHINE EVEN BRIGHTER.
IT WAS DREADFUL AT FIRST.
Whoa! What is this place?!
You're all old dudes!
Night Jobs
WASN'T IT? SHE WAS A LITTLE BABY MONKEY, FRESH FROM THE MOUNTAINS.
How dare you! We're old **hags**!
Ya punk!
RAR
SOY SAUCE AND... RICE?
The 10kg bag.*
THOSE DAMN HAGS, WORKING ME LIKE A DOG...
TREMBLE
TREMBLE
THAT VOICE...

*About 22lbs.

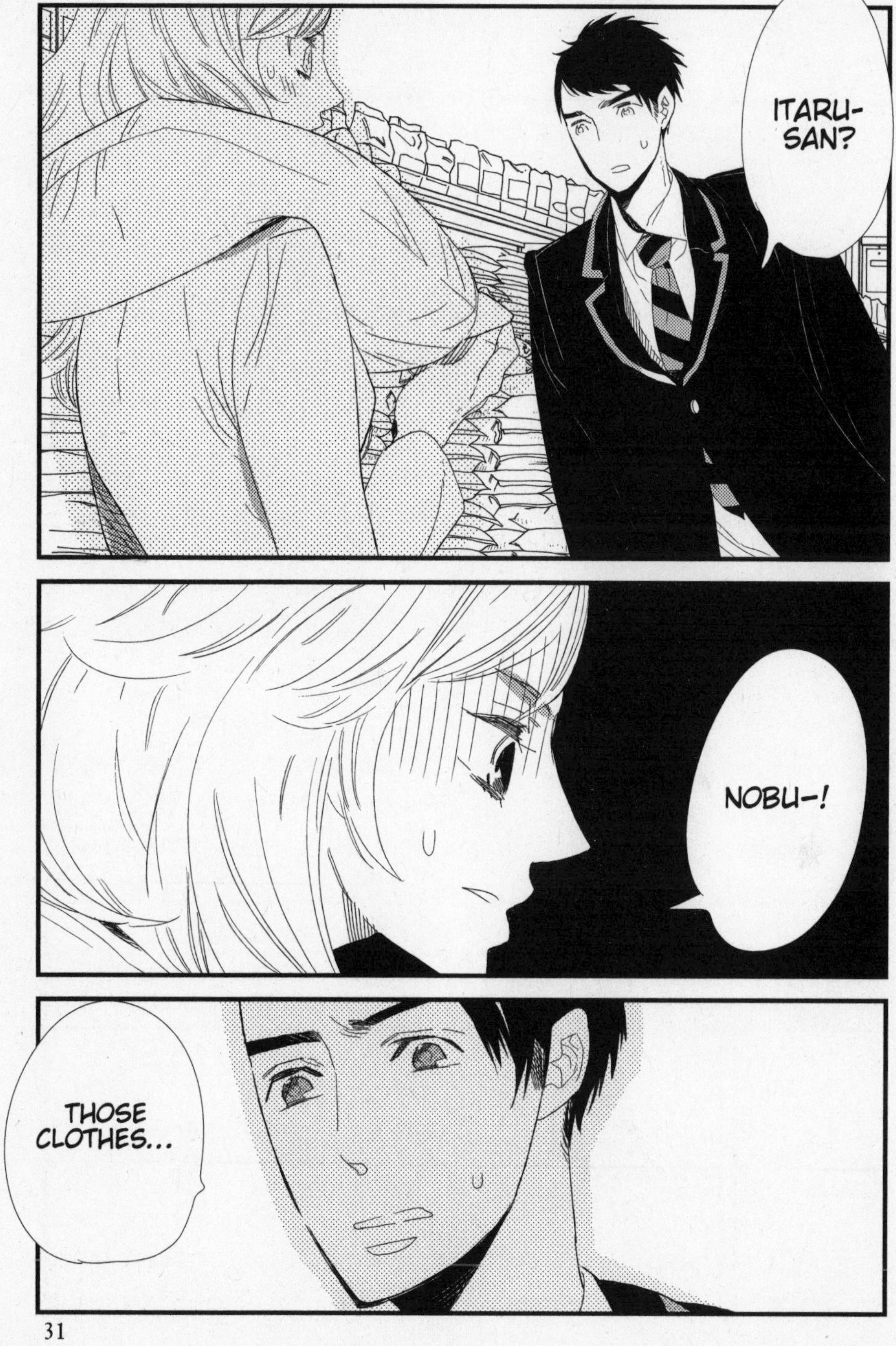
ITARU-SAN?
NOBU-!
THOSE CLOTHES...

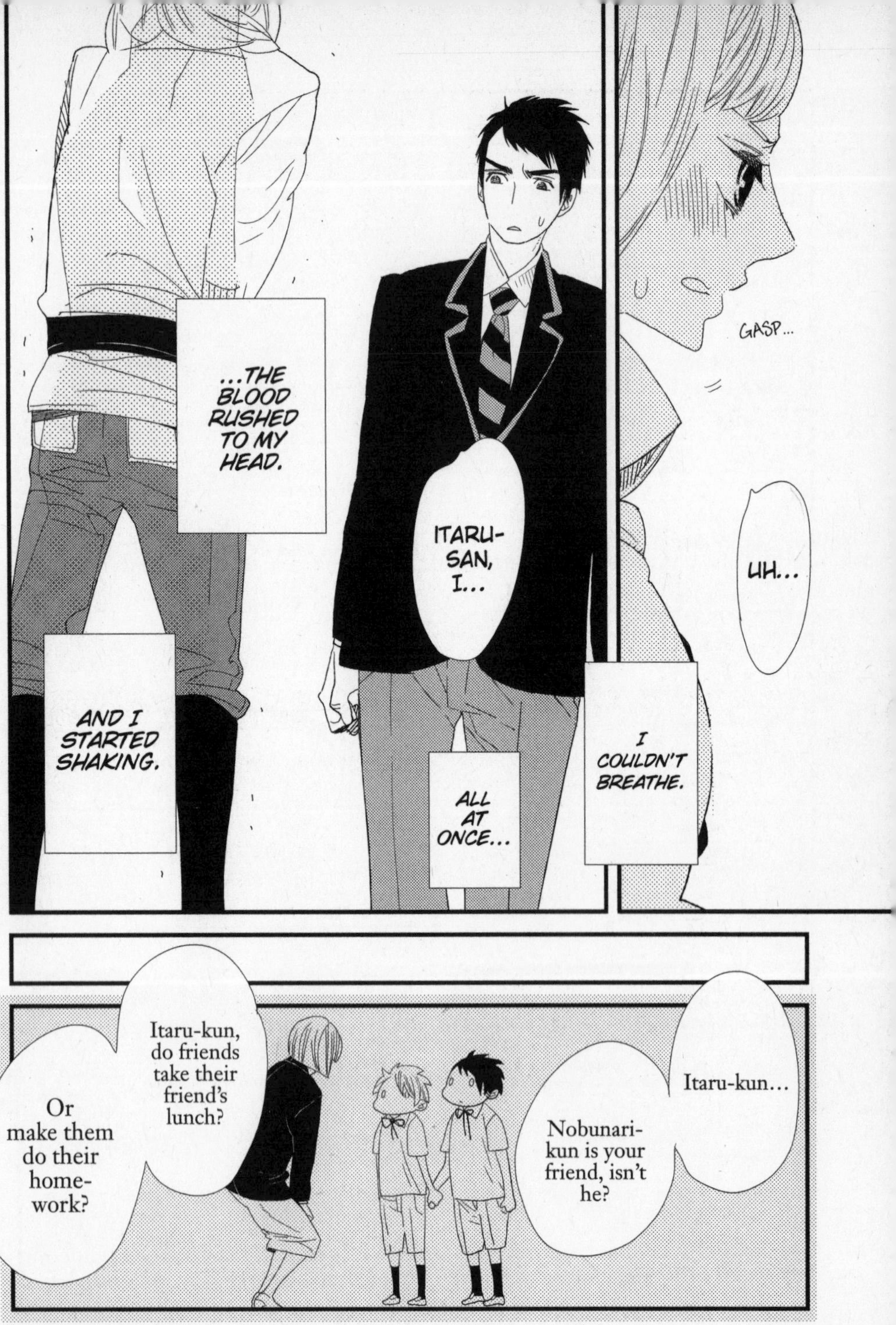
GASP...
UH...
I COULDN'T BREATHE.
ITARU-SAN, I...
ALL AT ONCE...
...THE BLOOD RUSHED TO MY HEAD.
AND I STARTED SHAKING.
Itaru-kun...
Nobunari-kun is your friend, isn't he?
Itaru-kun, do friends take their friend's lunch?
Or make them do their home-work?

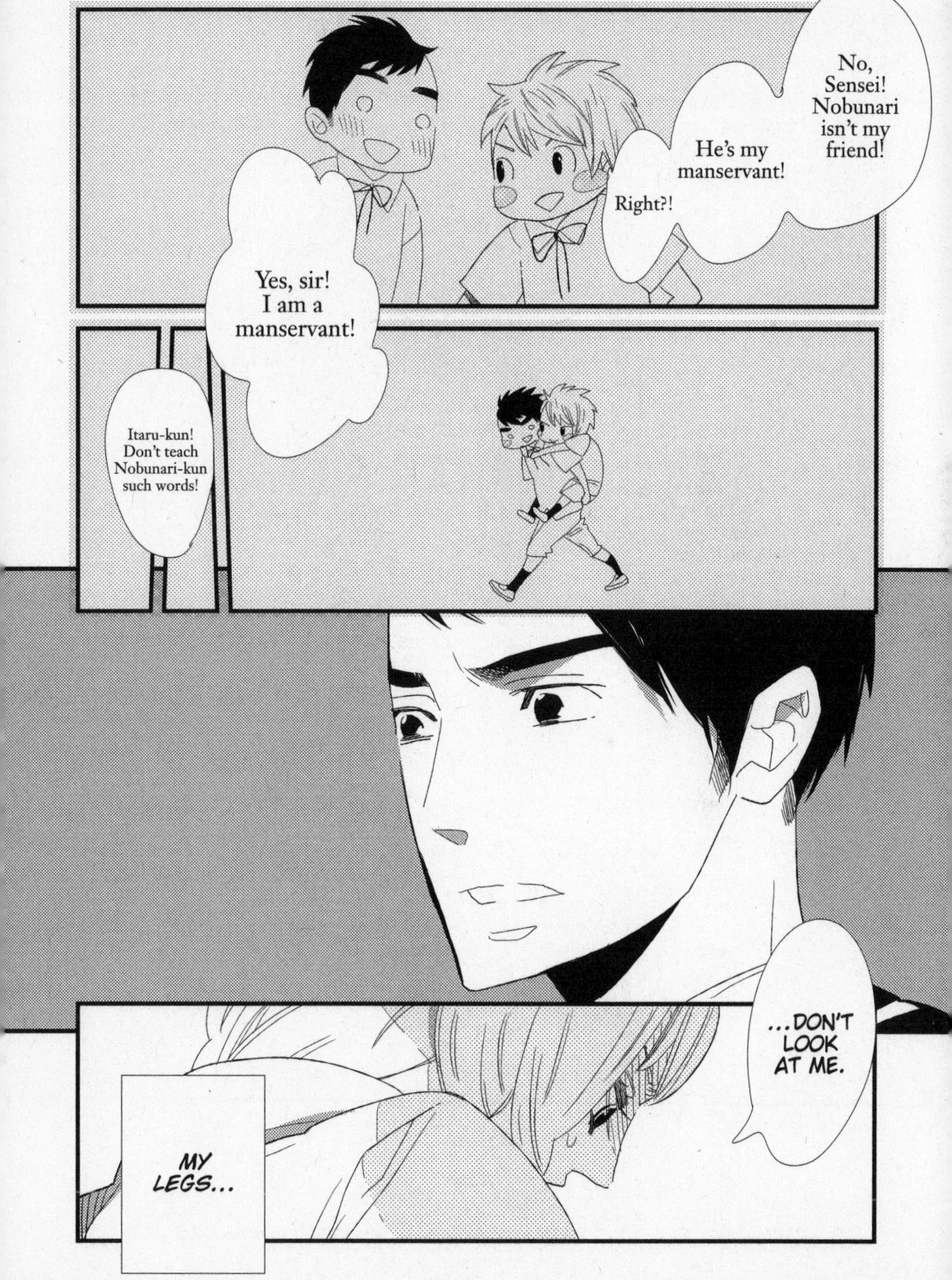
No, Sensei! Nobunari isn't my friend!
He's my manservant!
Right?!
Yes, sir! I am a manservant!
Itaru-kun! Don't teach Nobunari-kun such words!
...DON'T LOOK AT ME.
MY LEGS...

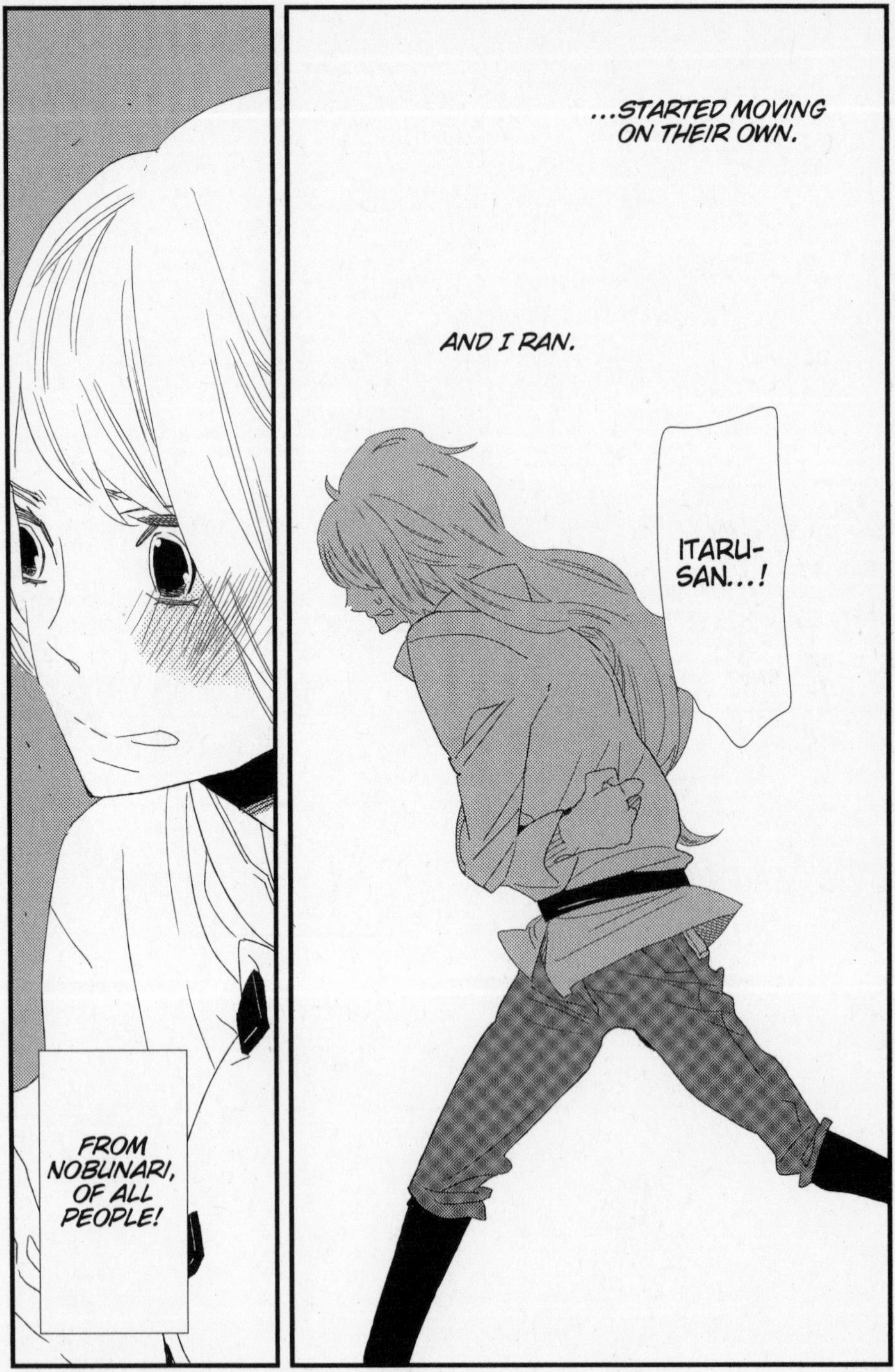
...STARTED MOVING ON THEIR OWN.
AND I RAN.
ITARU-SAN...!
FROM NOBUNARI, OF ALL PEOPLE!

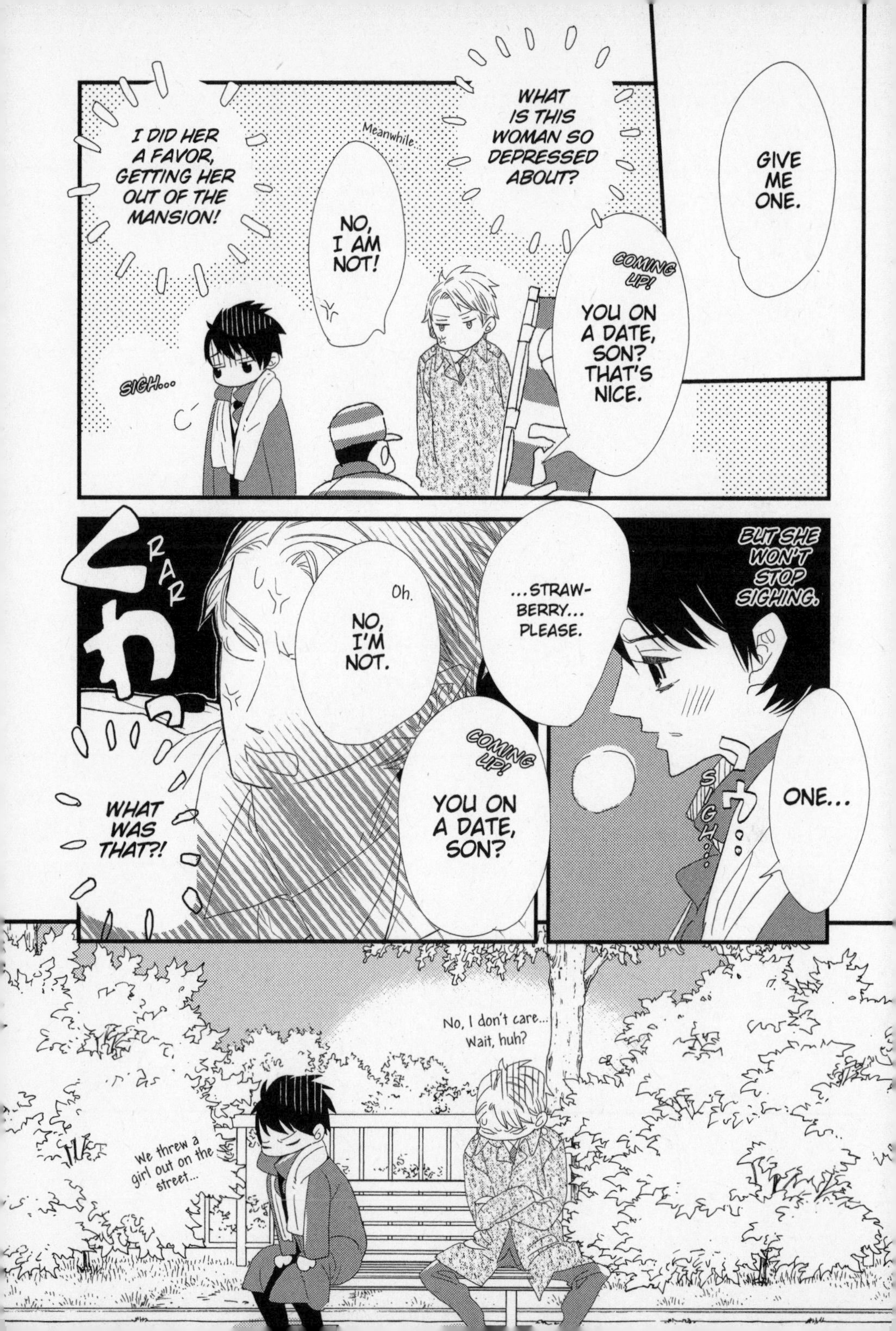
GIVE ME ONE.
WHAT IS THIS WOMAN SO DEPRESSED ABOUT?
COMING UP!
YOU ON A DATE, SON? THAT'S NICE.
Meanwhile...
NO, I AM NOT!
I DID HER A FAVOR, GETTING HER OUT OF THE MANSION!
SIGH...
BUT SHE WON'T STOP SIGHING.
ONE...
SIGH...
...STRAW-BERRY... PLEASE.
COMING UP!
YOU ON A DATE, SON?
Oh.
NO, I'M NOT.
RAR
WHAT WAS THAT?!
No, I don't care... Wait, huh?
We threw a girl out on the street...

the prince in his dark days
hico yamanaka

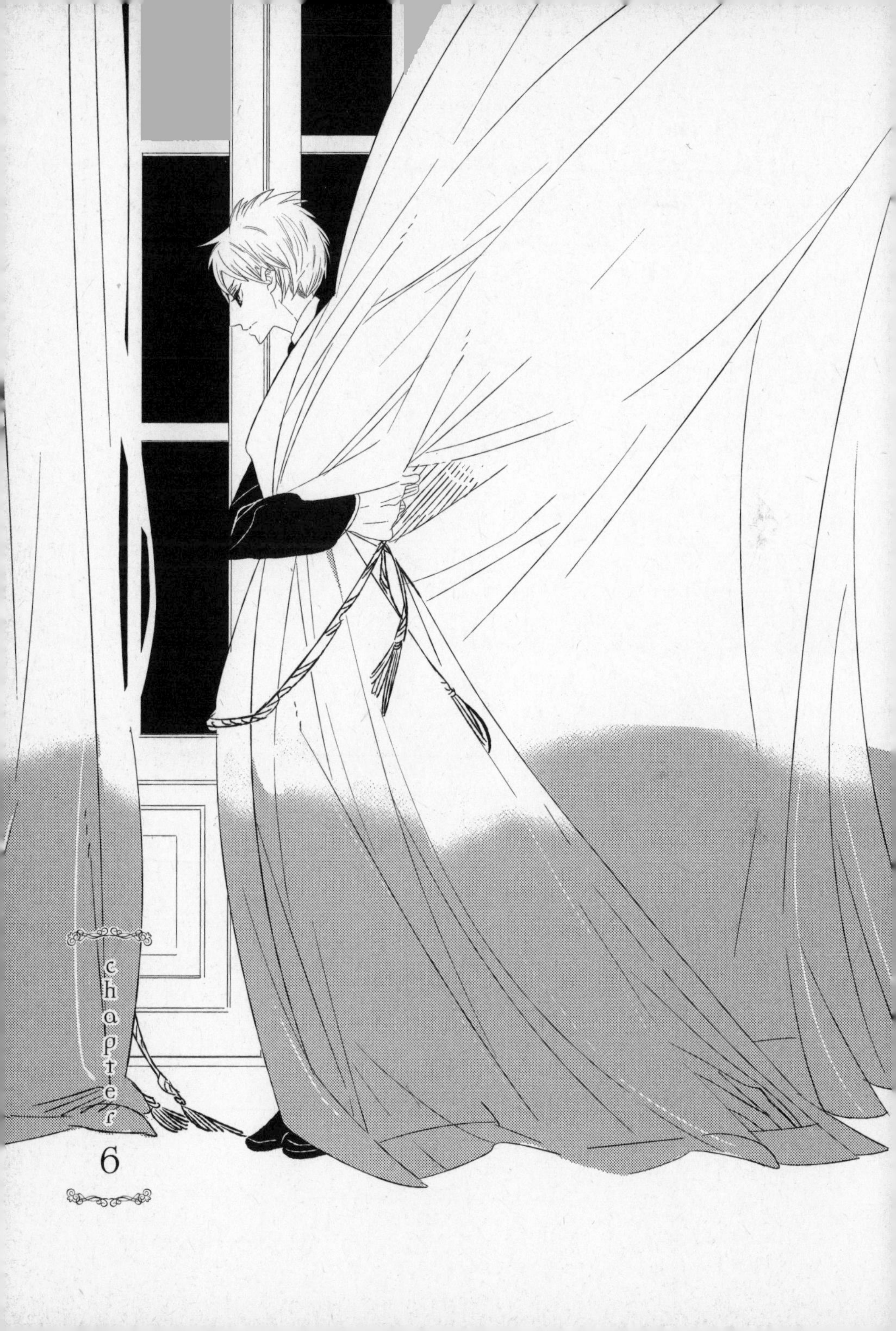
chapter
6

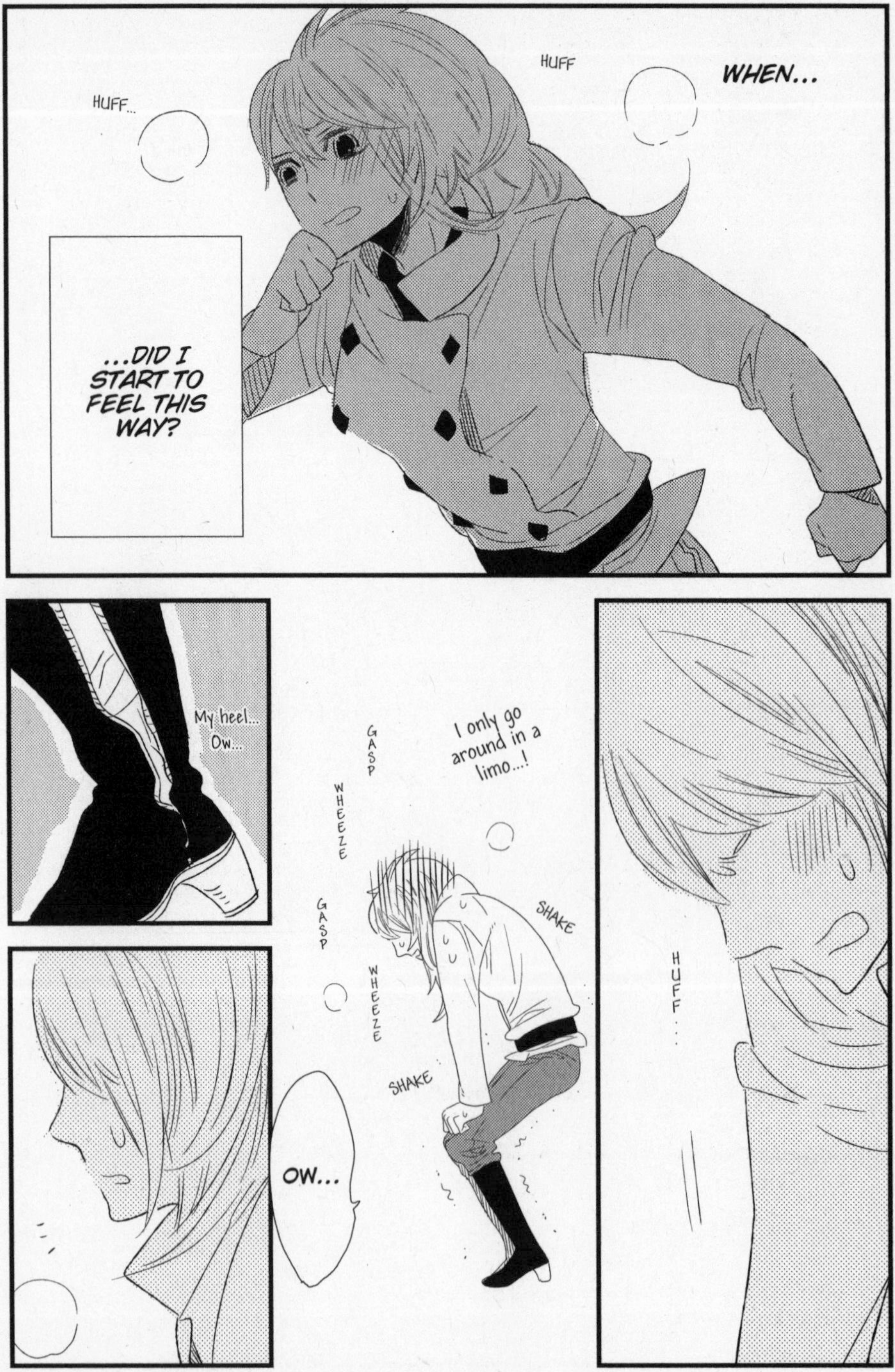
WHEN...
HUFF
HUFF...
...DID I START TO FEEL THIS WAY?
HUFF...
I only go around in a limo...!
GASP
WHEEZE
SHAKE
GASP
WHEEZE
SHAKE
OW...
My heel... Ow...

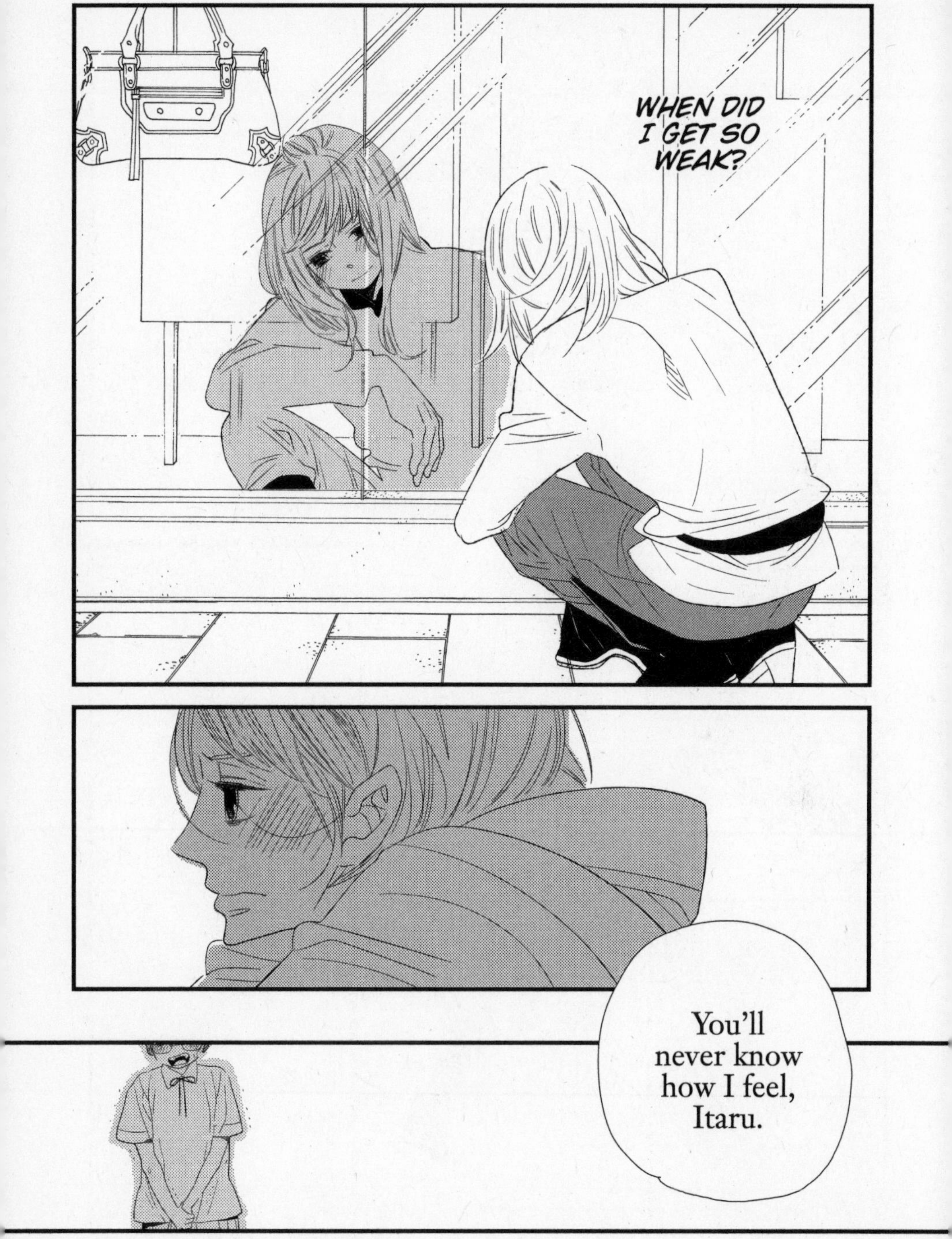
WHEN DID I GET SO WEAK?
You'll never know how I feel, Itaru.

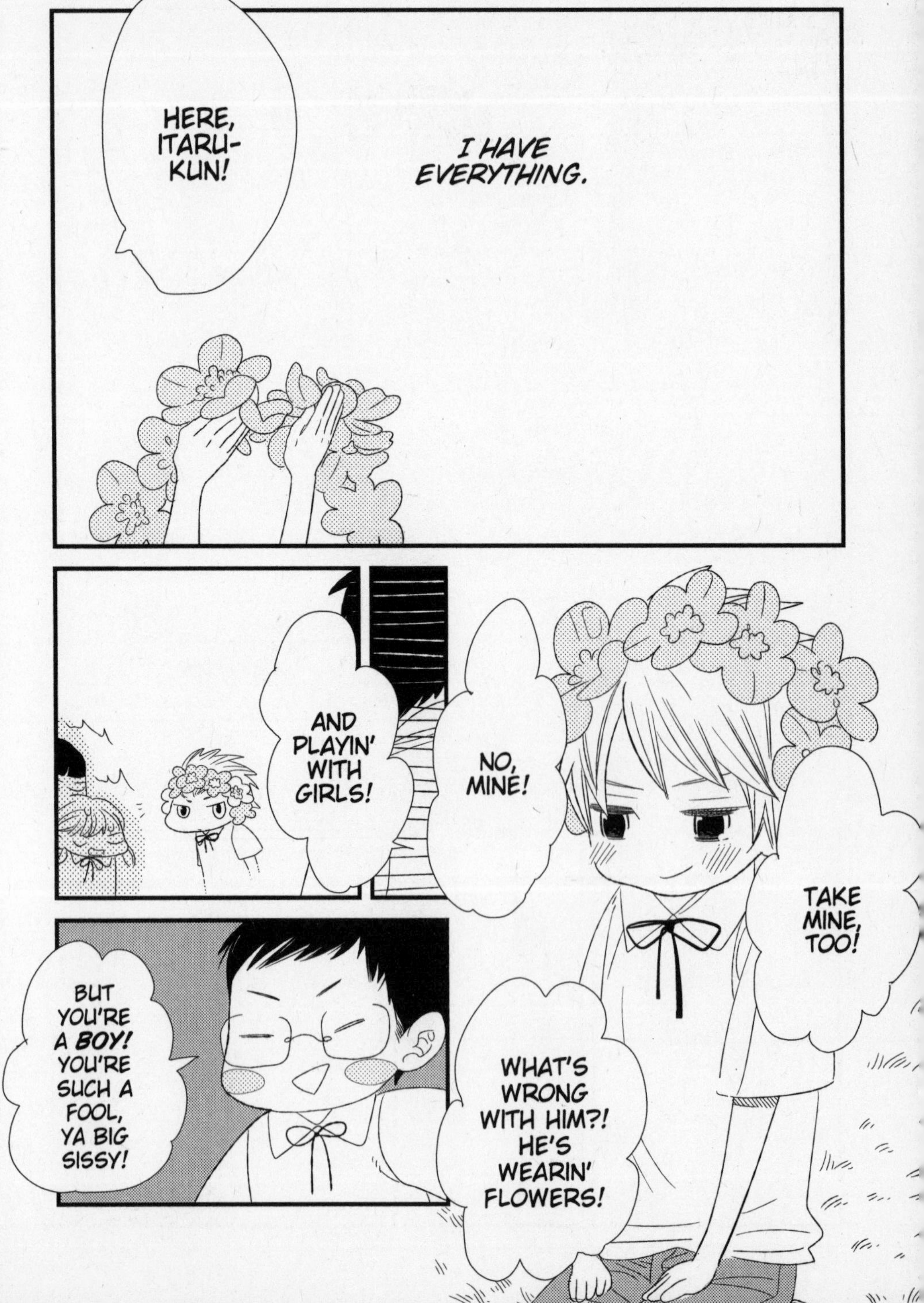
I HAVE EVERYTHING.
HERE, ITARU-KUN!
TAKE MINE, TOO!
NO, MINE!
WHAT'S WRONG WITH HIM?! HE'S WEARIN' FLOWERS!
AND PLAYIN' WITH GIRLS!
BUT YOU'RE A *BOY!* YOU'RE SUCH A FOOL, YA BIG SISSY!

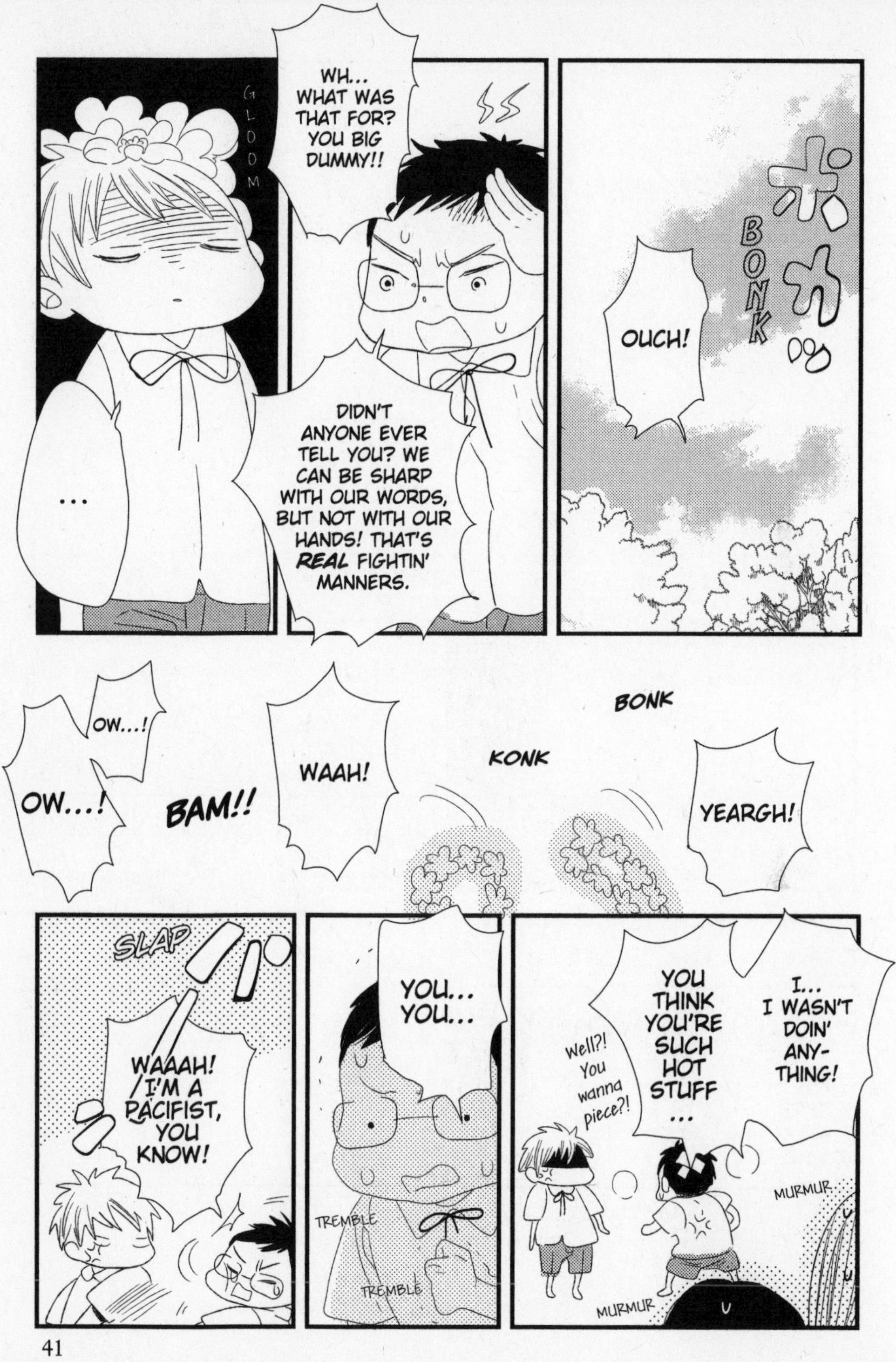
BONK
OUCH!
WH... WHAT WAS THAT FOR? YOU BIG DUMMY!!
DIDN'T ANYONE EVER TELL YOU? WE CAN BE SHARP WITH OUR WORDS, BUT NOT WITH OUR HANDS! THAT'S REAL FIGHTIN' MANNERS.
GLOOM
...
YEARGH!
BONK
KONK
WAAH!
BAM!!
OW...!
OW...!
I... I WASN'T DOIN' ANY-THING!
YOU THINK YOU'RE SUCH HOT STUFF ...
Well?! You wanna piece?!
MURMUR
MURMUR
YOU... YOU...
TREMBLE
TREMBLE
SLAP
WAAAH! I'M A PACIFIST, YOU KNOW!

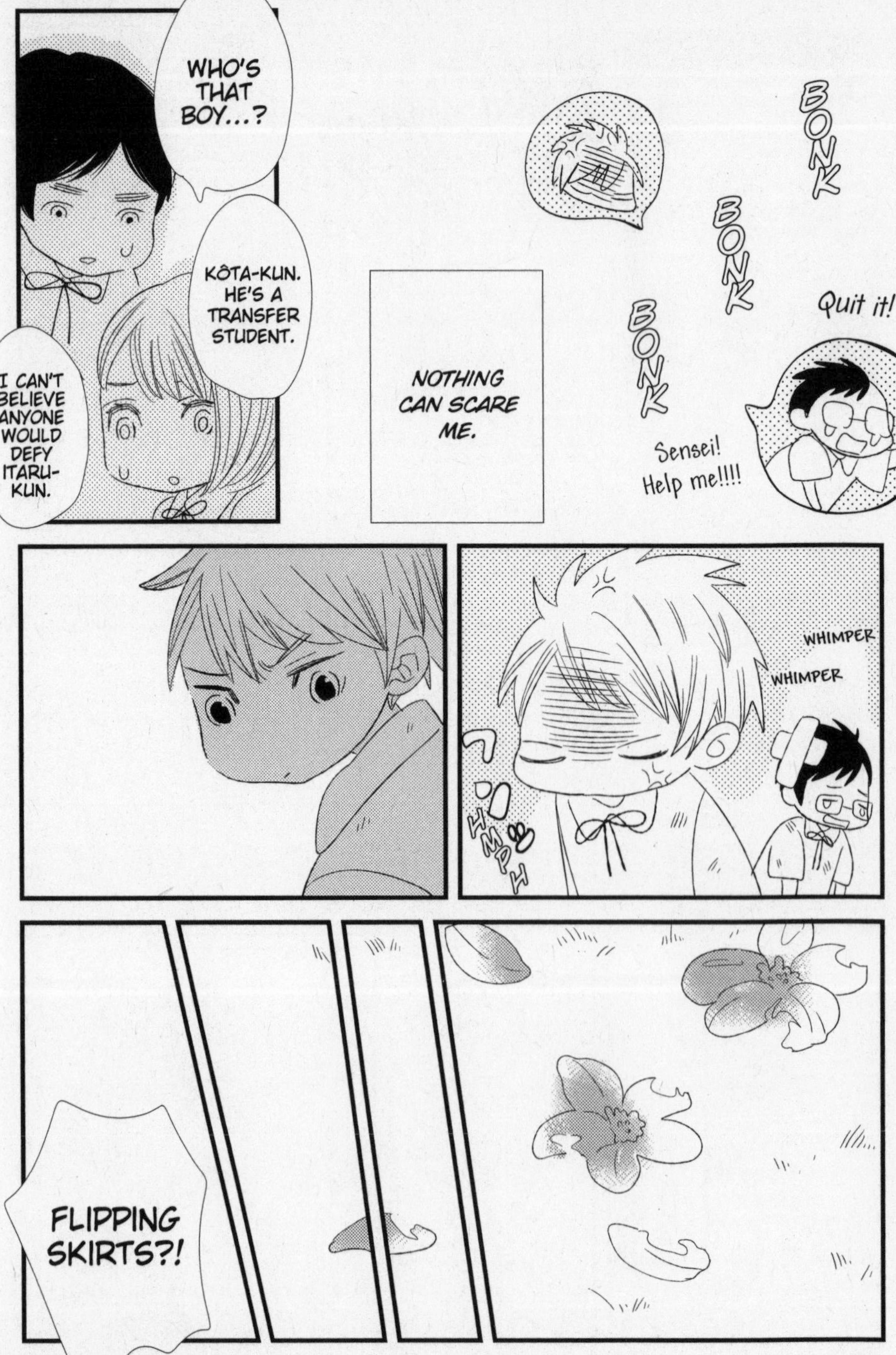
BONK
BONK
BONK
Quit it!
Sensei! Help me!!!!
NOTHING CAN SCARE ME.
WHO'S THAT BOY...?
KÔTA-KUN. HE'S A TRANSFER STUDENT.
I CAN'T BELIEVE ANYONE WOULD DEFY ITARU-KUN.
WHIMPER
WHIMPER
HMPH
FLIPPING SKIRTS?!

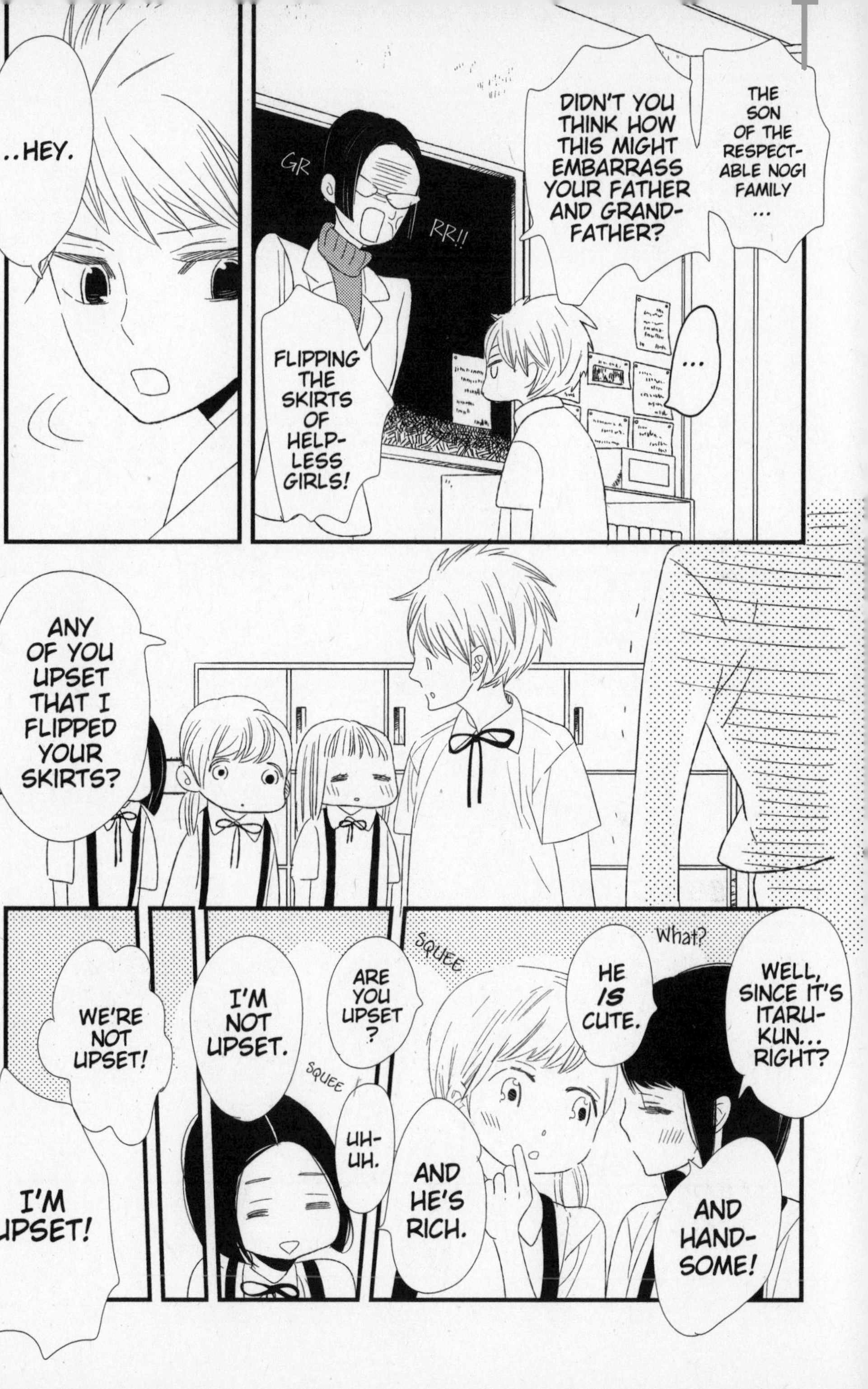
THE SON OF THE RESPECTABLE NOGI FAMILY...
DIDN'T YOU THINK HOW THIS MIGHT EMBARRASS YOUR FATHER AND GRANDFATHER?
GR
RR!!
FLIPPING THE SKIRTS OF HELPLESS GIRLS!
...
...HEY.
ANY OF YOU UPSET THAT I FLIPPED YOUR SKIRTS?
What?
WELL, SINCE IT'S ITARU-KUN... RIGHT?
HE *IS* CUTE.
AND HANDSOME!
SQUEE
AND HE'S RICH.
ARE YOU UPSET?
SQUEE
UH-UH.
I'M NOT UPSET.
WE'RE NOT UPSET!
I'M UPSET!

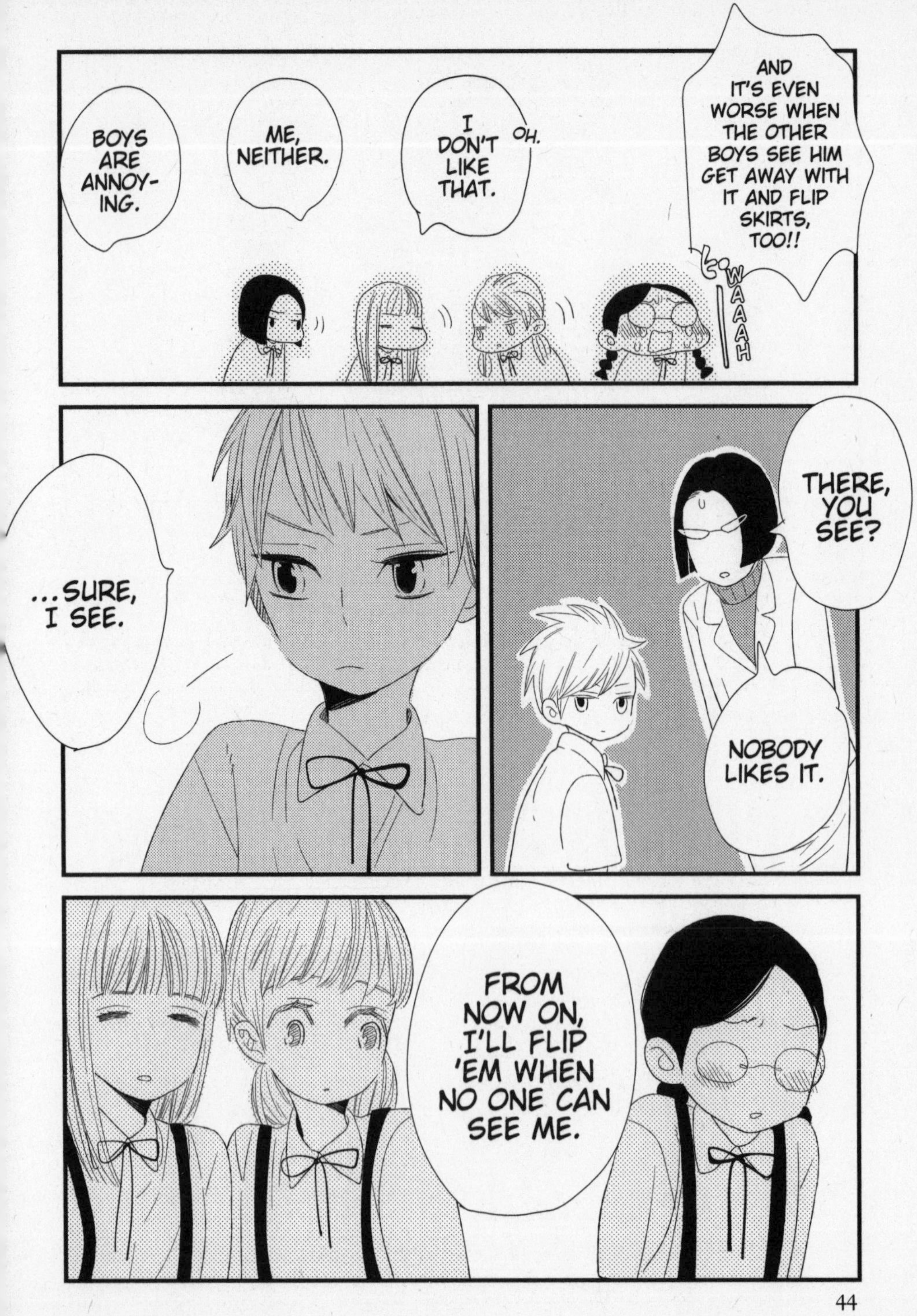

AND IT'S EVEN WORSE WHEN THE OTHER BOYS SEE HIM GET AWAY WITH IT AND FLIP SKIRTS, TOO!!
WAAAAH
OH.
I DON'T LIKE THAT.
ME, NEITHER.
BOYS ARE ANNOY-ING.
THERE, YOU SEE?
NOBODY LIKES IT.
...SURE, I SEE.
FROM NOW ON, I'LL FLIP 'EM WHEN NO ONE CAN SEE ME.

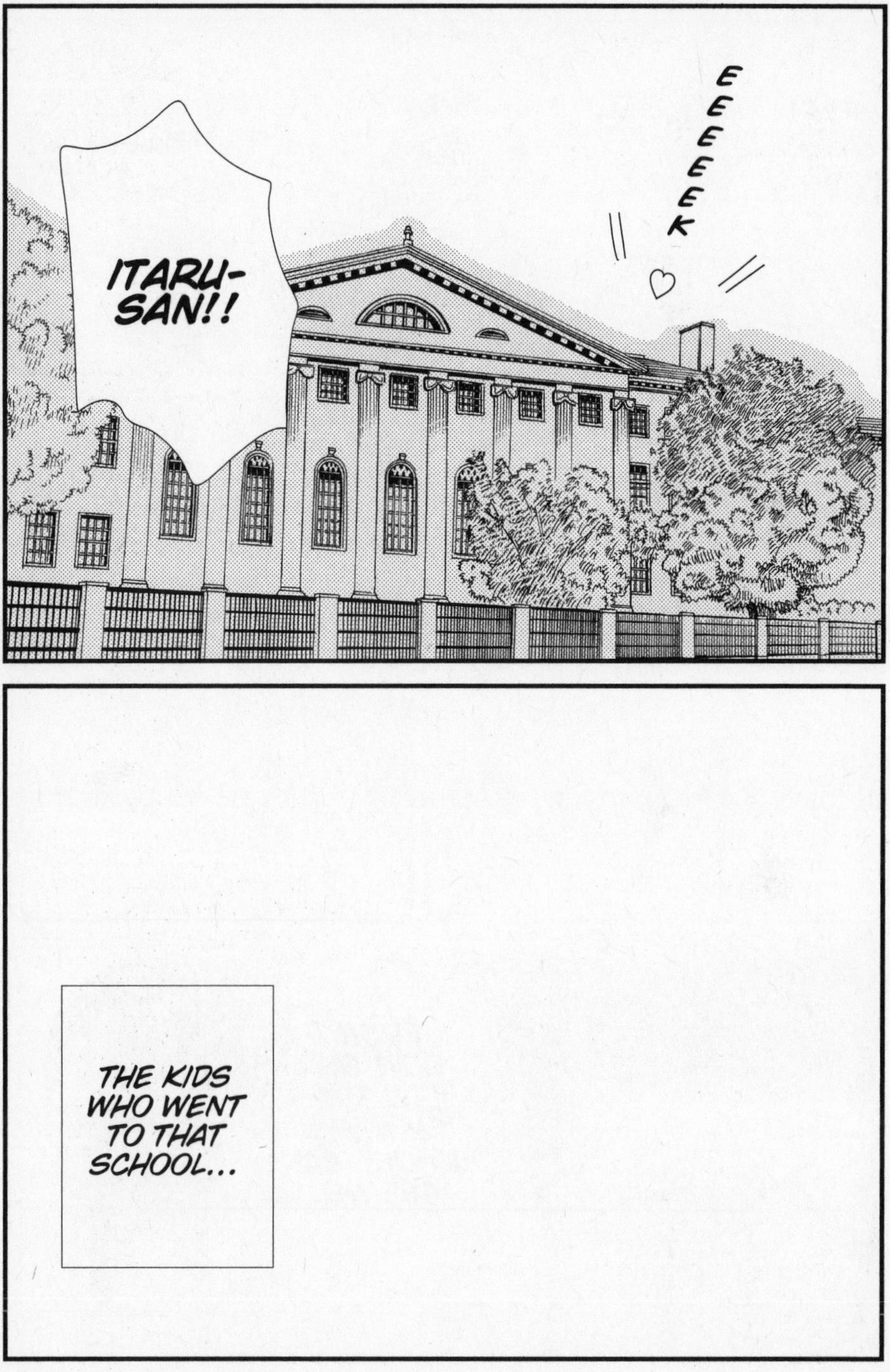
EEEEEK
ITARU-SAN!!
THE KIDS WHO WENT TO THAT SCHOOL...

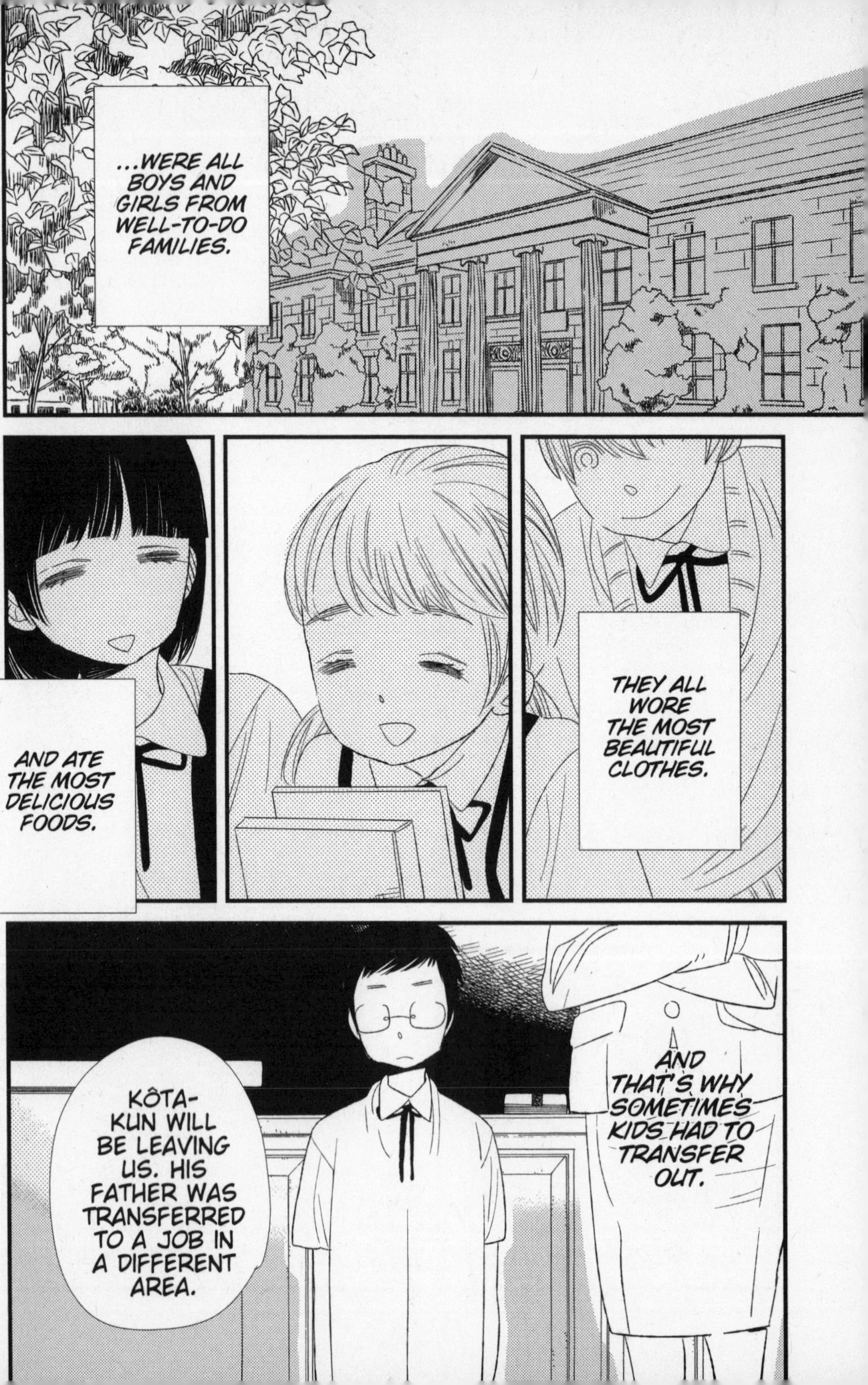
...WERE ALL BOYS AND GIRLS FROM WELL-TO-DO FAMILIES.
THEY ALL WORE THE MOST BEAUTIFUL CLOTHES.
AND ATE THE MOST DELICIOUS FOODS.
AND THAT'S WHY SOMETIMES KIDS HAD TO TRANSFER OUT.
KÔTA-KUN WILL BE LEAVING US. HIS FATHER WAS TRANSFERRED TO A JOB IN A DIFFERENT AREA.

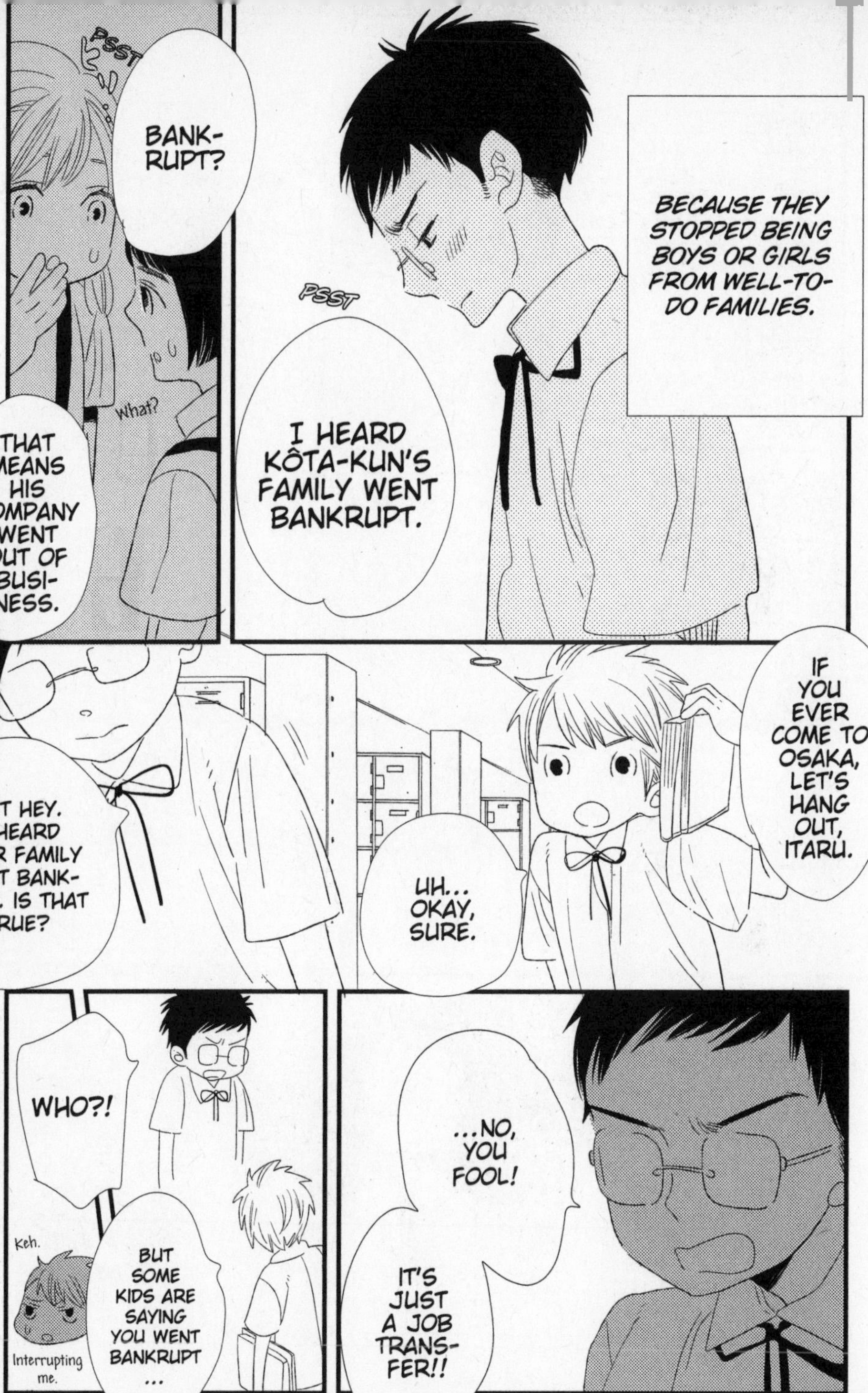
BECAUSE THEY STOPPED BEING BOYS OR GIRLS FROM WELL-TO-DO FAMILIES.
PSST
I HEARD KÔTA-KUN'S FAMILY WENT BANKRUPT.
PSST
BANK-RUPT?
What?
THAT MEANS HIS COMPANY WENT OUT OF BUSI-NESS.
IF YOU EVER COME TO OSAKA, LET'S HANG OUT, ITARU.
UH... OKAY, SURE.
BUT HEY. I HEARD YOUR FAMILY WENT BANK-RUPT. IS THAT TRUE?
...NO, YOU FOOL!
IT'S JUST A JOB TRANS-FER!!
WHO?!
BUT SOME KIDS ARE SAYING YOU WENT BANKRUPT ...
Keh.
Interrupting me.

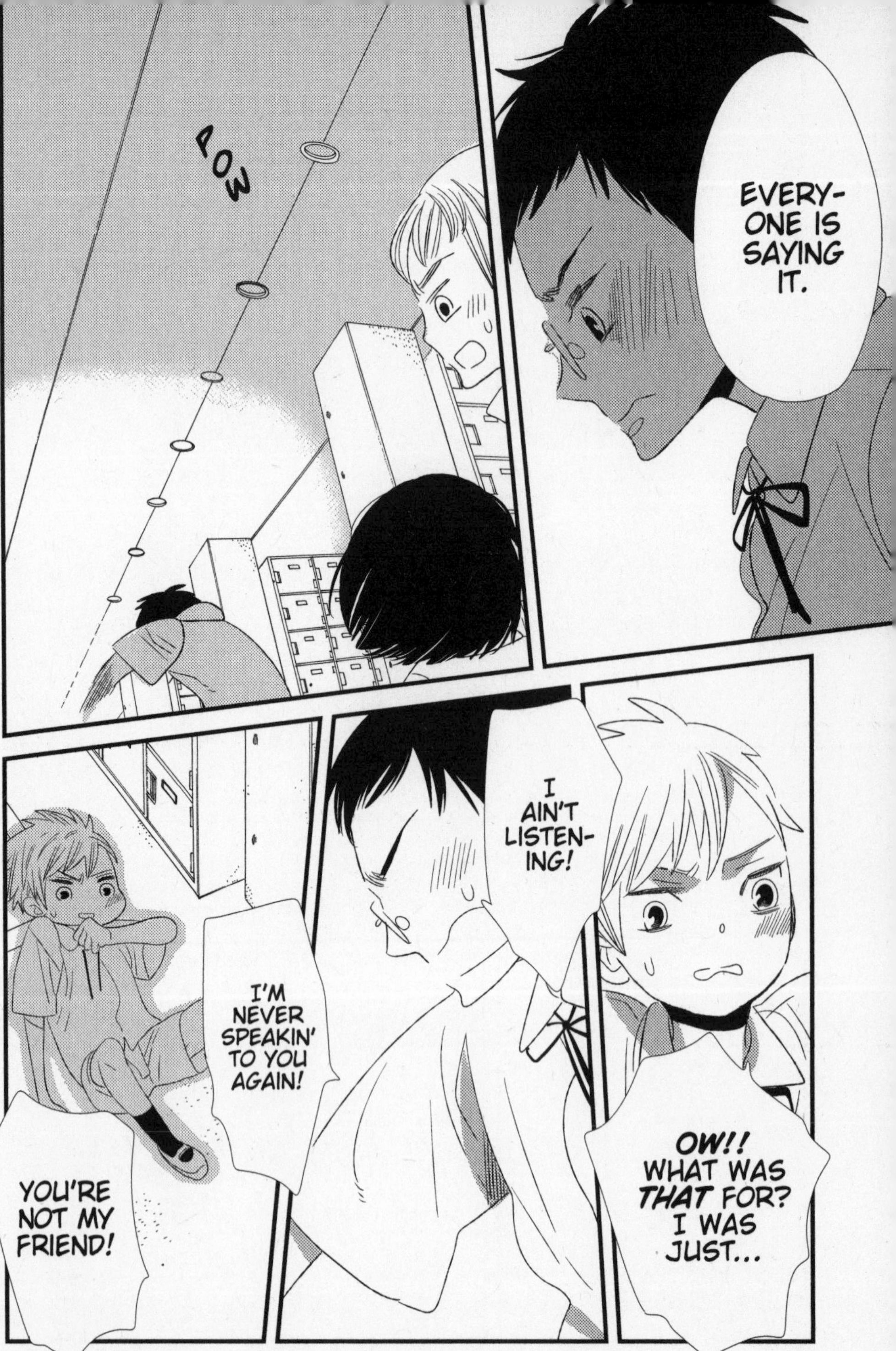
EVERY-ONE IS SAYING IT.
POW
OW!! WHAT WAS THAT FOR? I WAS JUST...
I AIN'T LISTEN-ING!
I'M NEVER SPEAKIN' TO YOU AGAIN!
YOU'RE NOT MY FRIEND!

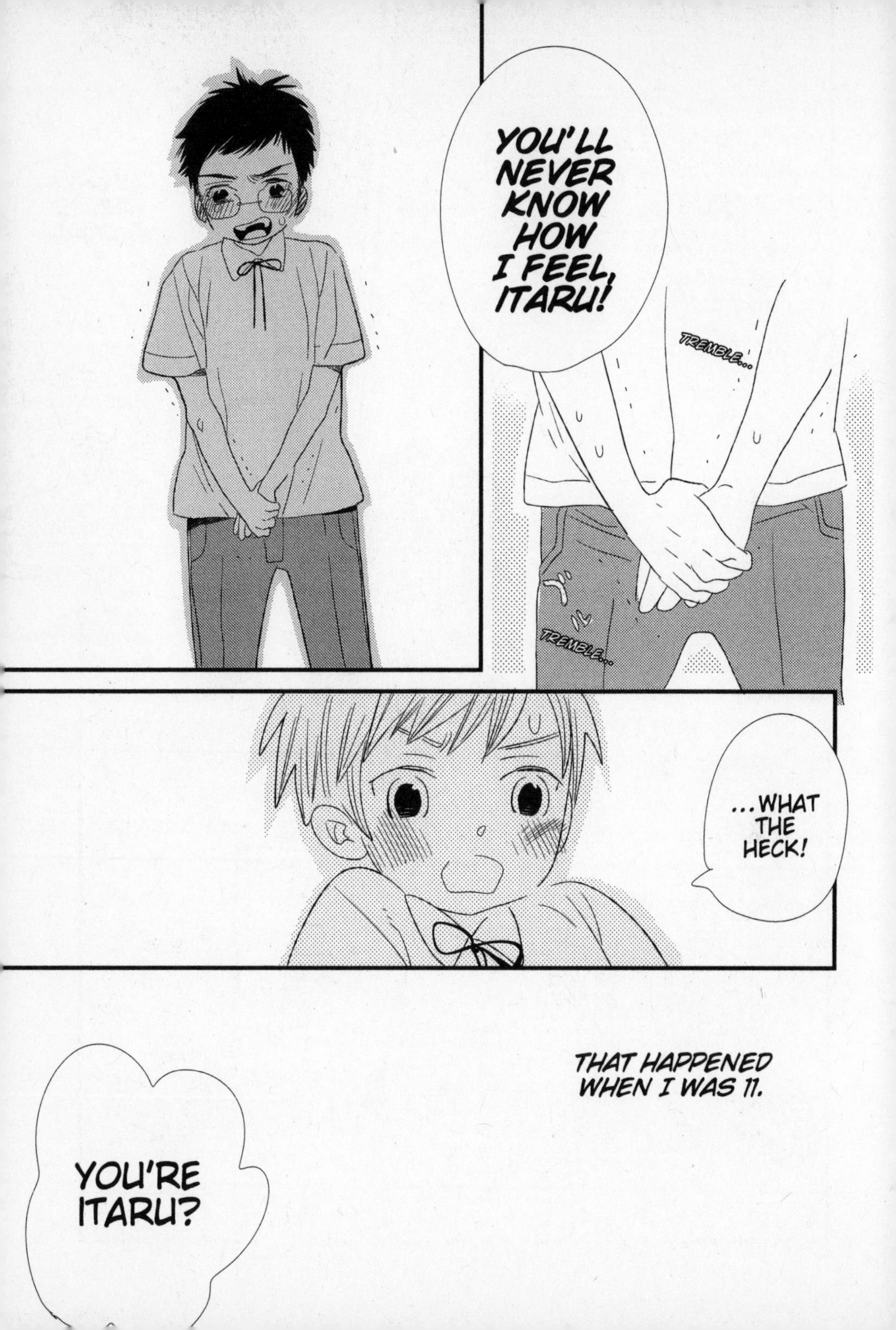
YOU'LL NEVER KNOW HOW I FEEL, ITARU!
TREMBLE...
TREMBLE...
...WHAT THE HECK!
THAT HAPPENED WHEN I WAS 11.
YOU'RE ITARU?

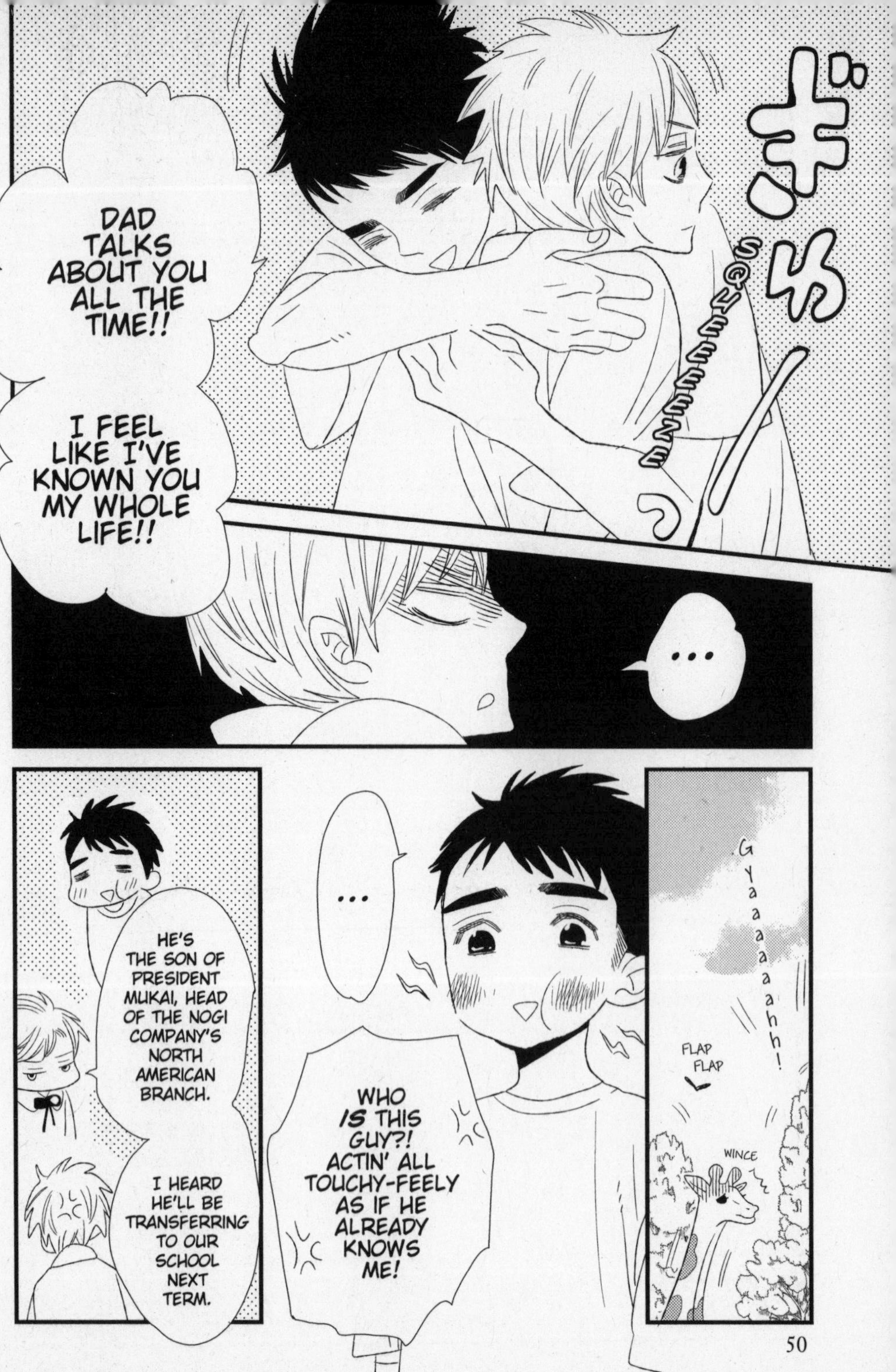
ぎゅっ
SQUEEEEEEZE
DAD TALKS ABOUT YOU ALL THE TIME!!
I FEEL LIKE I'VE KNOWN YOU MY WHOLE LIFE!!
...
Gyaaaaaahh!
FLAP FLAP
WINCE
...
WHO IS THIS GUY?! ACTIN' ALL TOUCHY-FEELY AS IF HE ALREADY KNOWS ME!
HE'S THE SON OF PRESIDENT MUKAI, HEAD OF THE NOGI COMPANY'S NORTH AMERICAN BRANCH.
I HEARD HE'LL BE TRANSFERRING TO OUR SCHOOL NEXT TERM.

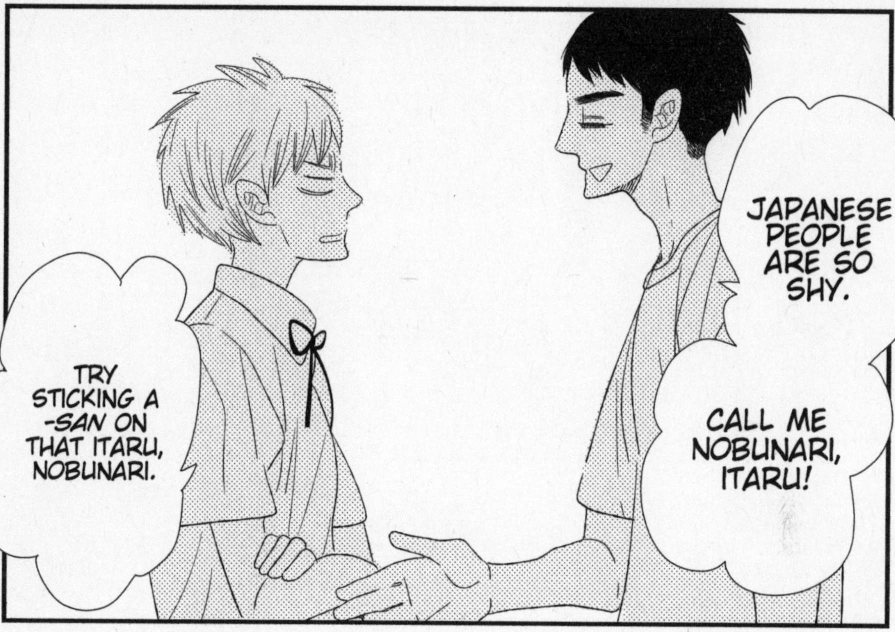
JAPANESE PEOPLE ARE SO SHY.
CALL ME NOBUNARI, ITARU!
TRY STICKING A -SAN ON THAT ITARU, NOBUNARI.

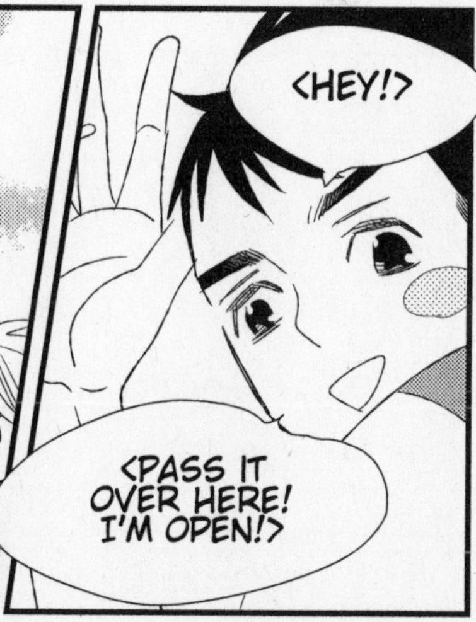
<HEY!>
<PASS IT OVER HERE! I'M OPEN!>

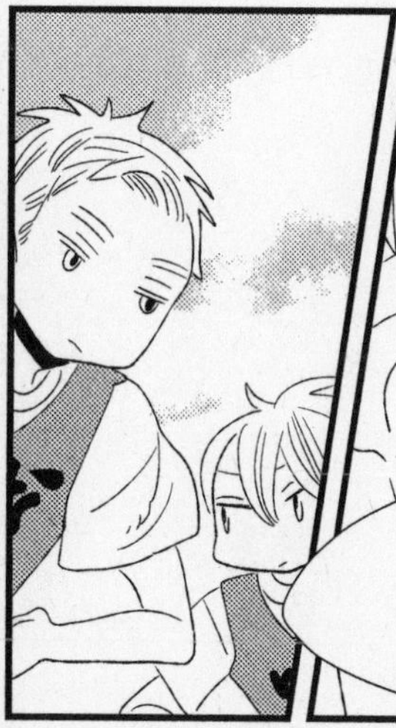

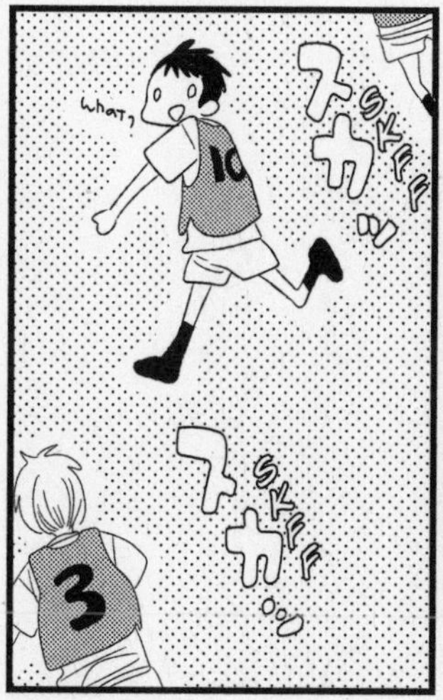
what,
SKFF
SKFF

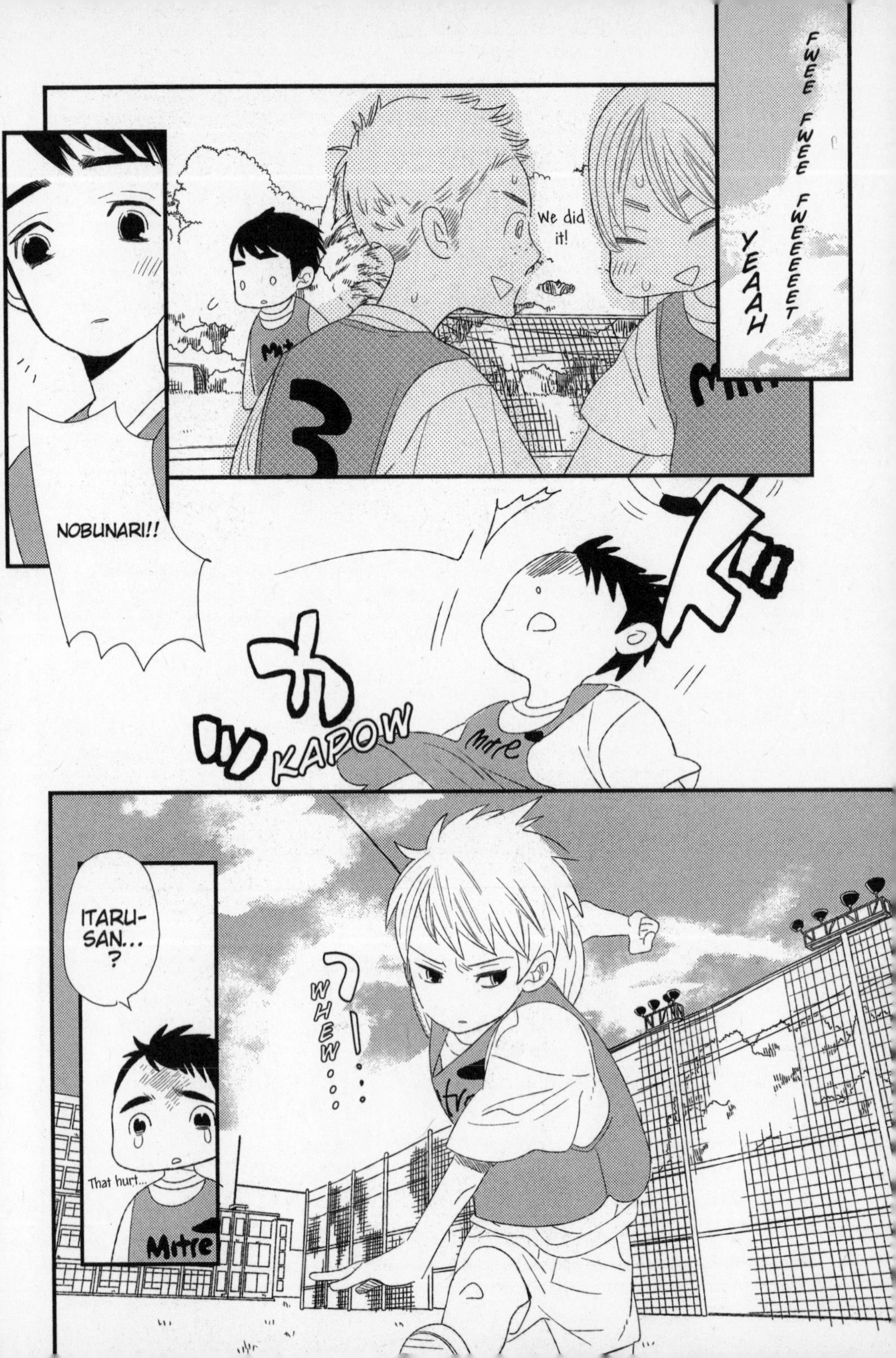
FWEE FWEE FWEEEEET
YEAAH
We did it!
NOBUNARI!!
KAPOW
WHEW...
ITARU-SAN...?
That hurt...

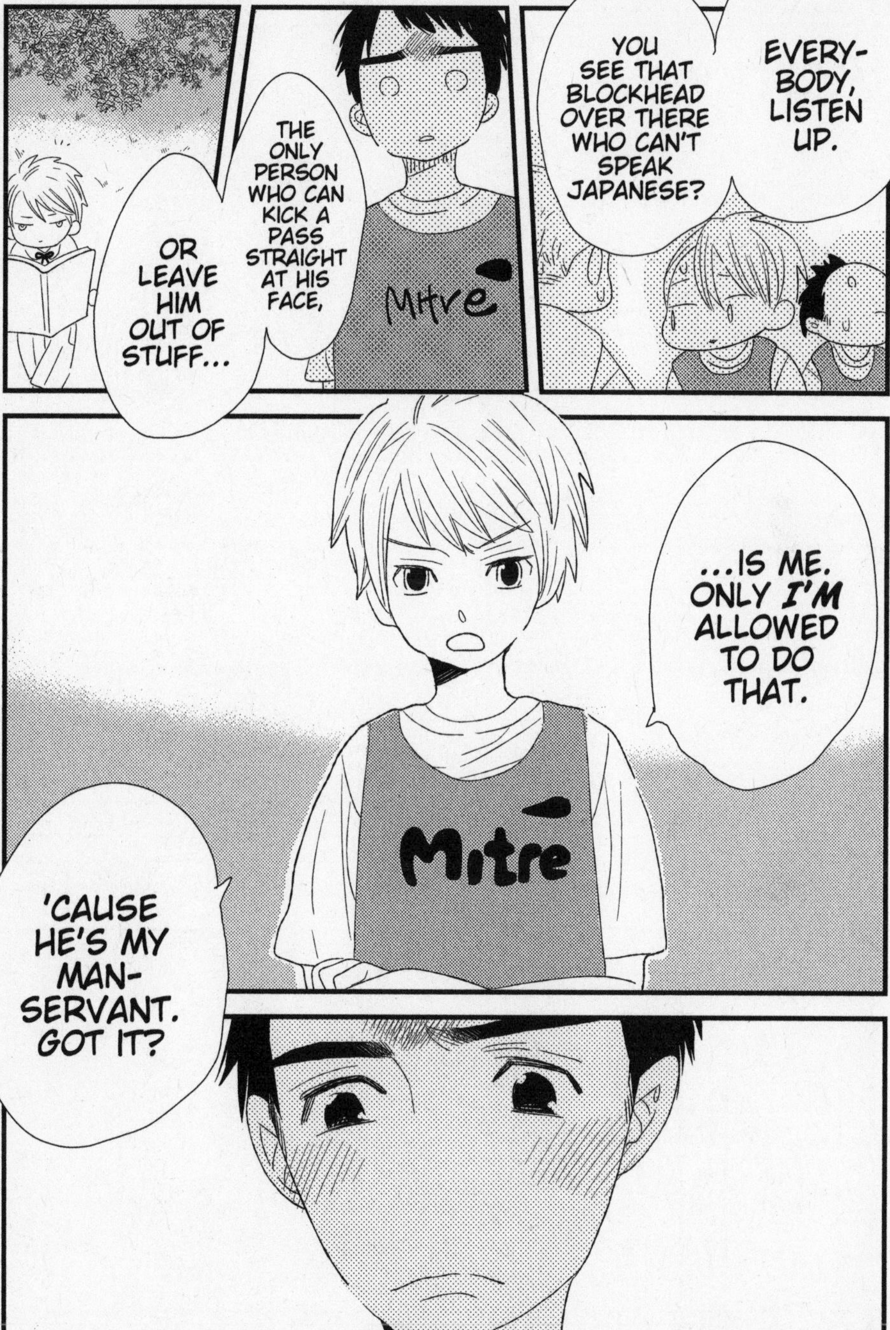
EVERY-BODY, LISTEN UP.
YOU SEE THAT BLOCKHEAD OVER THERE WHO CAN'T SPEAK JAPANESE?
Mitre
THE ONLY PERSON WHO CAN KICK A PASS STRAIGHT AT HIS FACE,
OR LEAVE HIM OUT OF STUFF...
...IS ME. ONLY *I'M* ALLOWED TO DO THAT.
Mitre
'CAUSE HE'S MY MAN-SERVANT. GOT IT?

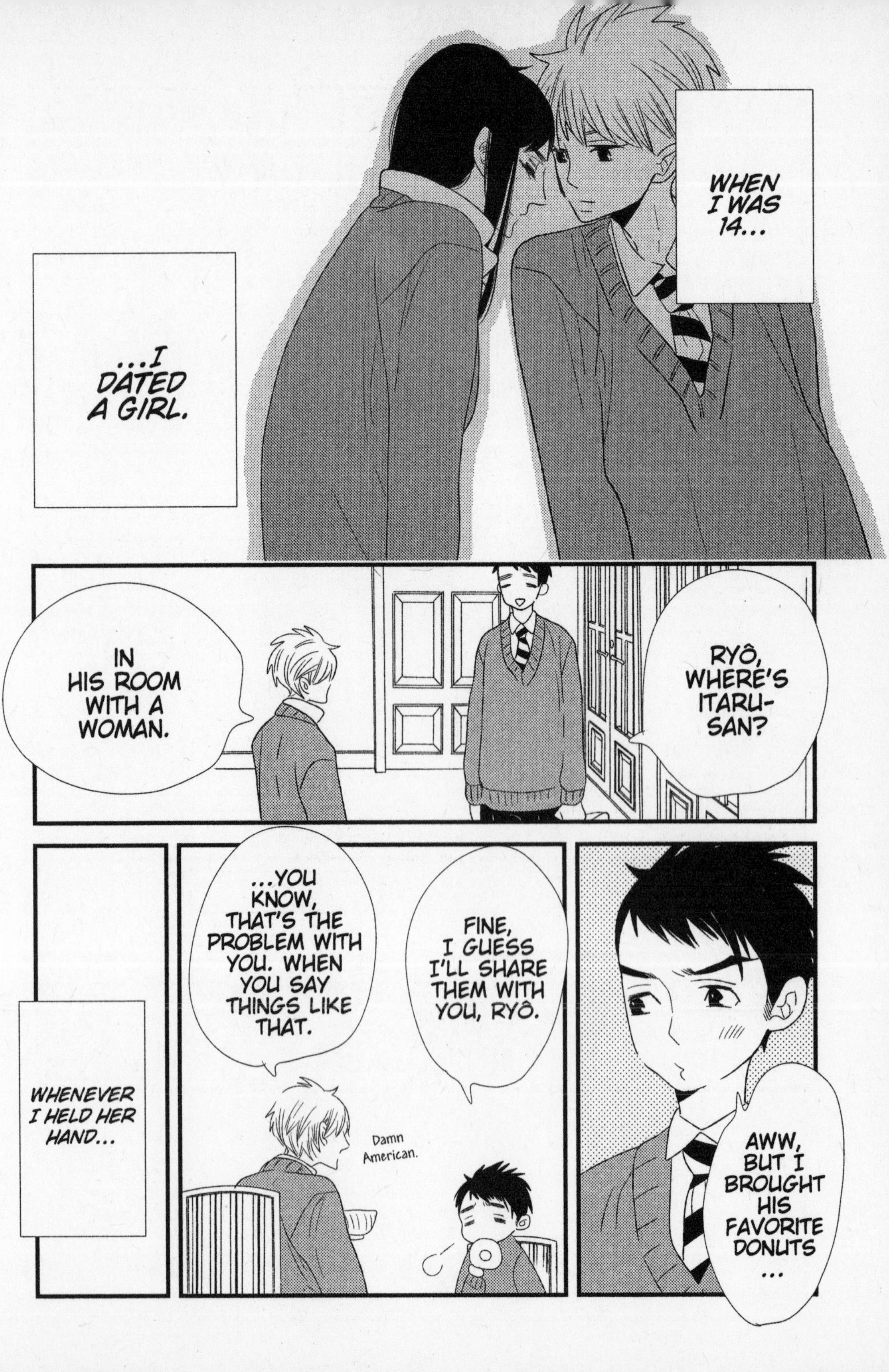
WHEN I WAS 14...
...I DATED A GIRL.
RYÔ, WHERE'S ITARU-SAN?
IN HIS ROOM WITH A WOMAN.
AWW, BUT I BROUGHT HIS FAVORITE DONUTS ...
FINE, I GUESS I'LL SHARE THEM WITH YOU, RYÔ.
...YOU KNOW, THAT'S THE PROBLEM WITH YOU. WHEN YOU SAY THINGS LIKE THAT.
Damn American.
WHENEVER I HELD HER HAND...

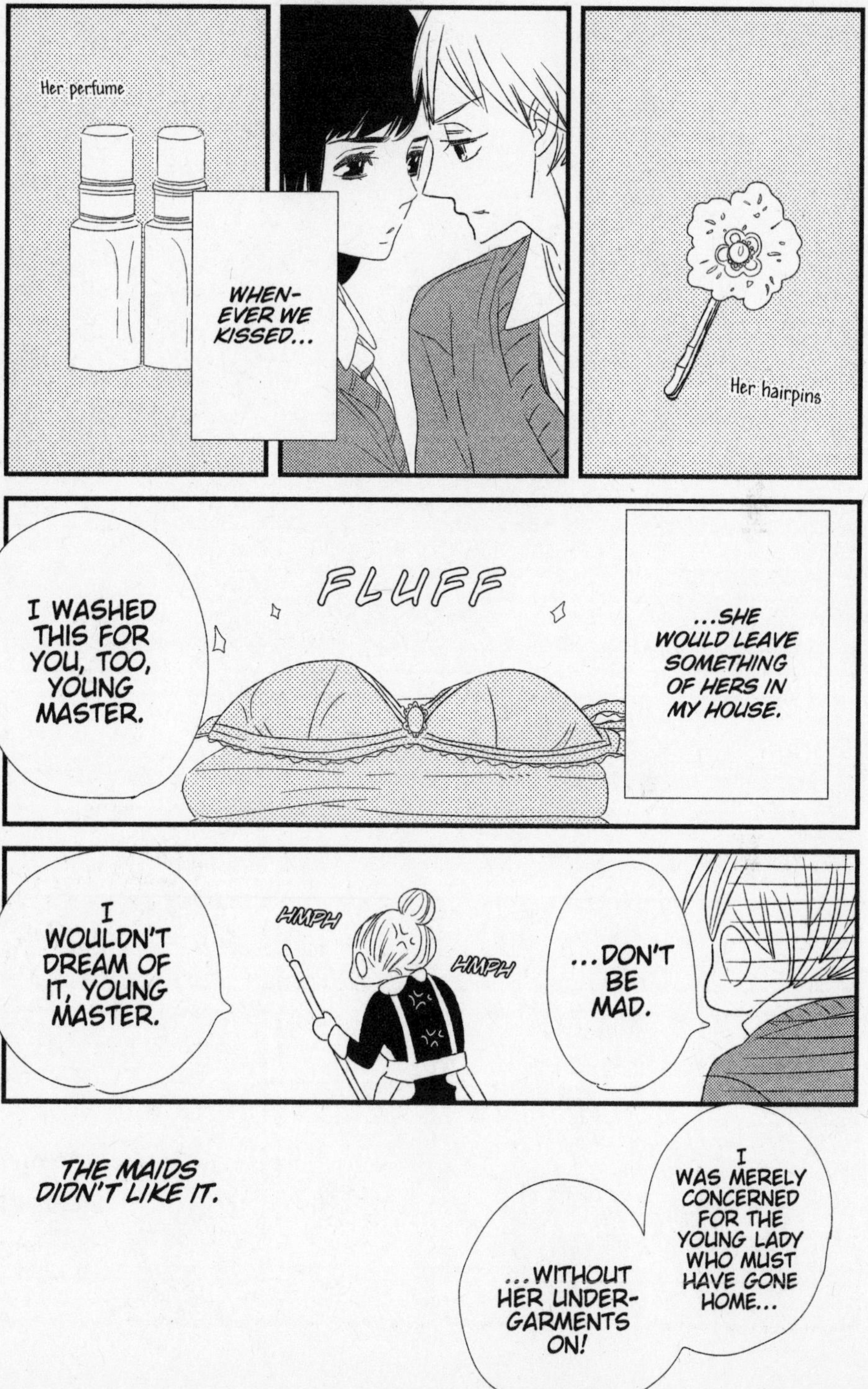
Her hairpins
WHEN-EVER WE KISSED...
Her perfume
...SHE WOULD LEAVE SOMETHING OF HERS IN MY HOUSE.
FLUFF
I WASHED THIS FOR YOU, TOO, YOUNG MASTER.
...DON'T BE MAD.
HMPH
HMPH
I WOULDN'T DREAM OF IT, YOUNG MASTER.
I WAS MERELY CONCERNED FOR THE YOUNG LADY WHO MUST HAVE GONE HOME...
...WITHOUT HER UNDER-GARMENTS ON!
THE MAIDS DIDN'T LIKE IT.

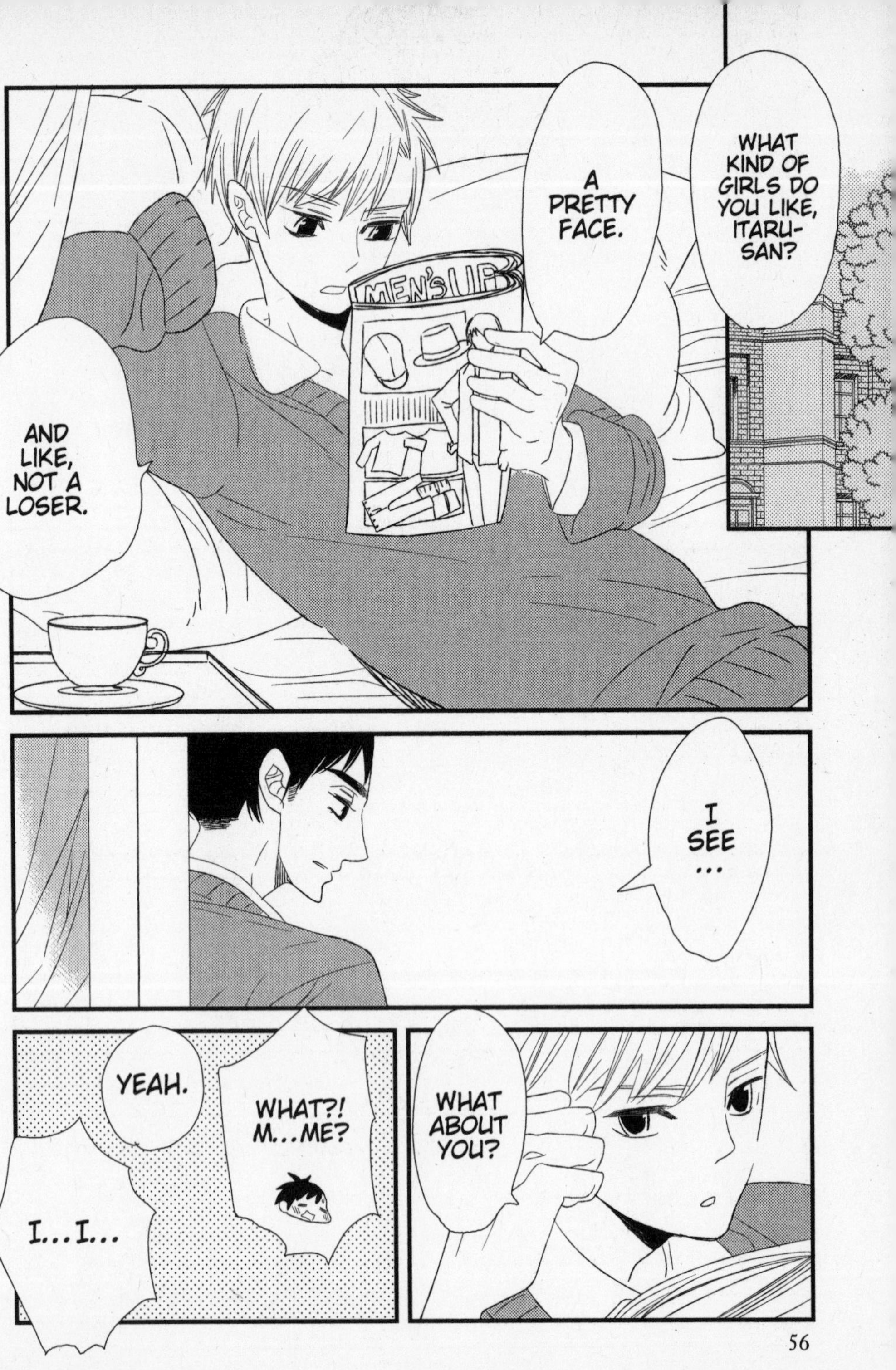
WHAT KIND OF GIRLS DO YOU LIKE, ITARU-SAN?
A PRETTY FACE.
AND LIKE, NOT A LOSER.
I SEE...
WHAT ABOUT YOU?
WHAT?! M...ME?
YEAH.
I...I...

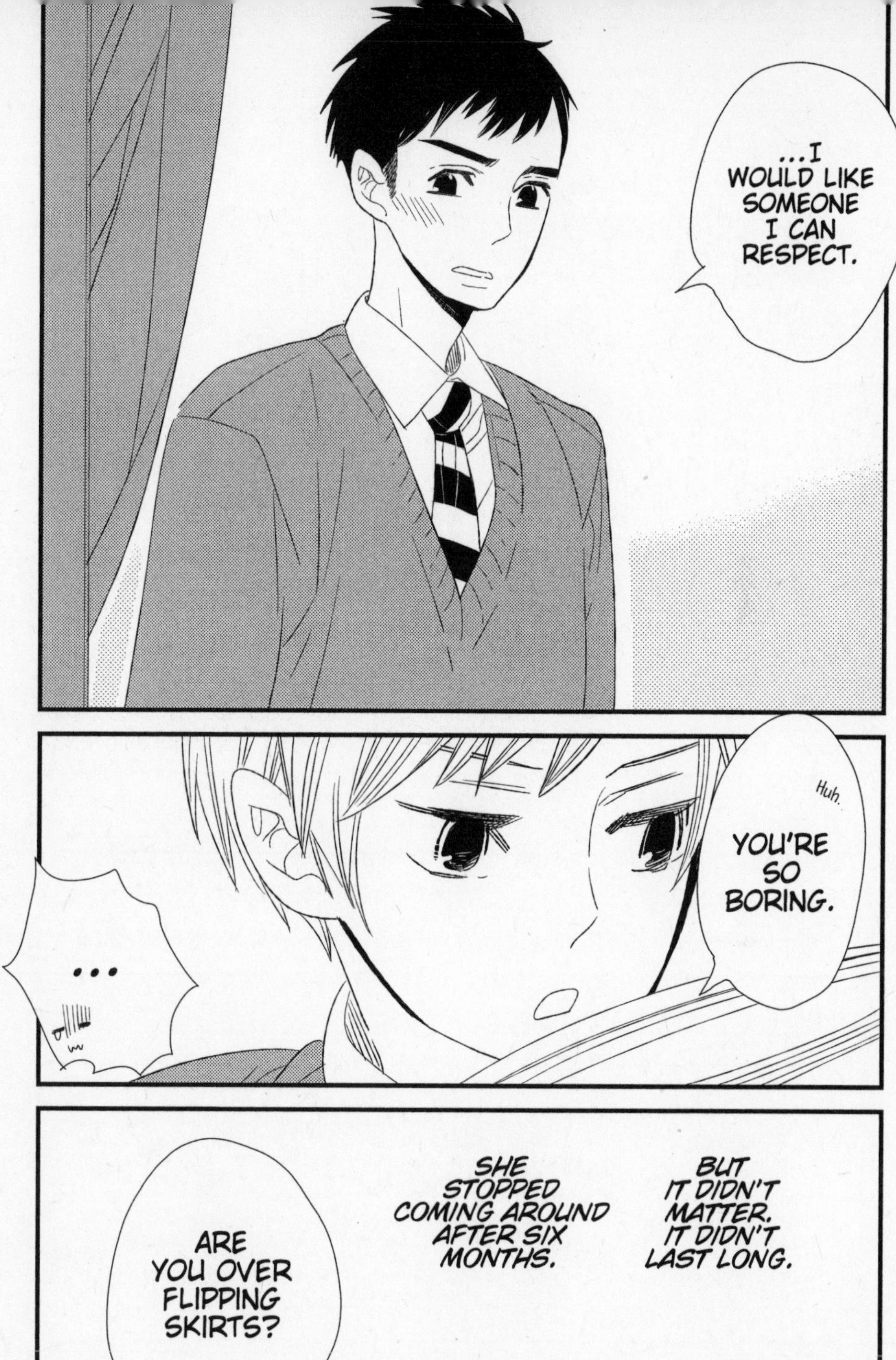
...I WOULD LIKE SOMEONE I CAN RESPECT.
Huh.
YOU'RE SO BORING.
...
BUT IT DIDN'T MATTER. IT DIDN'T LAST LONG.
SHE STOPPED COMING AROUND AFTER SIX MONTHS.
ARE YOU OVER FLIPPING SKIRTS?

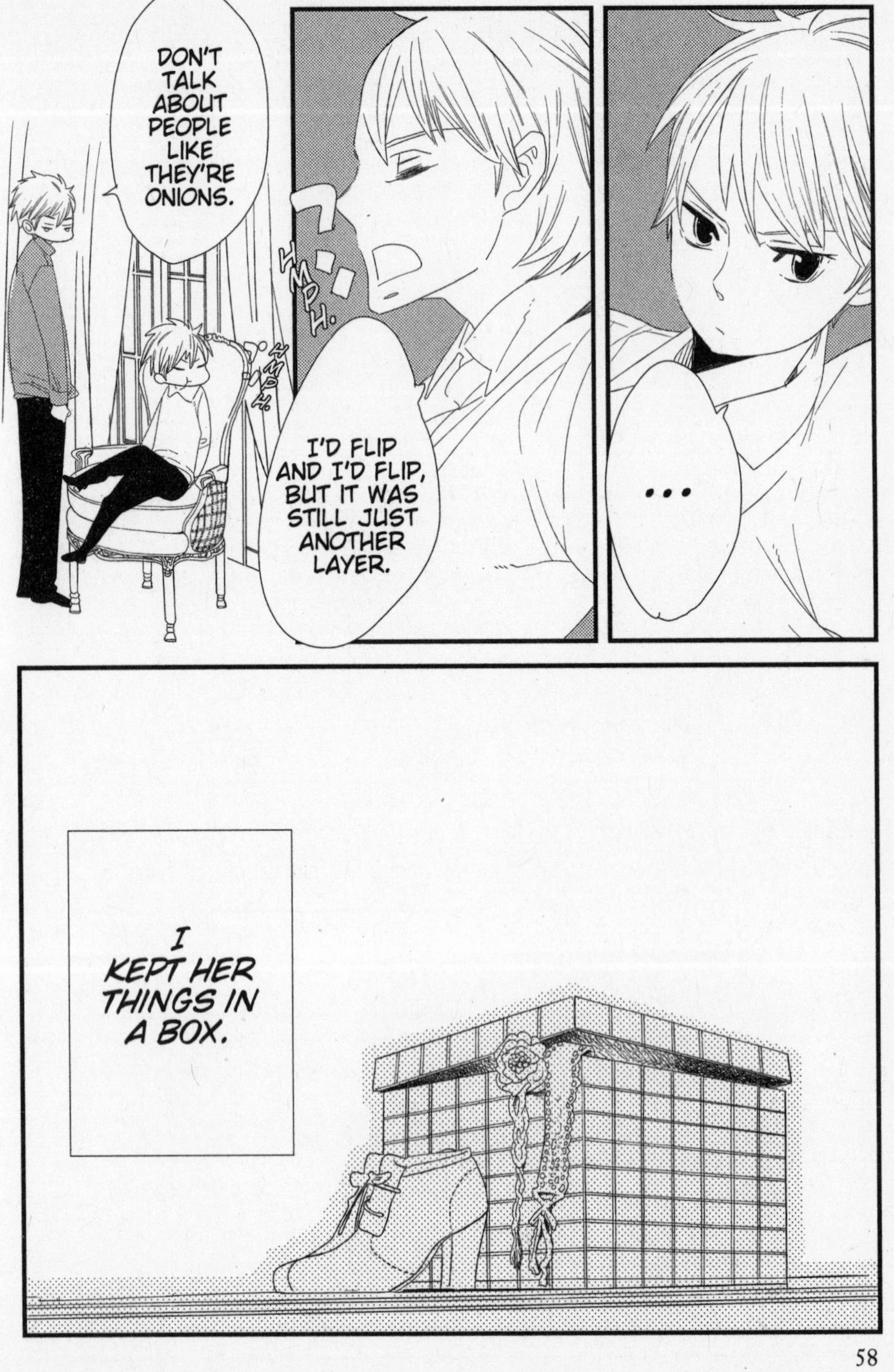
...
HMPH.
I'D FLIP AND I'D FLIP, BUT IT WAS STILL JUST ANOTHER LAYER.
HMPH.
DON'T TALK ABOUT PEOPLE LIKE THEY'RE ONIONS.
I KEPT HER THINGS IN A BOX.

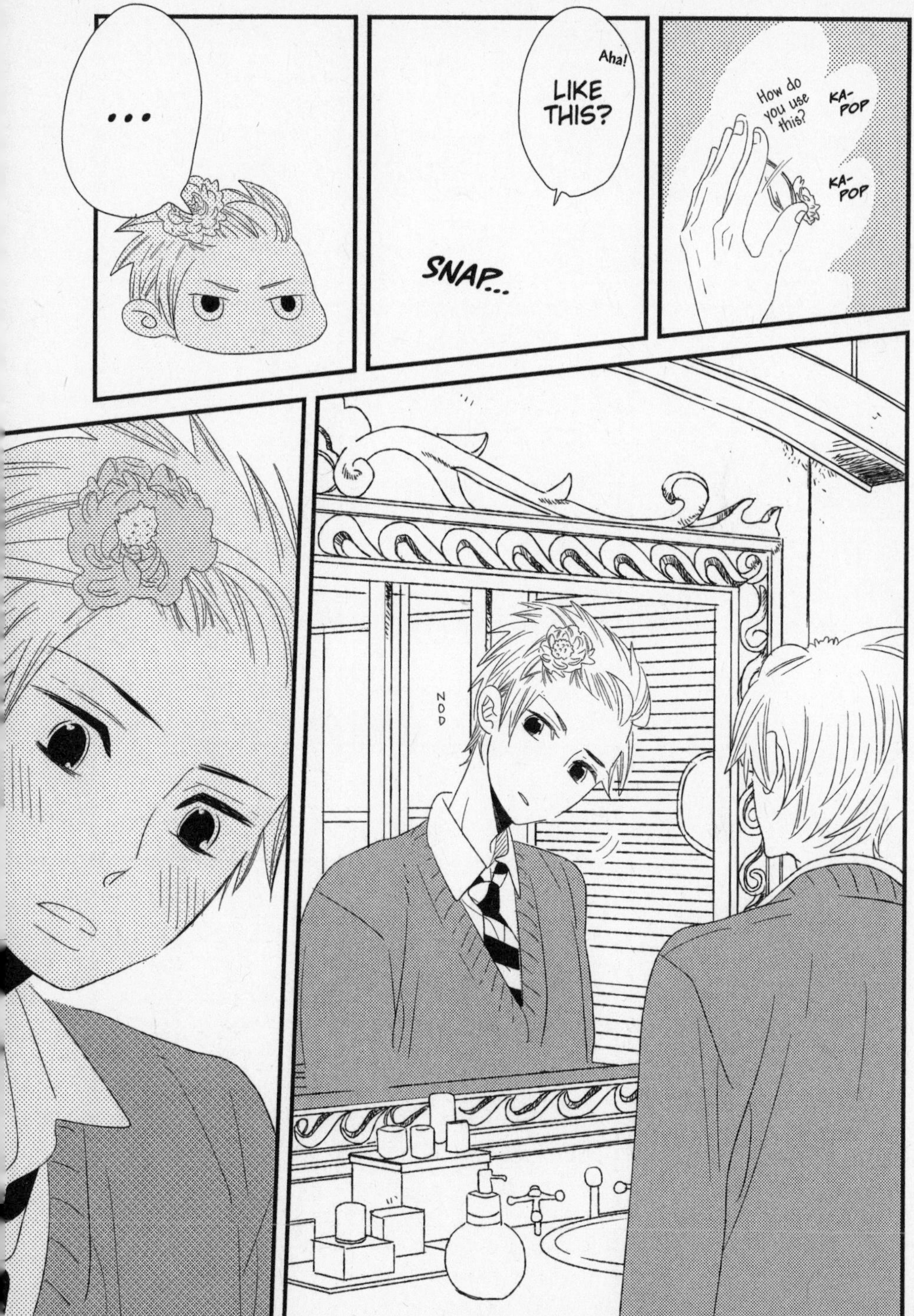
How do you use this?
KA-POP
KA-POP
Aha!
LIKE THIS?
SNAP...
...
NOD

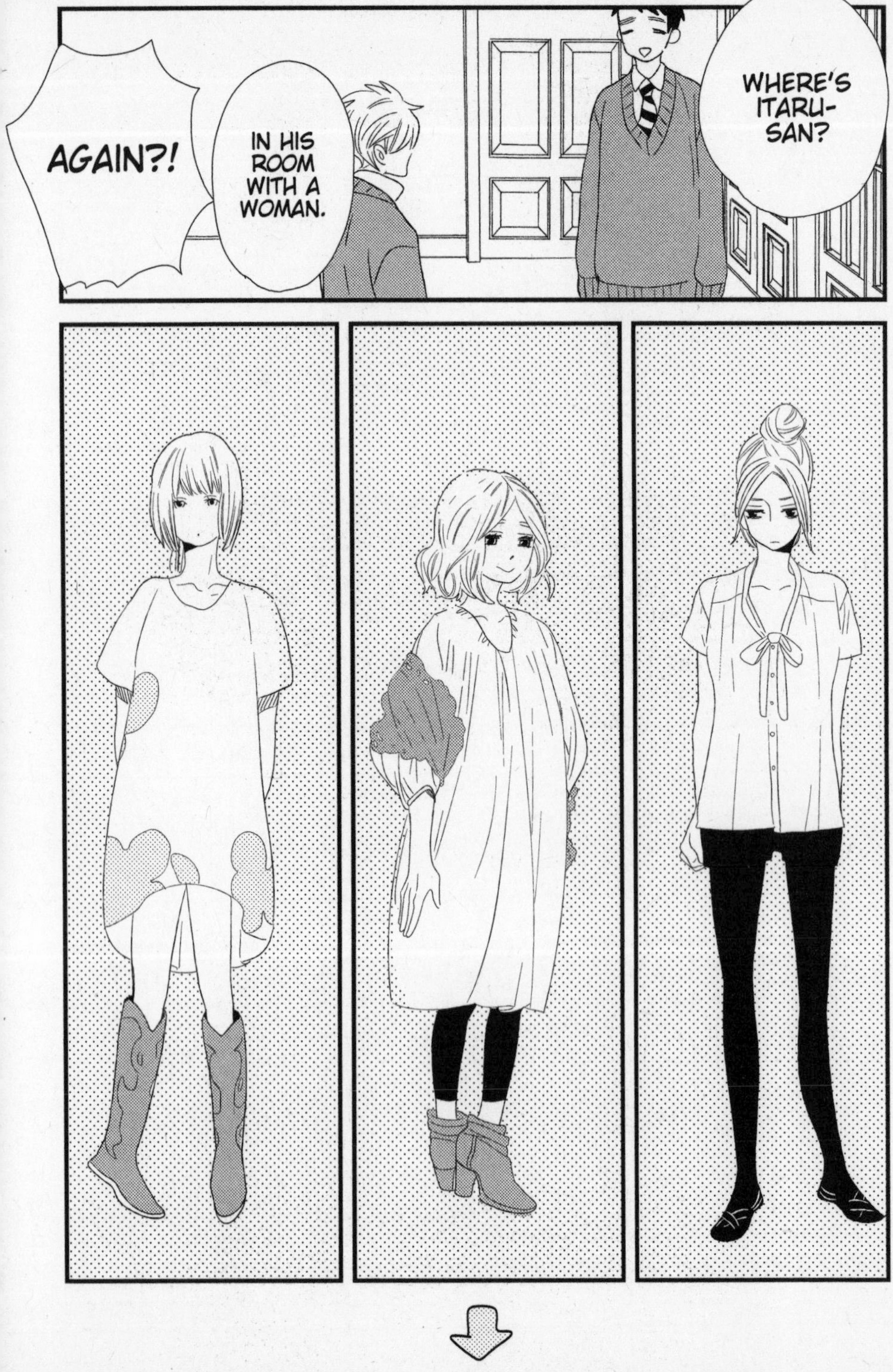
WHERE'S ITARU-SAN?
IN HIS ROOM WITH A WOMAN.
AGAIN?!

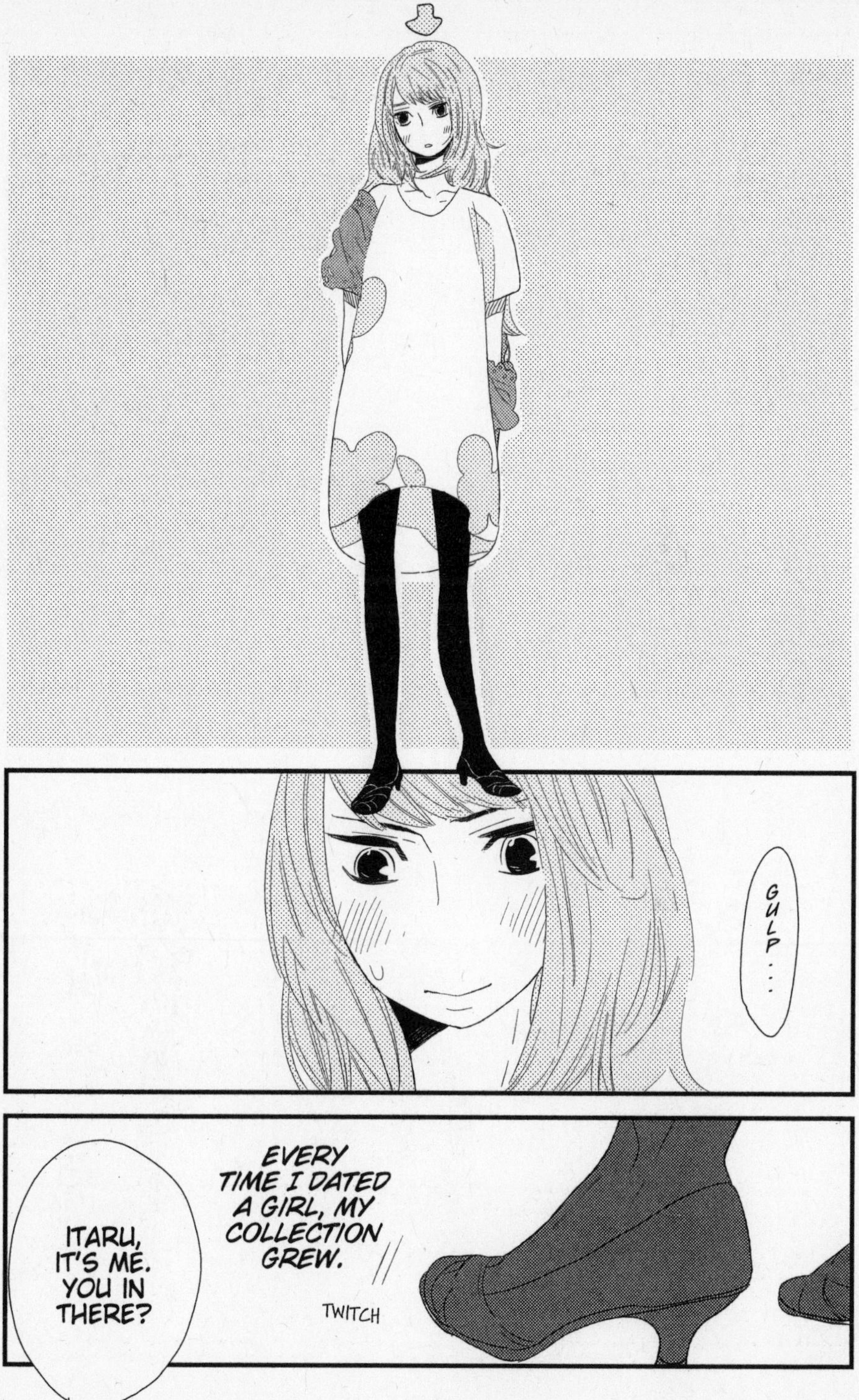
GULP...
EVERY TIME I DATED A GIRL, MY COLLECTION GREW.
TWITCH
ITARU, IT'S ME. YOU IN THERE?

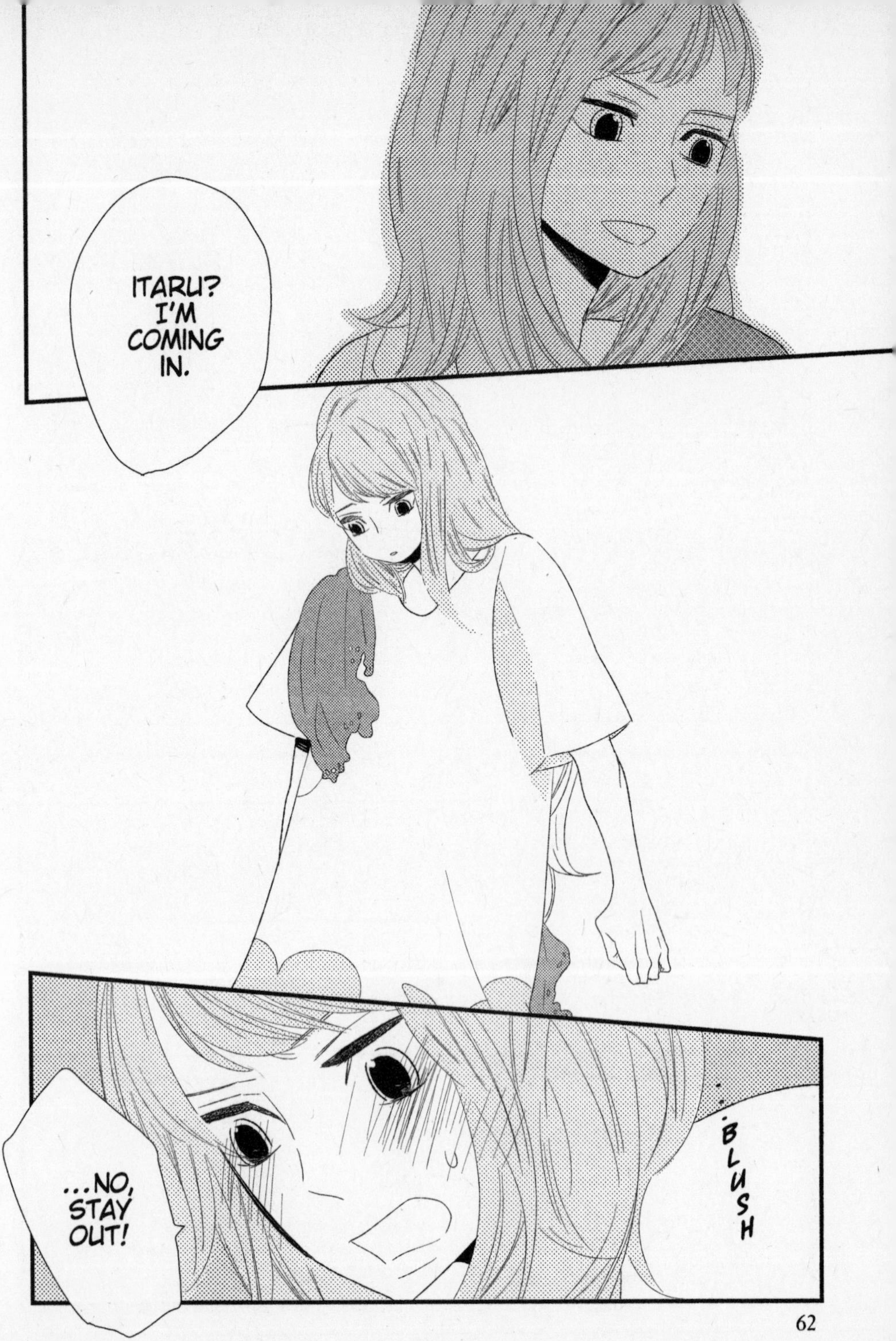

ITARU? I'M COMING IN.
...BLUSH
...NO, STAY OUT!

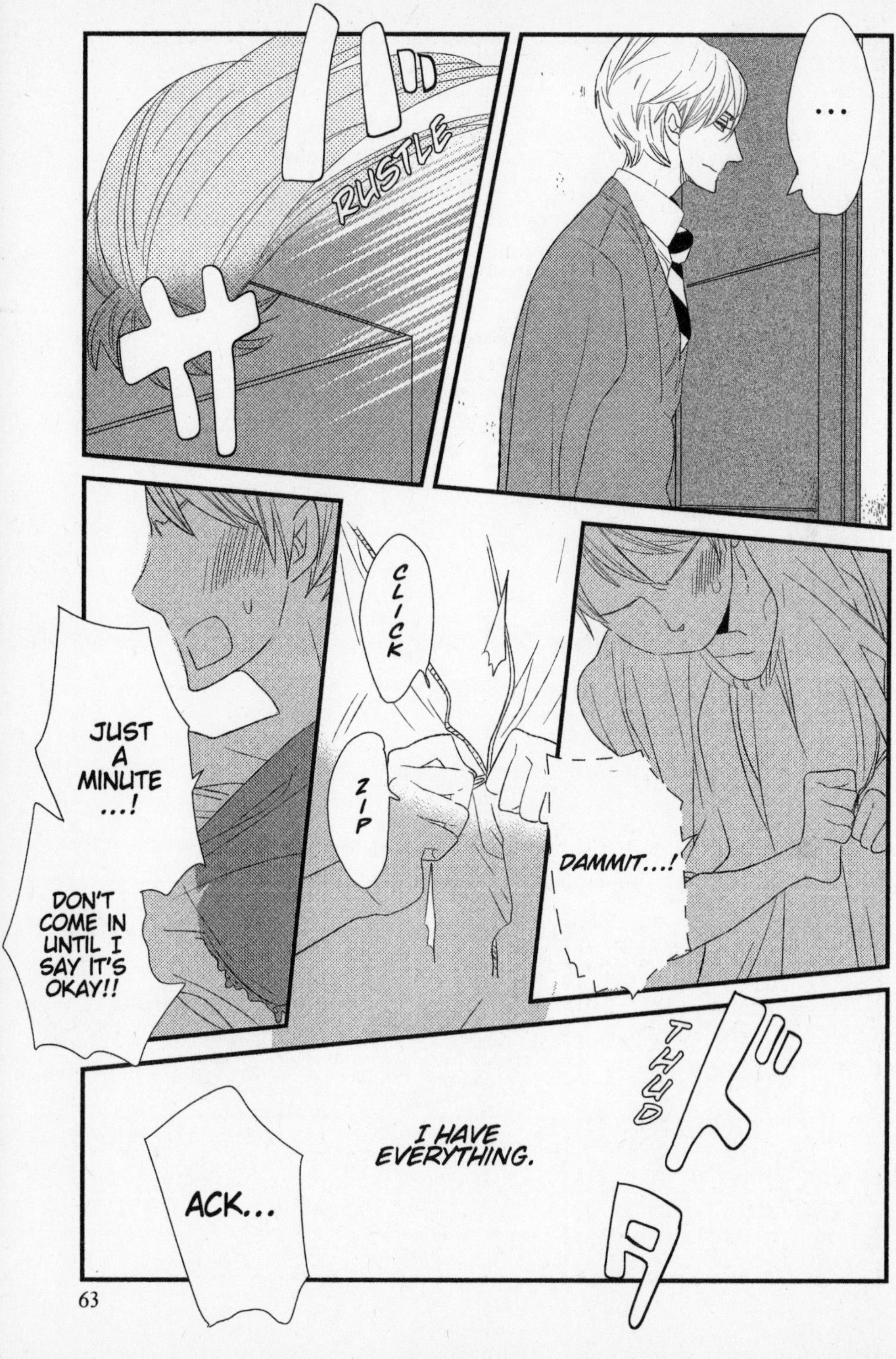
...
RUSTLE
DAMMIT...!
CLICK
ZIP
JUST A MINUTE ...!
DON'T COME IN UNTIL I SAY IT'S OKAY!!
THUD
I HAVE EVERYTHING.
ACK...

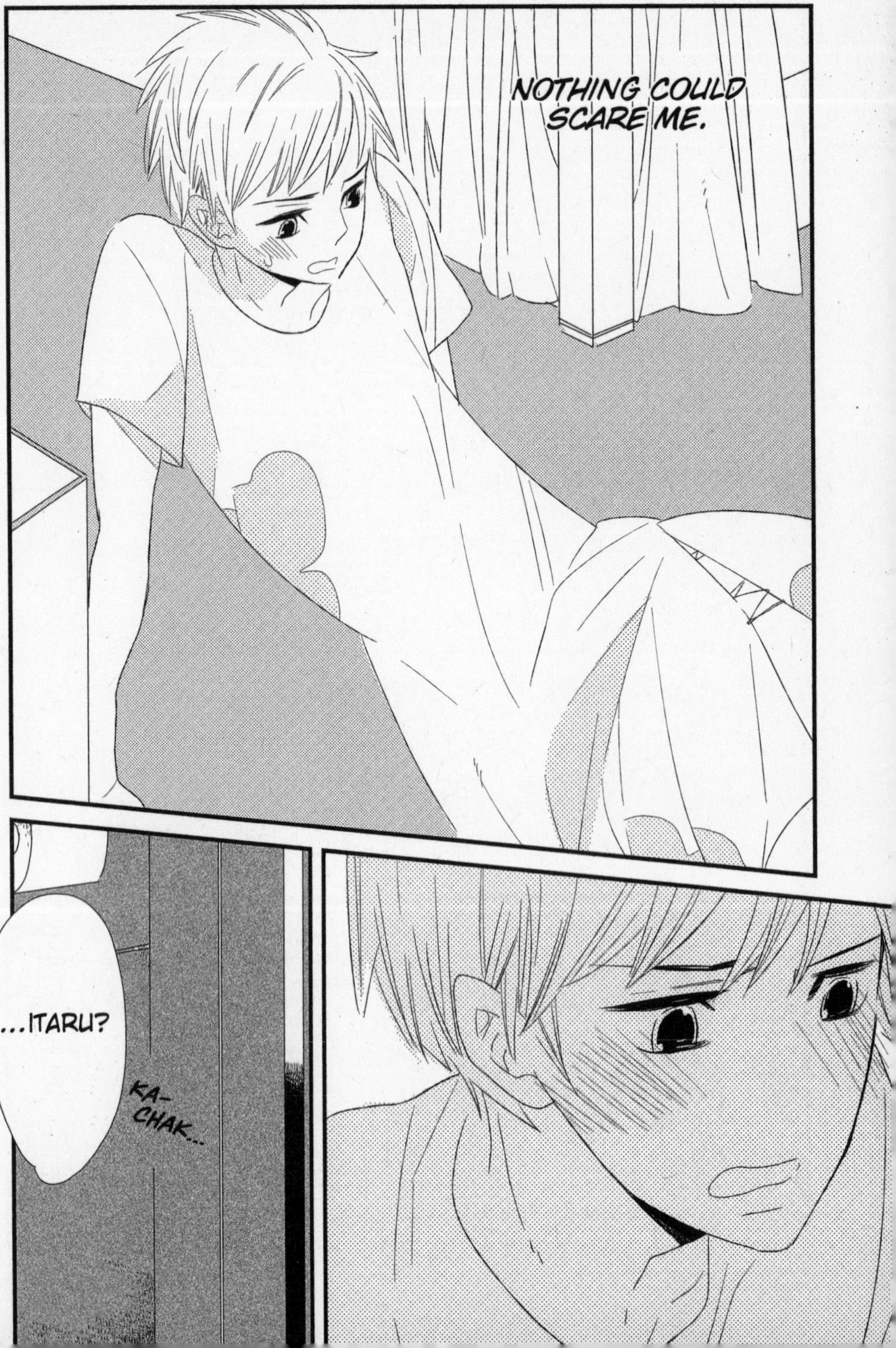
NOTHING COULD SCARE ME.
...ITARU?
KA-CHAK...

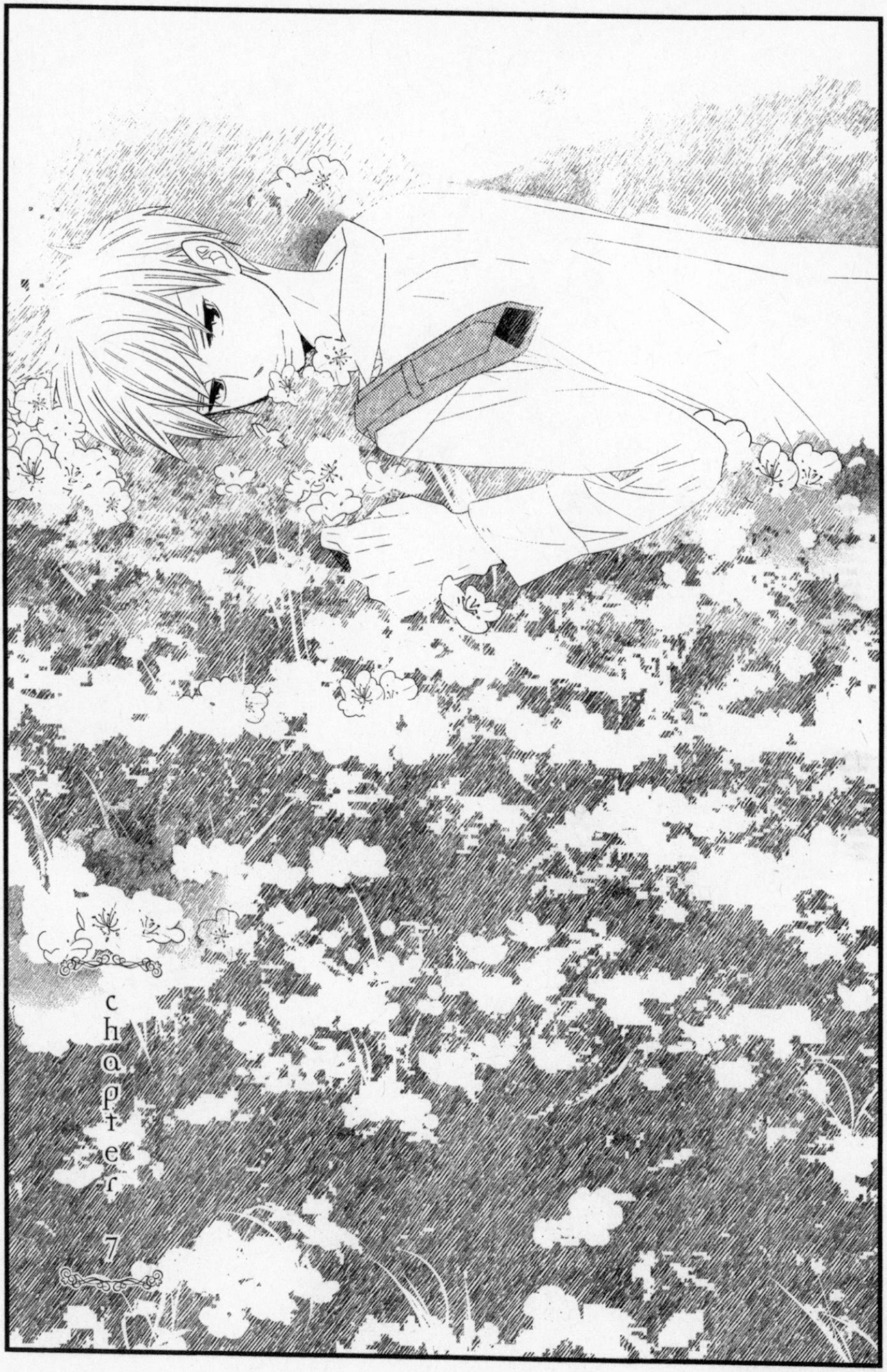
chapter 7

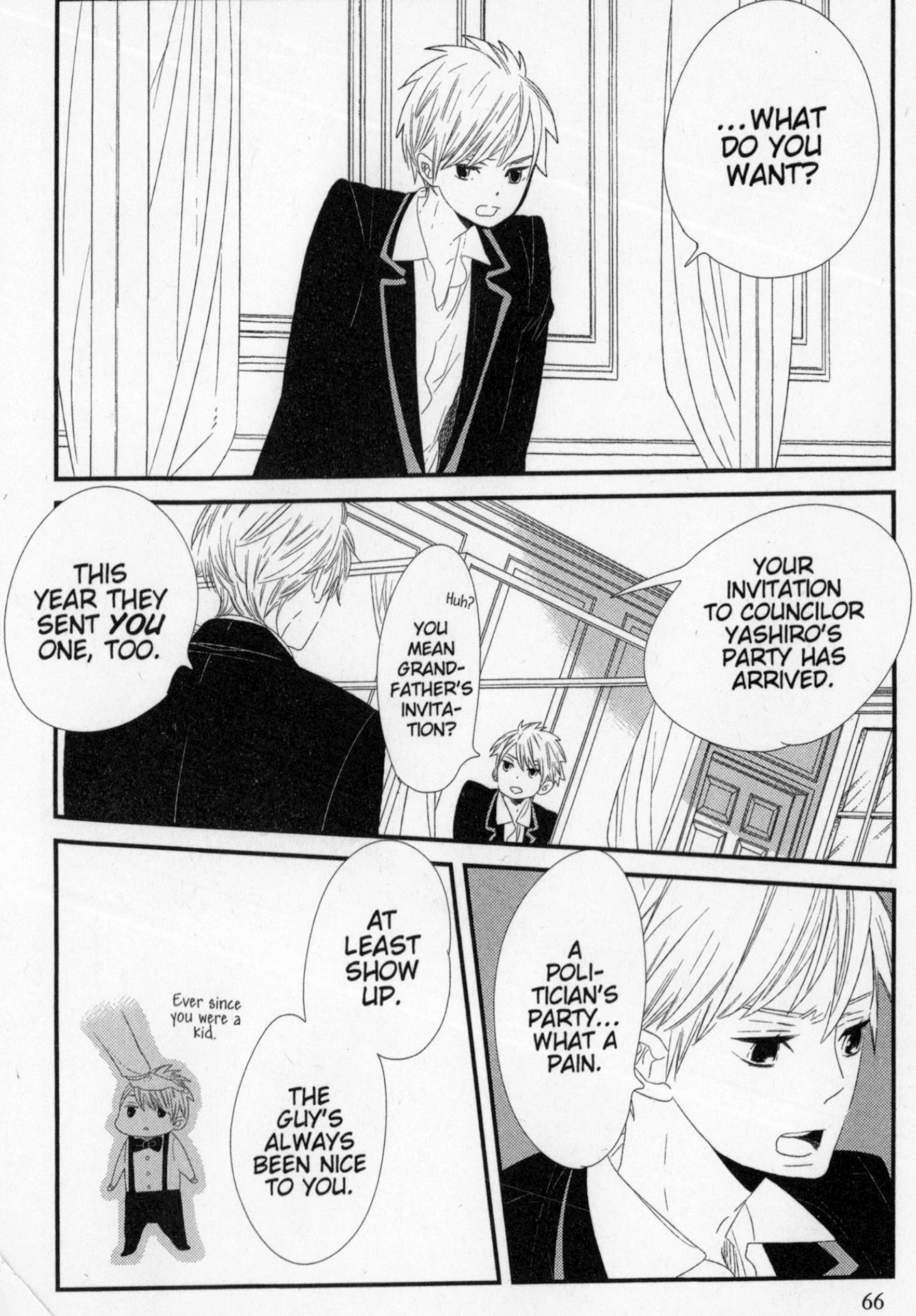
...WHAT DO YOU WANT?
YOUR INVITATION TO COUNCILOR YASHIRO'S PARTY HAS ARRIVED.
Huh?
YOU MEAN GRAND-FATHER'S INVITA-TION?
THIS YEAR THEY SENT *YOU* ONE, TOO.
A POLI-TICIAN'S PARTY... WHAT A PAIN.
AT LEAST SHOW UP.
THE GUY'S ALWAYS BEEN NICE TO YOU.
Ever since you were a kid.

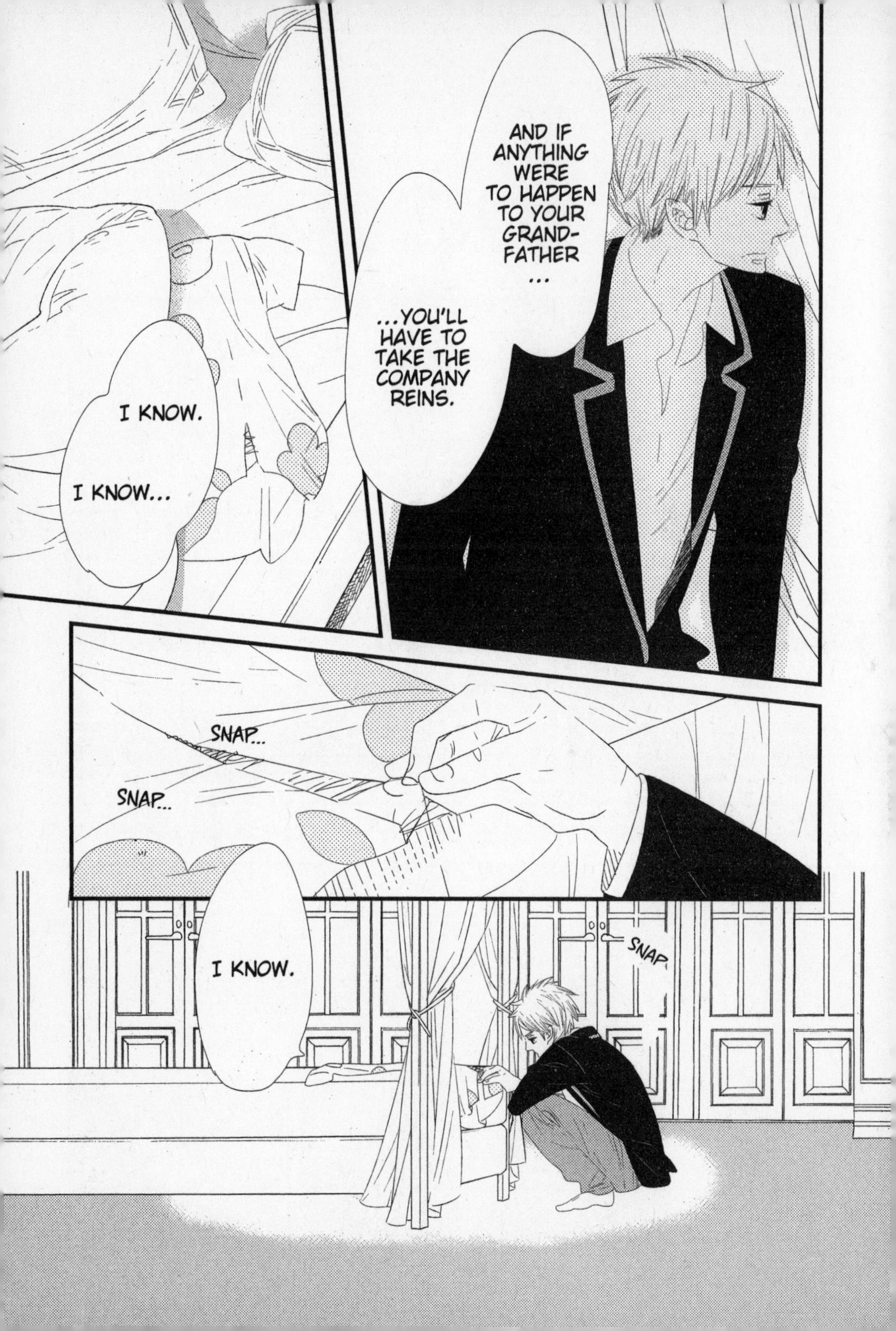
AND IF ANYTHING WERE TO HAPPEN TO YOUR GRAND-FATHER ...
...YOU'LL HAVE TO TAKE THE COMPANY REINS.
I KNOW.
I KNOW...
SNAP...
SNAP...
SNAP
I KNOW.

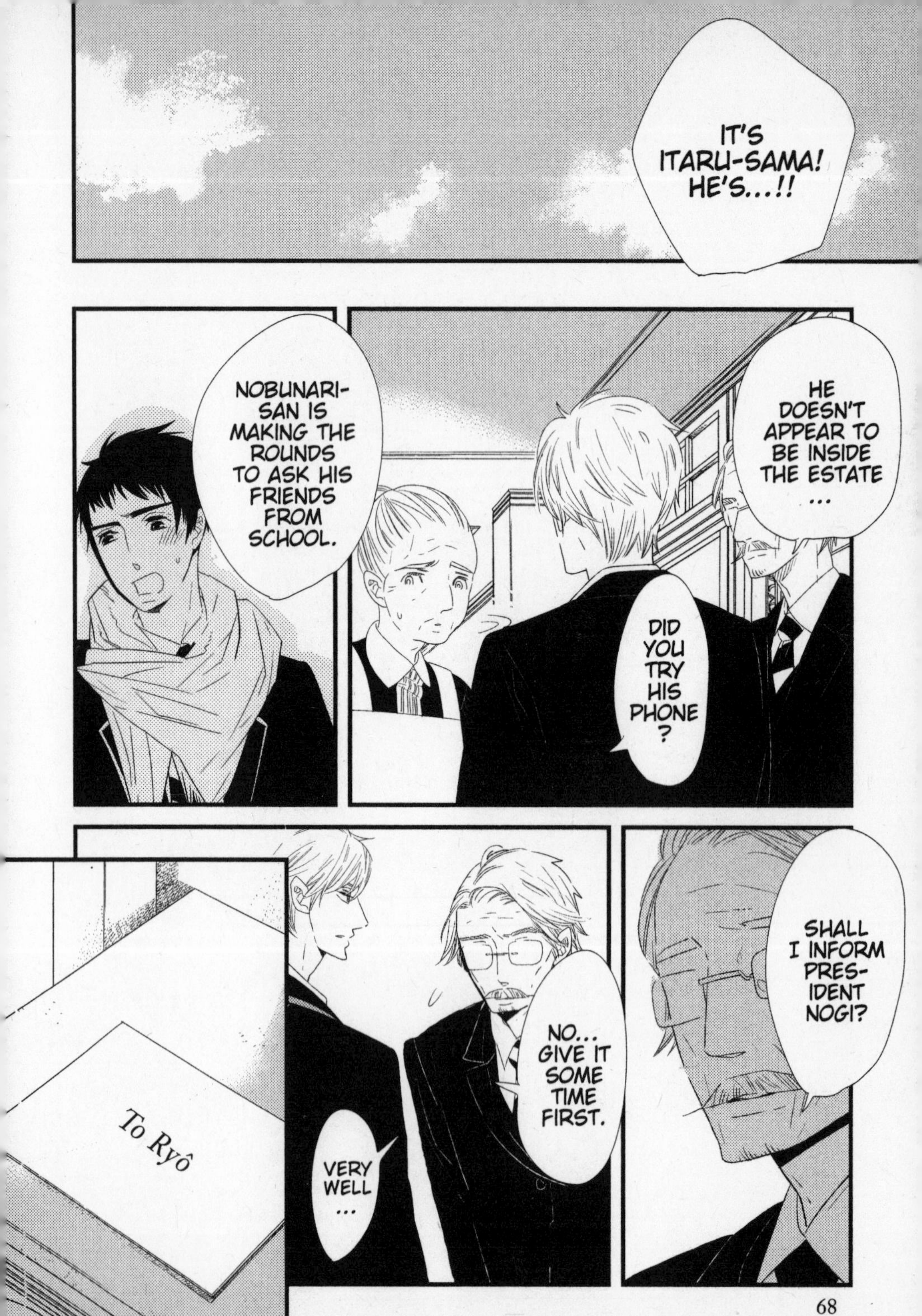
IT'S ITARU-SAMA! HE'S...!!
HE DOESN'T APPEAR TO BE INSIDE THE ESTATE ...
DID YOU TRY HIS PHONE ?
NOBUNARI-SAN IS MAKING THE ROUNDS TO ASK HIS FRIENDS FROM SCHOOL.
SHALL I INFORM PRES-IDENT NOGI?
NO... GIVE IT SOME TIME FIRST.
VERY WELL ...
To Ryô

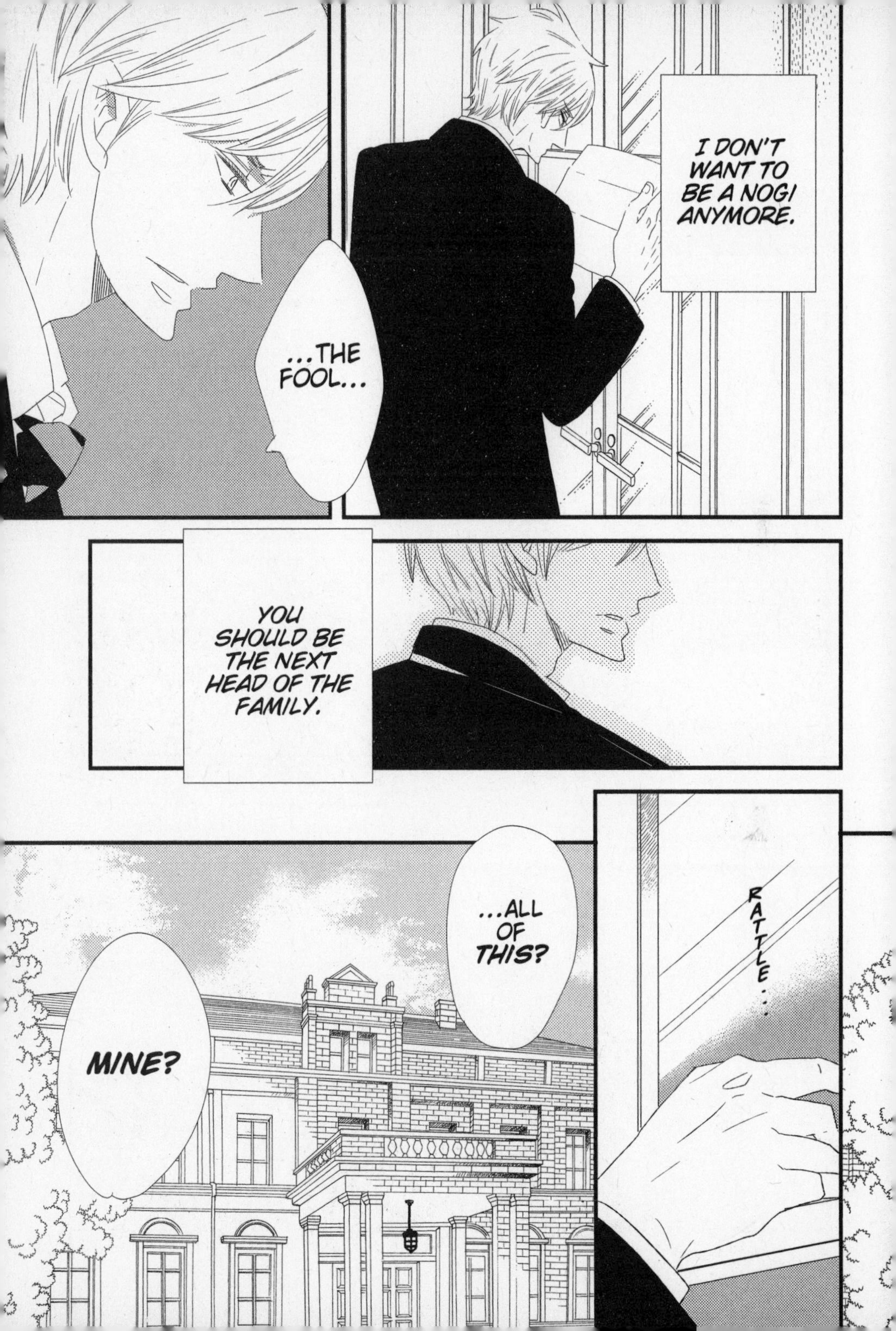
I DON'T WANT TO BE A NOGI ANYMORE.
...THE FOOL...
YOU SHOULD BE THE NEXT HEAD OF THE FAMILY.
RATTLE...
...ALL OF THIS?
MINE?

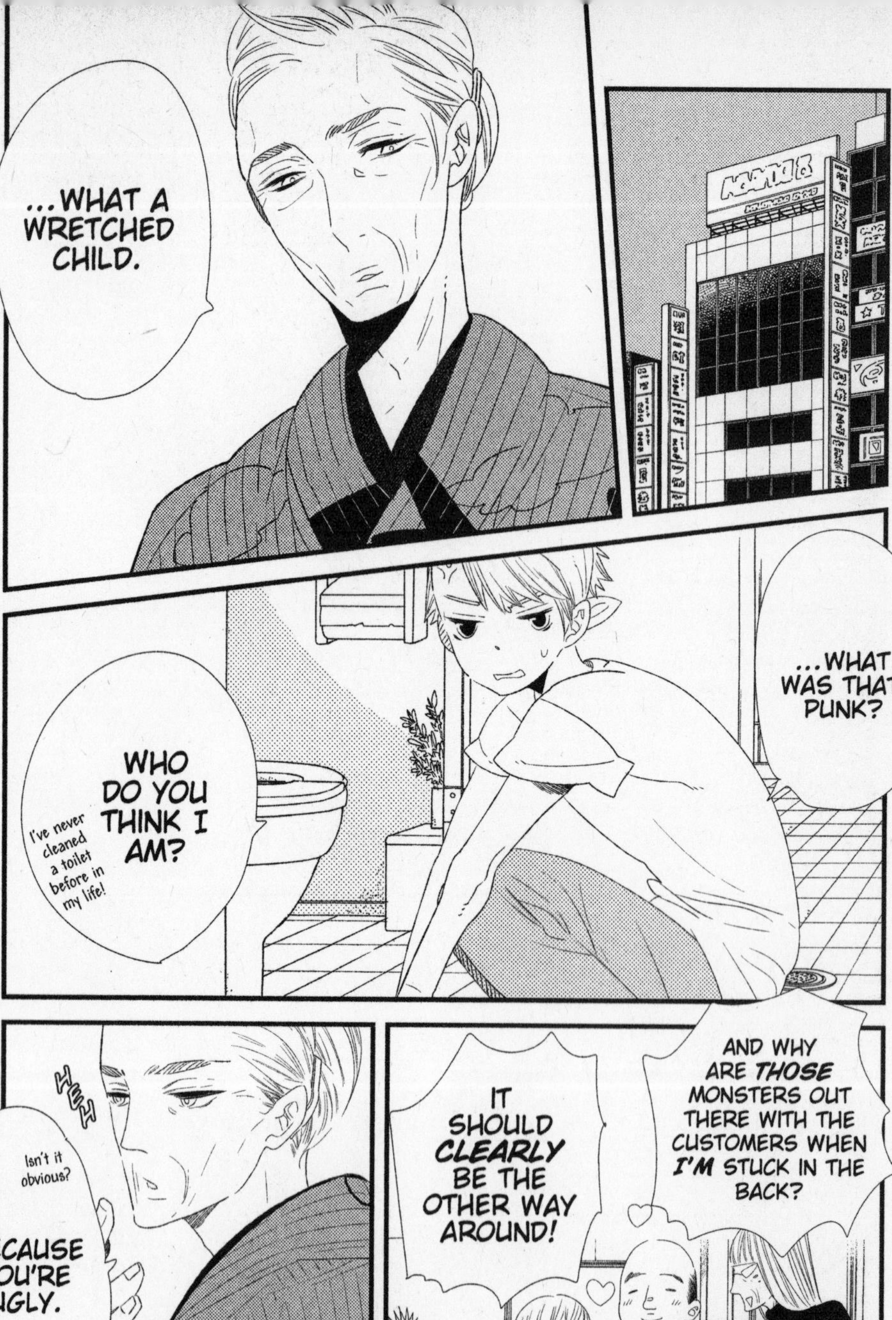
...WHAT A WRETCHED CHILD.
...WHAT WAS THAT, PUNK?
WHO DO YOU THINK I AM?
I've never cleaned a toilet before in my life!
AND WHY ARE *THOSE* MONSTERS OUT THERE WITH THE CUSTOMERS WHEN *I'M* STUCK IN THE BACK?
IT SHOULD *CLEARLY* BE THE OTHER WAY AROUND!
HEH
Isn't it obvious?
BECAUSE YOU'RE UGLY.

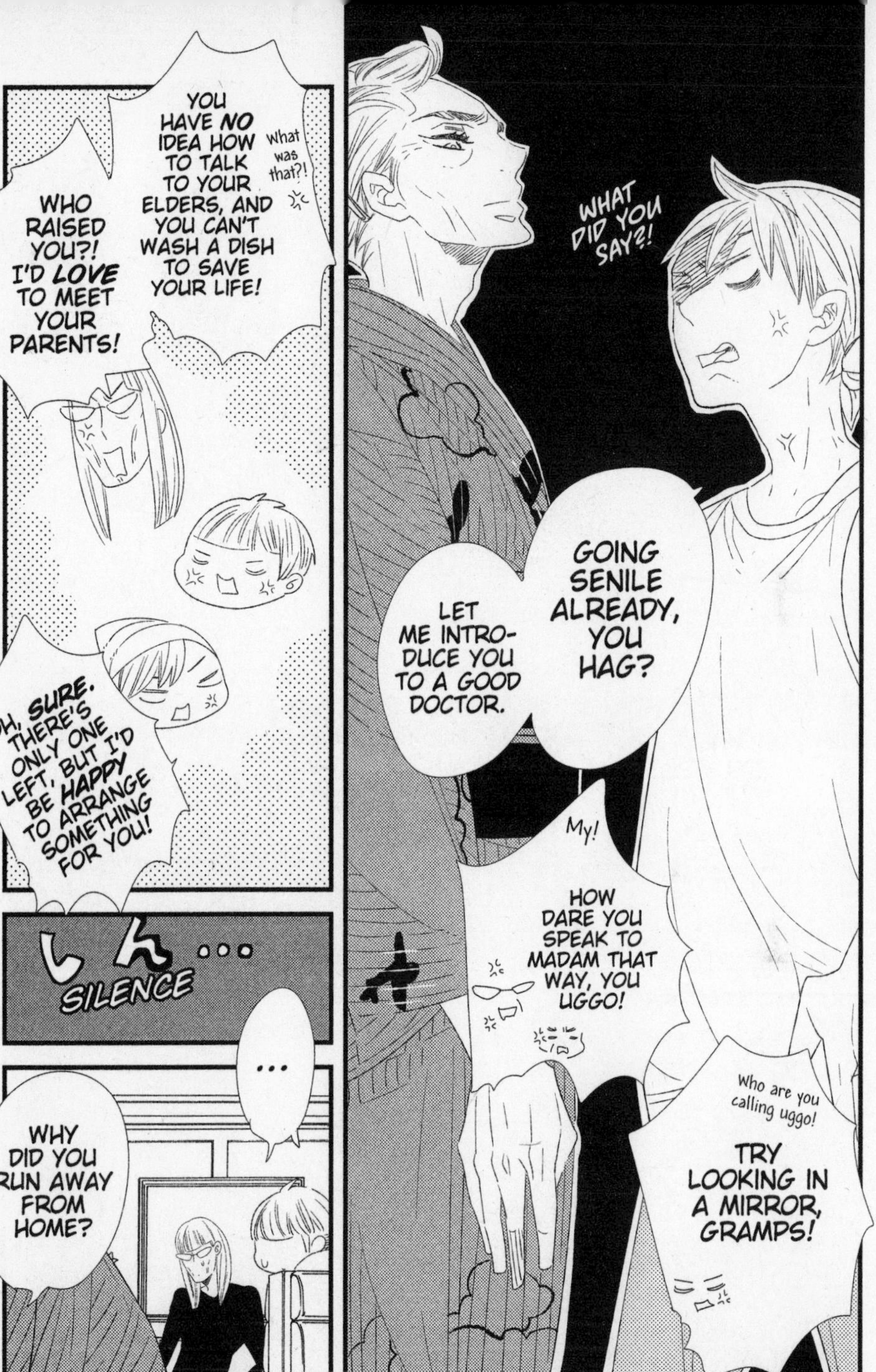
WHAT DID YOU SAY?!
GOING SENILE ALREADY, YOU HAG?
LET ME INTRO-DUCE YOU TO A GOOD DOCTOR.
My!
HOW DARE YOU SPEAK TO MADAM THAT WAY, YOU UGGO!
Who are you calling uggo!
TRY LOOKING IN A MIRROR, GRAMPS!
YOU HAVE NO IDEA HOW TO TALK TO YOUR ELDERS, AND YOU CAN'T WASH A DISH TO SAVE YOUR LIFE!
What was that?!
WHO RAISED YOU?! I'D LOVE TO MEET YOUR PARENTS!
OH, SURE. THERE'S ONLY ONE LEFT, BUT I'D BE HAPPY TO ARRANGE SOMETHING FOR YOU!
しん…
SILENCE
...
WHY DID YOU RUN AWAY FROM HOME?

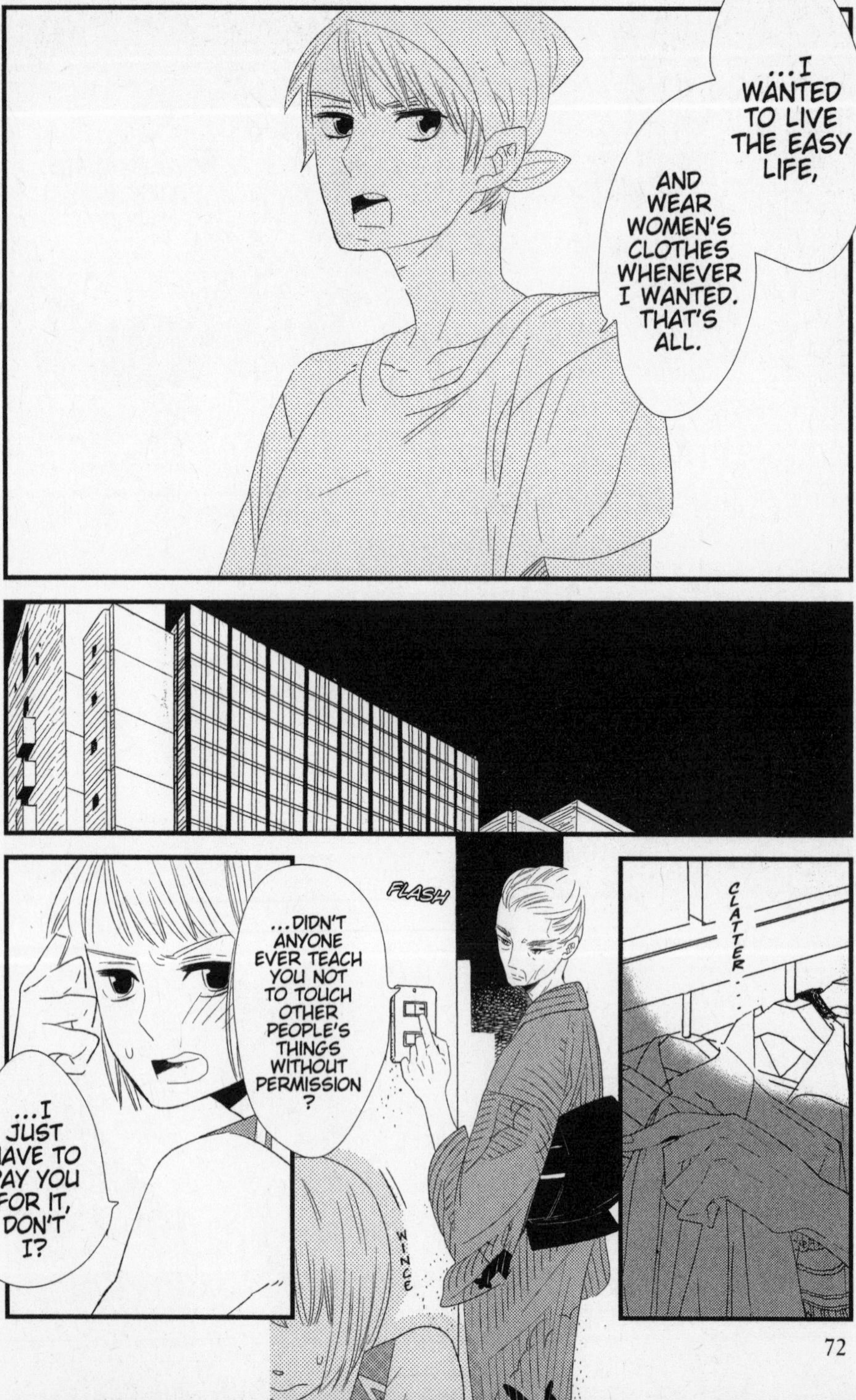
...I WANTED TO LIVE THE EASY LIFE,
AND WEAR WOMEN'S CLOTHES WHENEVER I WANTED. THAT'S ALL.
CLATTER...
FLASH
...DIDN'T ANYONE EVER TEACH YOU NOT TO TOUCH OTHER PEOPLE'S THINGS WITHOUT PERMISSION?
WINCE
...I JUST HAVE TO PAY YOU FOR IT, DON'T I?

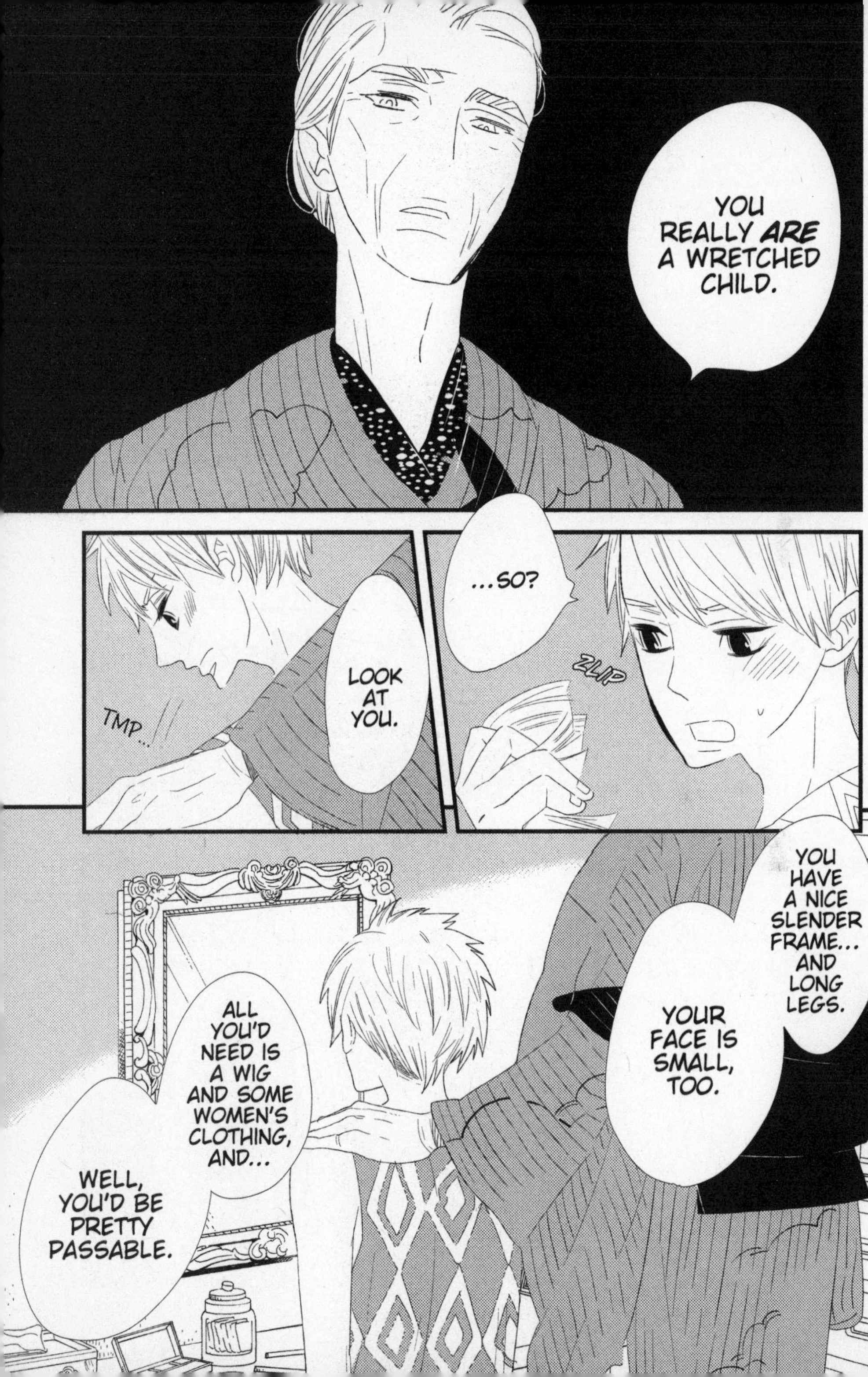
YOU REALLY ***ARE*** A WRETCHED CHILD.
...SO?
ZLIP
LOOK AT YOU.
TMP...
YOU HAVE A NICE SLENDER FRAME... AND LONG LEGS.
YOUR FACE IS SMALL, TOO.
ALL YOU'D NEED IS A WIG AND SOME WOMEN'S CLOTHING, AND...
WELL, YOU'D BE PRETTY PASSABLE.

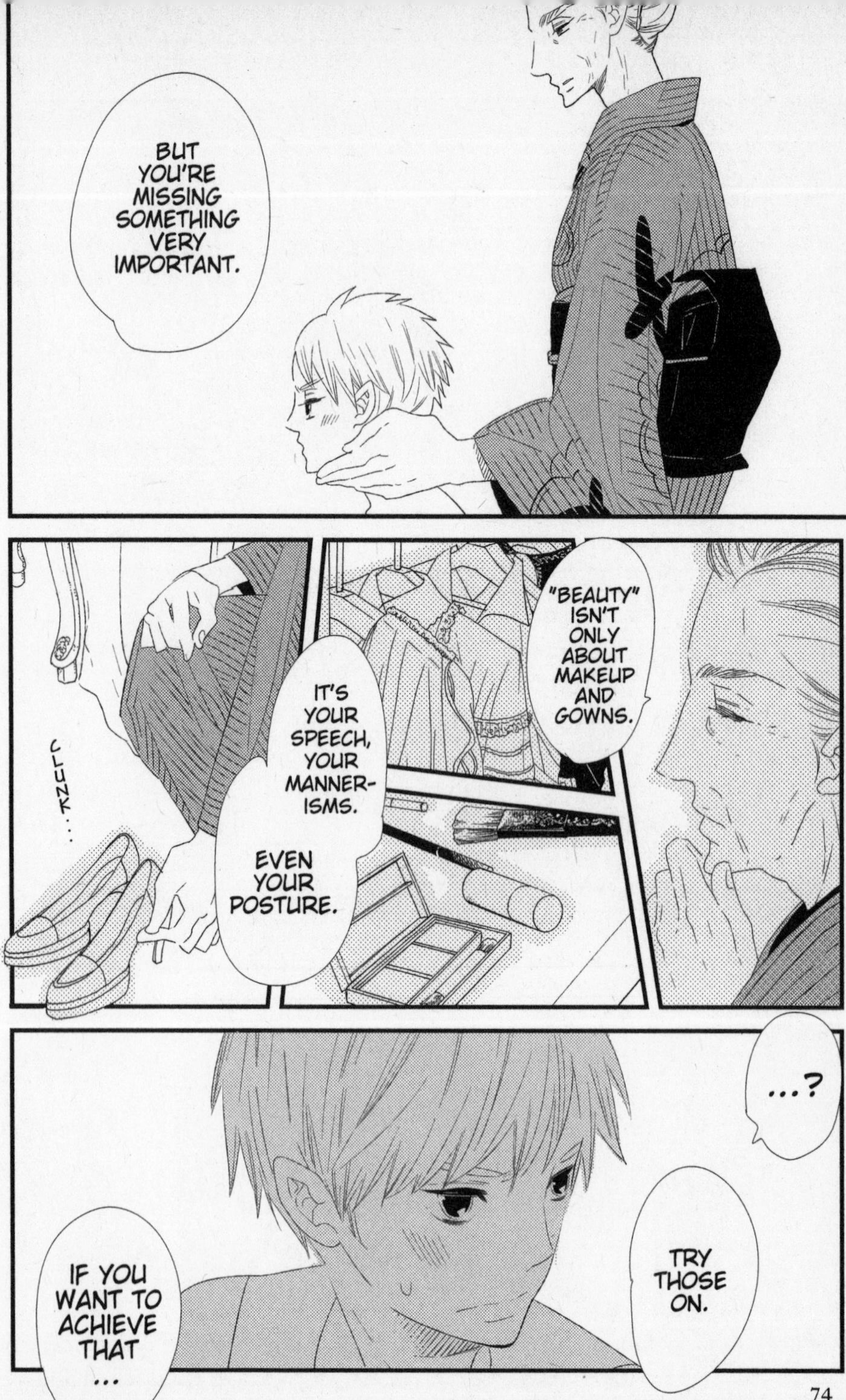
BUT YOU'RE MISSING SOMETHING VERY IMPORTANT.
"BEAUTY" ISN'T ONLY ABOUT MAKEUP AND GOWNS.
IT'S YOUR SPEECH, YOUR MANNERISMS.
EVEN YOUR POSTURE.
CLUNK...
...?
TRY THOSE ON.
IF YOU WANT TO ACHIEVE THAT...

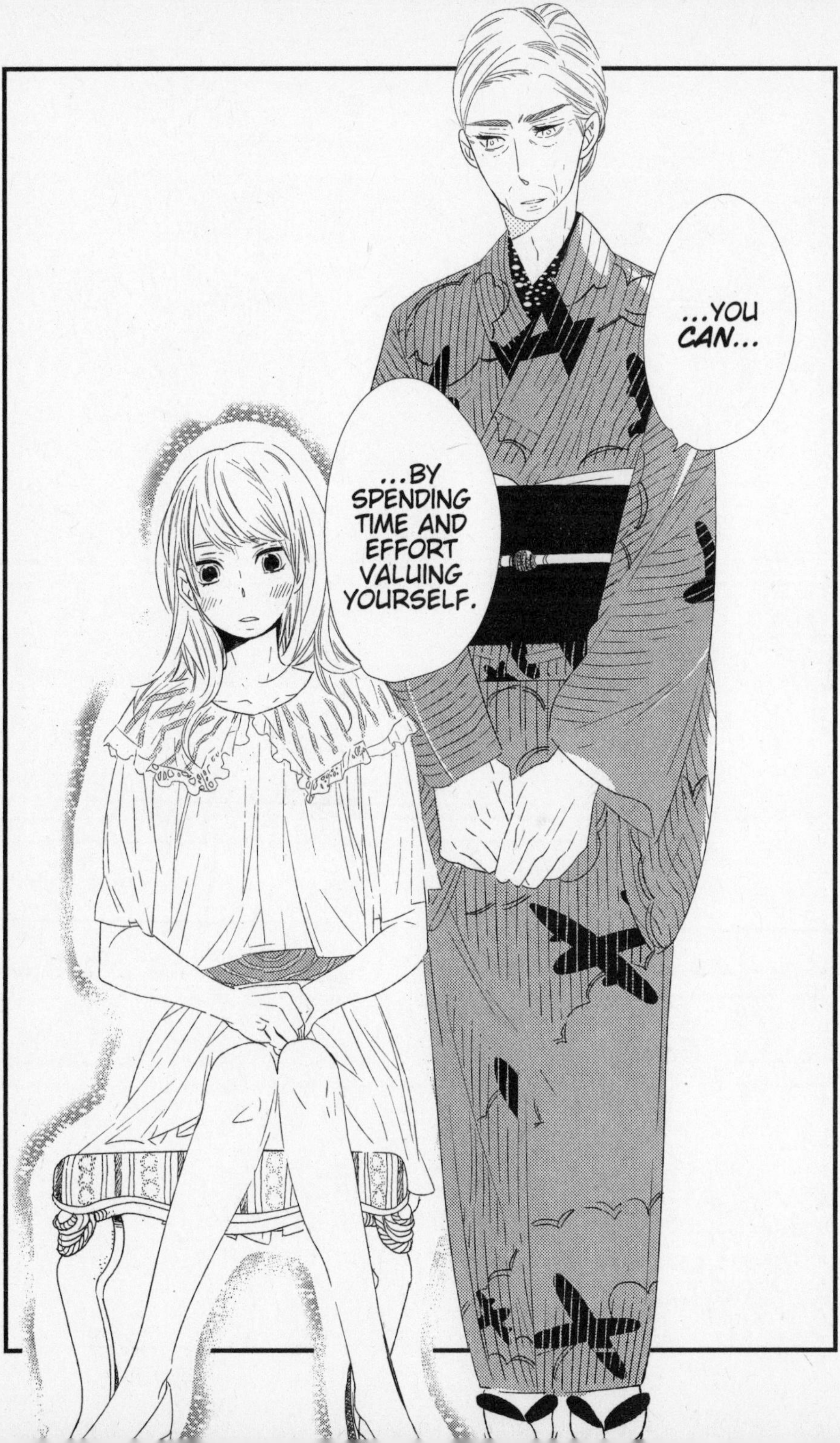
...YOU CAN...
...BY SPENDING TIME AND EFFORT VALUING YOURSELF.

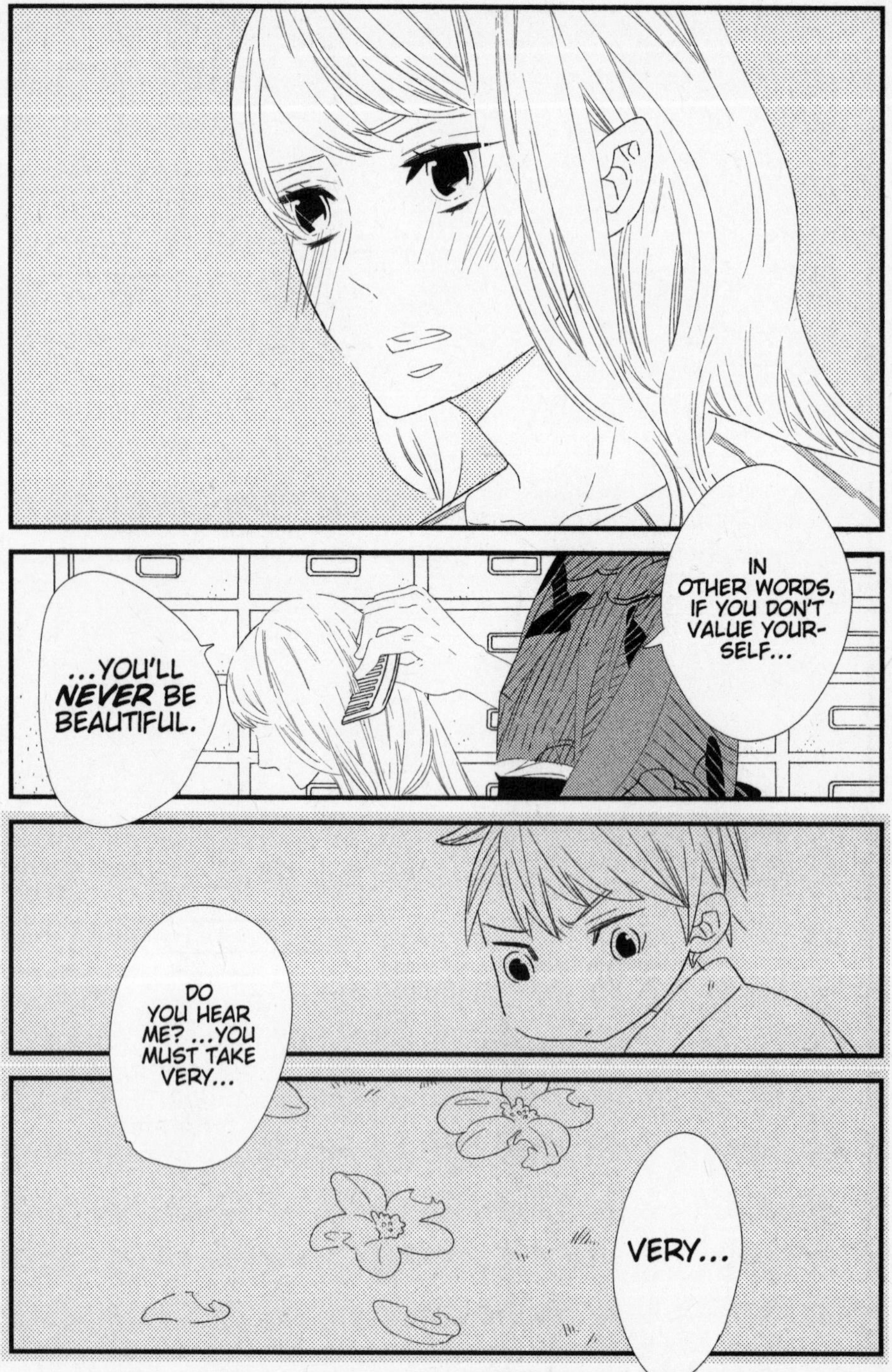
IN OTHER WORDS, IF YOU DON'T VALUE YOURSELF...
...YOU'LL *NEVER* BE BEAUTIFUL.
DO YOU HEAR ME? ...YOU MUST TAKE VERY...
VERY...

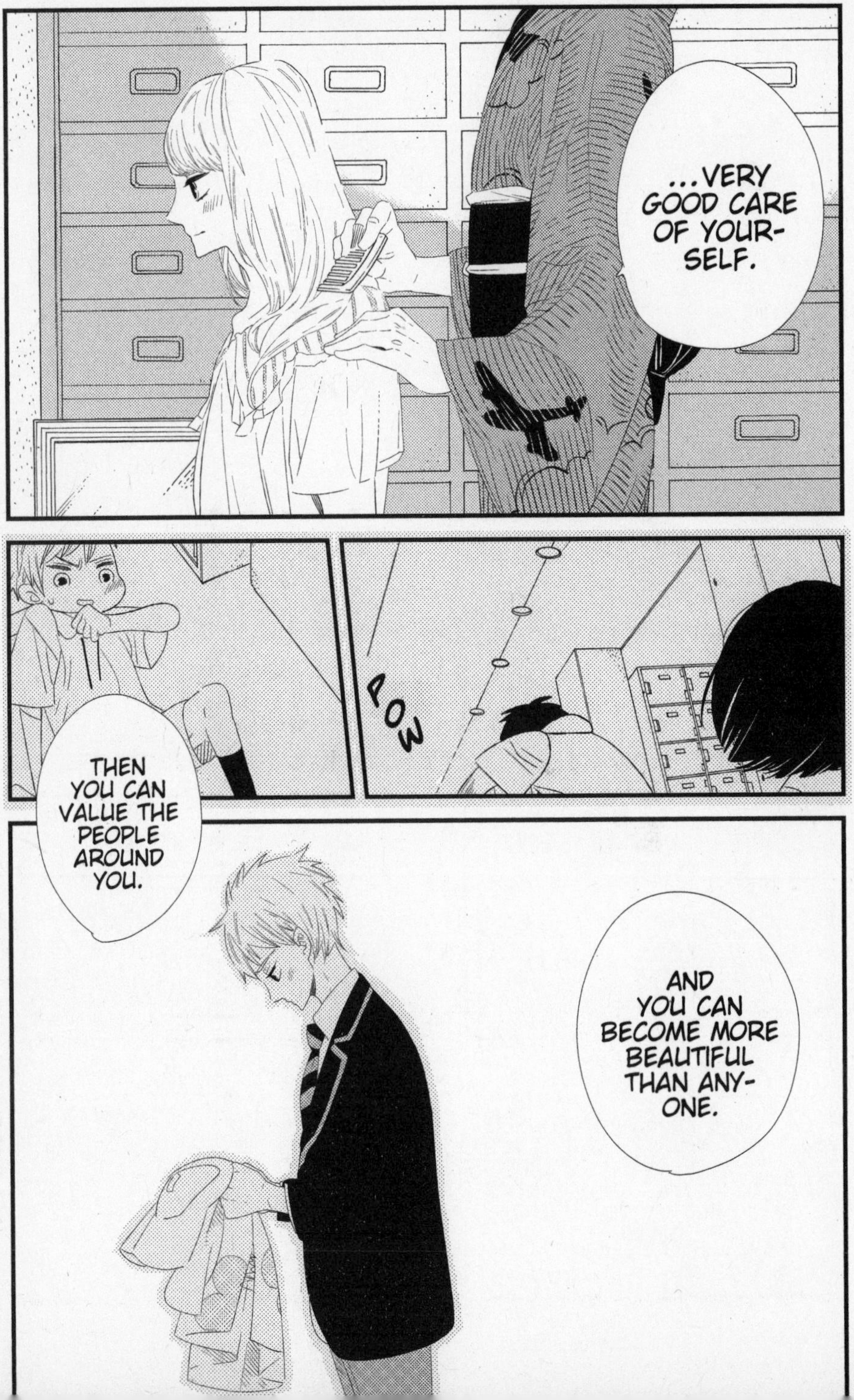
...VERY GOOD CARE OF YOUR-SELF.
POW
THEN YOU CAN VALUE THE PEOPLE AROUND YOU.
AND YOU CAN BECOME MORE BEAUTIFUL THAN ANY-ONE.

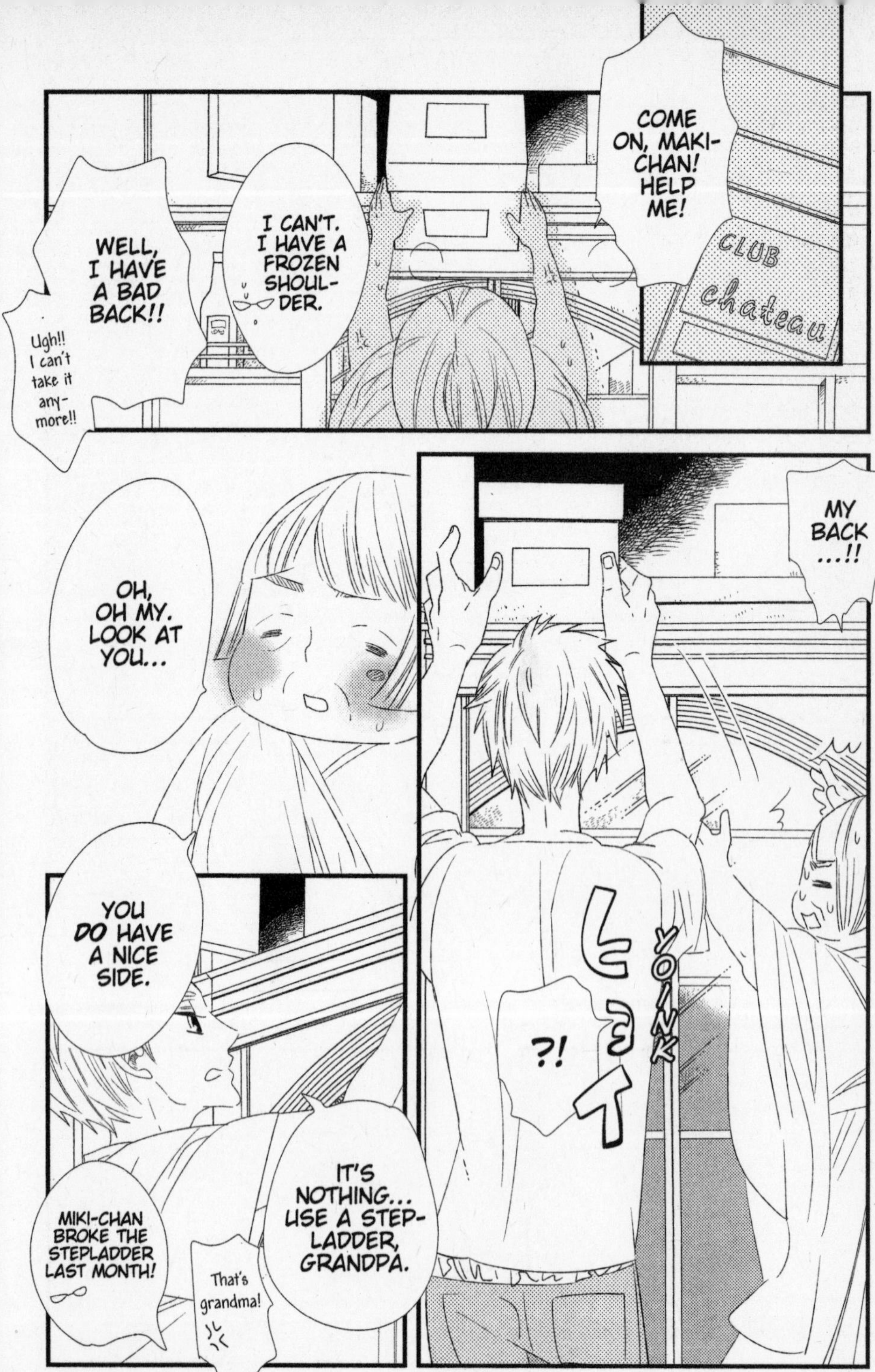
COME ON, MAKI-CHAN! HELP ME!
CLUB chateau
I CAN'T. I HAVE A FROZEN SHOULDER.
WELL, I HAVE A BAD BACK!!
Ugh!! I can't take it anymore!!
MY BACK ...!!
YOINK
?!
OH, OH MY. LOOK AT YOU...
YOU *DO* HAVE A NICE SIDE.
IT'S NOTHING... USE A STEP-LADDER, GRANDPA.
That's grandma!
MIKI-CHAN BROKE THE STEPLADDER LAST MONTH!

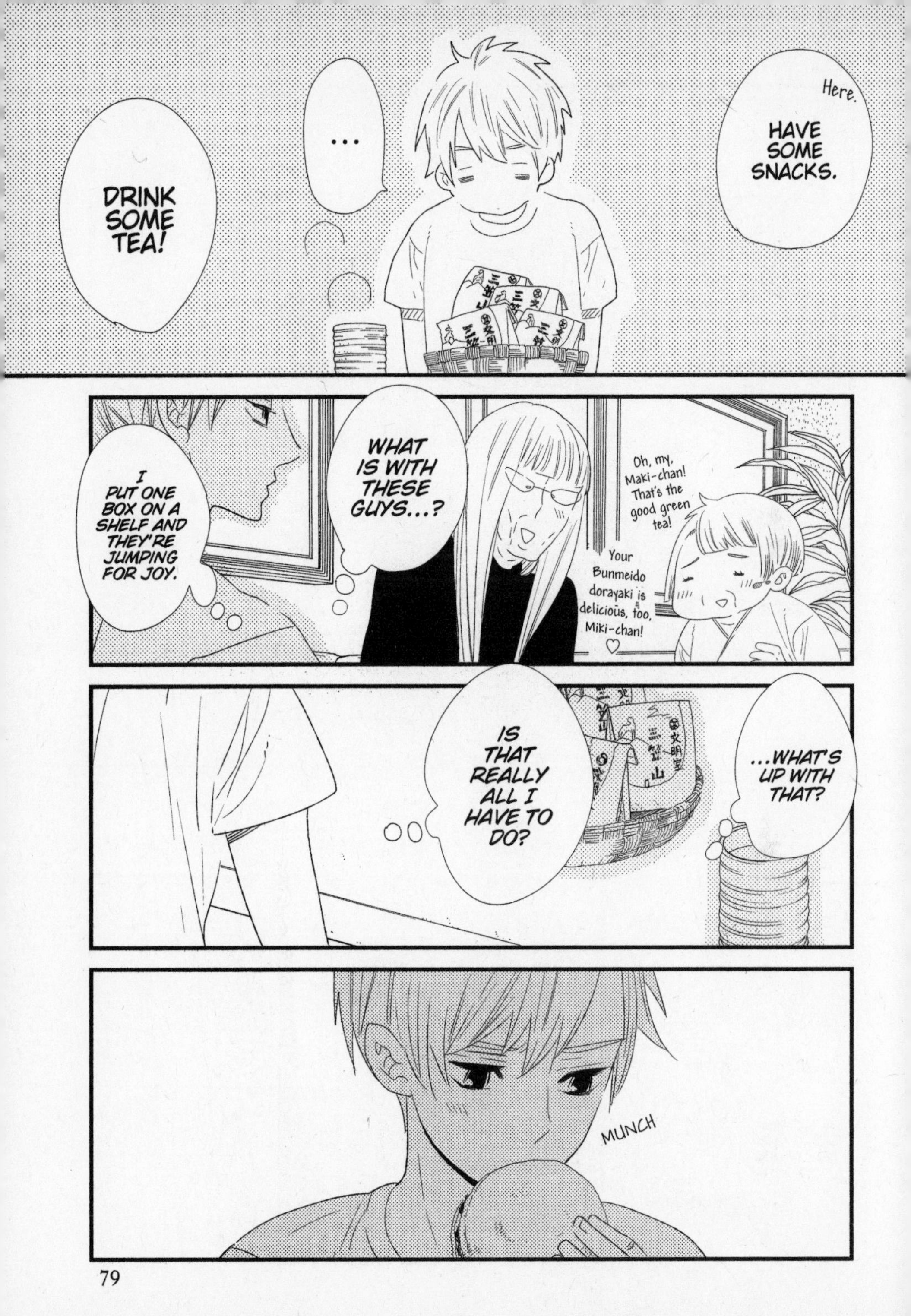
Here.
HAVE SOME SNACKS.
...
DRINK SOME TEA!
Oh, my, Maki-chan! That's the good green tea!
Your Bunmeido dorayaki is delicious, too, Miki-chan! ♡
WHAT IS WITH THESE GUYS...?
I PUT ONE BOX ON A SHELF AND THEY'RE JUMPING FOR JOY.
...WHAT'S UP WITH THAT?
IS THAT REALLY ALL I HAVE TO DO?
MUNCH

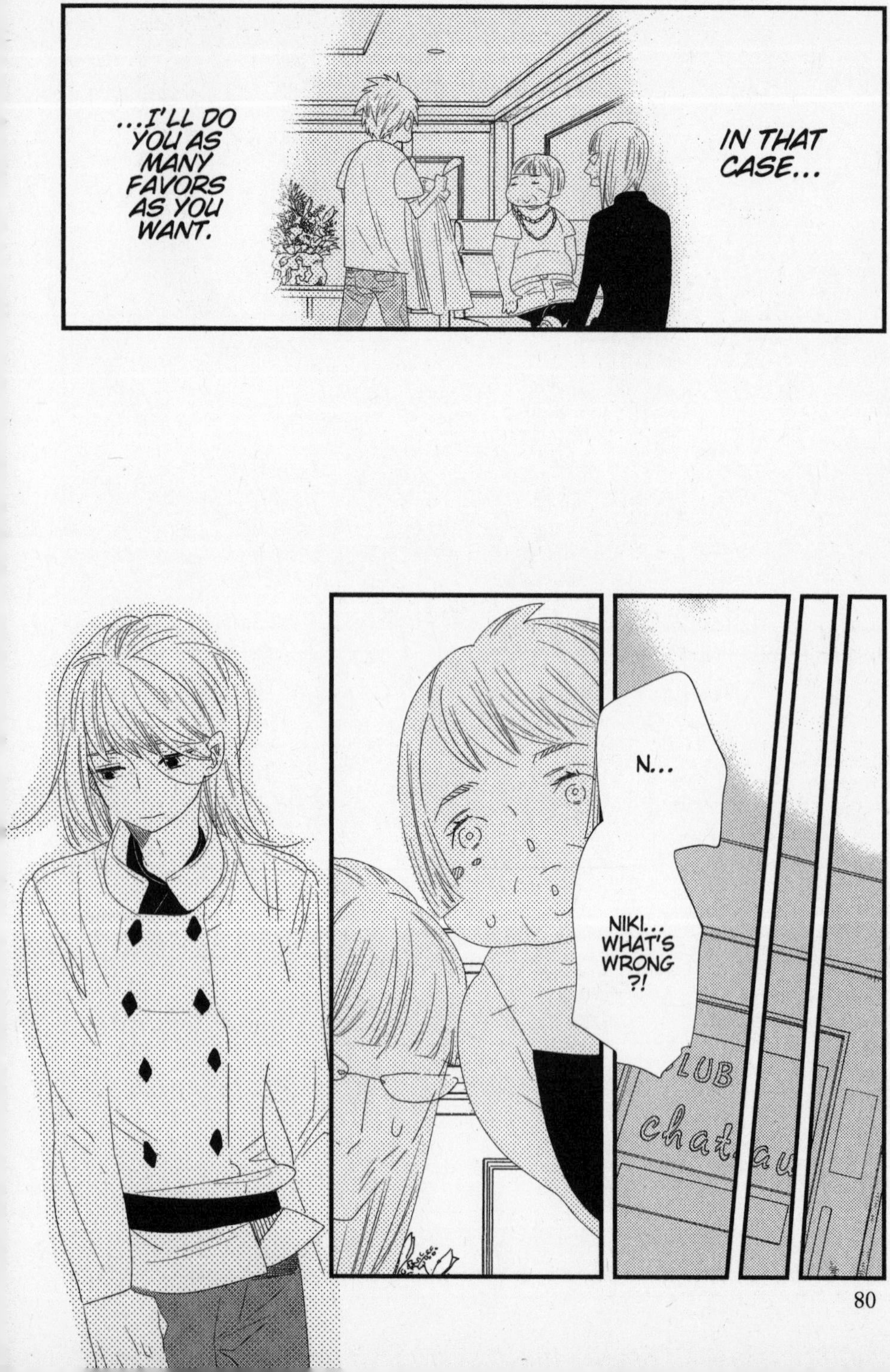
IN THAT CASE...
...I'LL DO YOU AS MANY FAVORS AS YOU WANT.
N...
NIKI... WHAT'S WRONG?!
CLUB chateau

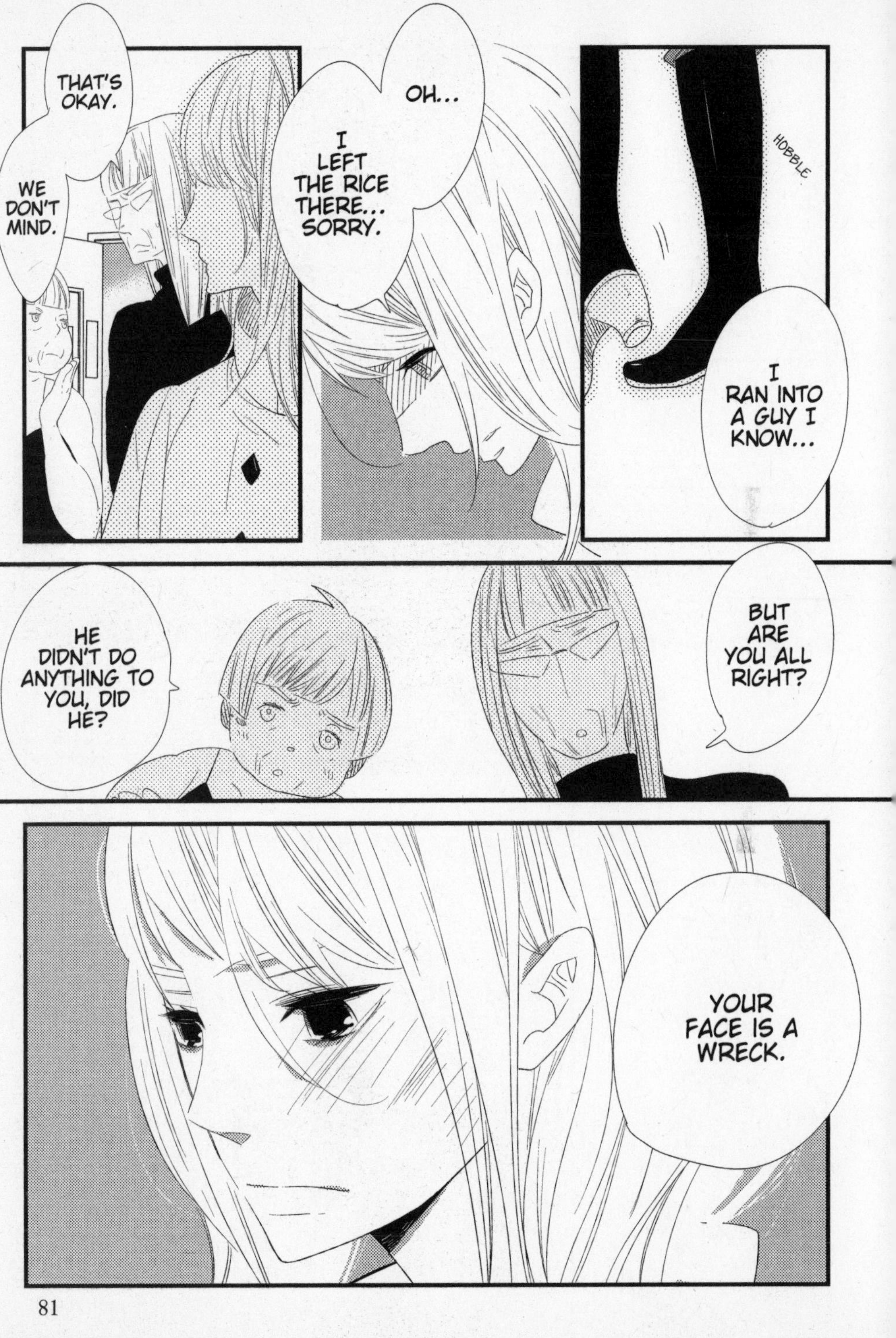
HOBBLE
I RAN INTO A GUY I KNOW...
OH...
I LEFT THE RICE THERE... SORRY.
THAT'S OKAY.
WE DON'T MIND.
BUT ARE YOU ALL RIGHT?
HE DIDN'T DO ANYTHING TO YOU, DID HE?
YOUR FACE IS A WRECK.

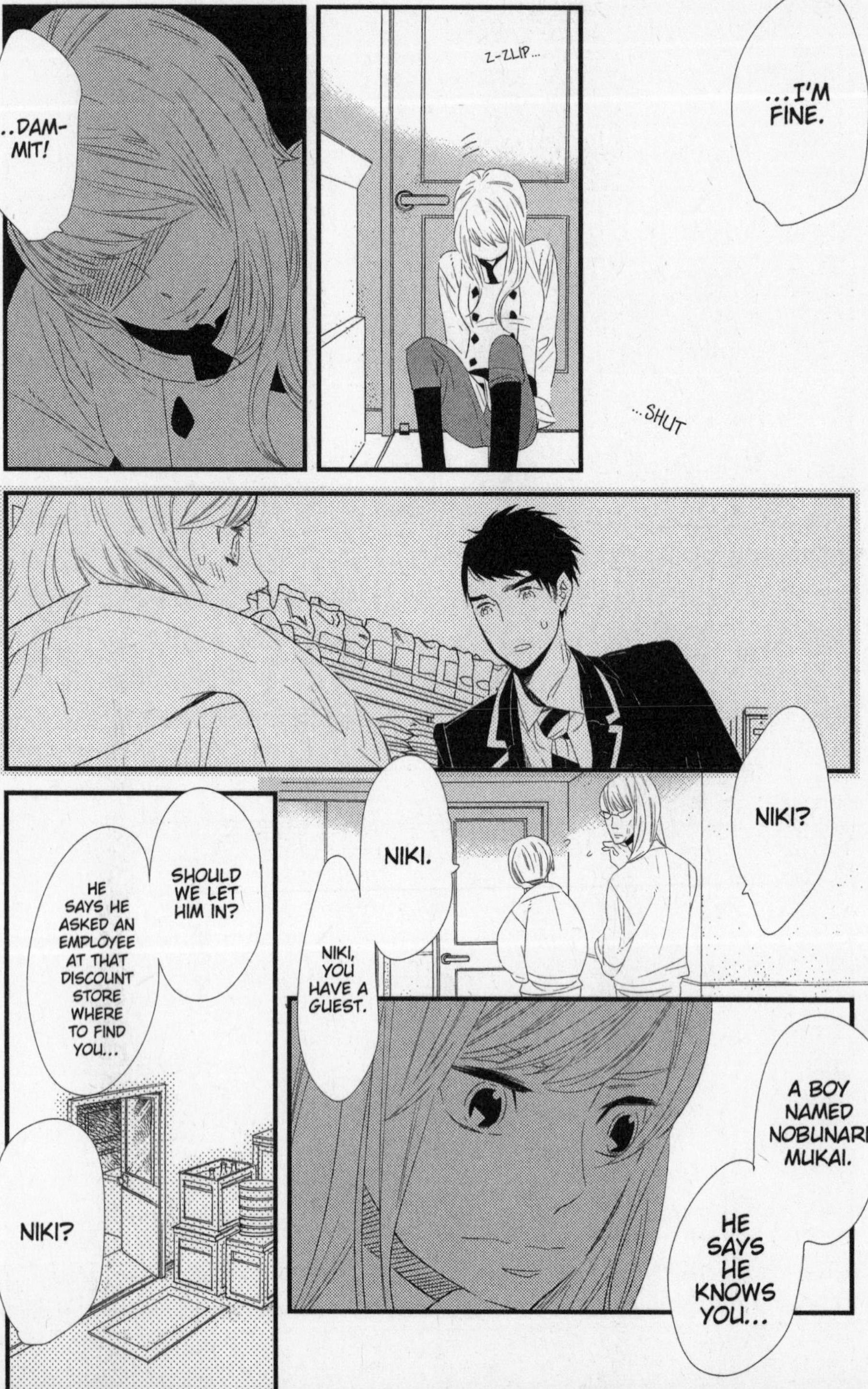
...I'M FINE.
Z-ZLIP...
...SHUT
...DAM-MIT!
NIKI?
NIKI.
NIKI, YOU HAVE A GUEST.
A BOY NAMED NOBUNARI MUKAI.
HE SAYS HE KNOWS YOU...
SHOULD WE LET HIM IN?
HE SAYS HE ASKED AN EMPLOYEE AT THAT DISCOUNT STORE WHERE TO FIND YOU...
NIKI?

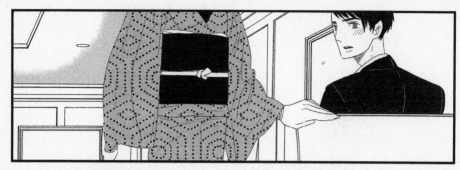

WHAT AM I
RUNNING FROM?

Traffic Safety

"I wanted to live the easy life."

FROM HOME?
FROM NOBUNARI!?

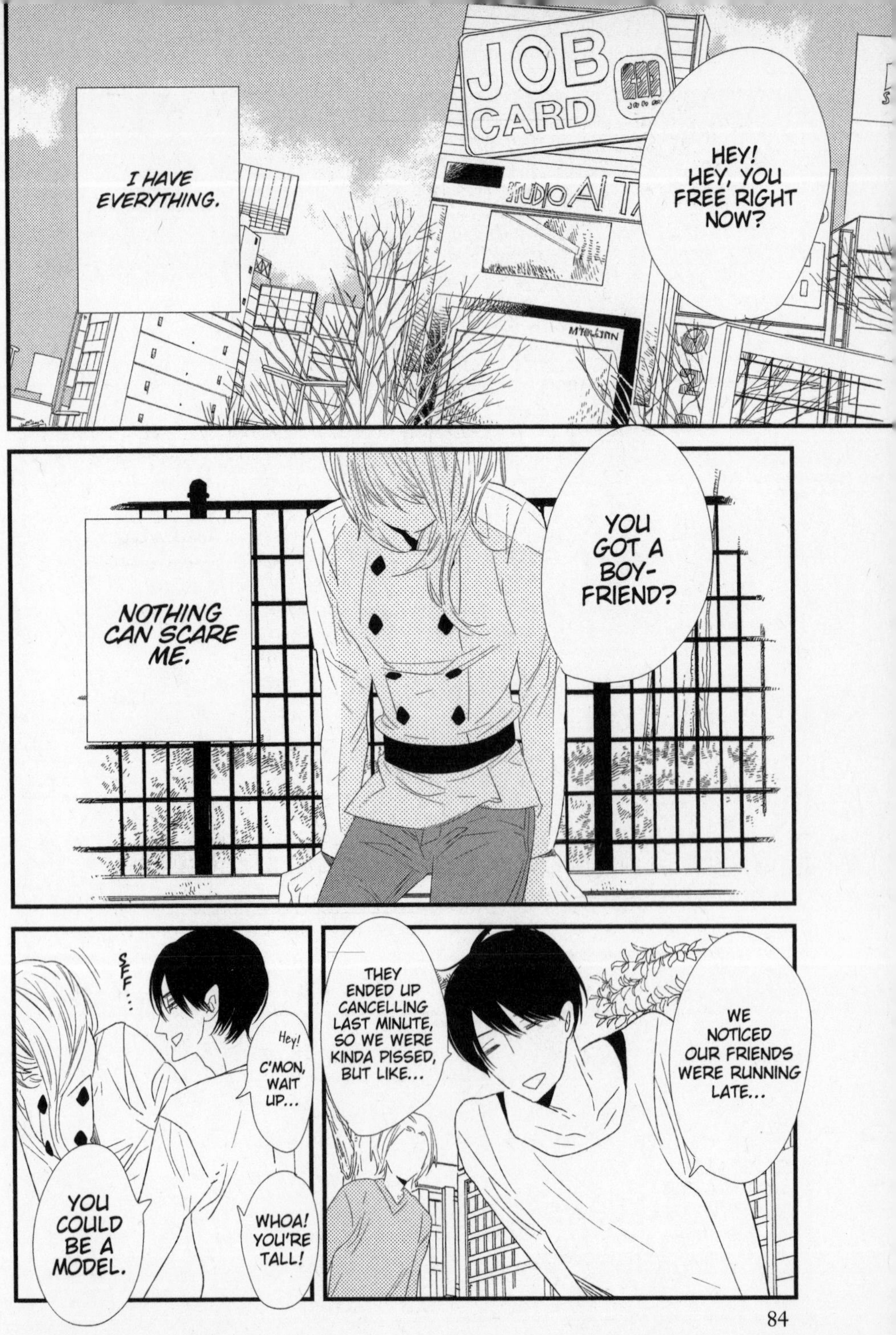
JOB CARD
HEY! HEY, YOU FREE RIGHT NOW?
I HAVE EVERYTHING.
YOU GOT A BOY-FRIEND?
NOTHING CAN SCARE ME.
WE NOTICED OUR FRIENDS WERE RUNNING LATE...
THEY ENDED UP CANCELLING LAST MINUTE, SO WE WERE KINDA PISSED, BUT LIKE...
Hey!
C'MON, WAIT UP...
SFF...
WHOA! YOU'RE TALL!
YOU COULD BE A MODEL.

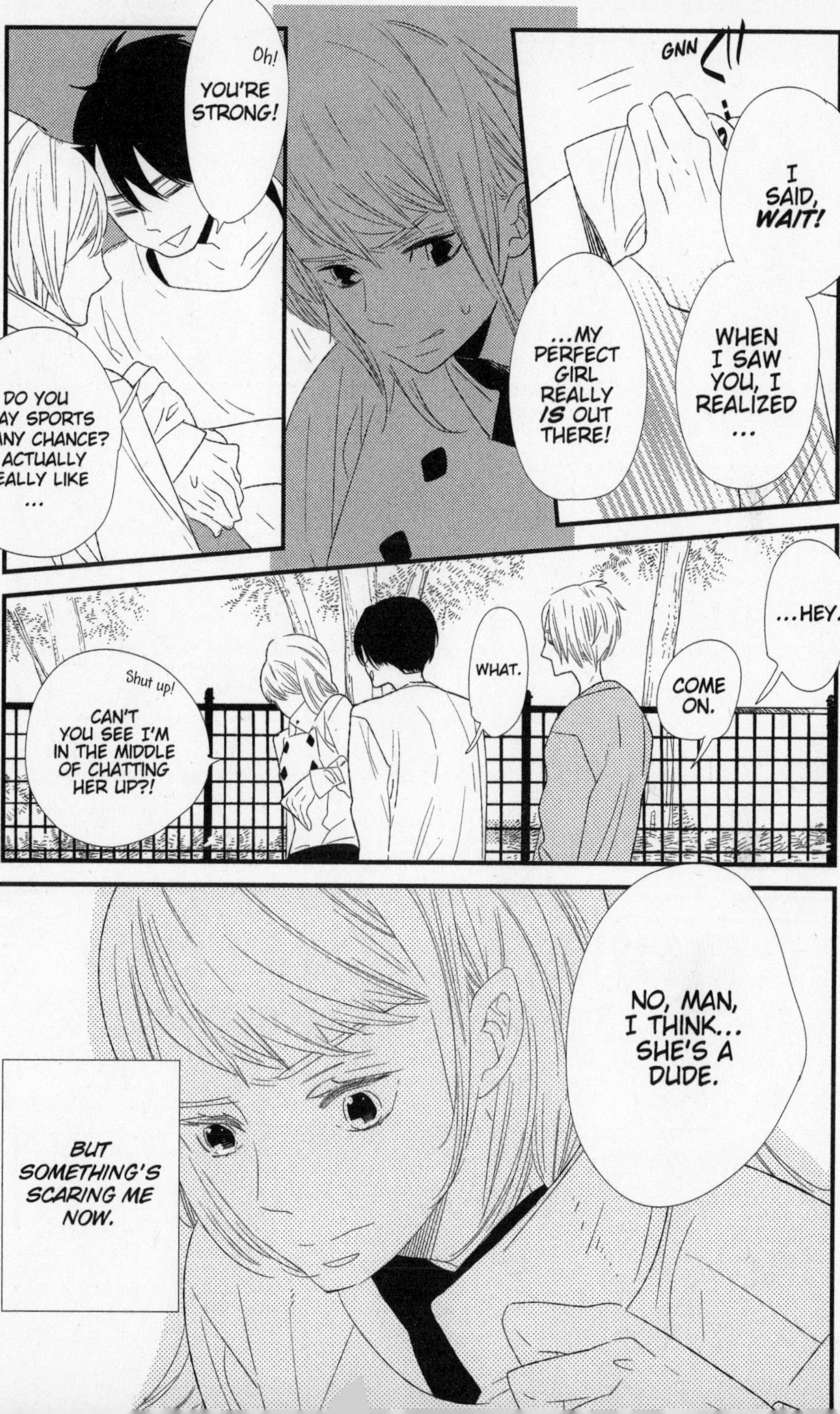
GNN
I SAID, *WAIT!*
WHEN I SAW YOU, I REALIZED ...
...MY PERFECT GIRL REALLY *IS* OUT THERE!
Oh!
YOU'RE STRONG!
DO YOU PLAY SPORTS BY ANY CHANCE? I ACTUALLY REALLY LIKE ...
...HEY.
COME ON.
WHAT.
Shut up!
CAN'T YOU SEE I'M IN THE MIDDLE OF CHATTING HER UP?!
NO, MAN, I THINK... SHE'S A DUDE.
BUT SOMETHING'S SCARING ME NOW.

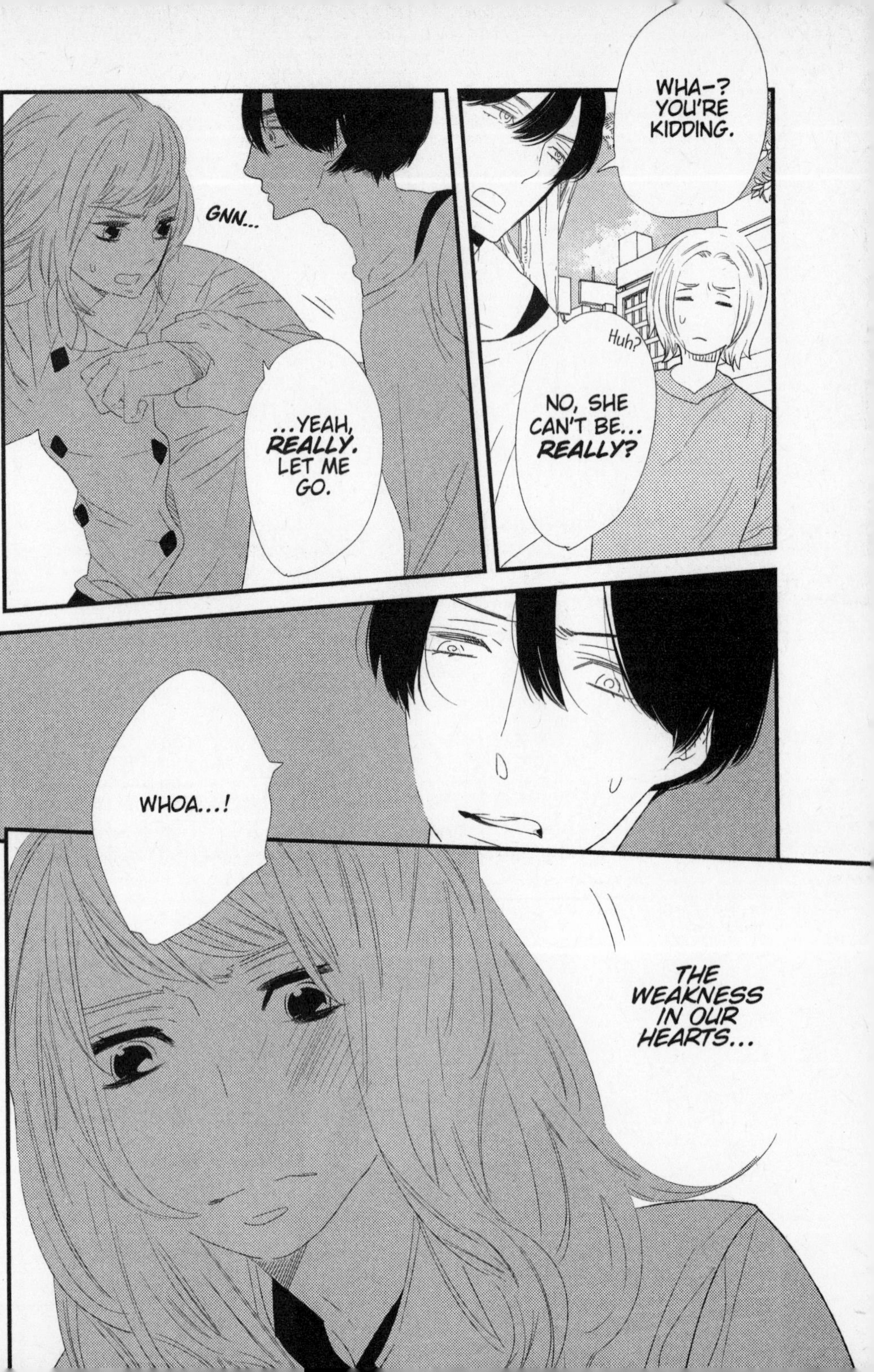
WHA-? YOU'RE KIDDING.
Huh?
NO, SHE CAN'T BE... REALLY?
GNN...
...YEAH, REALLY. LET ME GO.
WHOA...!
THE WEAKNESS IN OUR HEARTS...

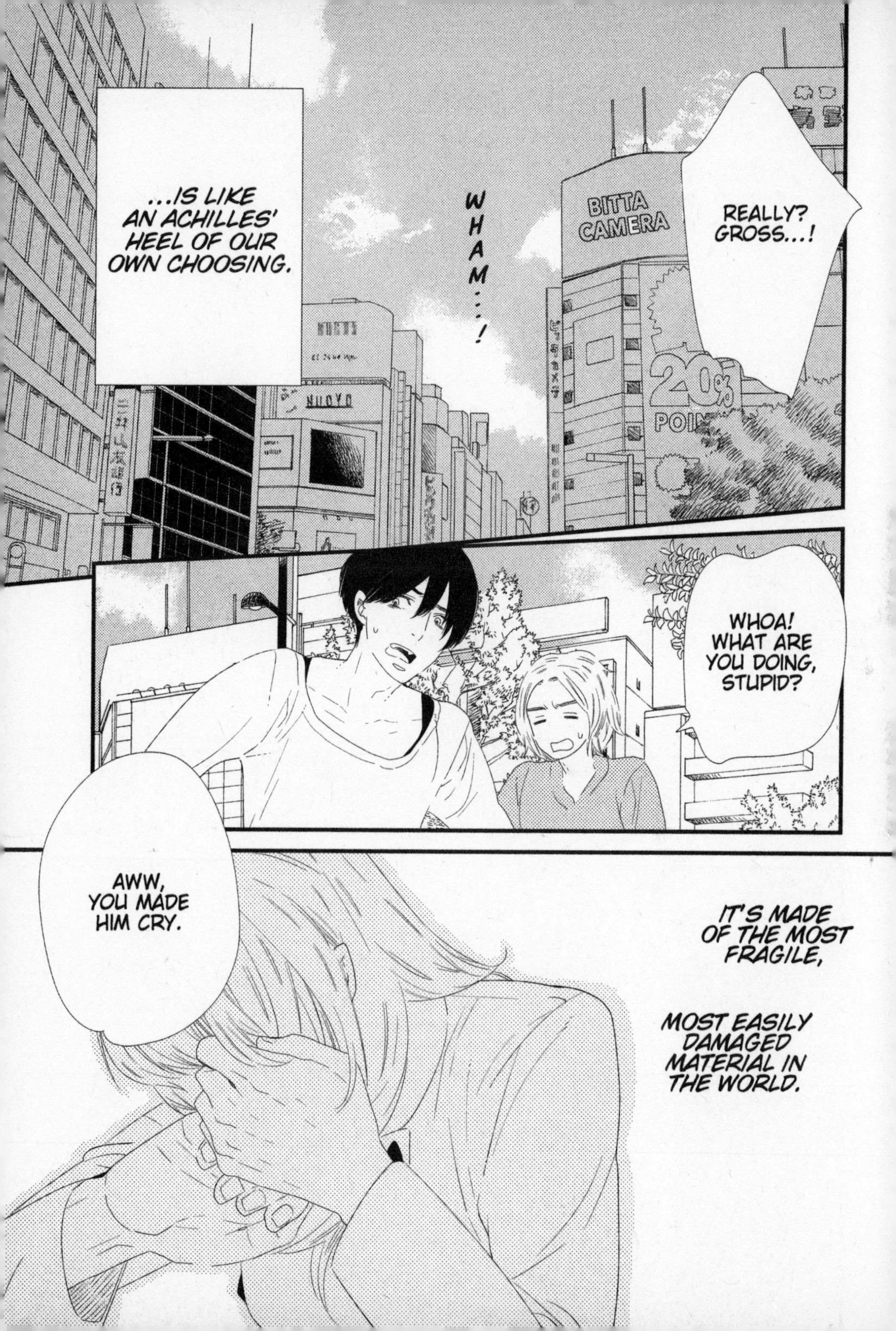
REALLY? GROSS...!
BITTA CAMERA
WHAM...!
...IS LIKE AN ACHILLES' HEEL OF OUR OWN CHOOSING.
WHOA! WHAT ARE YOU DOING, STUPID?
AWW, YOU MADE HIM CRY.
IT'S MADE OF THE MOST FRAGILE,
MOST EASILY DAMAGED MATERIAL IN THE WORLD.

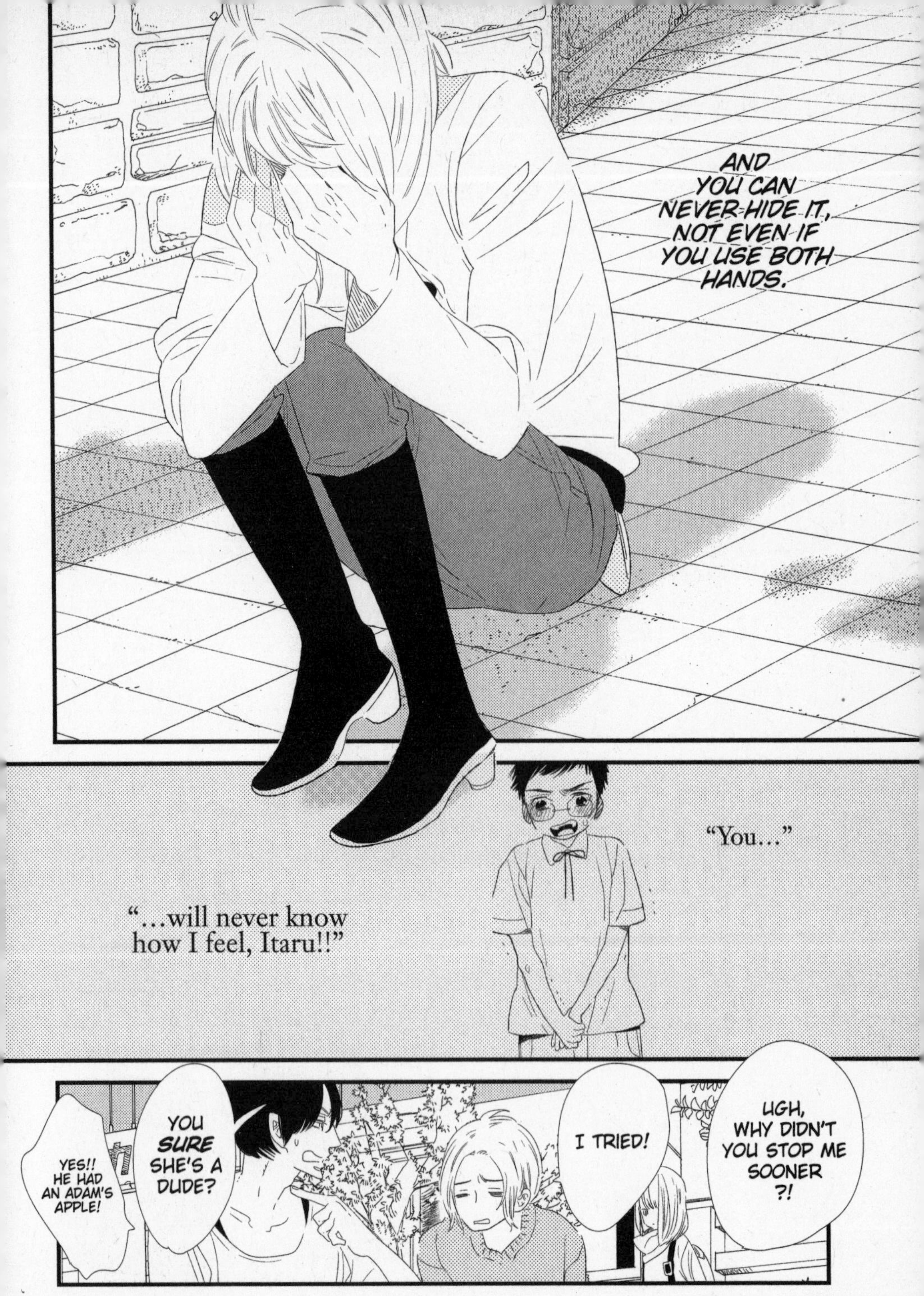
AND YOU CAN NEVER HIDE IT, NOT EVEN IF YOU USE BOTH HANDS.
"You…"
"…will never know how I feel, Itaru!!"
UGH, WHY DIDN'T YOU STOP ME SOONER?!
I TRIED!
YOU **SURE** SHE'S A DUDE?
YES!! HE HAD AN ADAM'S APPLE!

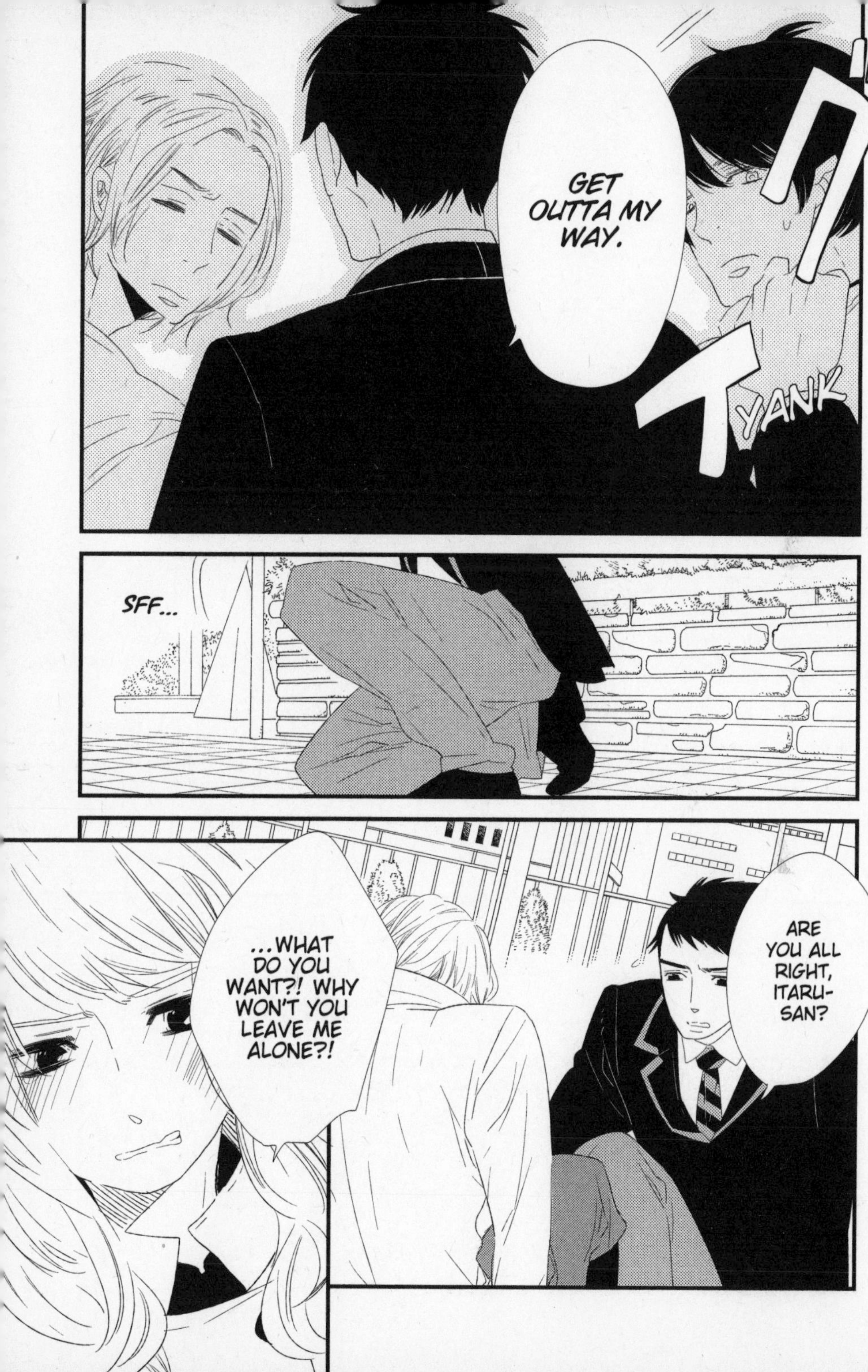
GET OUTTA MY WAY.
YANK
SFF...
ARE YOU ALL RIGHT, ITARU-SAN?
...WHAT DO YOU WANT?! WHY WON'T YOU LEAVE ME ALONE?!

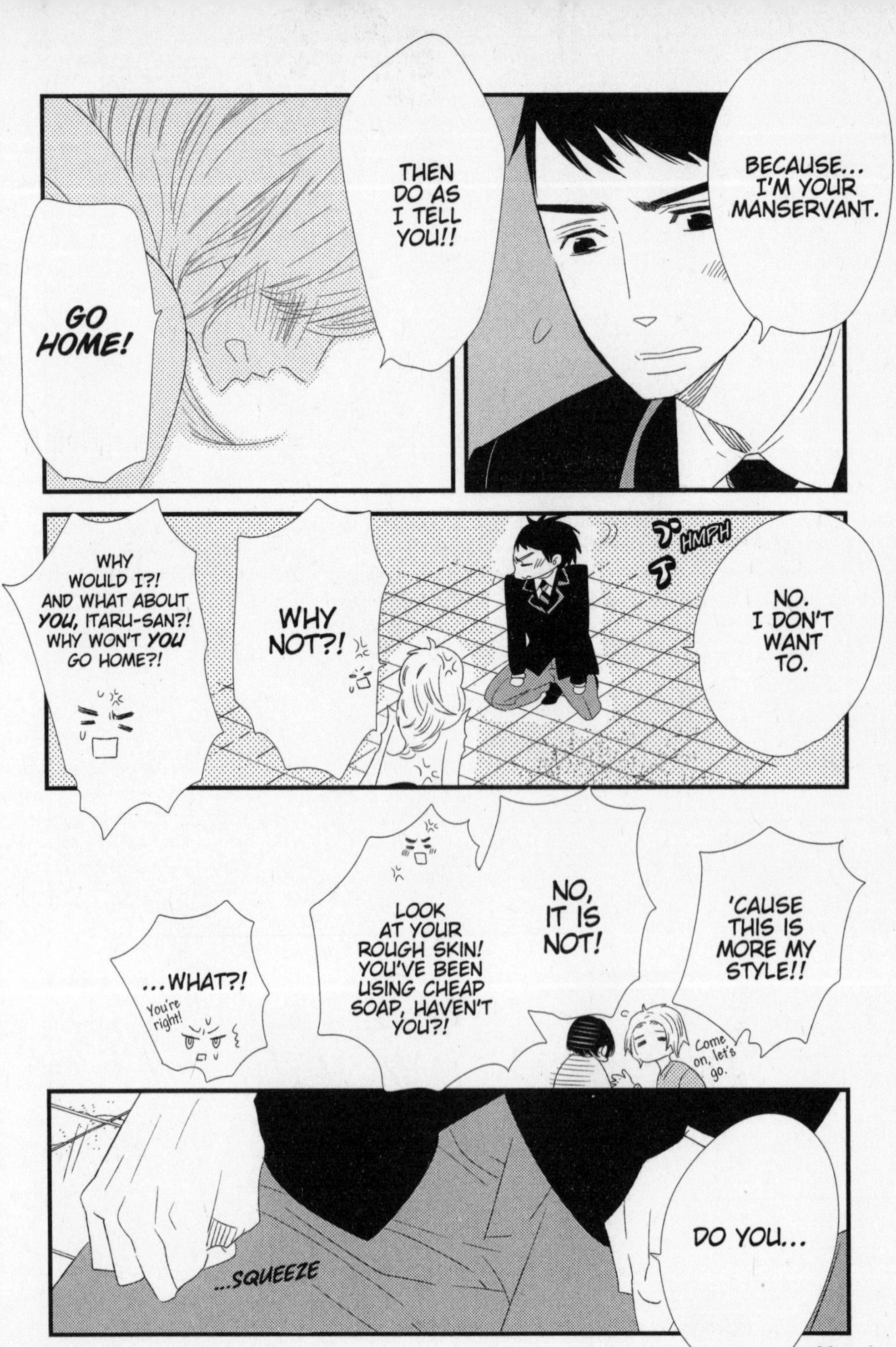
BECAUSE... I'M YOUR MANSERVANT.
THEN DO AS I TELL YOU!!
GO HOME!
HMPH
NO. I DON'T WANT TO.
WHY NOT?!
WHY WOULD I?! AND WHAT ABOUT YOU, ITARU-SAN?! WHY WON'T YOU GO HOME?!
'CAUSE THIS IS MORE MY STYLE!!
Come on, let's go.
NO, IT IS NOT!
LOOK AT YOUR ROUGH SKIN! YOU'VE BEEN USING CHEAP SOAP, HAVEN'T YOU?!
...WHAT?!
You're right!
DO YOU...
...SQUEEZE

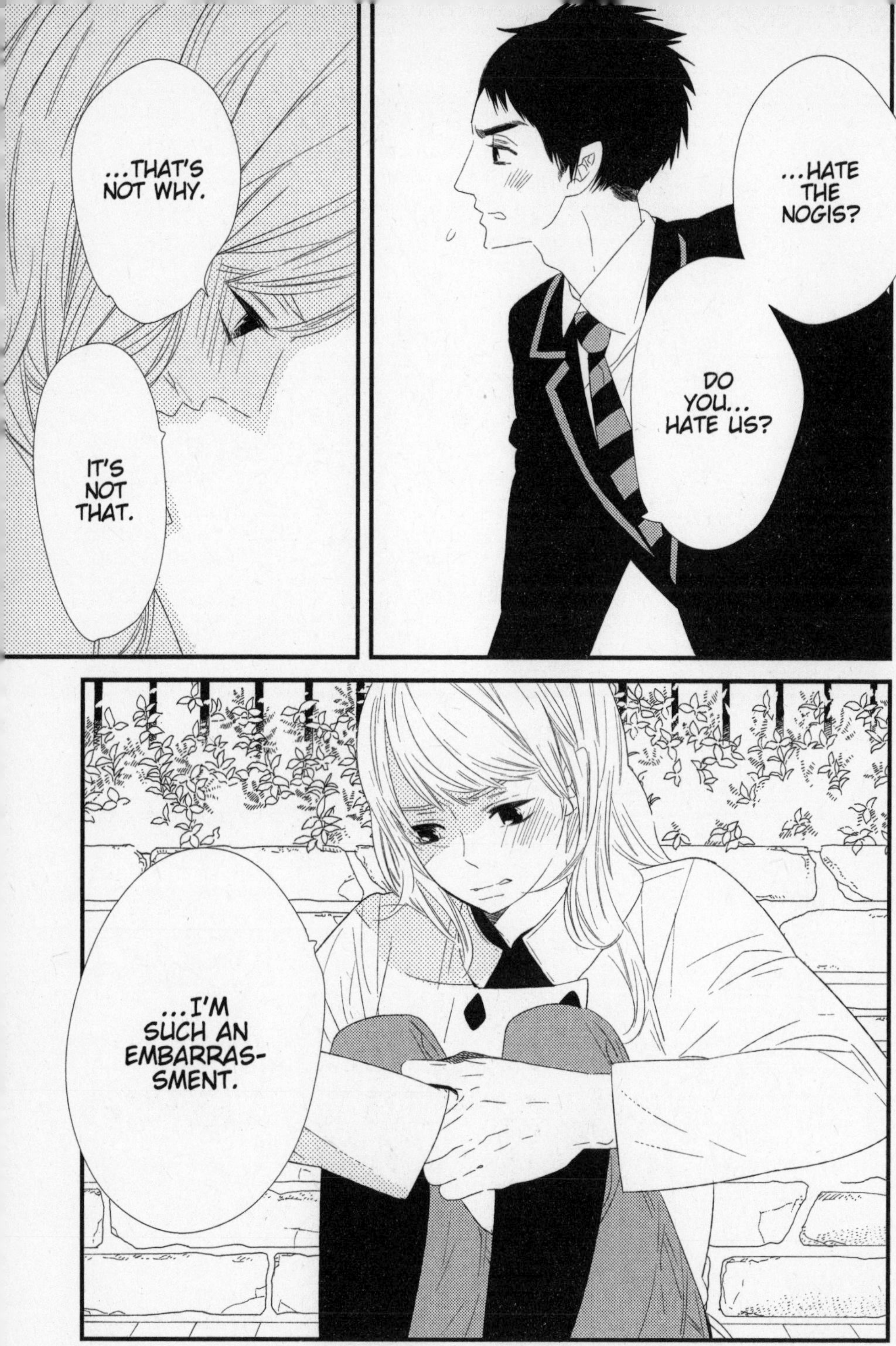
...HATE THE NOGIS?
DO YOU... HATE US?
...THAT'S NOT WHY.
IT'S NOT THAT.
...I'M SUCH AN EMBARRASSMENT.

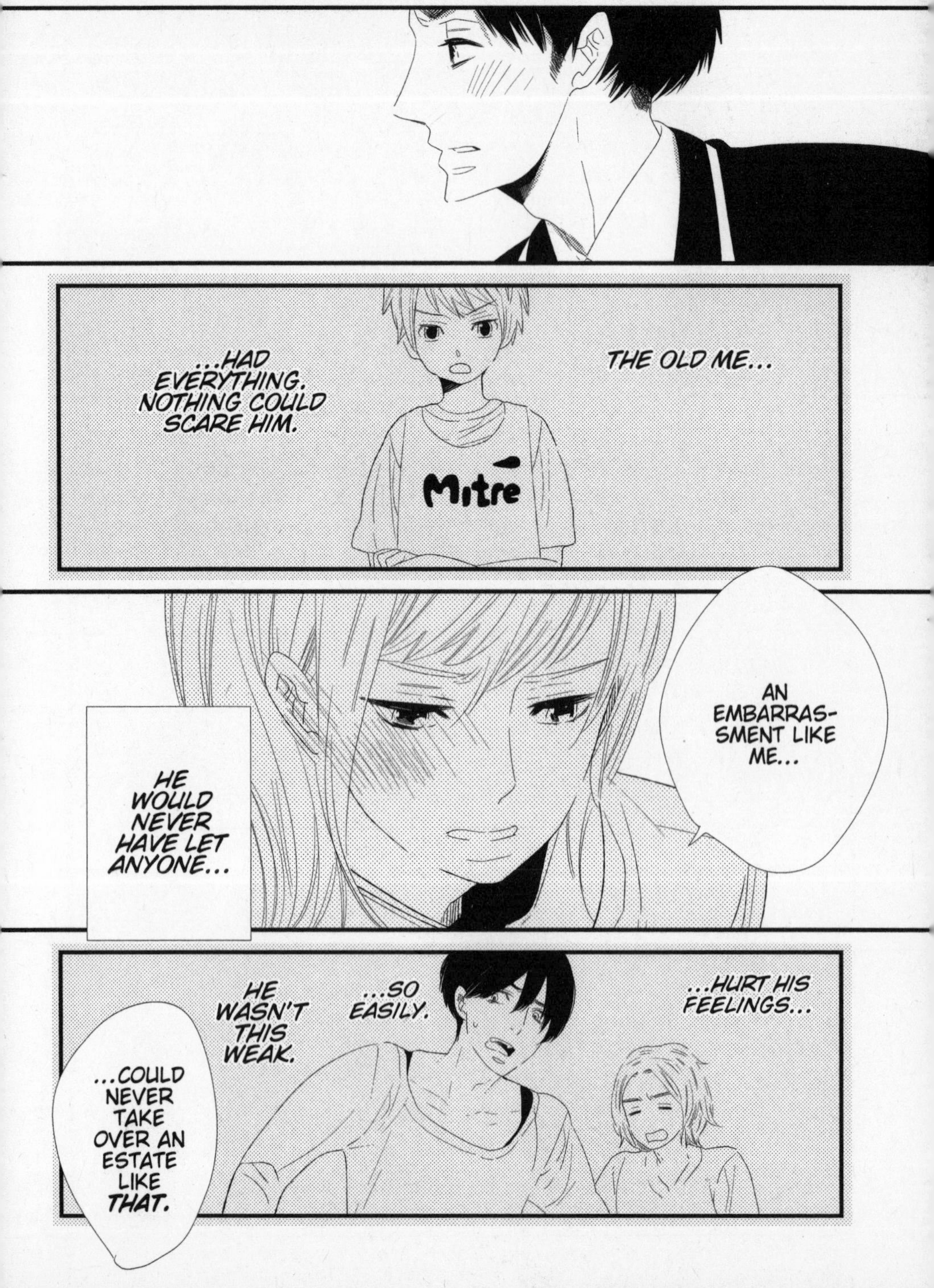
THE OLD ME...
...HAD EVERYTHING. NOTHING COULD SCARE HIM.
Mitre
AN EMBARRAS-SMENT LIKE ME...
HE WOULD NEVER HAVE LET ANYONE...
...HURT HIS FEELINGS...
...SO EASILY.
HE WASN'T THIS WEAK.
...COULD NEVER TAKE OVER AN ESTATE LIKE THAT.

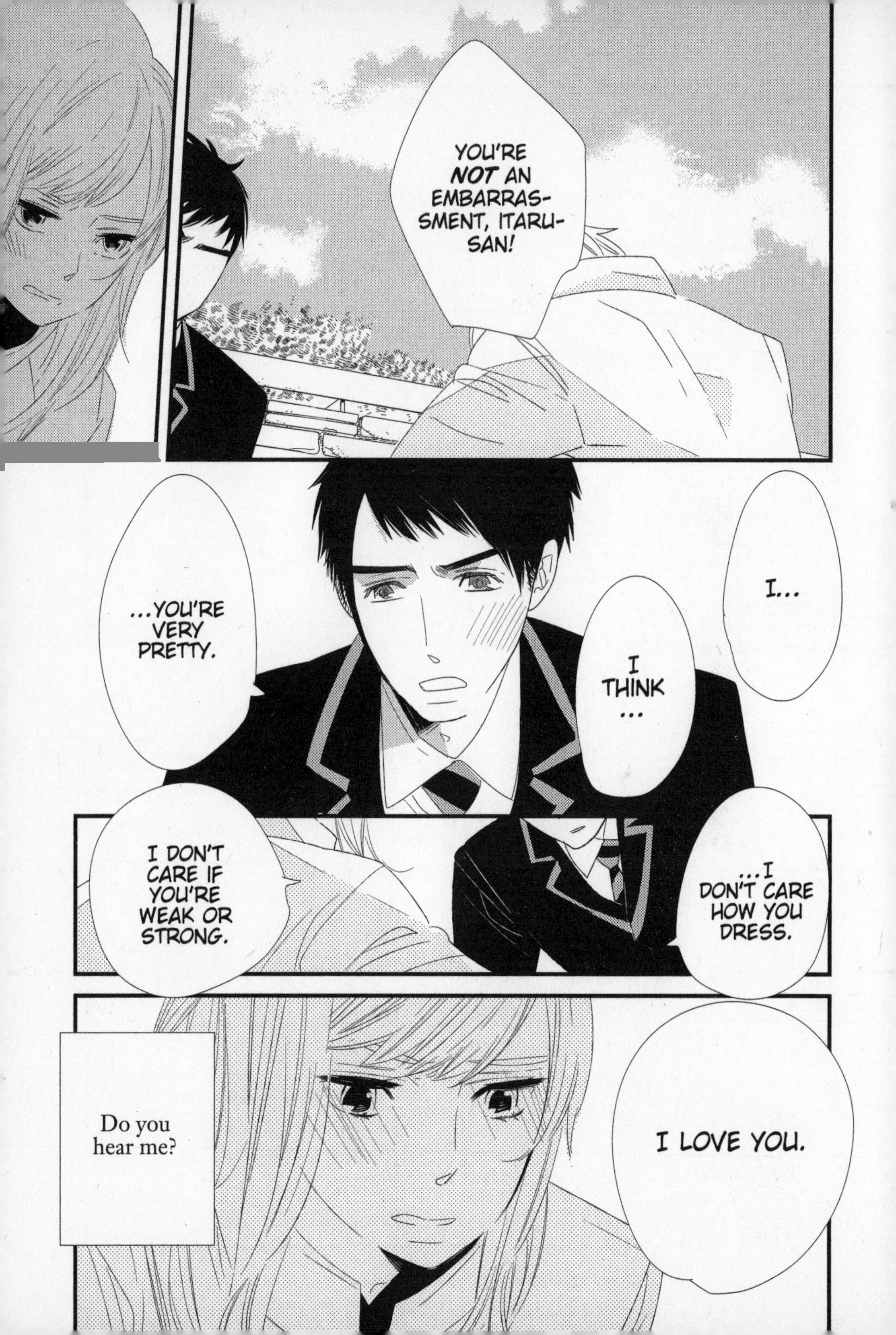
YOU'RE NOT AN EMBARRAS-SMENT, ITARU-SAN!
I...
I THINK...
...YOU'RE VERY PRETTY.
...I DON'T CARE HOW YOU DRESS.
I DON'T CARE IF YOU'RE WEAK OR STRONG.
I LOVE YOU.
Do you hear me?

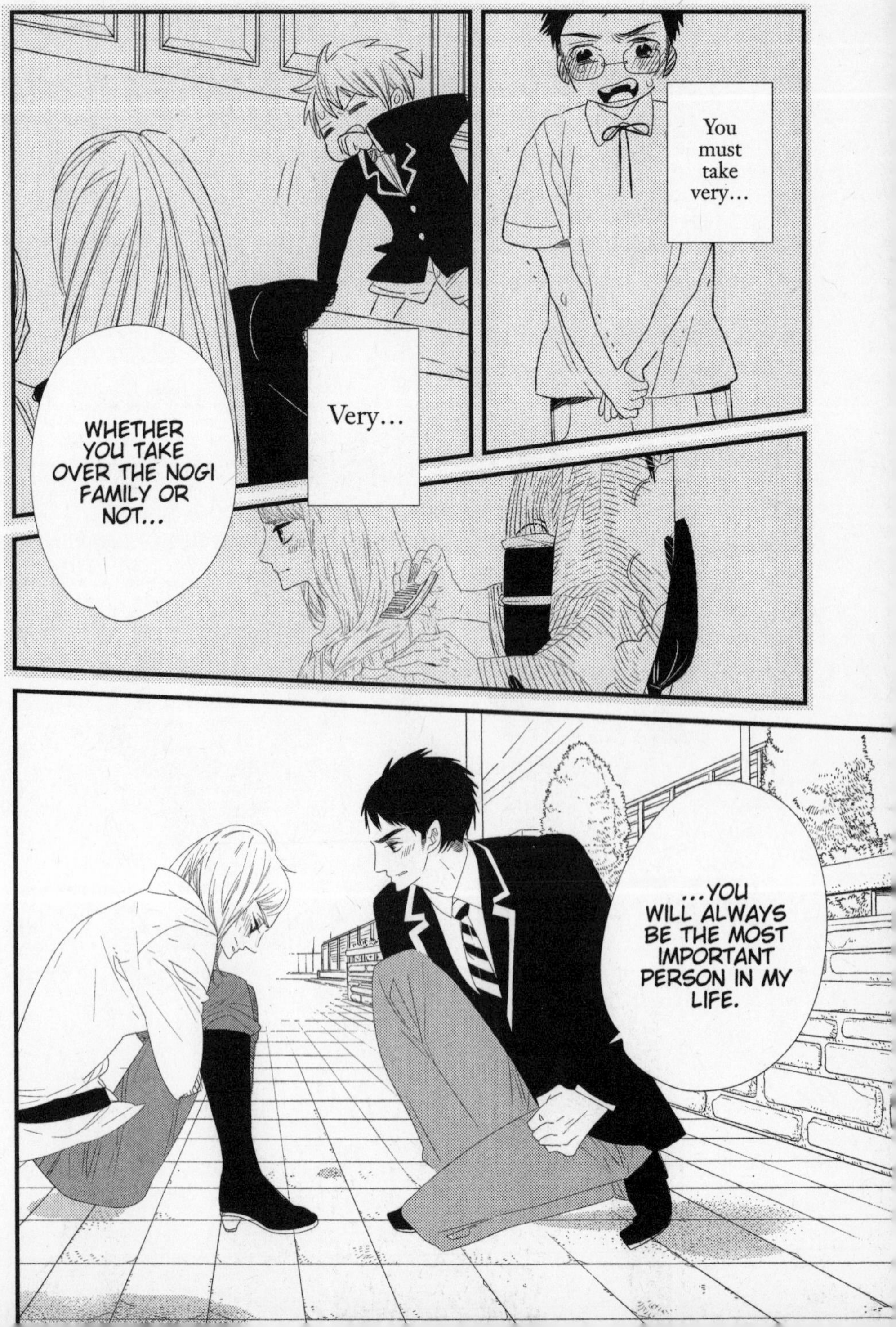
You must take very…
Very…
WHETHER YOU TAKE OVER THE NOGI FAMILY OR NOT…
…YOU WILL ALWAYS BE THE MOST IMPORTANT PERSON IN MY LIFE.

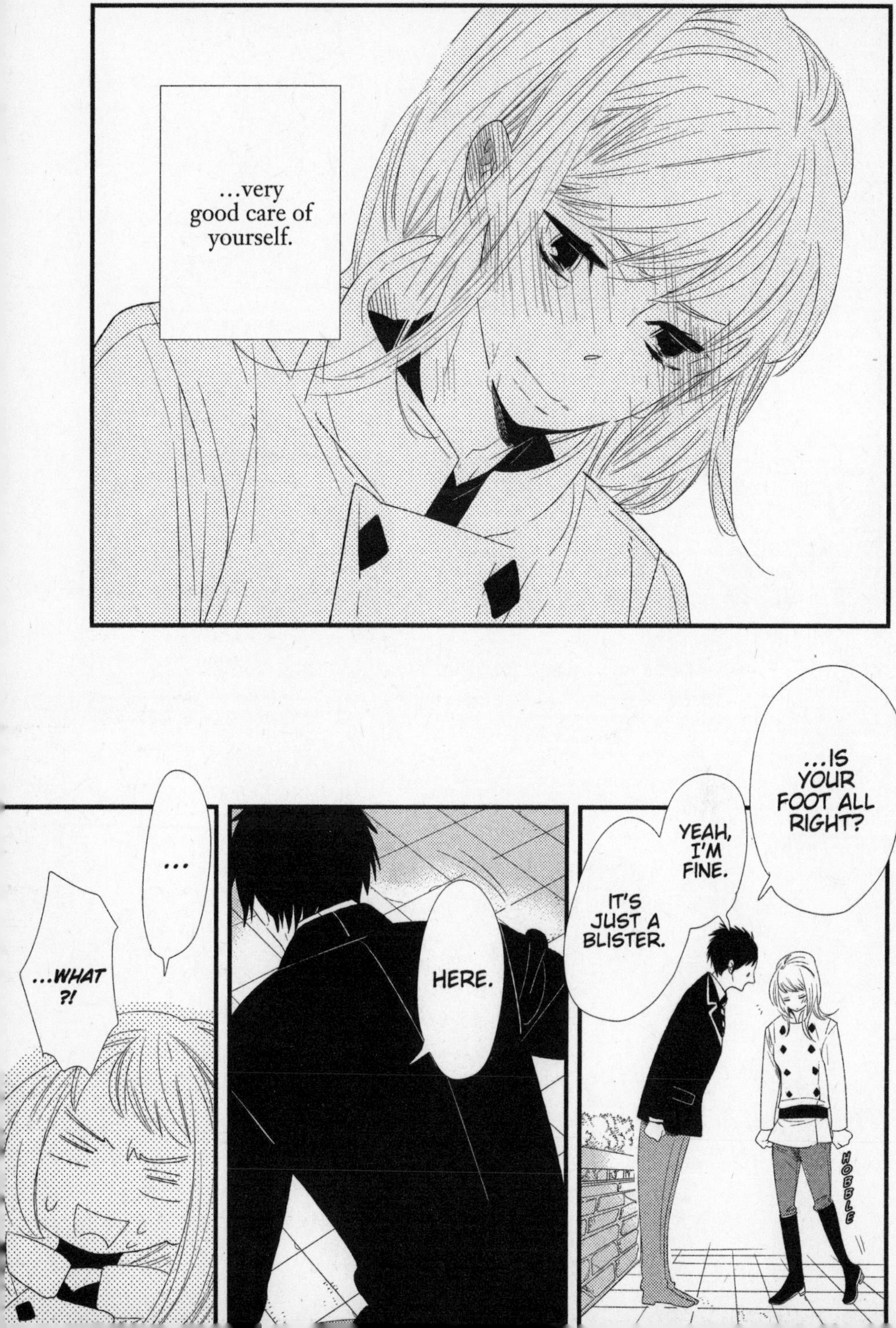
...very good care of yourself.
...IS YOUR FOOT ALL RIGHT?
YEAH, I'M FINE.
IT'S JUST A BLISTER.
HOBBLE
HERE.
...
...WHAT?!

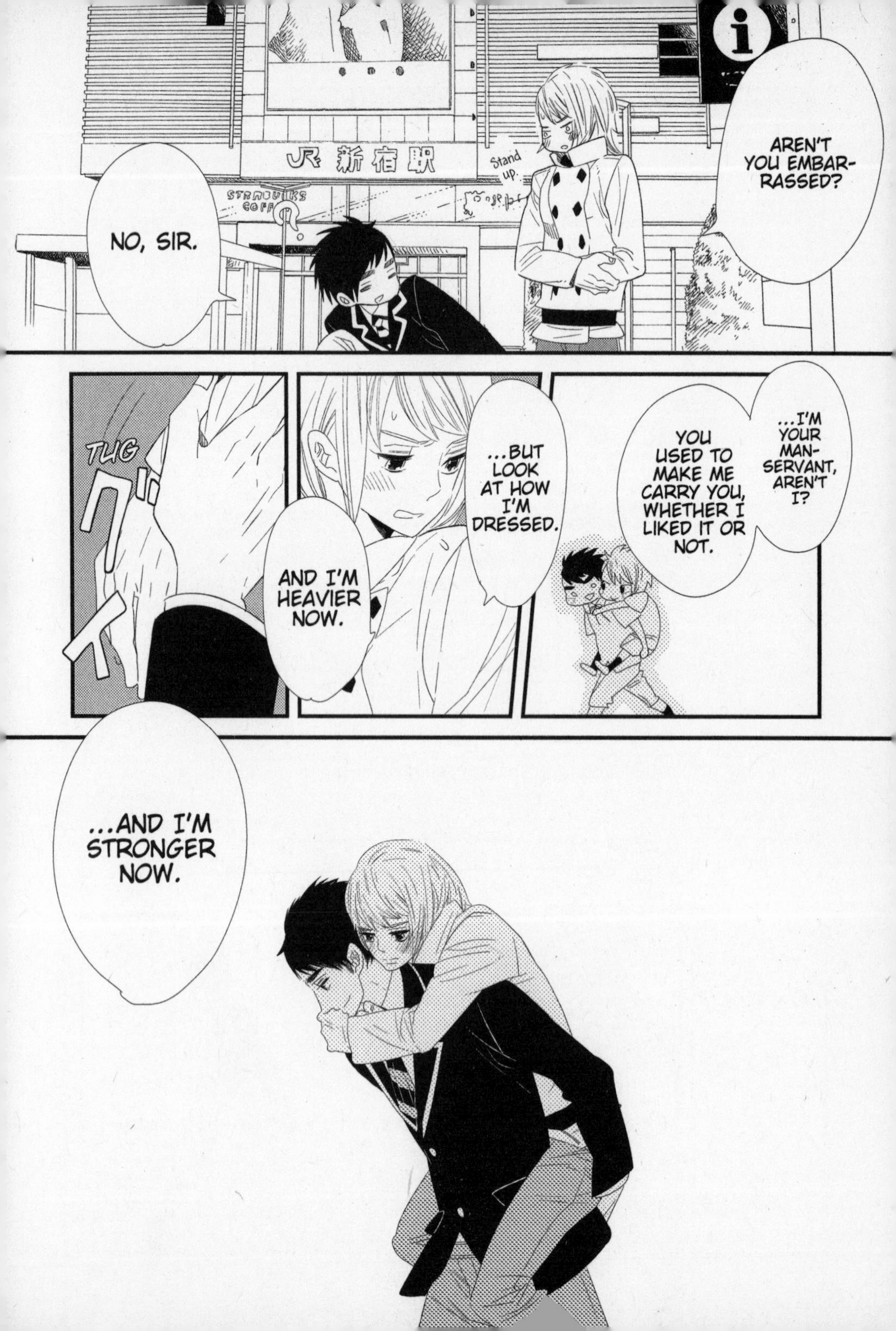
ARE'NT YOU EMBAR-RASSED?
Stand up.
新宿駅
NO, SIR.
...I'M YOUR MAN-SERVANT, AREN'T I?
YOU USED TO MAKE ME CARRY YOU, WHETHER I LIKED IT OR NOT.
...BUT LOOK AT HOW I'M DRESSED.
AND I'M HEAVIER NOW.
TUG
...AND I'M STRONGER NOW.

chapter 8

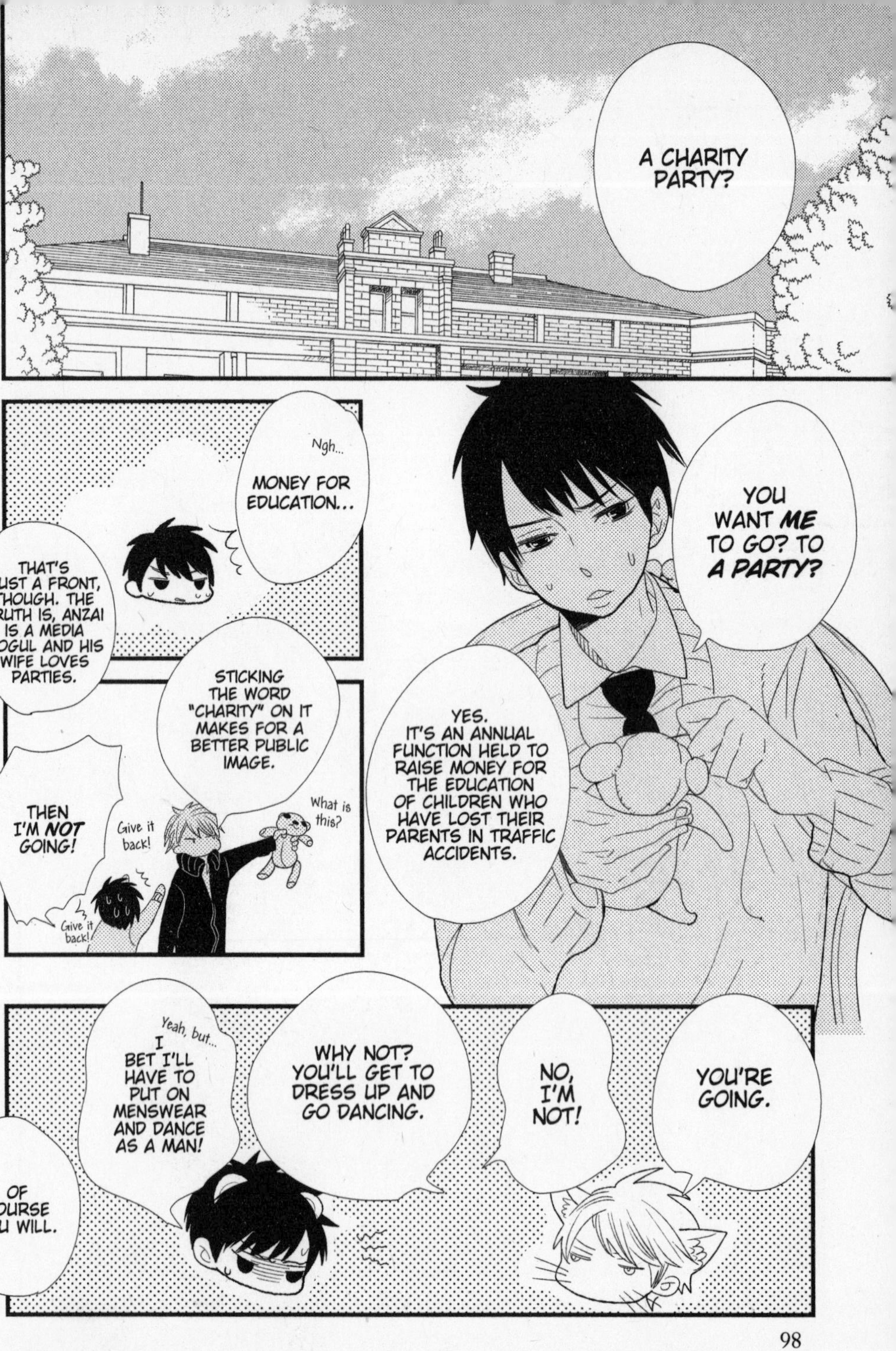
A CHARITY PARTY?
YOU WANT ME TO GO? TO A PARTY?
YES. IT'S AN ANNUAL FUNCTION HELD TO RAISE MONEY FOR THE EDUCATION OF CHILDREN WHO HAVE LOST THEIR PARENTS IN TRAFFIC ACCIDENTS.
Ngh...
MONEY FOR EDUCATION...
THAT'S JUST A FRONT, THOUGH. THE TRUTH IS, ANZAI IS A MEDIA MOGUL AND HIS WIFE LOVES PARTIES.
STICKING THE WORD "CHARITY" ON IT MAKES FOR A BETTER PUBLIC IMAGE.
What is this?
Give it back!
THEN I'M NOT GOING!
Give it back!
YOU'RE GOING.
NO, I'M NOT!
WHY NOT? YOU'LL GET TO DRESS UP AND GO DANCING.
Yeah, but...
I BET I'LL HAVE TO PUT ON MENSWEAR AND DANCE AS A MAN!
OF COURSE YOU WILL.

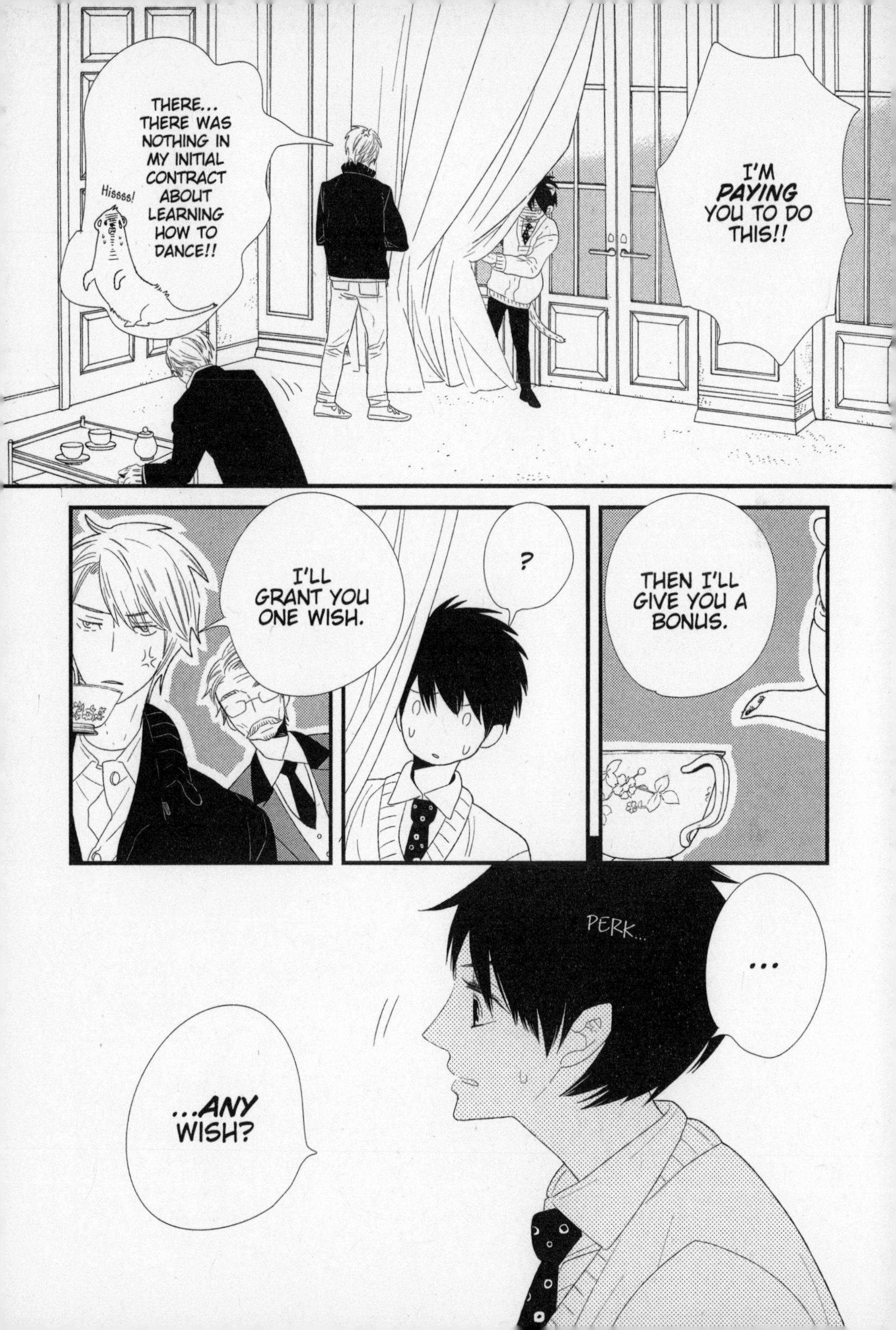
I'M PAYING YOU TO DO THIS!!
THERE... THERE WAS NOTHING IN MY INITIAL CONTRACT ABOUT LEARNING HOW TO DANCE!!
Hissss!
THEN I'LL GIVE YOU A BONUS.
?
I'LL GRANT YOU ONE WISH.
...
PERK...
...ANY WISH?

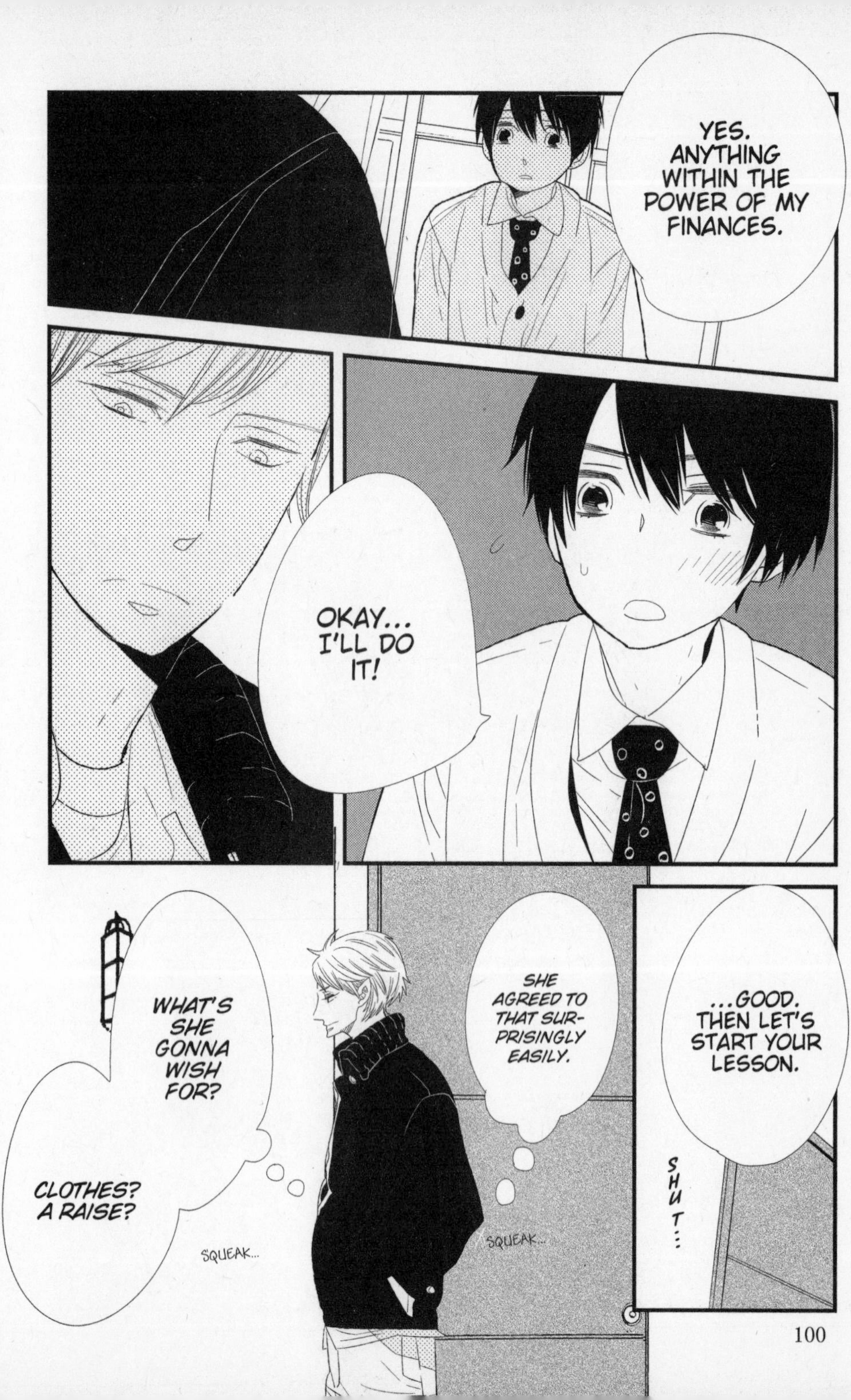
YES. ANYTHING WITHIN THE POWER OF MY FINANCES.
OKAY... I'LL DO IT!
...GOOD. THEN LET'S START YOUR LESSON.
SHUT...
SHE AGREED TO THAT SUR-PRISINGLY EASILY.
WHAT'S SHE GONNA WISH FOR?
SQUEAK...
CLOTHES? A RAISE?
SQUEAK...

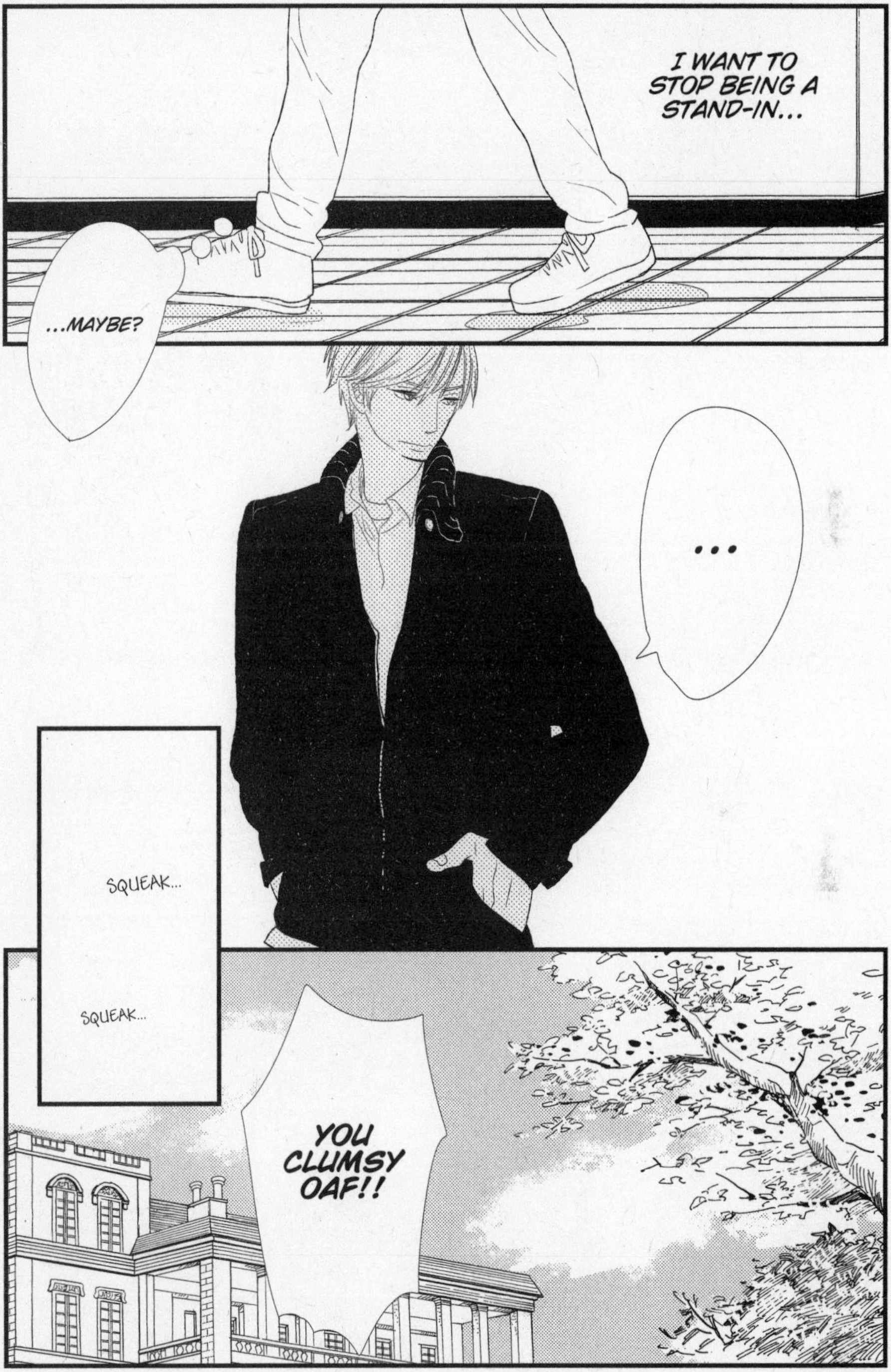
I WANT TO STOP BEING A STAND-IN...
...MAYBE?
...
SQUEAK...
SQUEAK...
YOU CLUMSY OAF!!

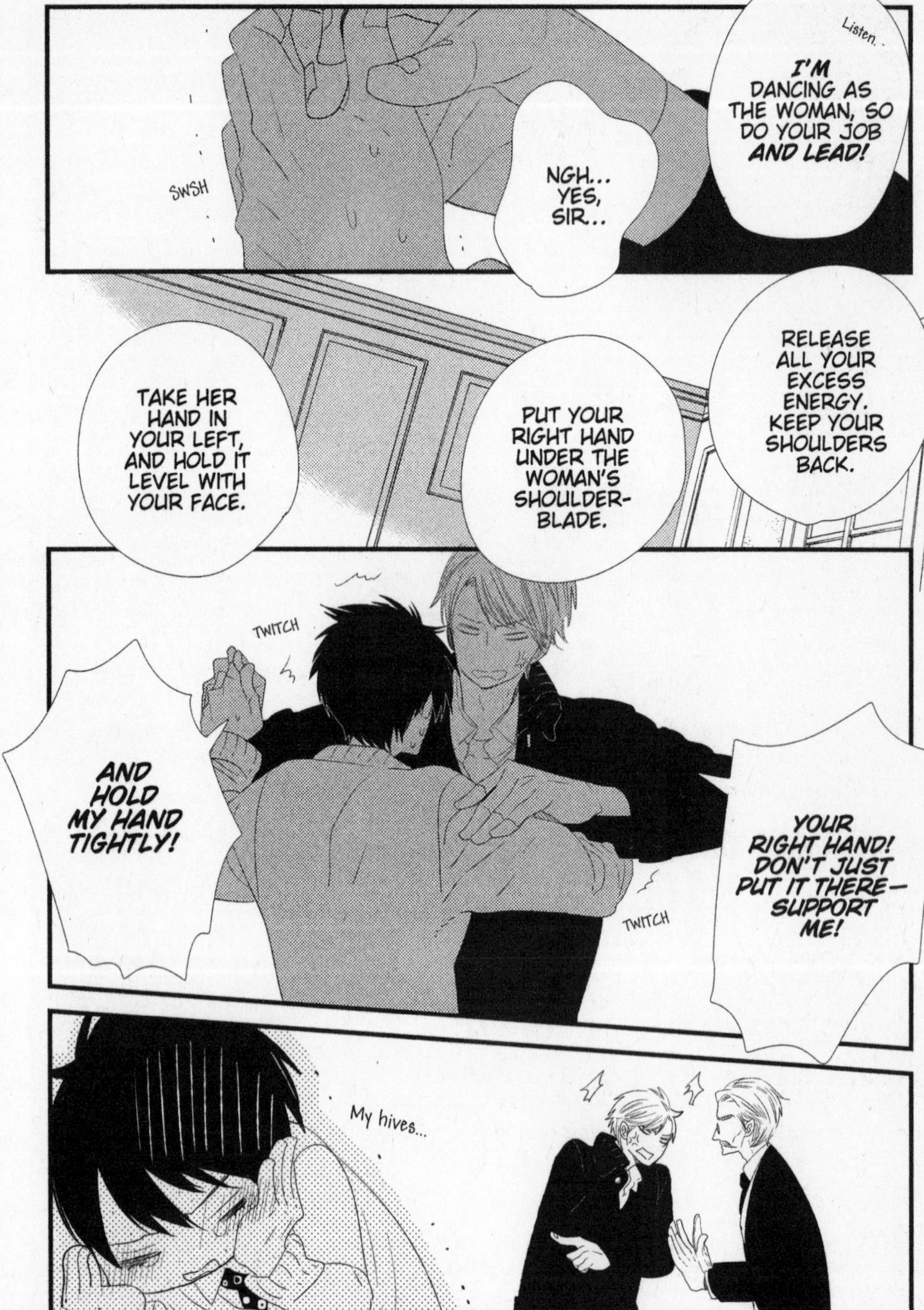
Listen...
I'M DANCING AS THE WOMAN, SO DO YOUR JOB AND LEAD!
NGH... YES, SIR...
SWSH
RELEASE ALL YOUR EXCESS ENERGY. KEEP YOUR SHOULDERS BACK.
PUT YOUR RIGHT HAND UNDER THE WOMAN'S SHOULDER-BLADE.
TAKE HER HAND IN YOUR LEFT, AND HOLD IT LEVEL WITH YOUR FACE.
YOUR RIGHT HAND! DON'T JUST PUT IT THERE—SUPPORT ME!
TWITCH
TWITCH
AND HOLD MY HAND TIGHTLY!
My hives...

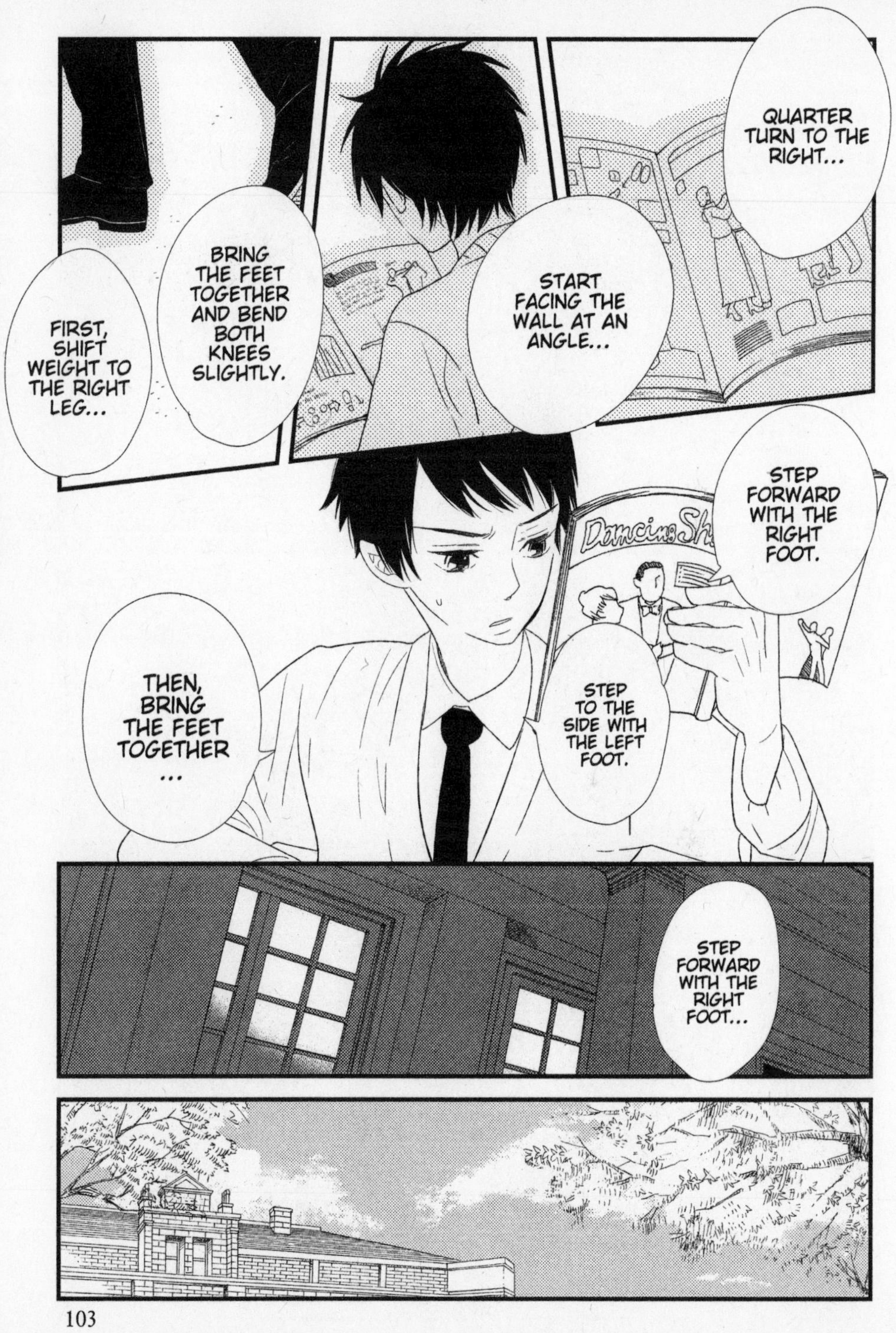
QUARTER TURN TO THE RIGHT...
START FACING THE WALL AT AN ANGLE...
BRING THE FEET TOGETHER AND BEND BOTH KNEES SLIGHTLY.
FIRST, SHIFT WEIGHT TO THE RIGHT LEG...
STEP FORWARD WITH THE RIGHT FOOT.
STEP TO THE SIDE WITH THE LEFT FOOT.
THEN, BRING THE FEET TOGETHER ...
STEP FORWARD WITH THE RIGHT FOOT...

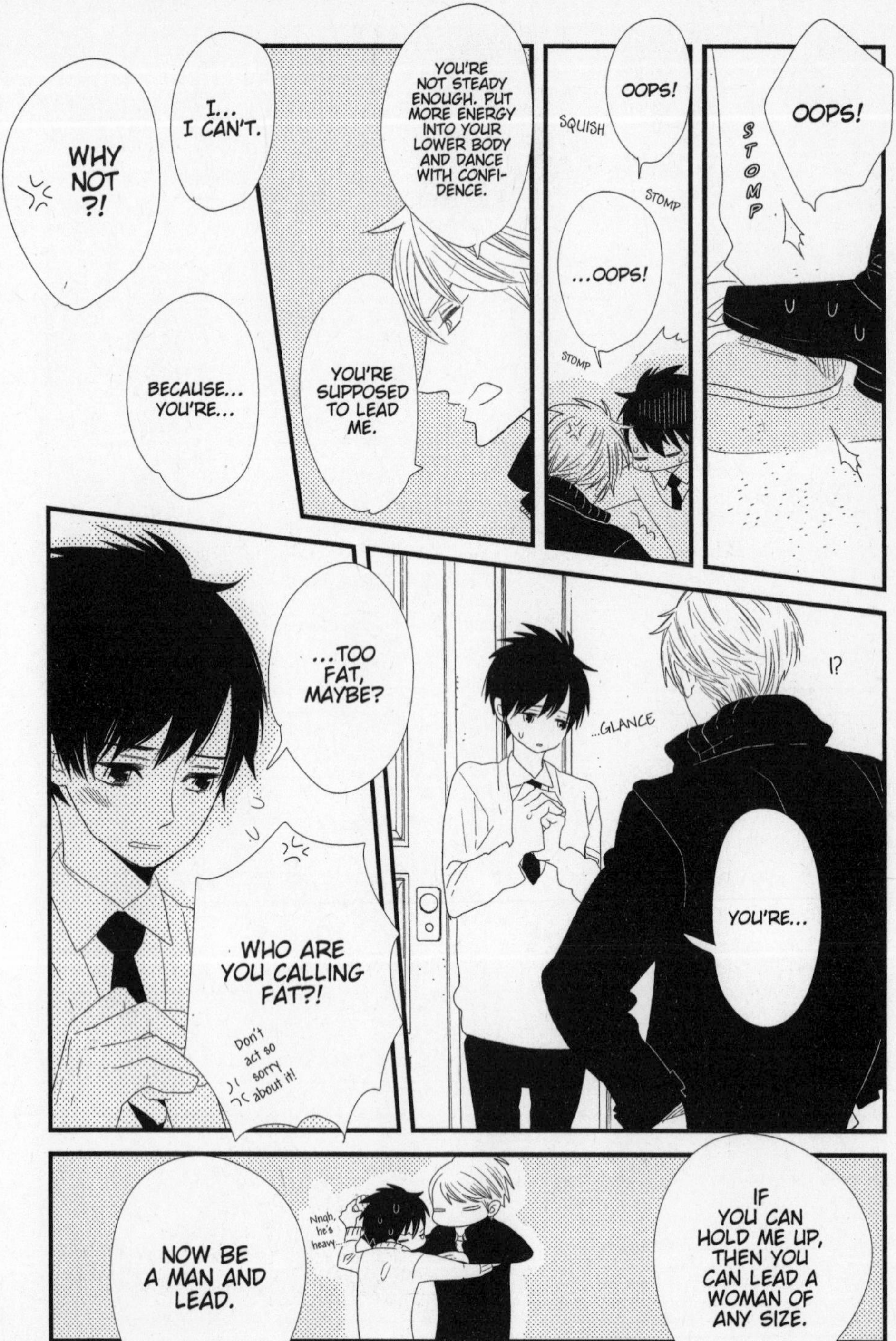

OOPS!
STOMP
OOPS!
SQUISH
STOMP
...OOPS!
STOMP
YOU'RE NOT STEADY ENOUGH. PUT MORE ENERGY INTO YOUR LOWER BODY AND DANCE WITH CONFI-DENCE.
YOU'RE SUPPOSED TO LEAD ME.
I... I CAN'T.
WHY NOT ?!
BECAUSE... YOU'RE...
!?
...GLANCE
YOU'RE...
...TOO FAT, MAYBE?
WHO ARE YOU CALLING FAT?!
Don't act so sorry about it!
IF YOU CAN HOLD ME UP, THEN YOU CAN LEAD A WOMAN OF ANY SIZE.
Nngh, he's heavy...
NOW BE A MAN AND LEAD.

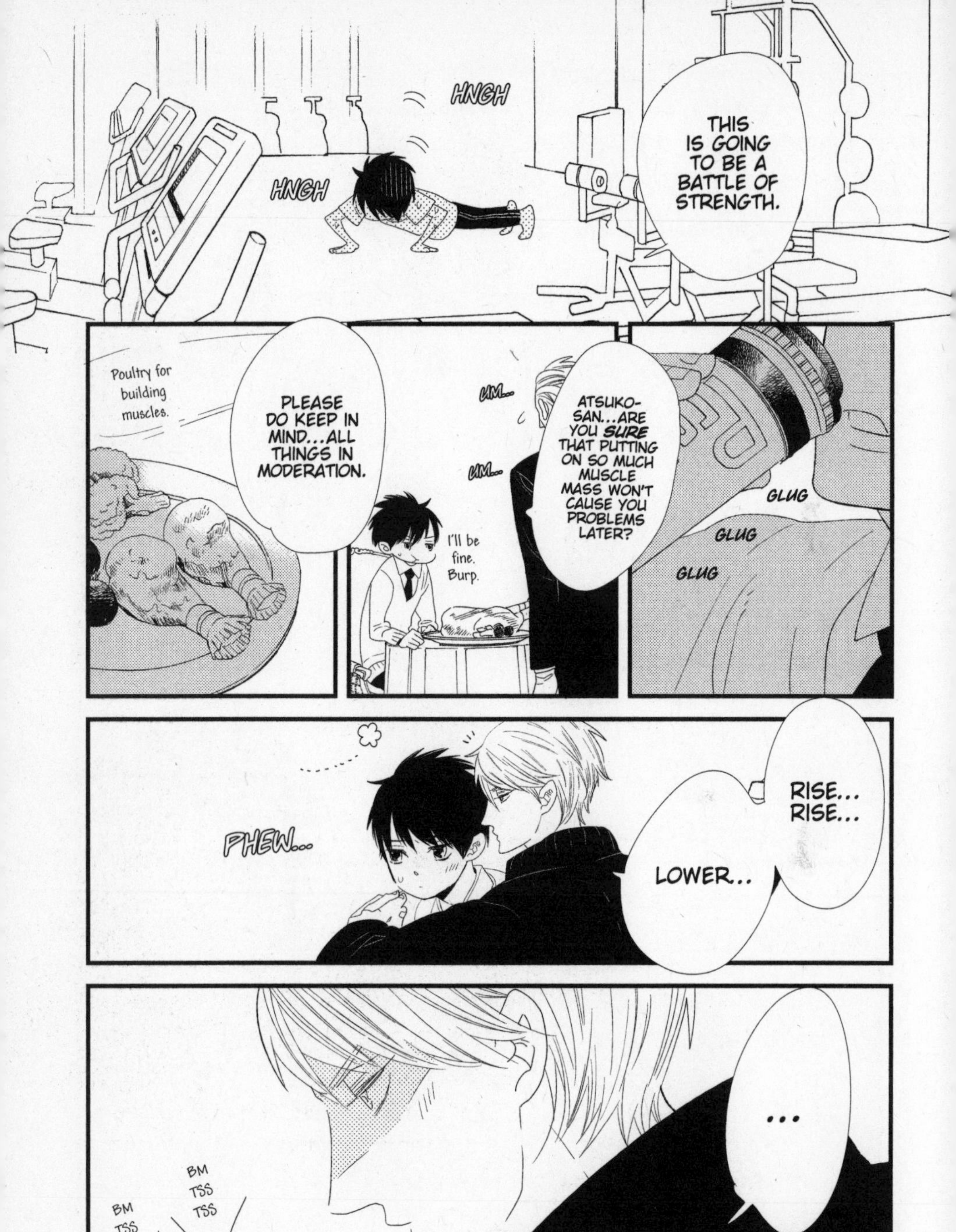
THIS IS GOING TO BE A BATTLE OF STRENGTH.
HNGH
HNGH
GLUG
GLUG
GLUG
ATSUKO-SAN...ARE YOU SURE THAT PUTTING ON SO MUCH MUSCLE MASS WON'T CAUSE YOU PROBLEMS LATER?
UM...
UM...
I'll be fine. Burp.
PLEASE DO KEEP IN MIND...ALL THINGS IN MODERATION.
Poultry for building muscles.
RISE... RISE...
LOWER...
PHEW...
...
BM TSS TSS
BM TSS TSS

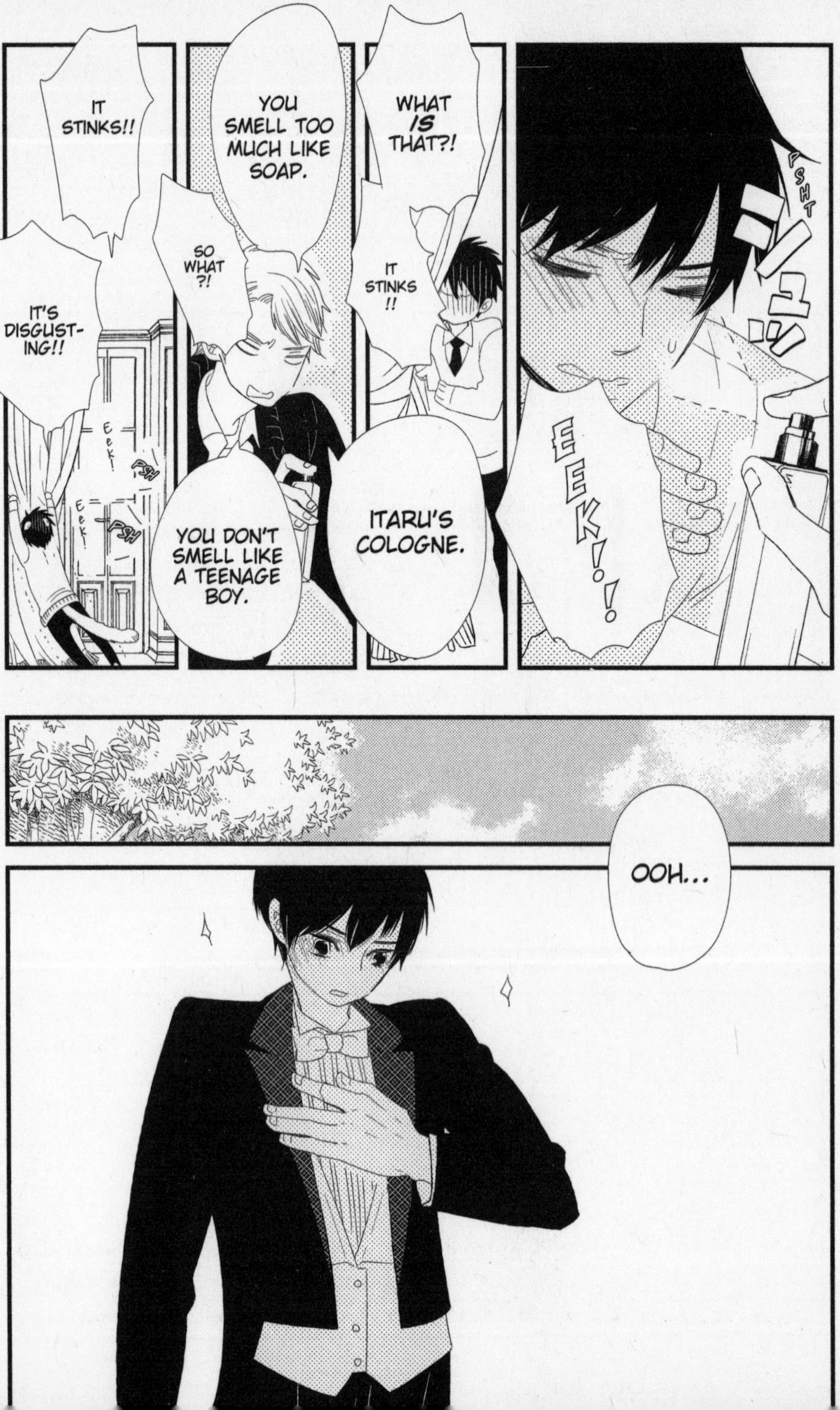
PSHT
EEK!!
WHAT IS THAT?!
IT STINKS!!
ITARU'S COLOGNE.
YOU SMELL TOO MUCH LIKE SOAP.
SO WHAT?!
YOU DON'T SMELL LIKE A TEENAGE BOY.
IT STINKS!!
IT'S DISGUSTING!!
Eek!
PSH
Eek!
PSH
OOH...

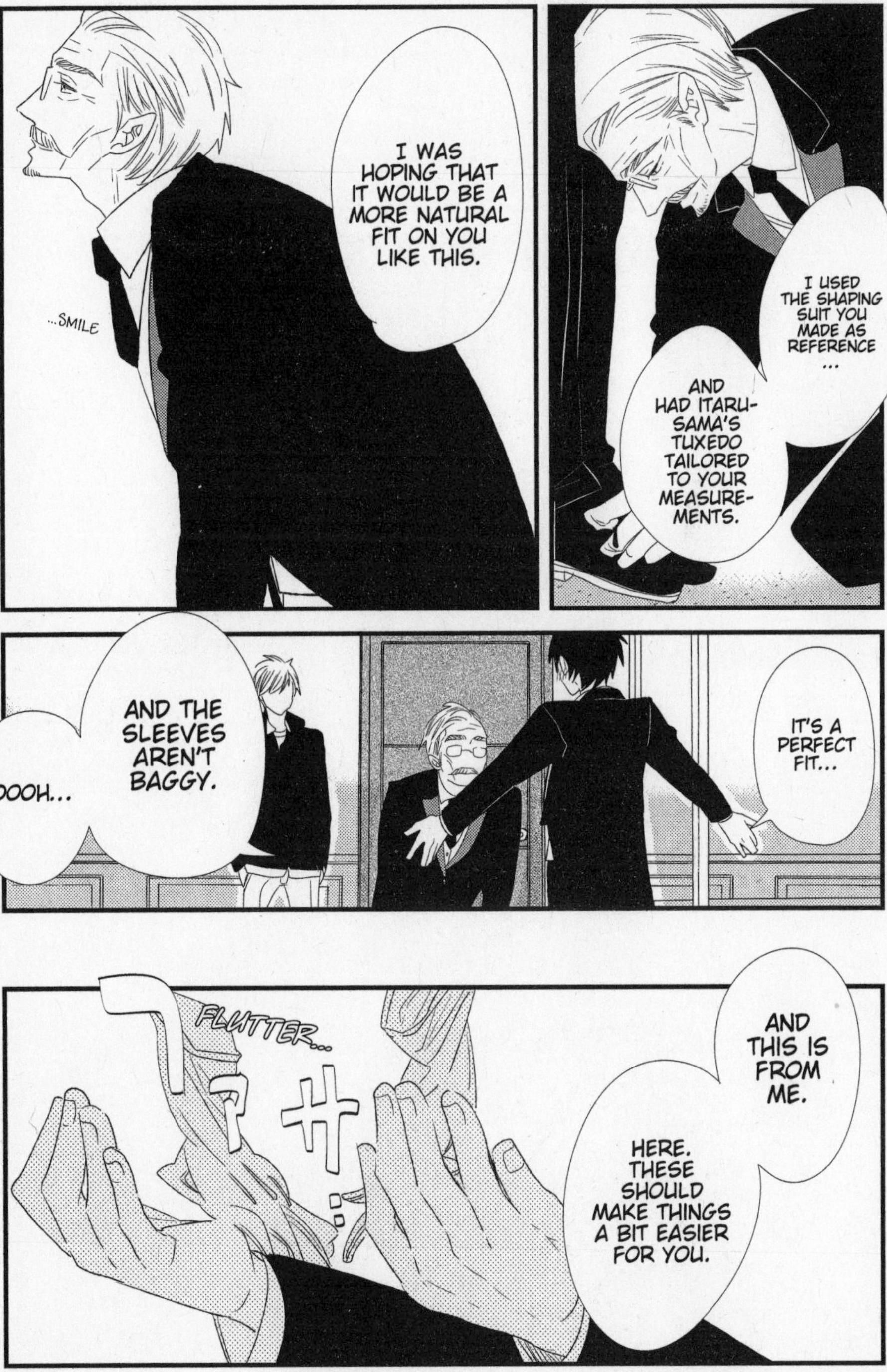
I USED THE SHAPING SUIT YOU MADE AS REFERENCE ...
AND HAD ITARU-SAMA'S TUXEDO TAILORED TO YOUR MEASUREMENTS.
I WAS HOPING THAT IT WOULD BE A MORE NATURAL FIT ON YOU LIKE THIS.
...SMILE
IT'S A PERFECT FIT...
AND THE SLEEVES AREN'T BAGGY.
OOOH...
AND THIS IS FROM ME.
HERE. THESE SHOULD MAKE THINGS A BIT EASIER FOR YOU.
FLUTTER...
ファサ

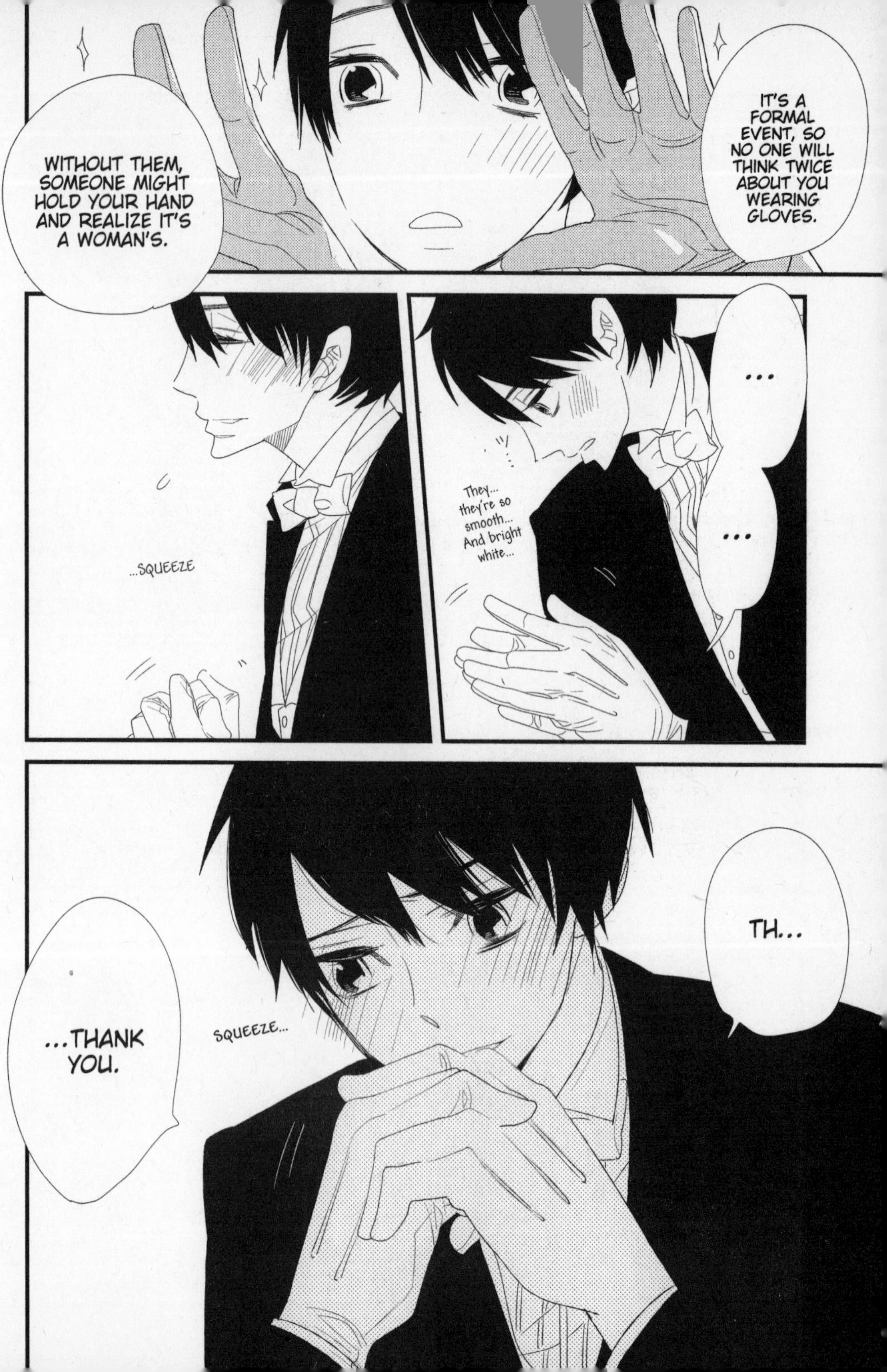
IT'S A FORMAL EVENT, SO NO ONE WILL THINK TWICE ABOUT YOU WEARING GLOVES.
WITHOUT THEM, SOMEONE MIGHT HOLD YOUR HAND AND REALIZE IT'S A WOMAN'S.
...
They... they're so smooth... And bright white...
...
...SQUEEZE
TH...
SQUEEZE...
...THANK YOU.

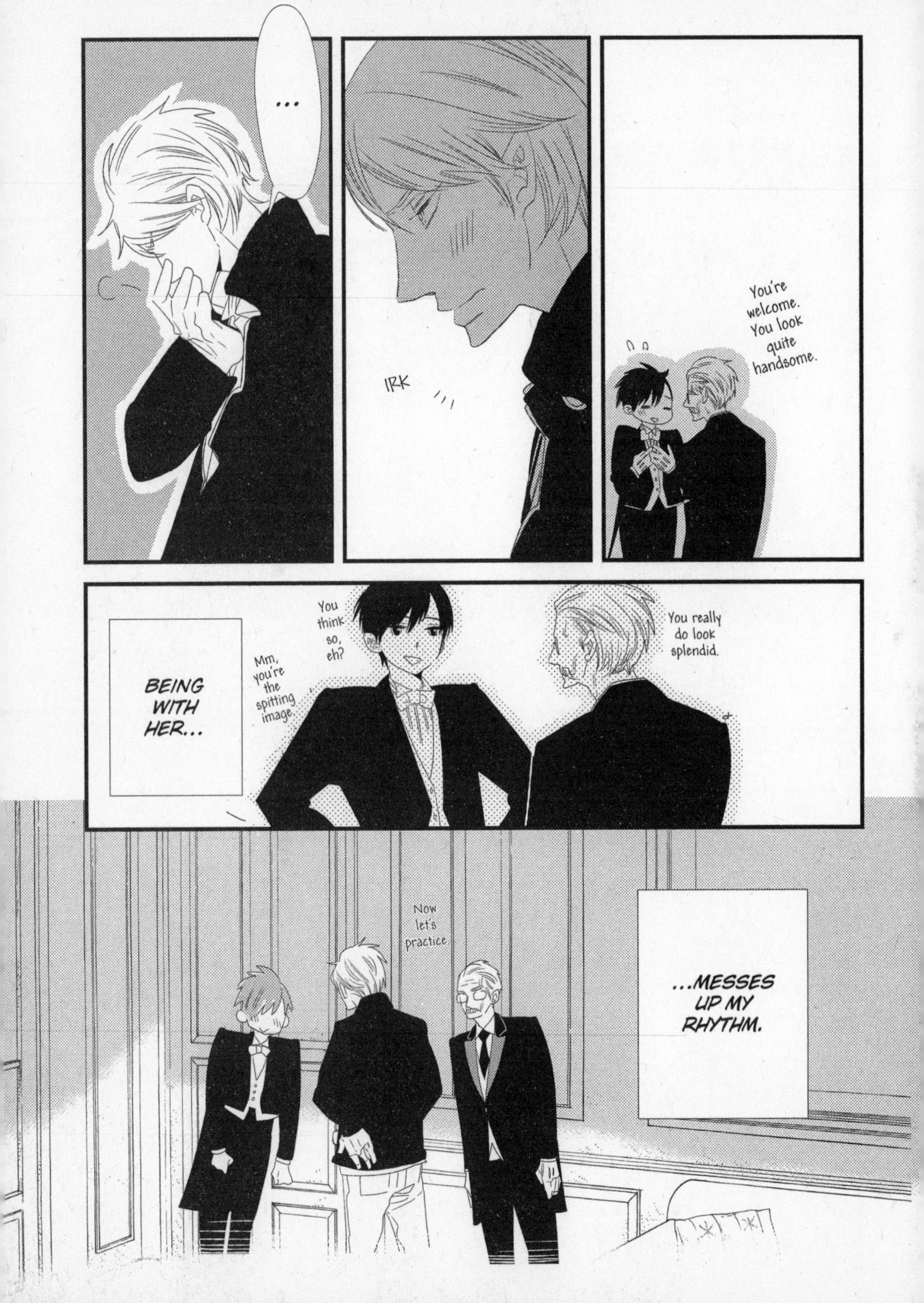
You're welcome. You look quite handsome.
IRK
...
You really do look splendid.
You think so, eh?
Mm, you're the spitting image.
BEING WITH HER...
...MESSES UP MY RHYTHM.
Now let's practice.

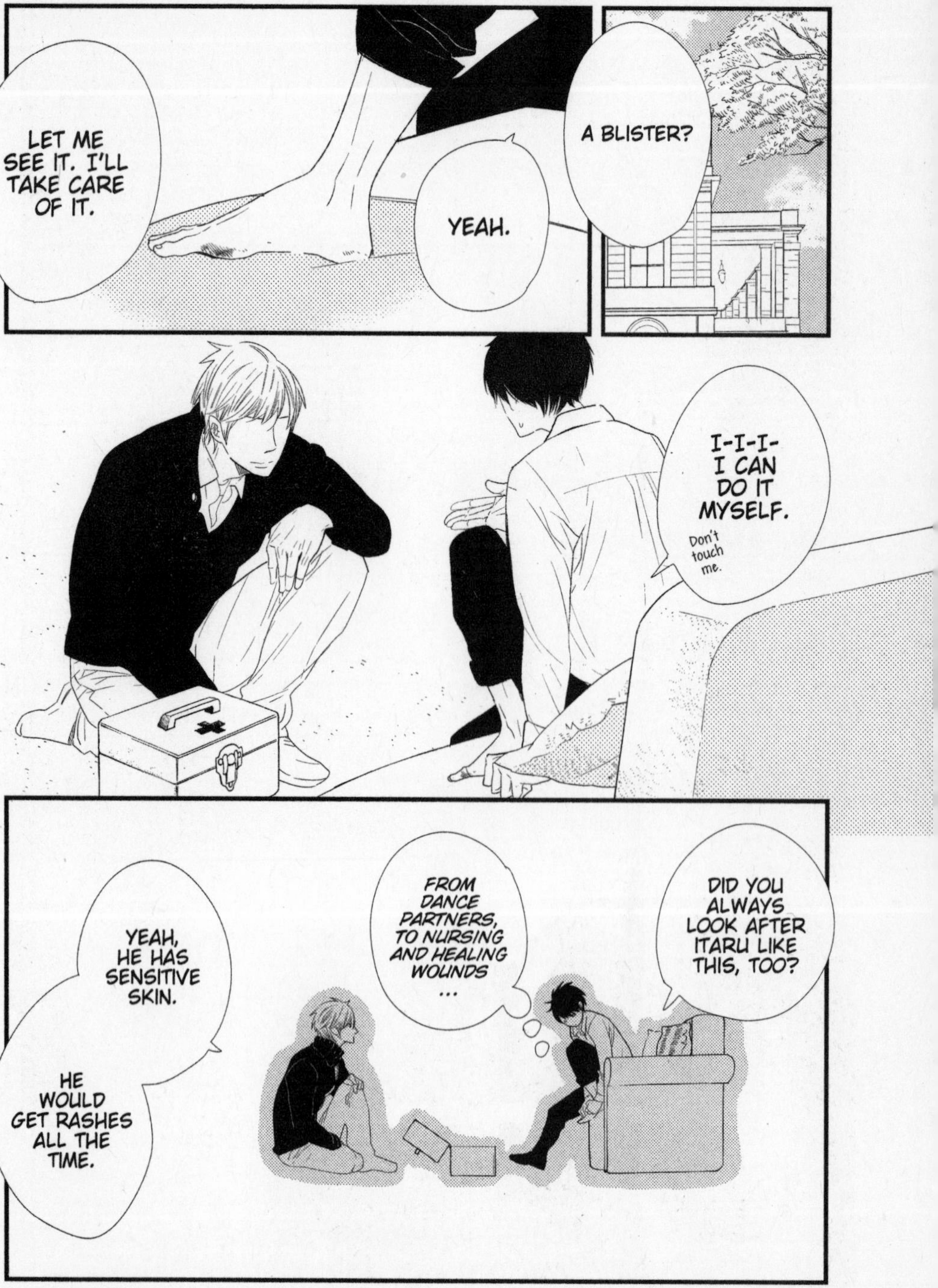
A BLISTER?
YEAH.
LET ME SEE IT. I'LL TAKE CARE OF IT.
I-I-I- I CAN DO IT MYSELF.
Don't touch me.
DID YOU ALWAYS LOOK AFTER ITARU LIKE THIS, TOO?
FROM DANCE PARTNERS, TO NURSING AND HEALING WOUNDS ...
YEAH, HE HAS SENSITIVE SKIN.
HE WOULD GET RASHES ALL THE TIME.

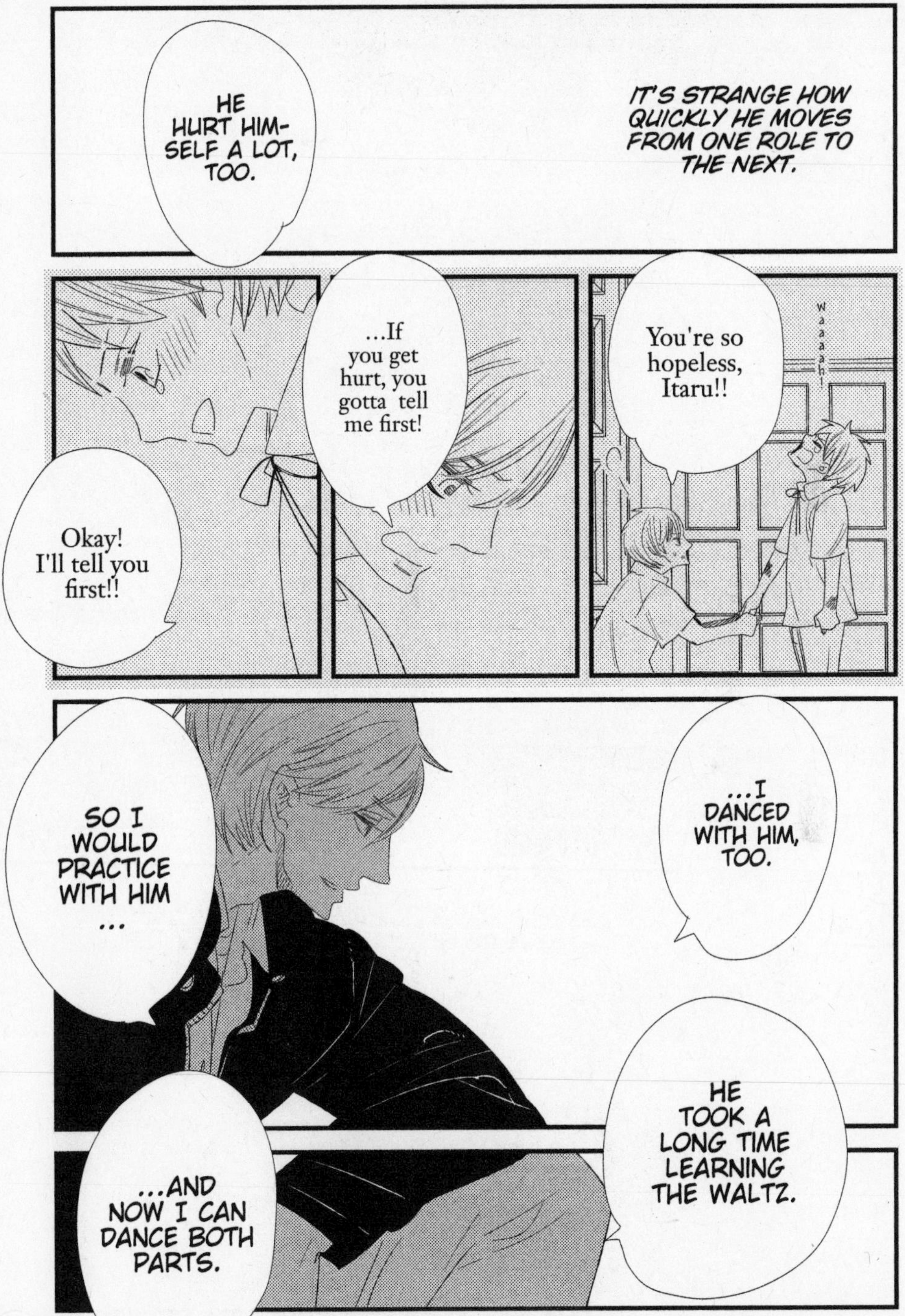
IT'S STRANGE HOW QUICKLY HE MOVES FROM ONE ROLE TO THE NEXT.
HE HURT HIM-SELF A LOT, TOO.
Waaaah!
You're so hopeless, Itaru!!
...If you get hurt, you gotta tell me first!
Okay! I'll tell you first!!
...I DANCED WITH HIM, TOO.
SO I WOULD PRACTICE WITH HIM ...
HE TOOK A LONG TIME LEARNING THE WALTZ.
...AND NOW I CAN DANCE BOTH PARTS.

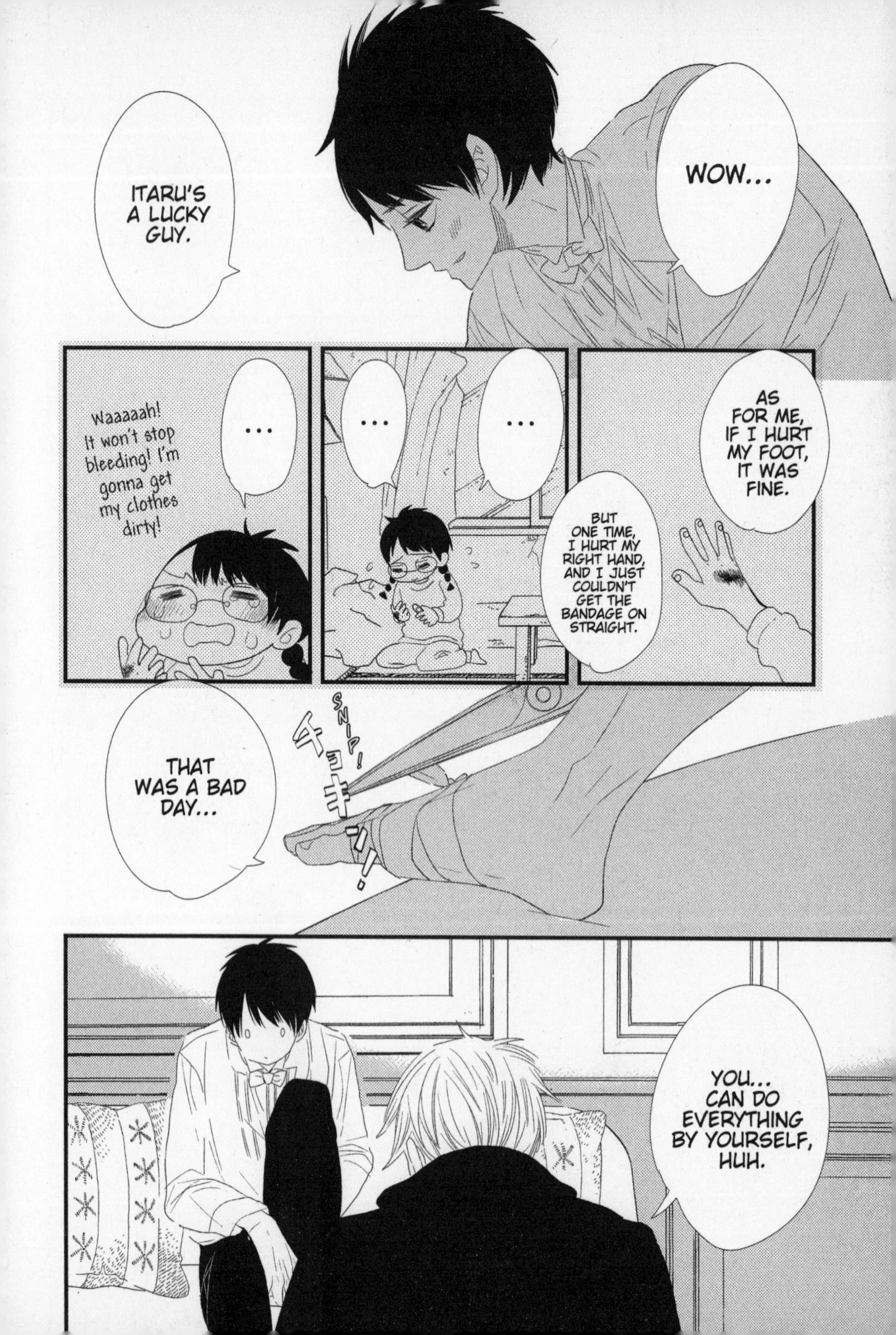
WOW...
ITARU'S A LUCKY GUY.
AS FOR ME, IF I HURT MY FOOT, IT WAS FINE.
BUT ONE TIME, I HURT MY RIGHT HAND, AND I JUST COULDN'T GET THE BANDAGE ON STRAIGHT.
...
...
...
Waaaaah! It won't stop bleeding! I'm gonna get my clothes dirty!
チョキン!
SNIP!
THAT WAS A BAD DAY...
YOU... CAN DO EVERYTHING BY YOURSELF, HUH.

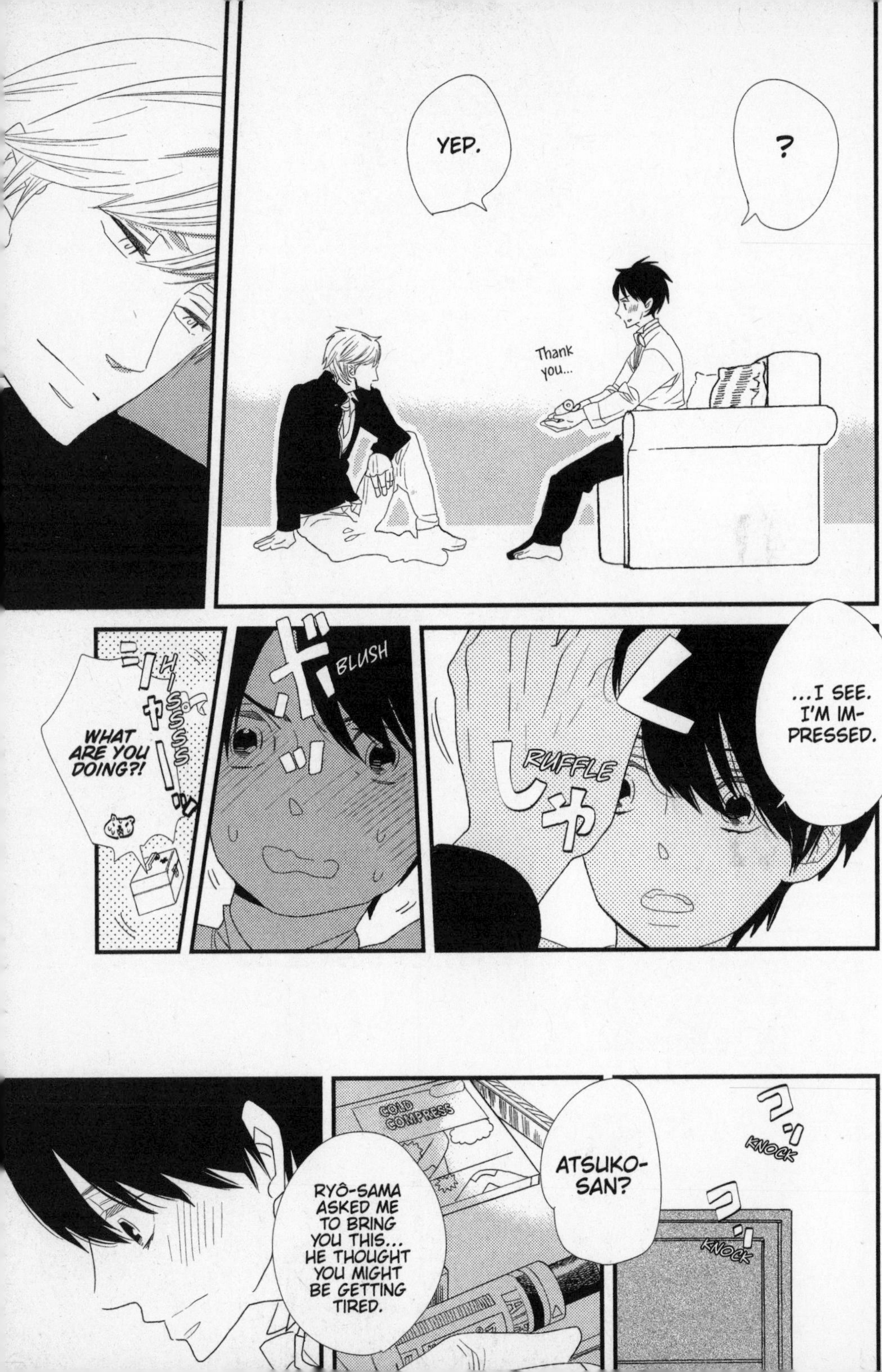
?
YEP.
Thank you...
...I SEE. I'M IM-PRESSED.
RUFFLE
BLUSH
HISSSS
WHAT ARE YOU DOING?!
KNOCK
KNOCK
ATSUKO-SAN?
COLD COMPRESS
RYÔ-SAMA ASKED ME TO BRING YOU THIS... HE THOUGHT YOU MIGHT BE GETTING TIRED.

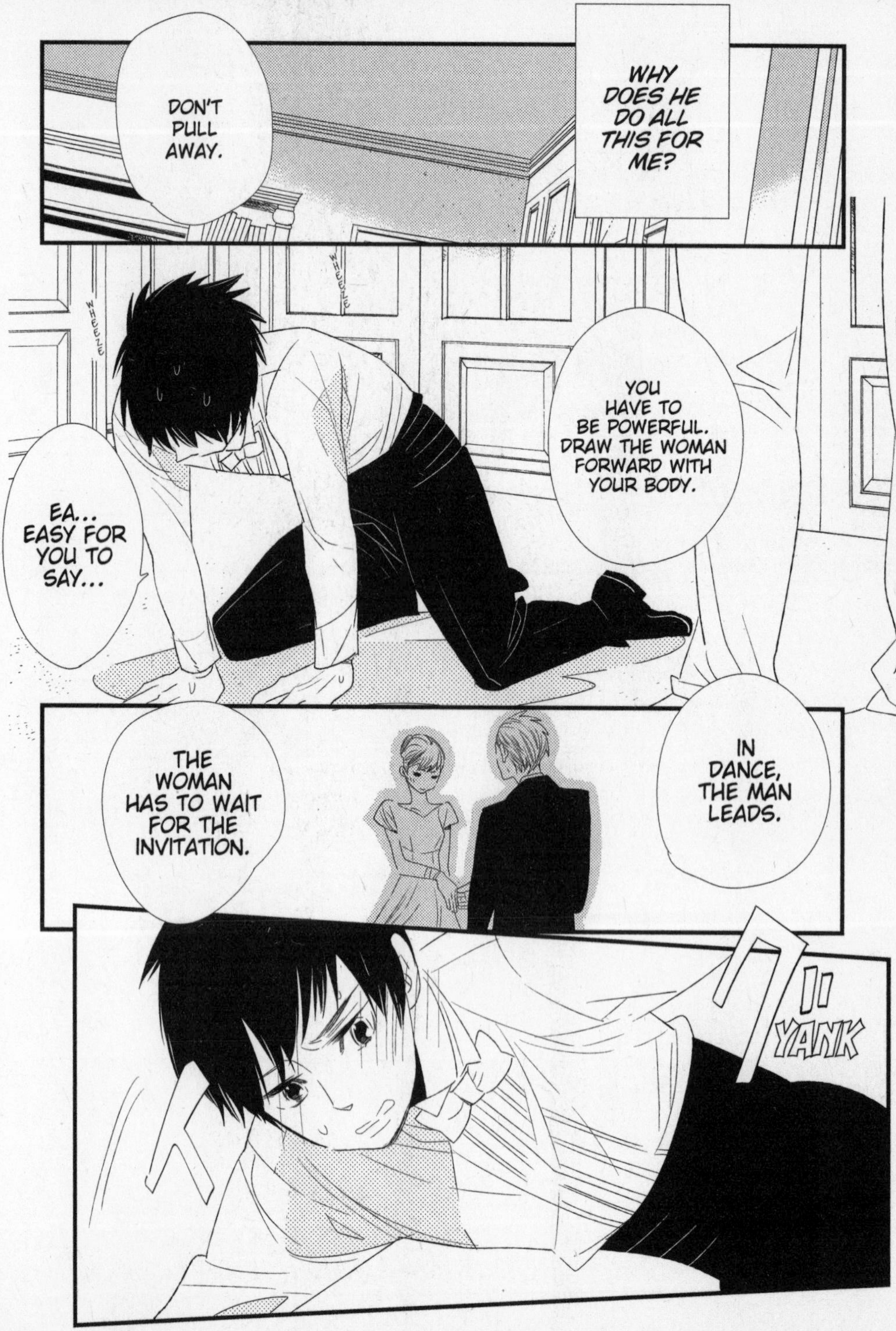
WHY DOES HE DO ALL THIS FOR ME?
DON'T PULL AWAY.
WHEEZE
YOU HAVE TO BE POWERFUL. DRAW THE WOMAN FORWARD WITH YOUR BODY.
WHEEZE
EA... EASY FOR YOU TO SAY...
IN DANCE, THE MAN LEADS.
THE WOMAN HAS TO WAIT FOR THE INVITATION.
YANK

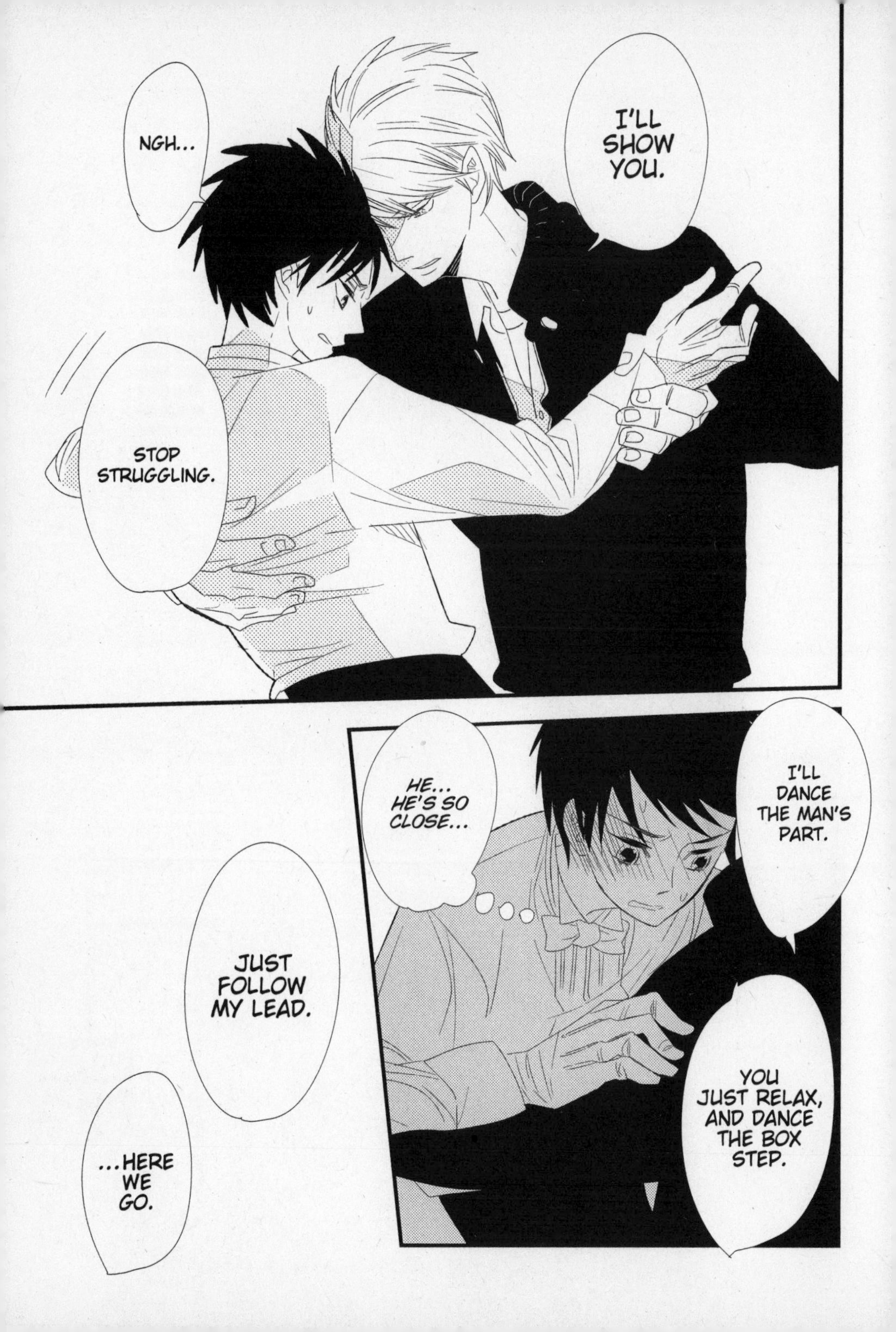

I'LL SHOW YOU.
NGH...
STOP STRUGGLING.
I'LL DANCE THE MAN'S PART.
HE... HE'S SO CLOSE...
YOU JUST RELAX, AND DANCE THE BOX STEP.
JUST FOLLOW MY LEAD.
...HERE WE GO.

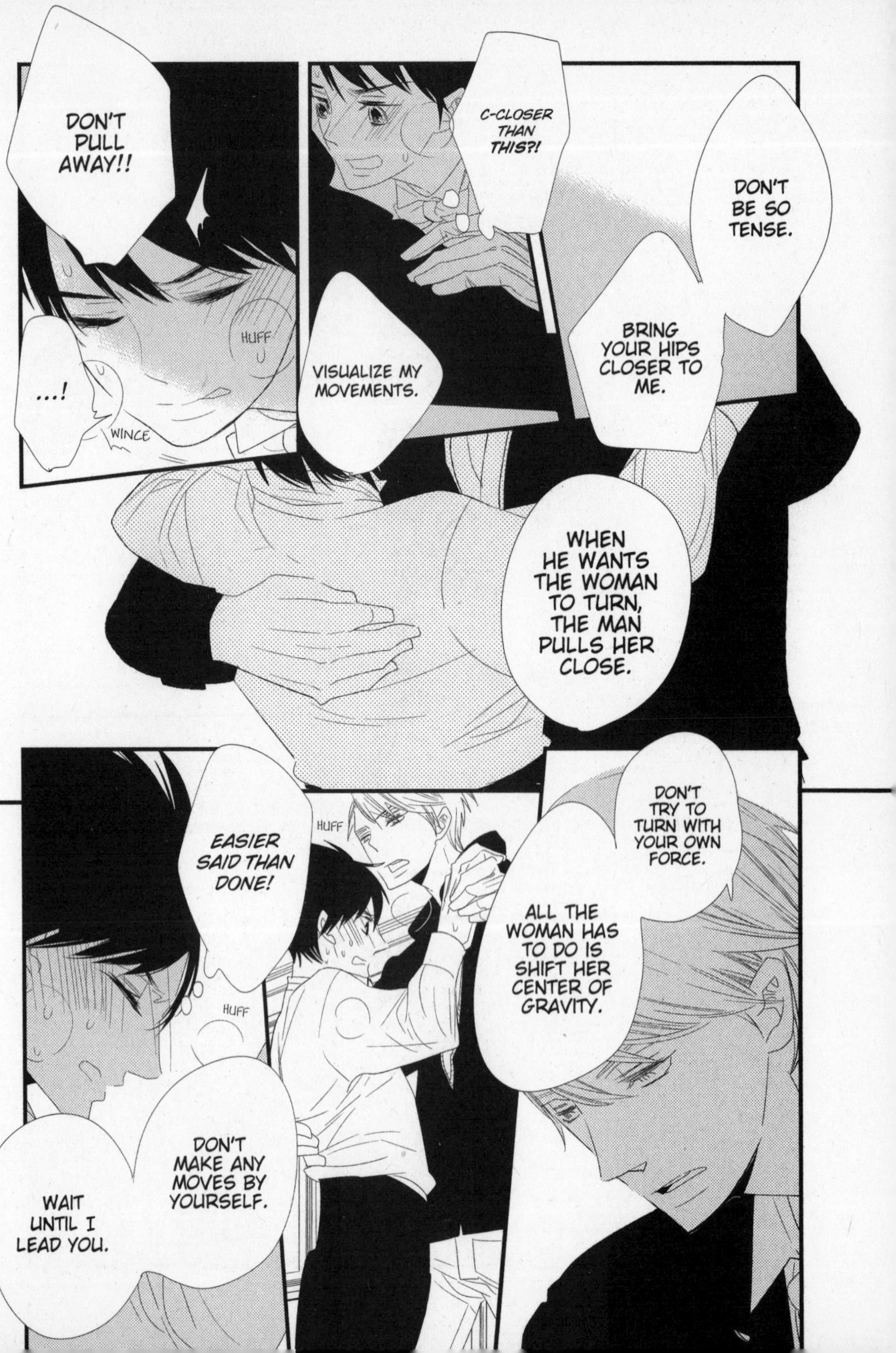
DON'T BE SO TENSE.
BRING YOUR HIPS CLOSER TO ME.
C-CLOSER THAN THIS?!
VISUALIZE MY MOVEMENTS.
DON'T PULL AWAY!!
HUFF
...!
WINCE
WHEN HE WANTS THE WOMAN TO TURN, THE MAN PULLS HER CLOSE.
DON'T TRY TO TURN WITH YOUR OWN FORCE.
ALL THE WOMAN HAS TO DO IS SHIFT HER CENTER OF GRAVITY.
HUFF
EASIER SAID THAN DONE!
HUFF
DON'T MAKE ANY MOVES BY YOURSELF.
WAIT UNTIL I LEAD YOU.

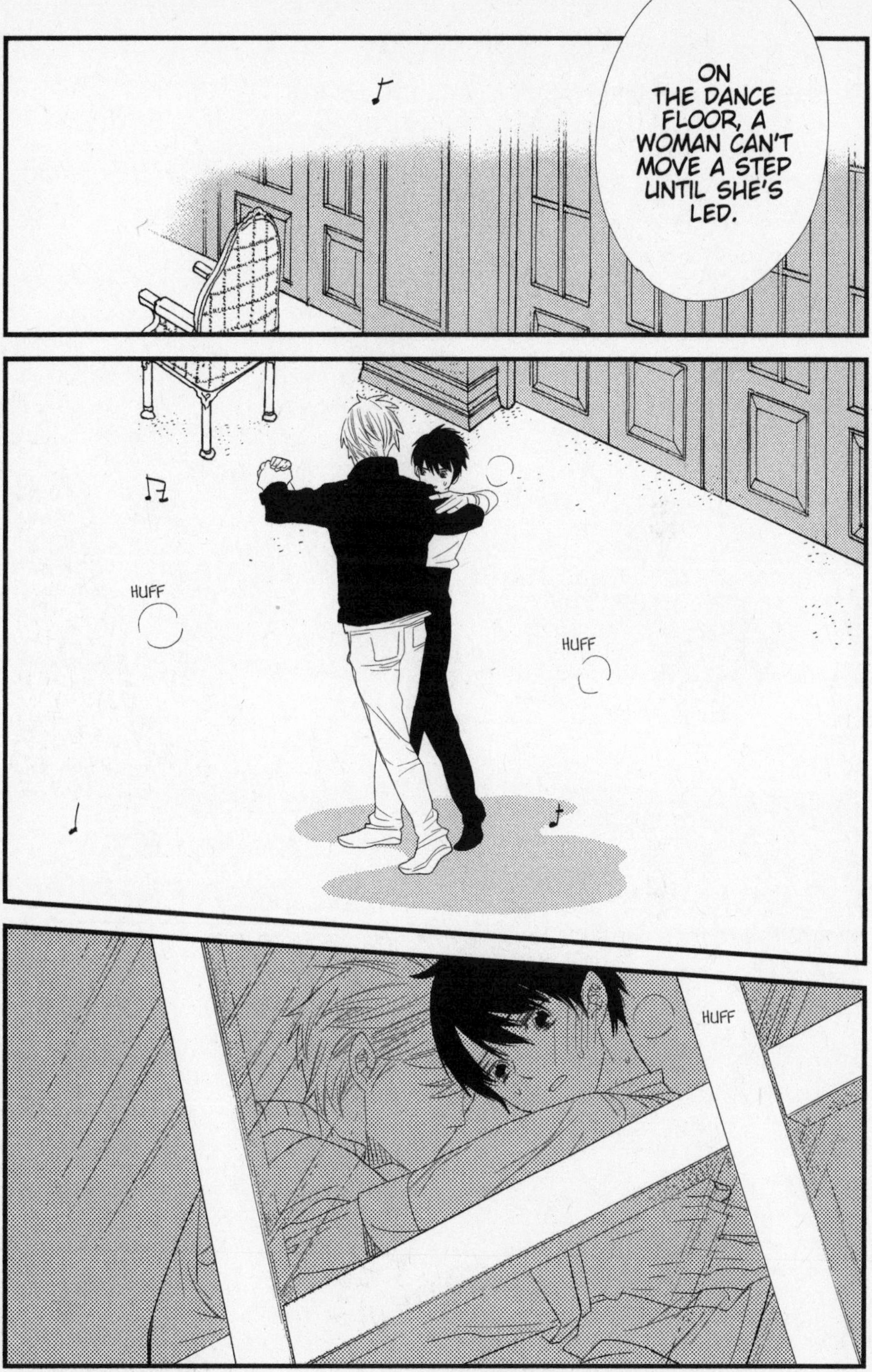
ON THE DANCE FLOOR, A WOMAN CAN'T MOVE A STEP UNTIL SHE'S LED.
HUFF
HUFF
HUFF

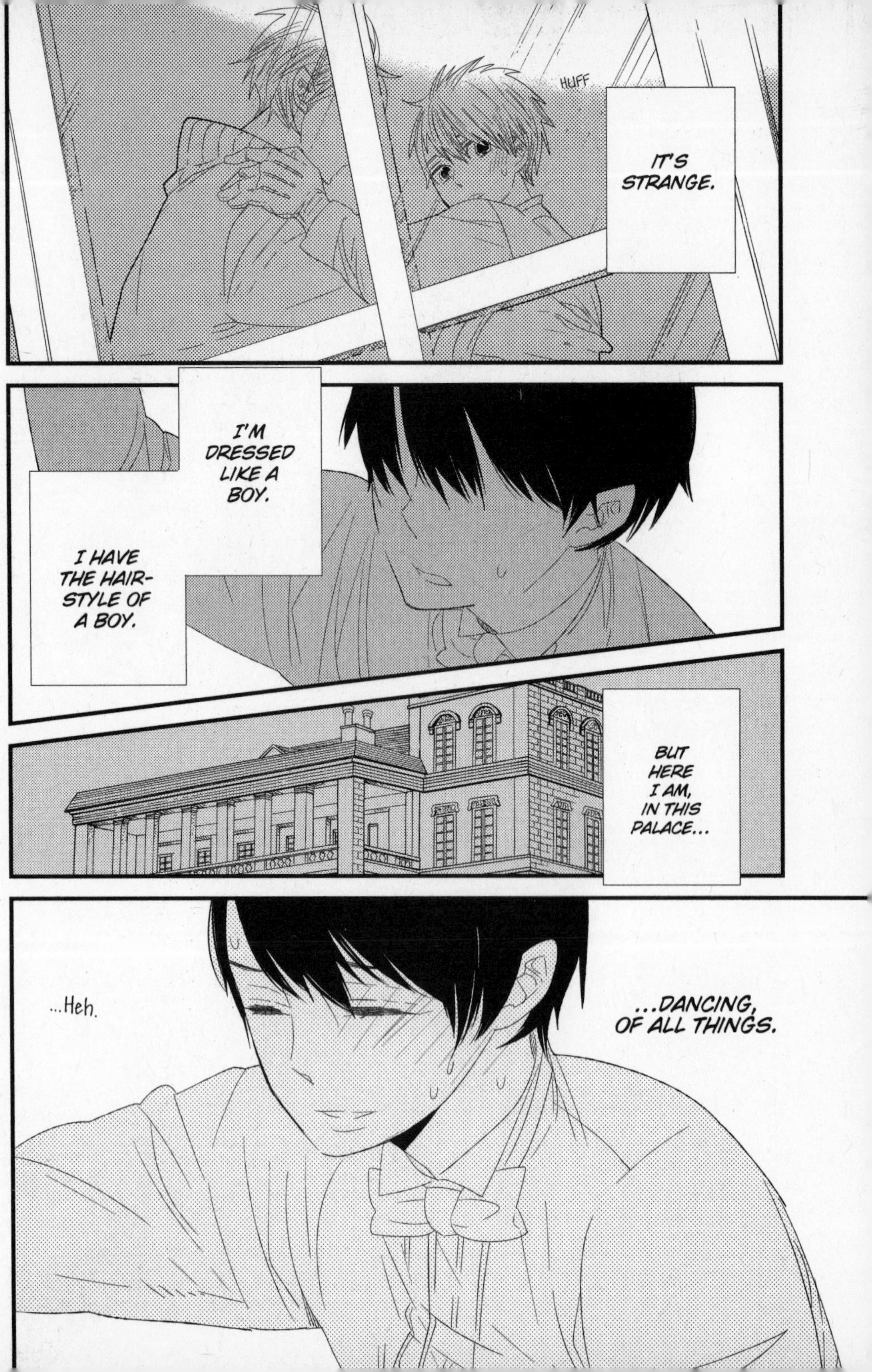
HUFF
IT'S STRANGE.
I'M DRESSED LIKE A BOY.
I HAVE THE HAIR-STYLE OF A BOY.
BUT HERE I AM, IN THIS PALACE...
...DANCING, OF ALL THINGS.
...Heh.

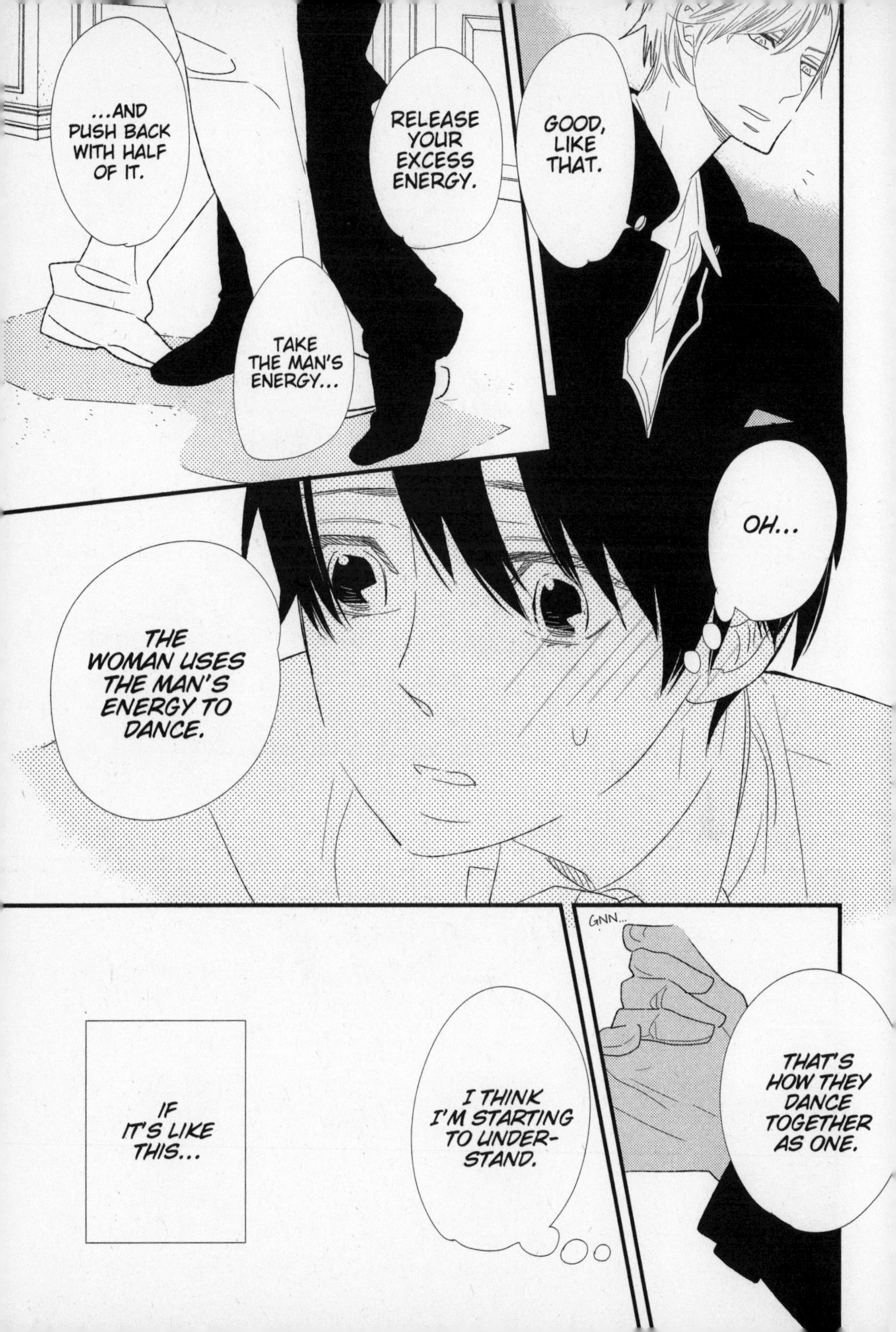
GOOD, LIKE THAT.
RELEASE YOUR EXCESS ENERGY.
TAKE THE MAN'S ENERGY...
...AND PUSH BACK WITH HALF OF IT.
OH...
THE WOMAN USES THE MAN'S ENERGY TO DANCE.
THAT'S HOW THEY DANCE TOGETHER AS ONE.
GNN...
I THINK I'M STARTING TO UNDER-STAND.
IF IT'S LIKE THIS...

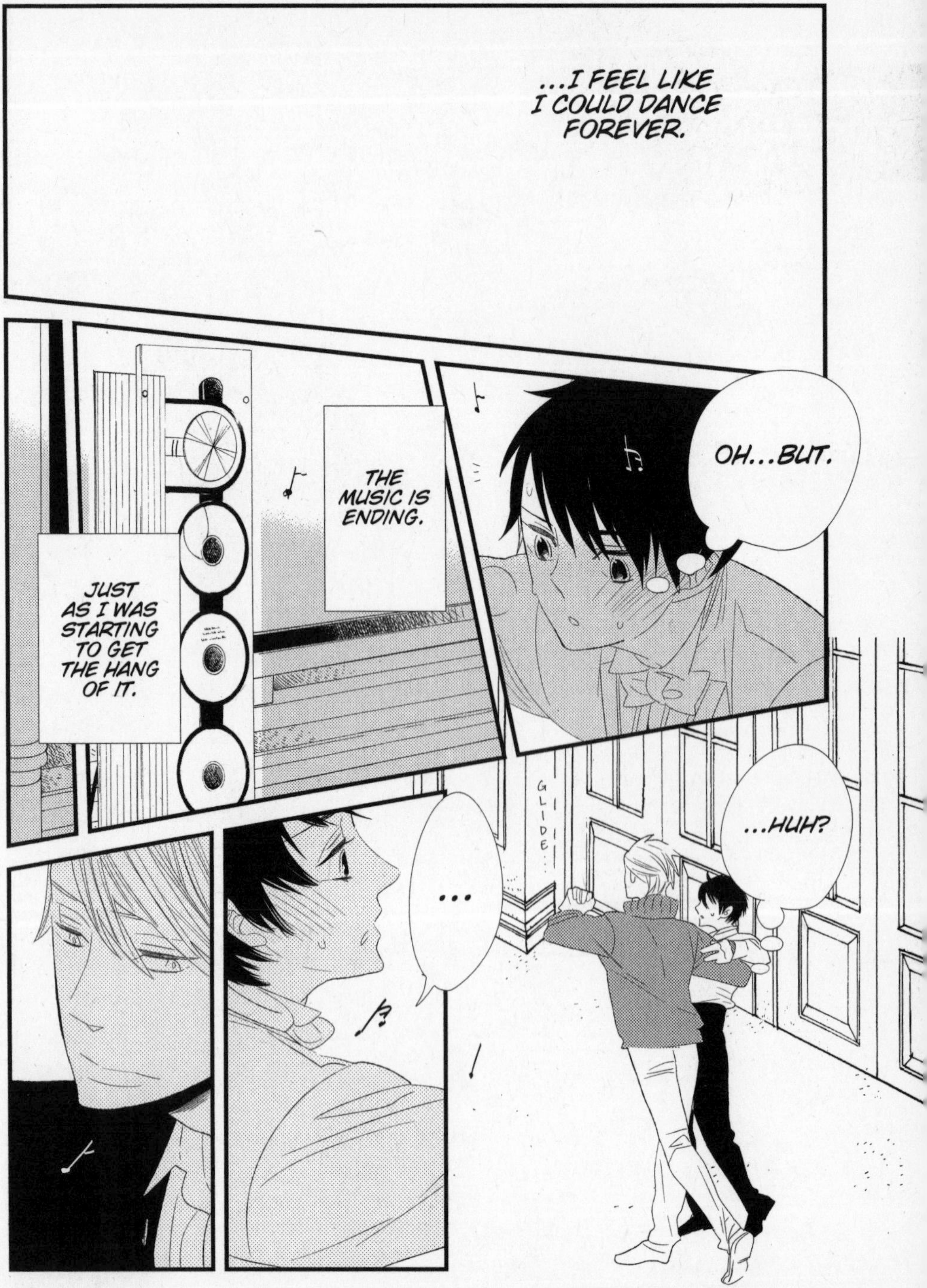
...I FEEL LIKE I COULD DANCE FOREVER.
OH...BUT.
THE MUSIC IS ENDING.
JUST AS I WAS STARTING TO GET THE HANG OF IT.
...HUH?
GLIDE...
...

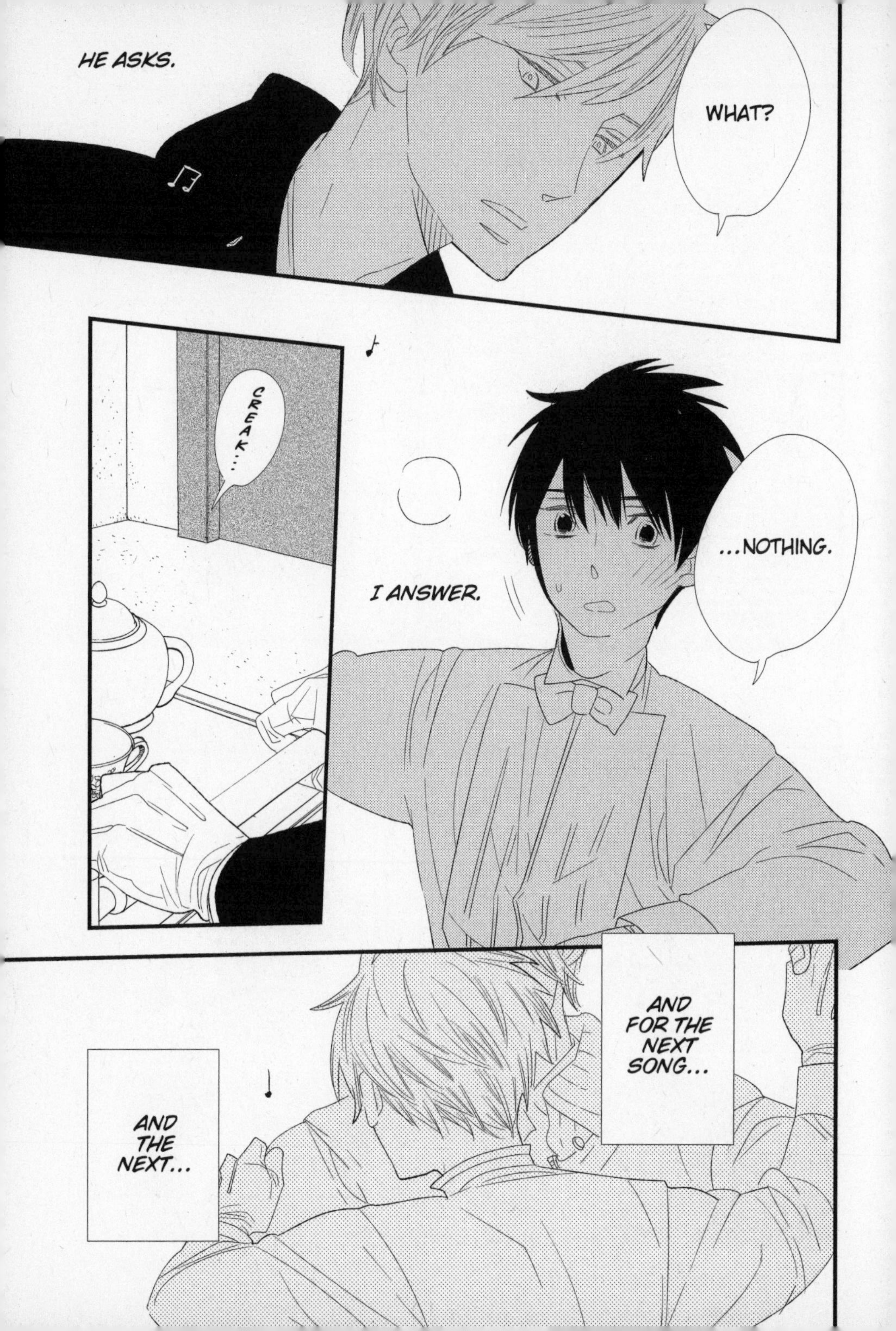
WHAT?
HE ASKS.
...NOTHING.
I ANSWER.
CREAK...
AND FOR THE NEXT SONG...
AND THE NEXT...

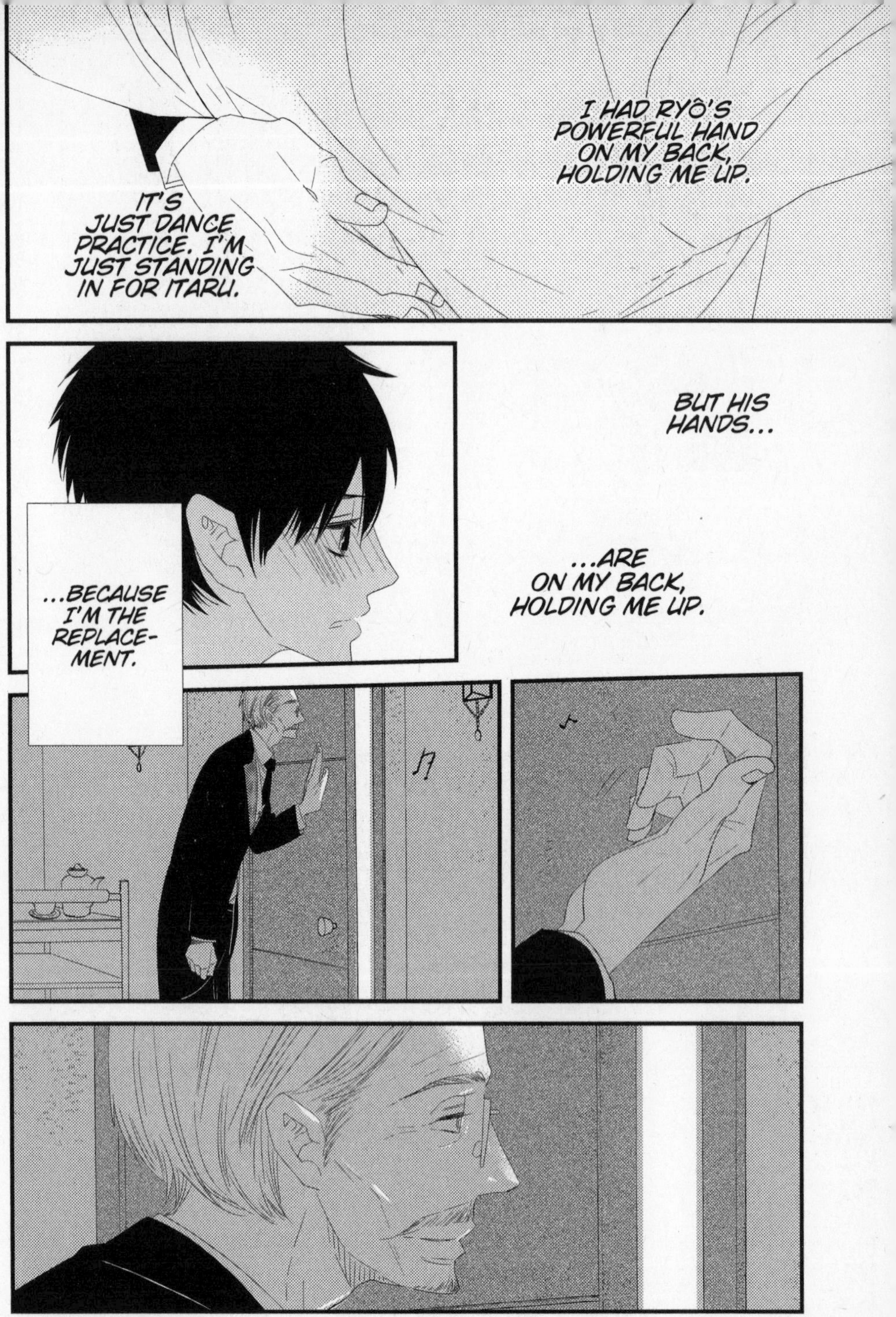
I HAD RYÔ'S POWERFUL HAND ON MY BACK, HOLDING ME UP.
IT'S JUST DANCE PRACTICE. I'M JUST STANDING IN FOR ITARU.
BUT HIS HANDS...
...ARE ON MY BACK, HOLDING ME UP.
...BECAUSE I'M THE REPLACE-MENT.

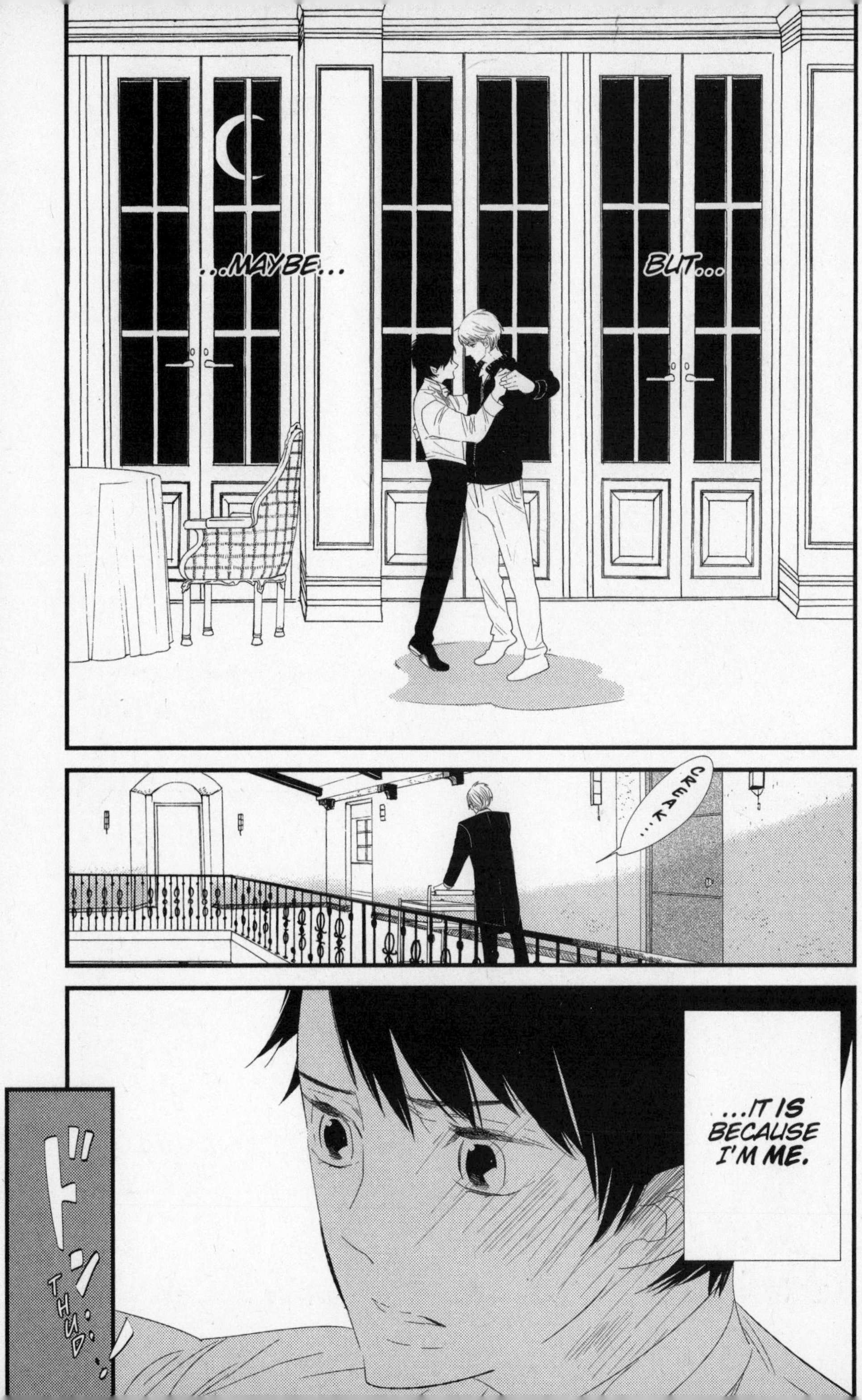
BUT...
...MAYBE...
CREAK...
...IT IS BECAUSE I'M ME.
ドン
THUD

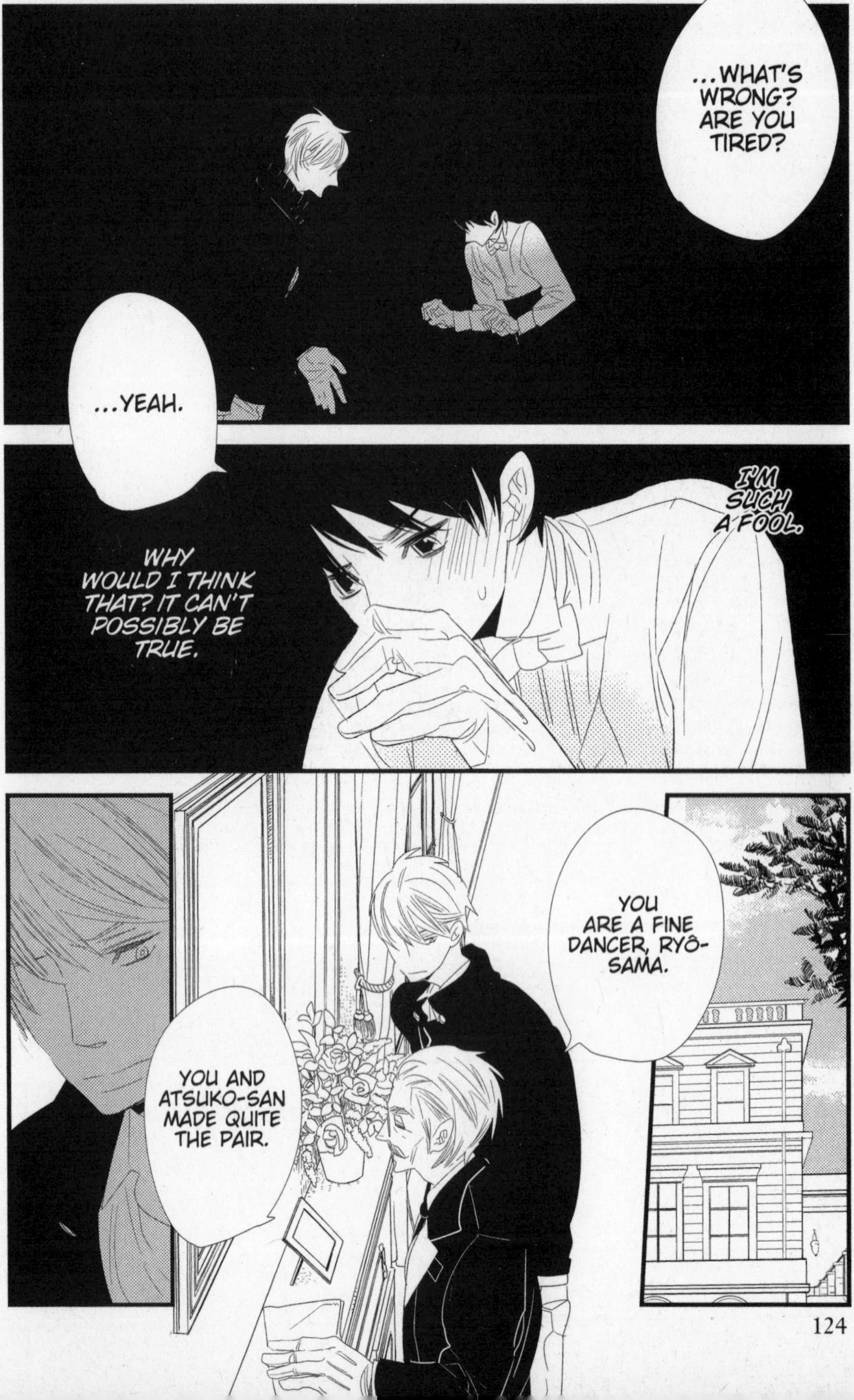
...WHAT'S WRONG? ARE YOU TIRED?
...YEAH.
I'M SUCH A FOOL.
WHY WOULD I THINK THAT? IT CAN'T POSSIBLY BE TRUE.
YOU ARE A FINE DANCER, RYÔ-SAMA.
YOU AND ATSUKO-SAN MADE QUITE THE PAIR.

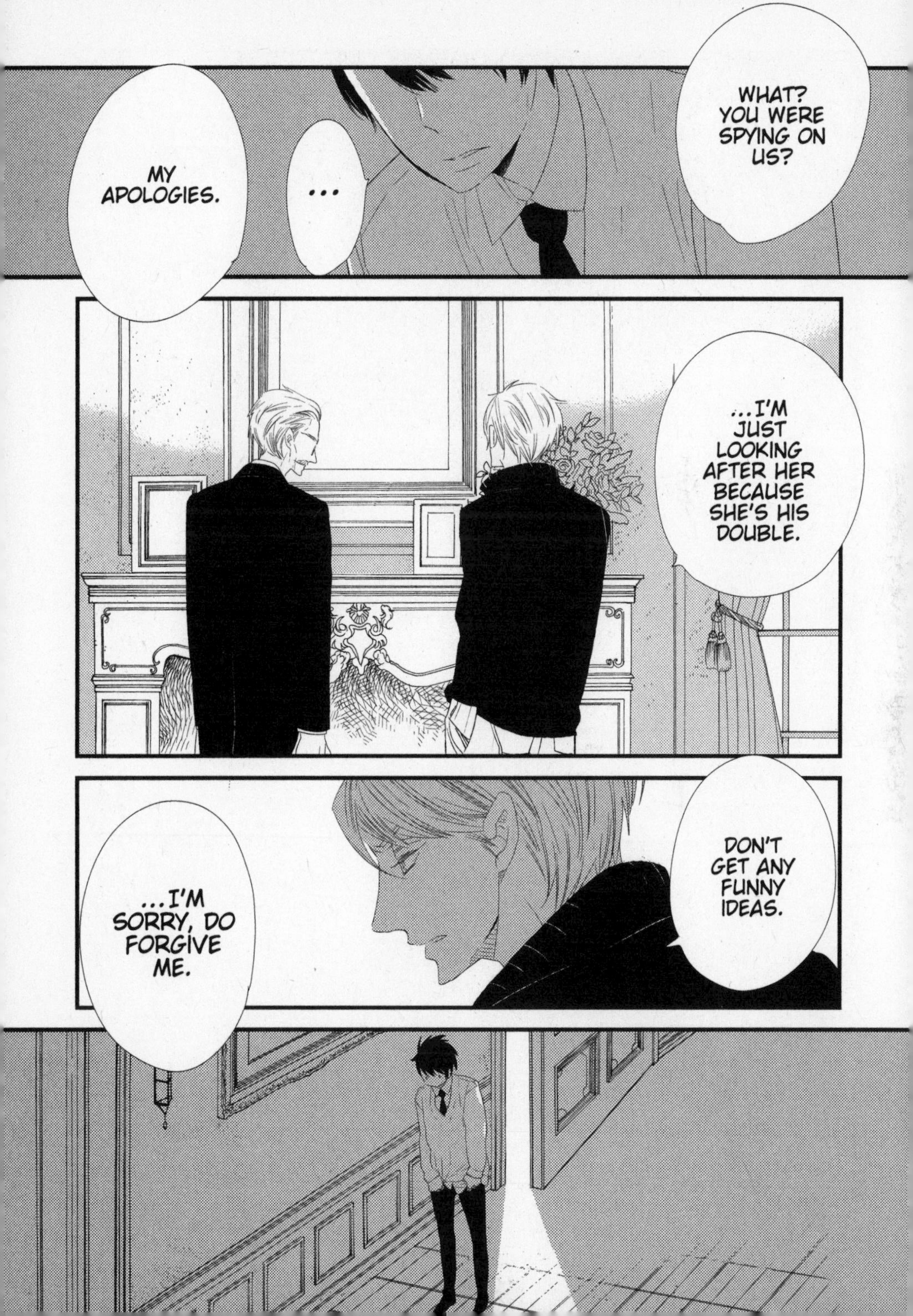
WHAT? YOU WERE SPYING ON US?
...
MY APOLOGIES.
...I'M JUST LOOKING AFTER HER BECAUSE SHE'S HIS DOUBLE.
DON'T GET ANY FUNNY IDEAS.
...I'M SORRY, DO FORGIVE ME.

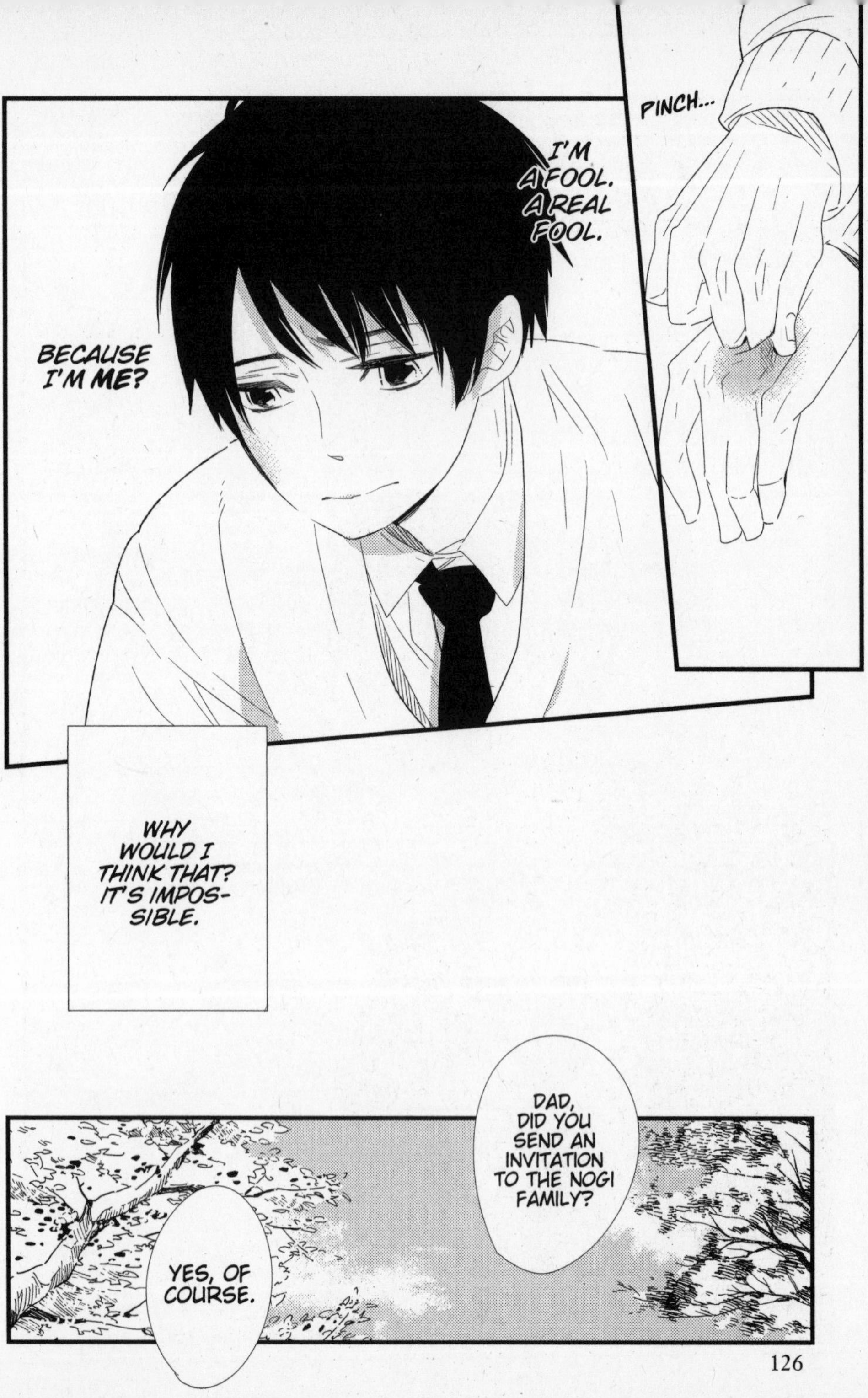
PINCH...
I'M A FOOL. A REAL FOOL.
BECAUSE I'M ME?
WHY WOULD I THINK THAT? IT'S IMPOS-SIBLE.
DAD, DID YOU SEND AN INVITATION TO THE NOGI FAMILY?
YES, OF COURSE.

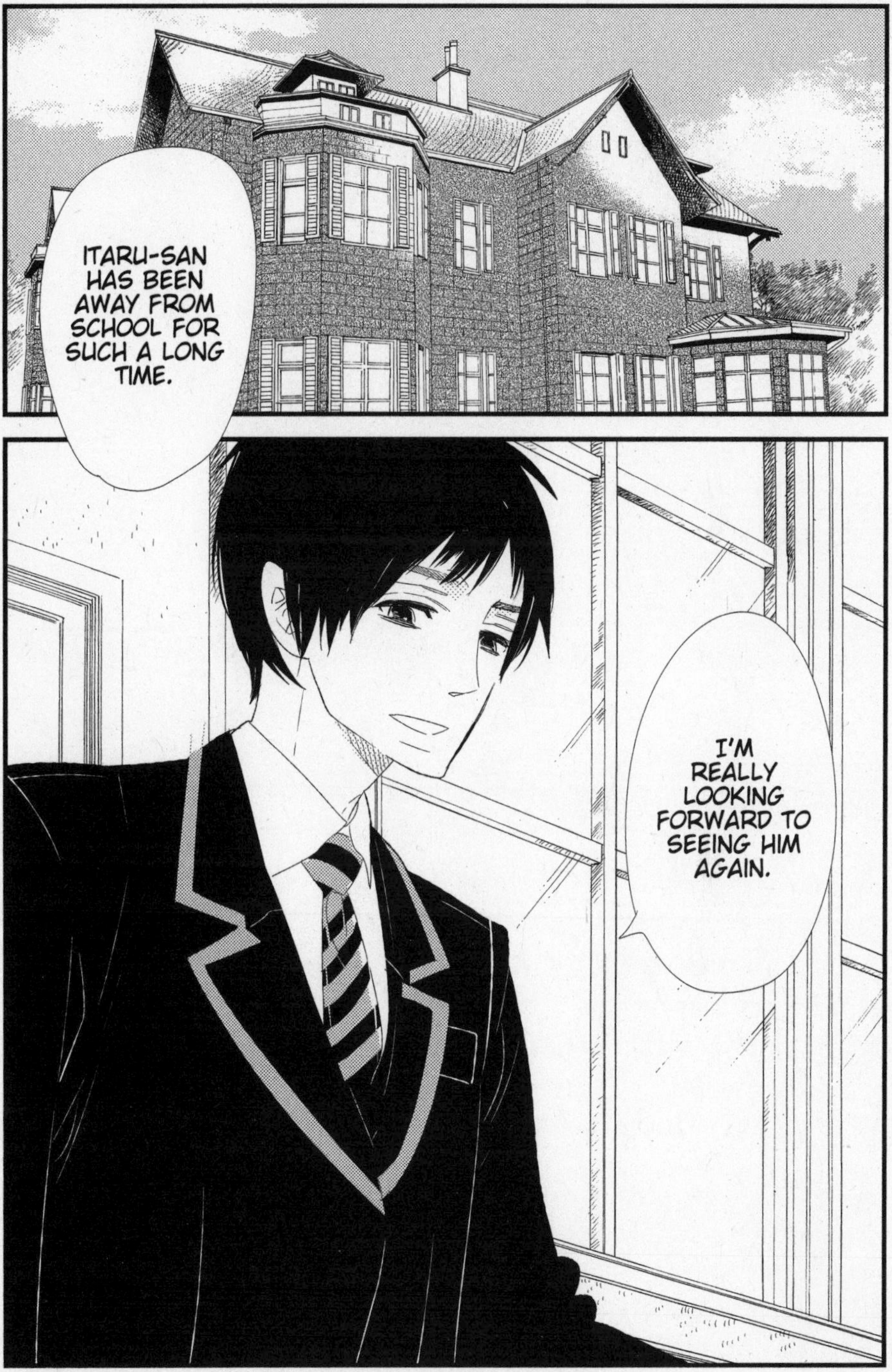
ITARU-SAN HAS BEEN AWAY FROM SCHOOL FOR SUCH A LONG TIME.
I'M REALLY LOOKING FORWARD TO SEEING HIM AGAIN.

the prince in his dark days
hico yamanaka

chapter 9

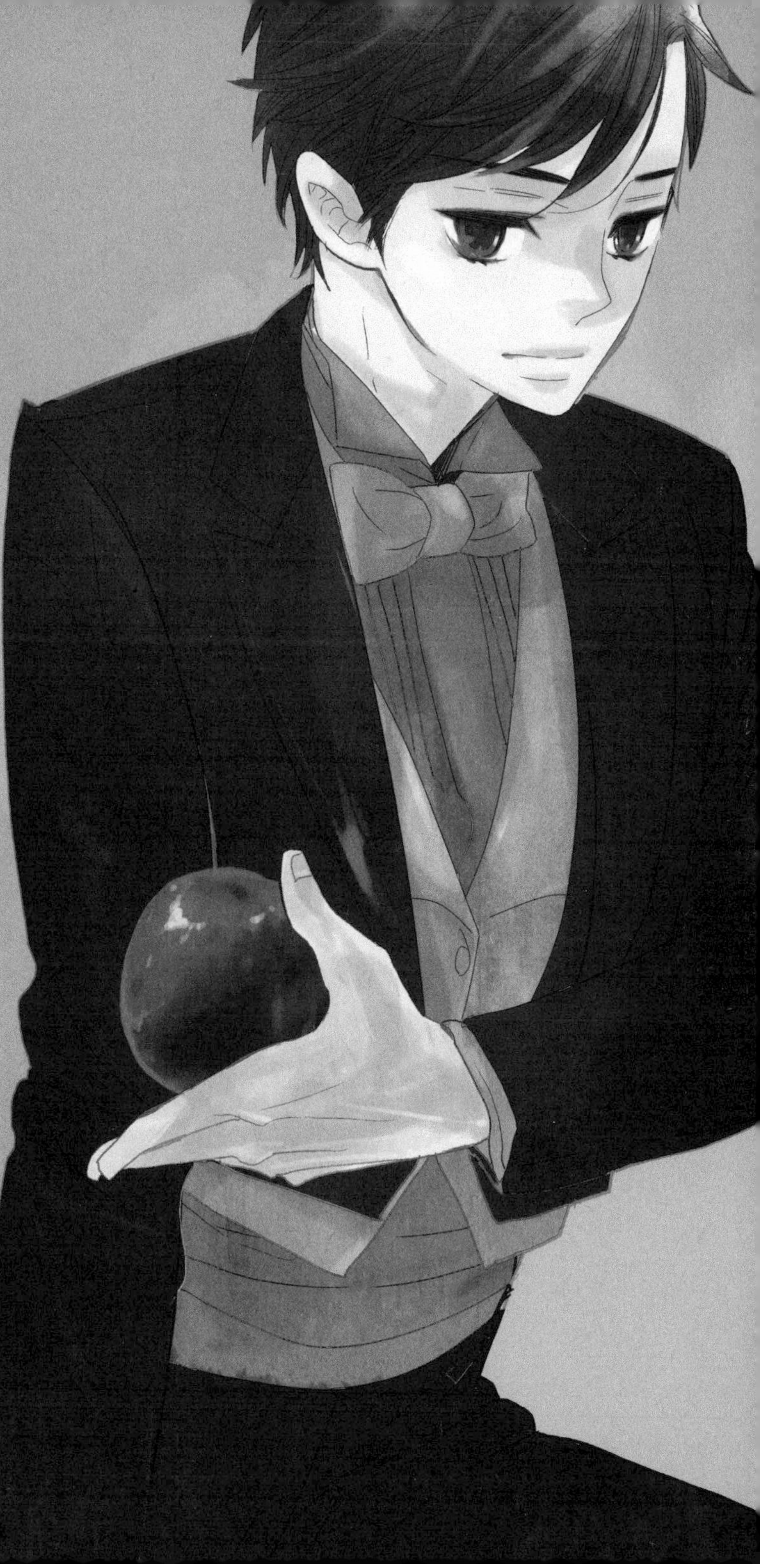

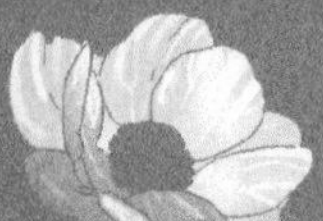

The prince in his dark days
Hico Yamanaka

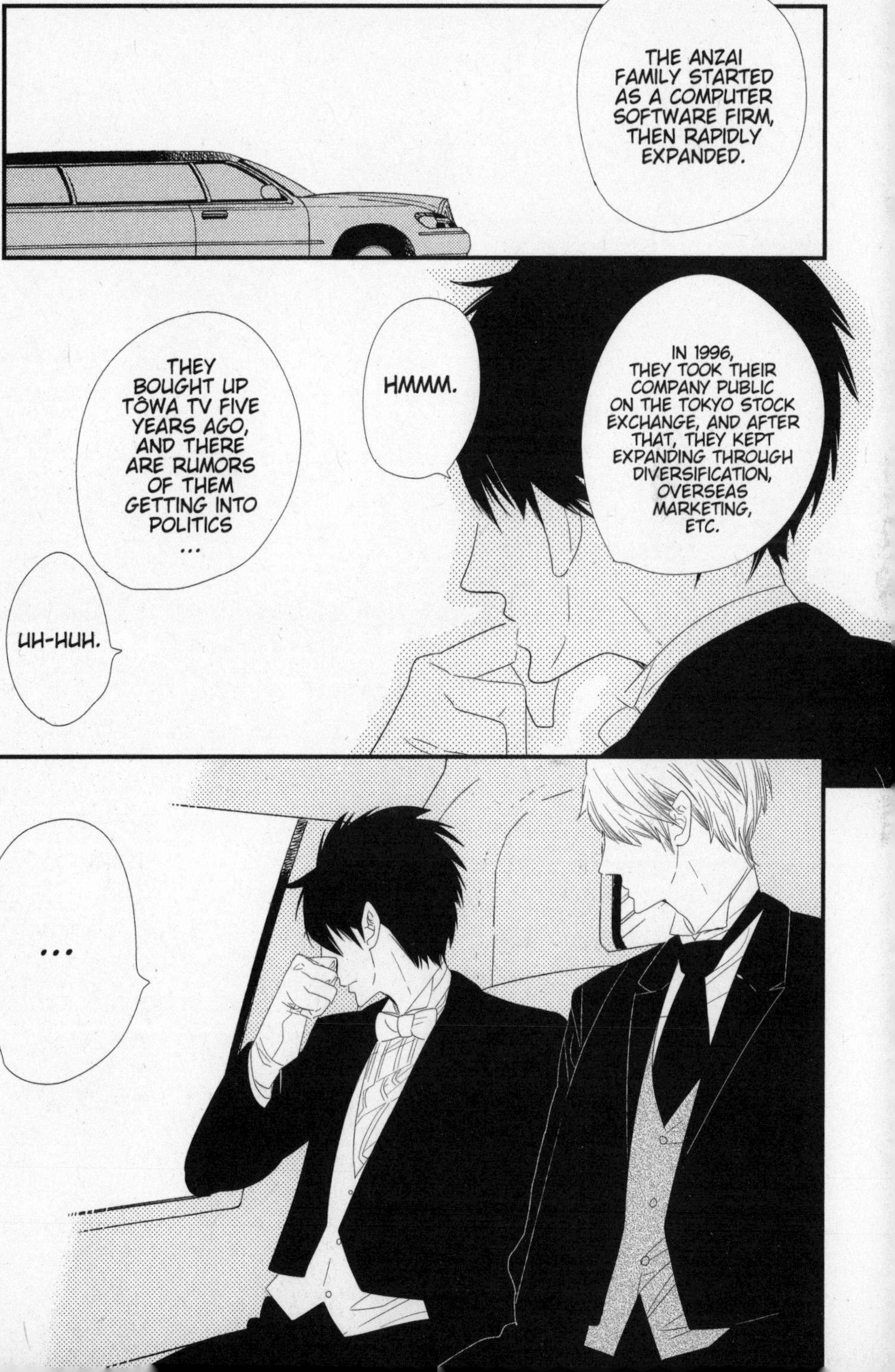
THE ANZAI FAMILY STARTED AS A COMPUTER SOFTWARE FIRM, THEN RAPIDLY EXPANDED.
IN 1996, THEY TOOK THEIR COMPANY PUBLIC ON THE TOKYO STOCK EXCHANGE, AND AFTER THAT, THEY KEPT EXPANDING THROUGH DIVERSIFICATION, OVERSEAS MARKETING, ETC.
HMMM.
THEY BOUGHT UP TÔWA TV FIVE YEARS AGO, AND THERE ARE RUMORS OF THEM GETTING INTO POLITICS ...
UH-HUH.
...

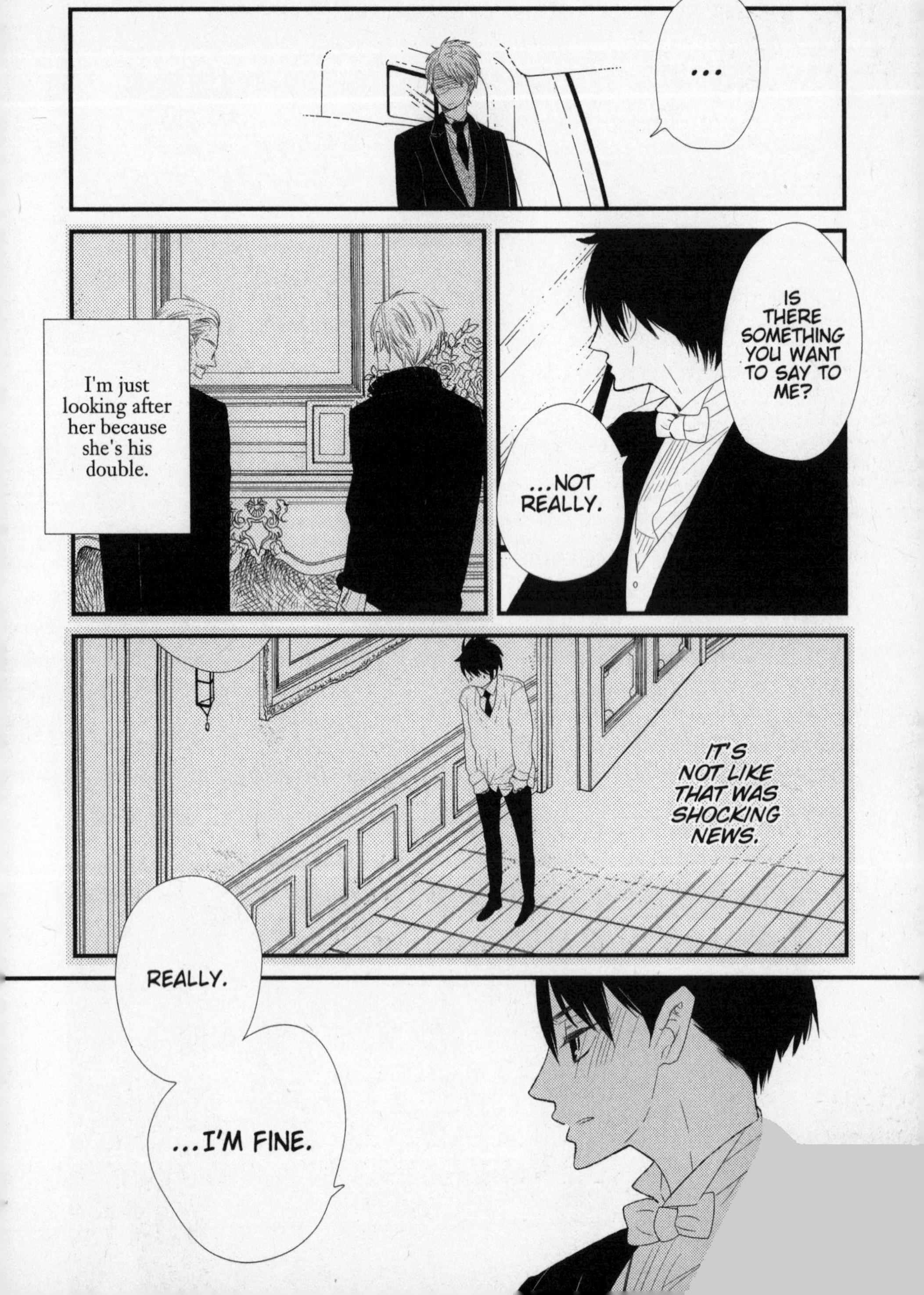
...
IS THERE SOMETHING YOU WANT TO SAY TO ME?
...NOT REALLY.
I'm just looking after her because she's his double.
IT'S NOT LIKE THAT WAS SHOCKING NEWS.
REALLY.
...I'M FINE.

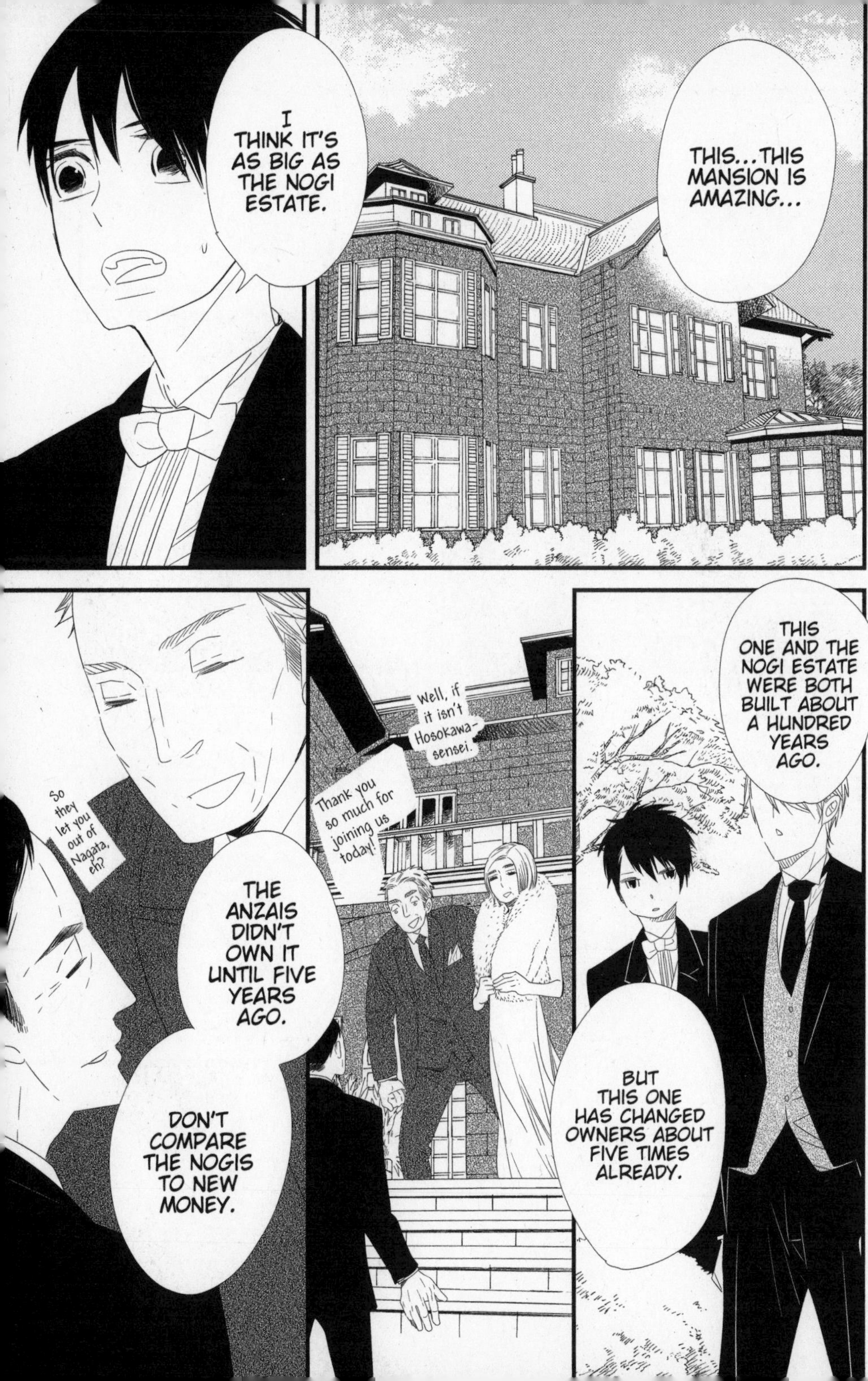
THIS...THIS MANSION IS AMAZING...
I THINK IT'S AS BIG AS THE NOGI ESTATE.
THIS ONE AND THE NOGI ESTATE WERE BOTH BUILT ABOUT A HUNDRED YEARS AGO.
BUT THIS ONE HAS CHANGED OWNERS ABOUT FIVE TIMES ALREADY.
Well, if it isn't Hosokawa-sensei.
Thank you so much for joining us today!
So they let you out of Nagata, eh?
THE ANZAIS DIDN'T OWN IT UNTIL FIVE YEARS AGO.
DON'T COMPARE THE NOGIS TO NEW MONEY.

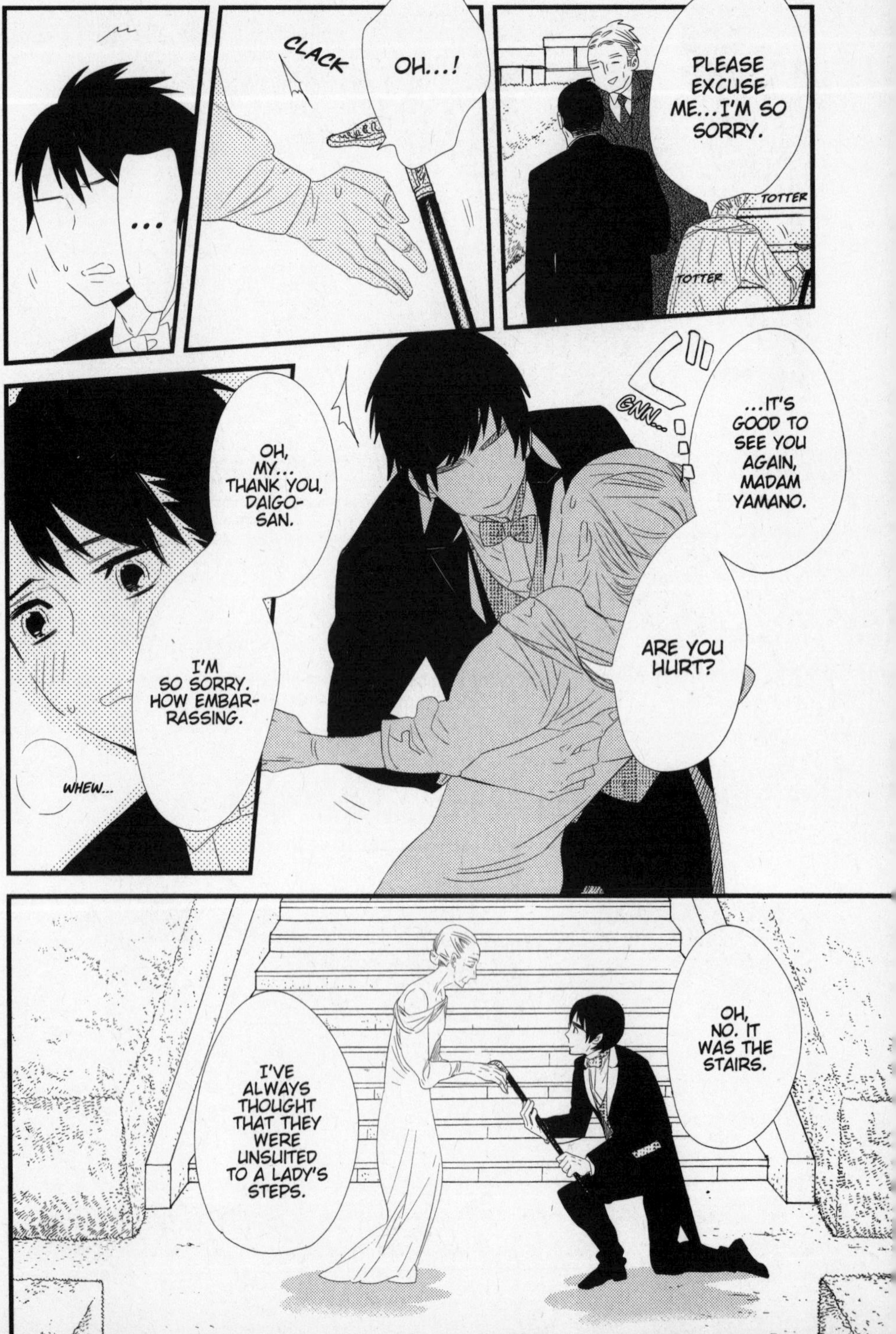
PLEASE EXCUSE ME...I'M SO SORRY.
TOTTER
TOTTER
CLACK
OH...!
...
GNN...
...IT'S GOOD TO SEE YOU AGAIN, MADAM YAMANO.
ARE YOU HURT?
OH, MY... THANK YOU, DAIGO-SAN.
I'M SO SORRY. HOW EMBARRASSING.
WHEW...
OH, NO. IT WAS THE STAIRS.
I'VE ALWAYS THOUGHT THAT THEY WERE UNSUITED TO A LADY'S STEPS.

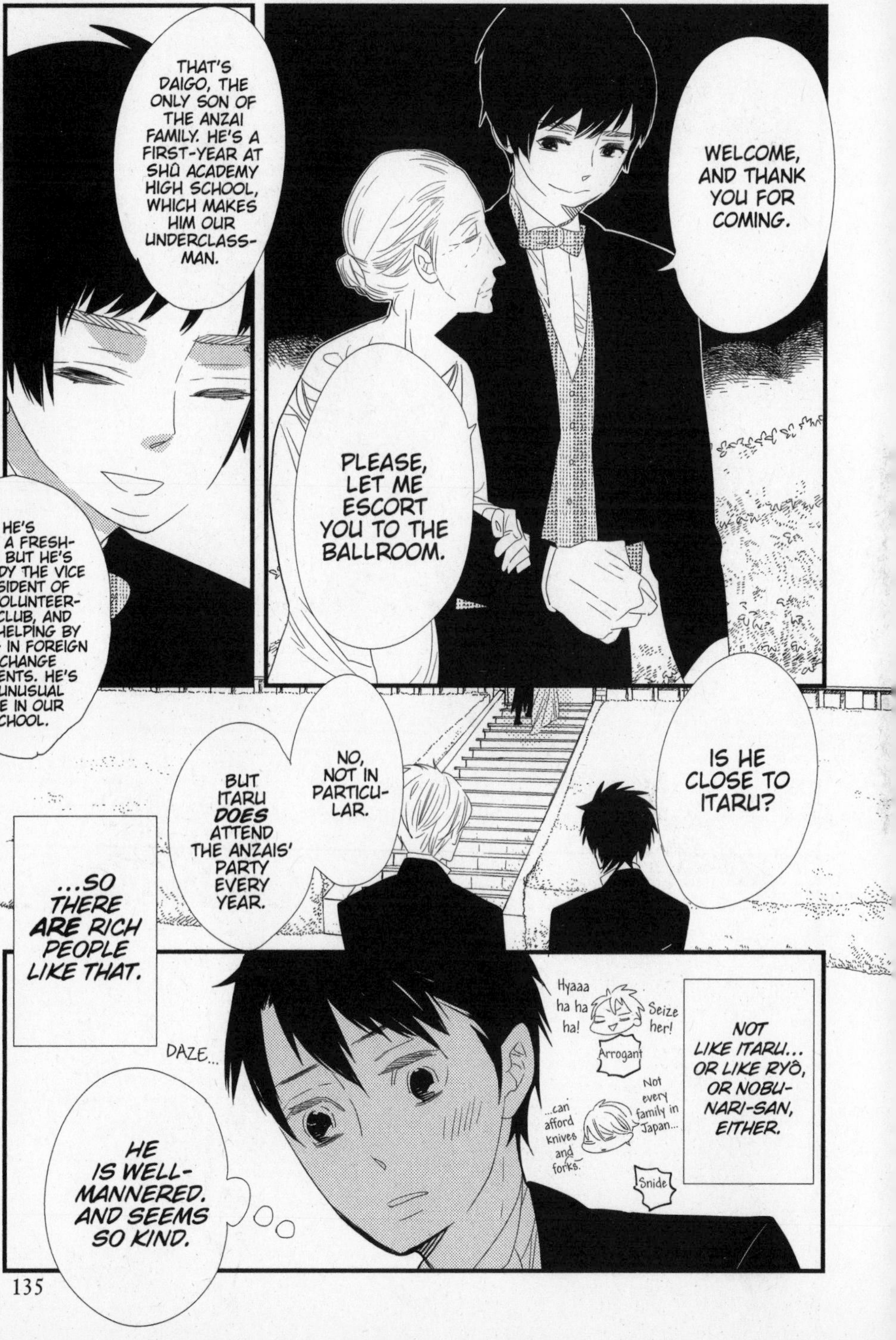
WELCOME, AND THANK YOU FOR COMING.
PLEASE, LET ME ESCORT YOU TO THE BALLROOM.
THAT'S DAIGO, THE ONLY SON OF THE ANZAI FAMILY. HE'S A FIRST-YEAR AT SHÛ ACADEMY HIGH SCHOOL, WHICH MAKES HIM OUR UNDERCLASSMAN.
HE'S ONLY A FRESHMAN, BUT HE'S ALREADY THE VICE PRESIDENT OF THE VOLUNTEERING CLUB, AND HE'S HELPING BY TAKING IN FOREIGN EXCHANGE STUDENTS. HE'S AN UNUSUAL TYPE IN OUR SCHOOL.
IS HE CLOSE TO ITARU?
NO, NOT IN PARTICULAR.
BUT ITARU DOES ATTEND THE ANZAIS' PARTY EVERY YEAR.
...SO THERE ARE RICH PEOPLE LIKE THAT.
NOT LIKE ITARU... OR LIKE RYÔ, OR NOBUNARI-SAN, EITHER.
Seize her!
Hyaaa ha ha ha!
Arrogant
Not every family in Japan...
...can afford knives and forks.
Snide
DAZE...
HE IS WELL-MANNERED. AND SEEMS SO KIND.

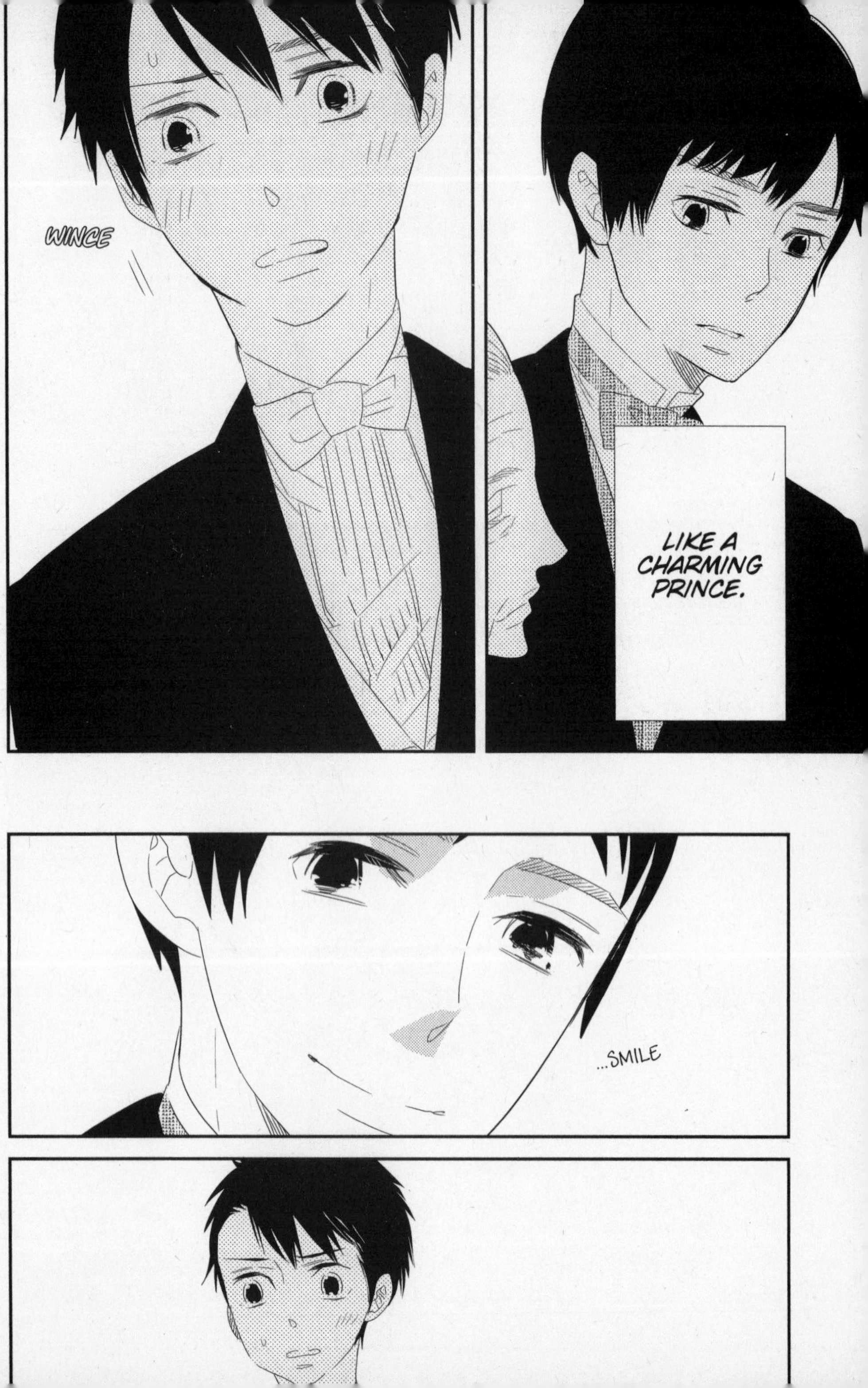
LIKE A CHARMING PRINCE.
WINCE
...SMILE

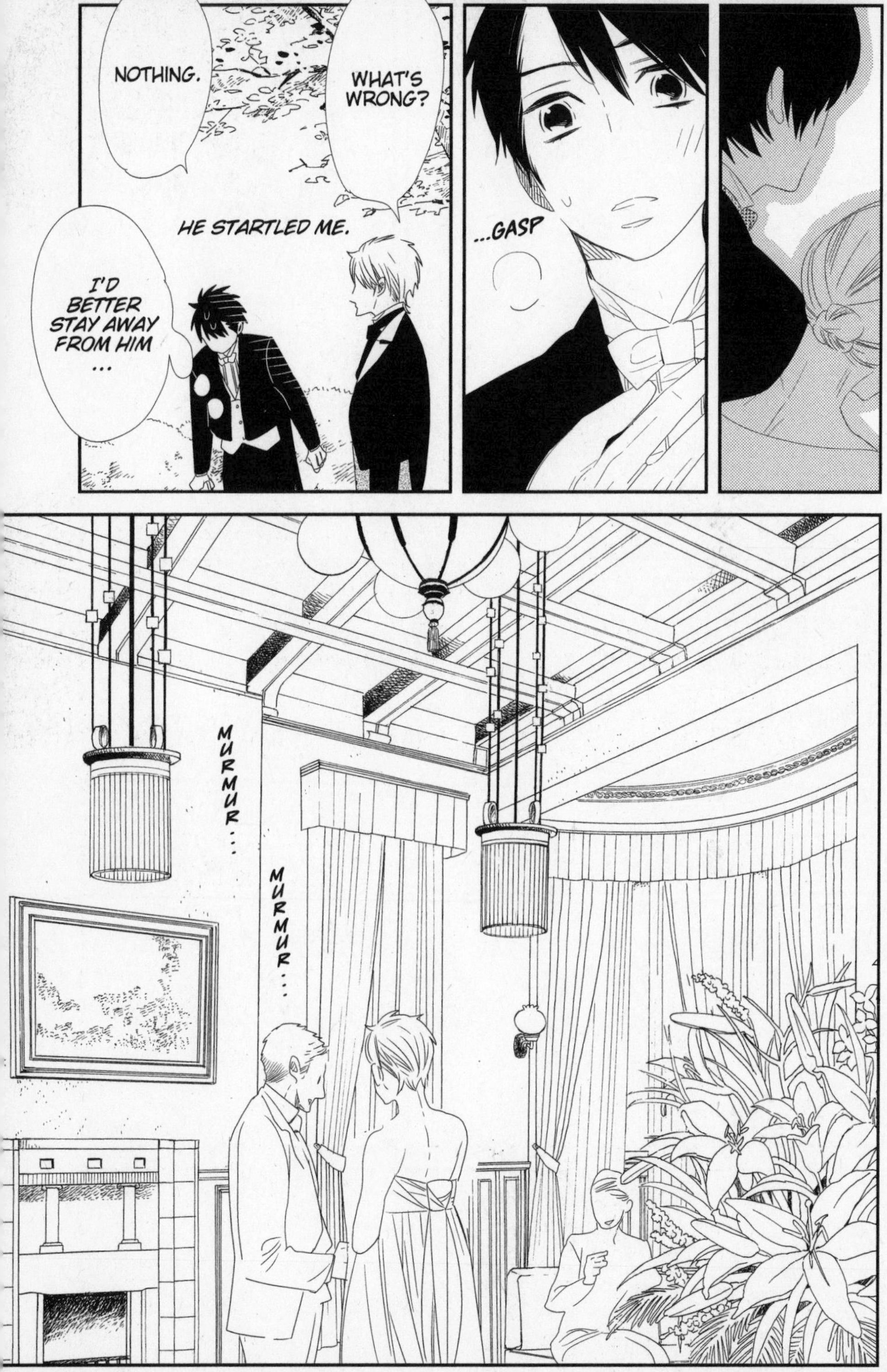
...GASP
WHAT'S WRONG?
NOTHING.
HE STARTLED ME.
I'D BETTER STAY AWAY FROM HIM ...
MURMUR...
MURMUR...

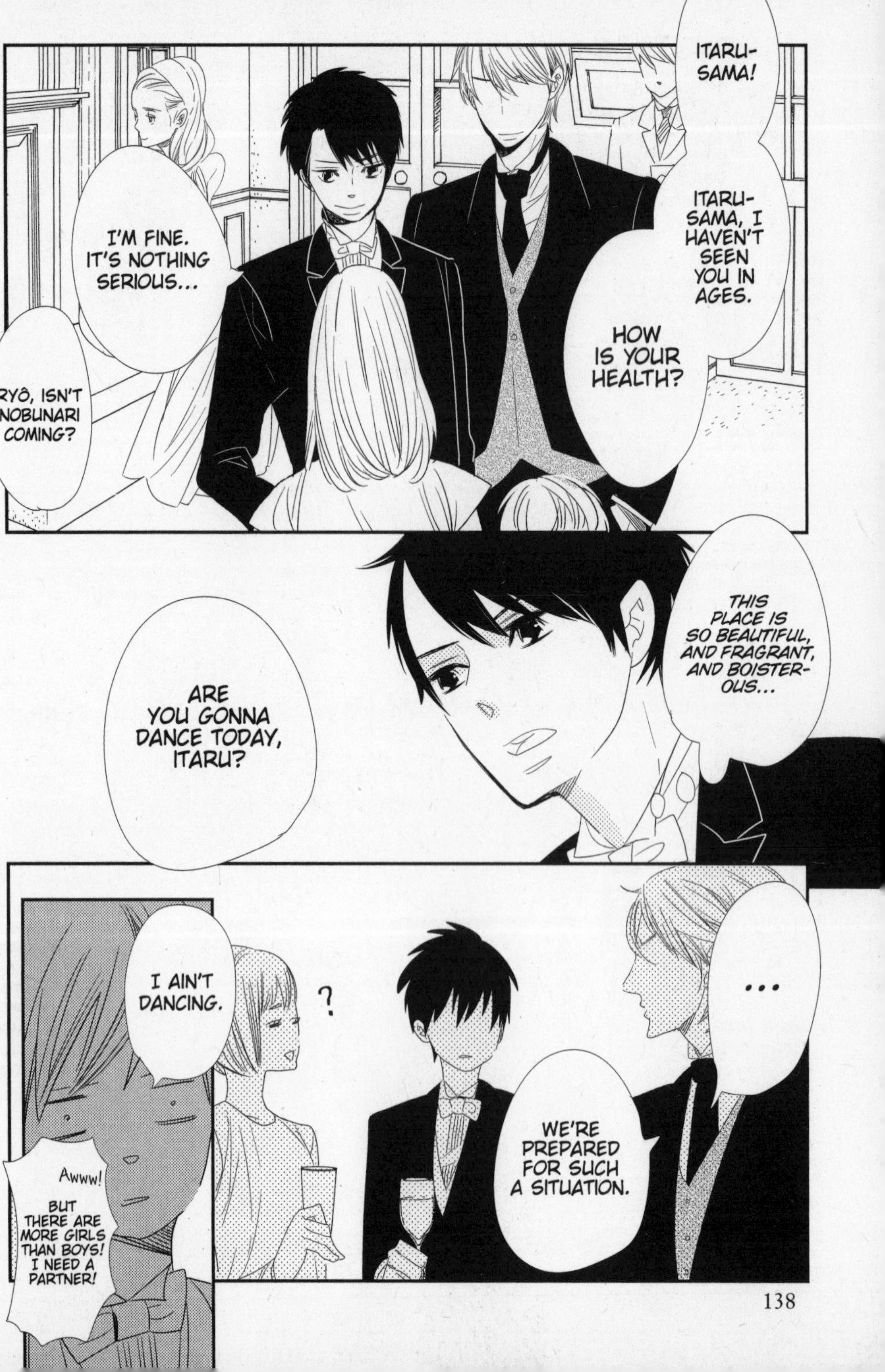
ITARU-SAMA!
ITARU-SAMA, I HAVEN'T SEEN YOU IN AGES.
HOW IS YOUR HEALTH?
I'M FINE. IT'S NOTHING SERIOUS...
RYÔ, ISN'T NOBUNARI COMING?
THIS PLACE IS SO BEAUTIFUL, AND FRAGRANT, AND BOISTER-OUS...
ARE YOU GONNA DANCE TODAY, ITARU?
...
WE'RE PREPARED FOR SUCH A SITUATION.
?
I AIN'T DANCING.
Awww!
BUT THERE ARE MORE GIRLS THAN BOYS! I NEED A PARTNER!

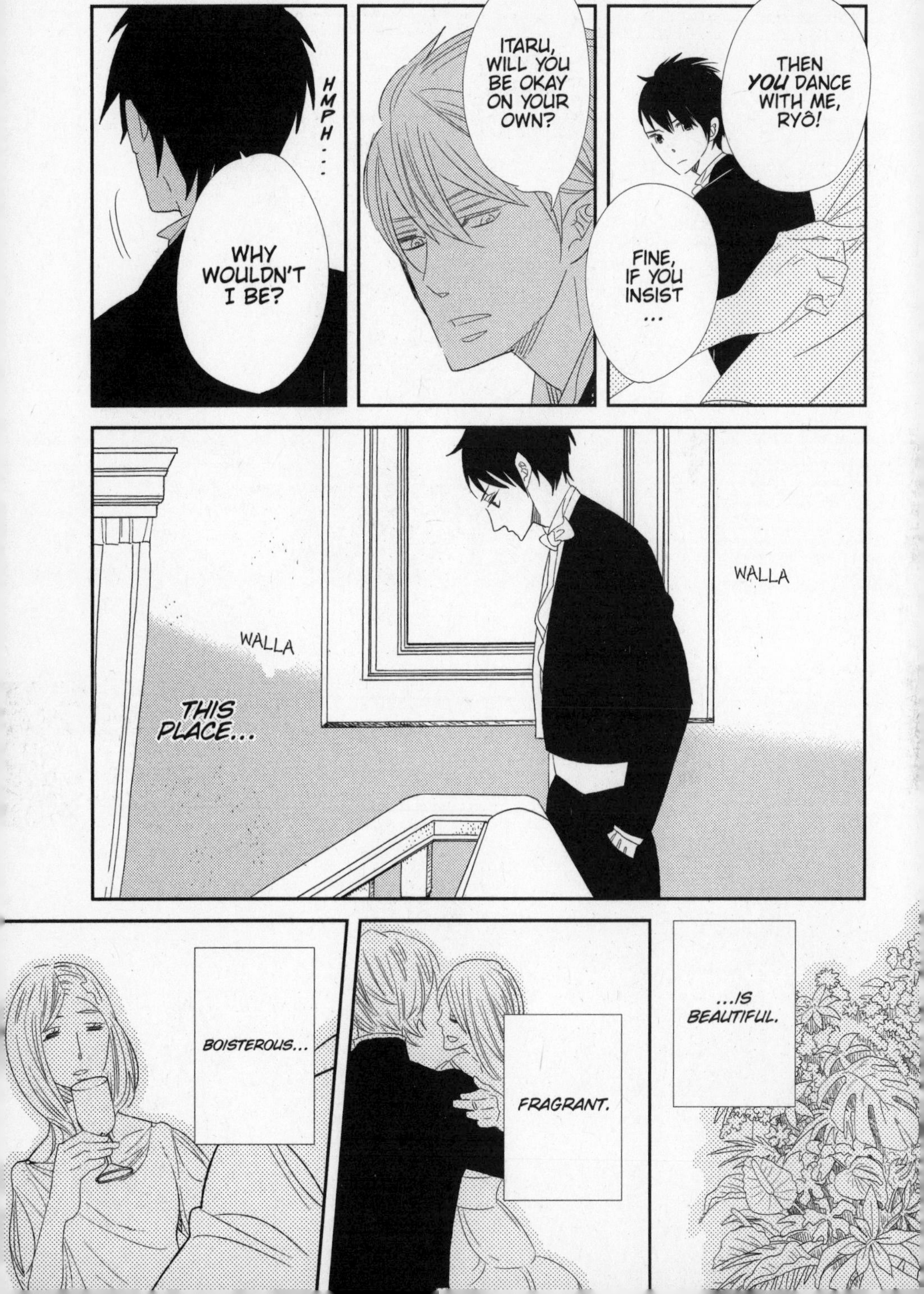
THEN YOU DANCE WITH ME, RYÔ!
FINE, IF YOU INSIST...
ITARU, WILL YOU BE OKAY ON YOUR OWN?
HMPH...
WHY WOULDN'T I BE?
WALLA
WALLA
THIS PLACE...
...IS BEAUTIFUL.
FRAGRANT.
BOISTEROUS...

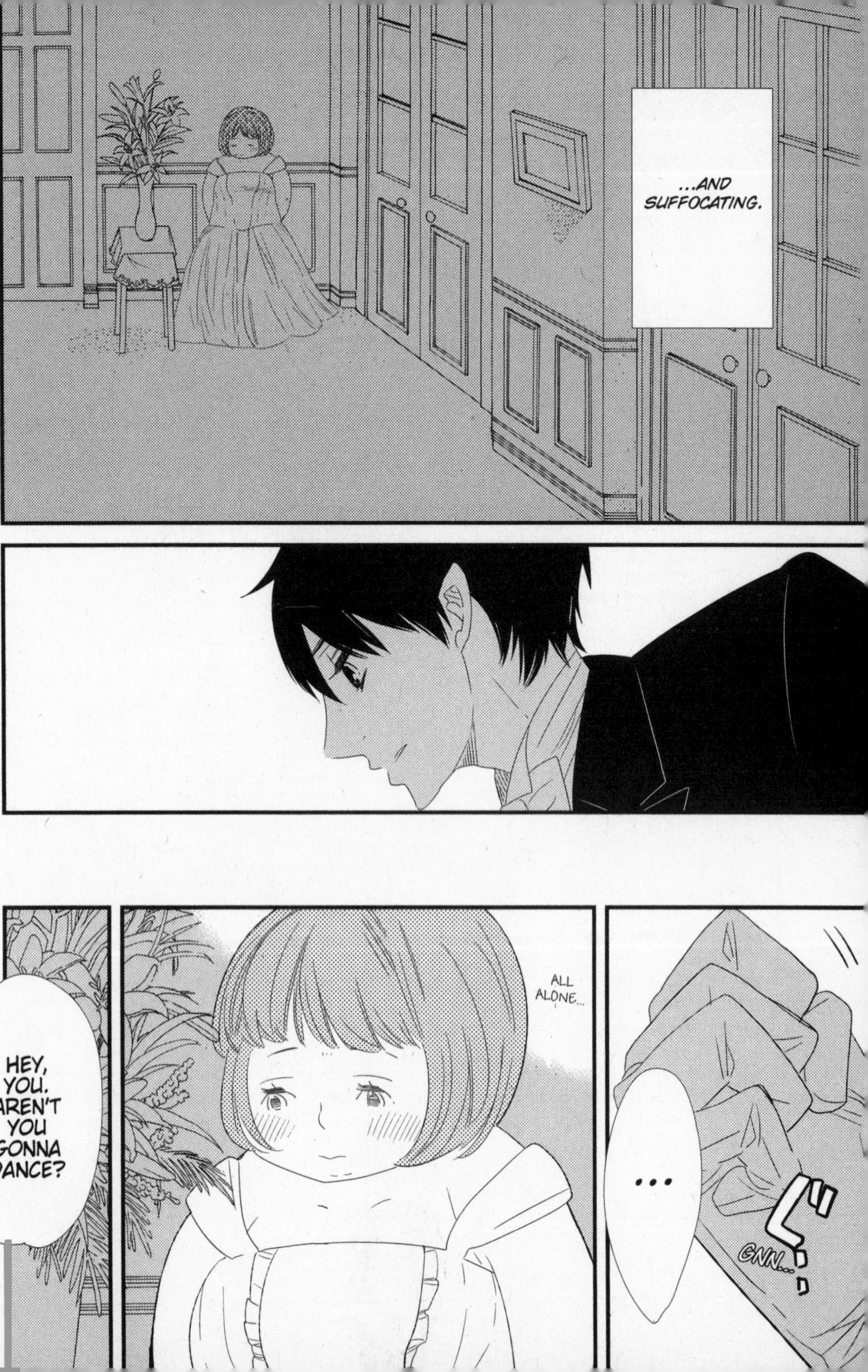
...AND SUFFOCATING.
...
ALL ALONE...
HEY, YOU. AREN'T YOU GONNA DANCE?
GNN...

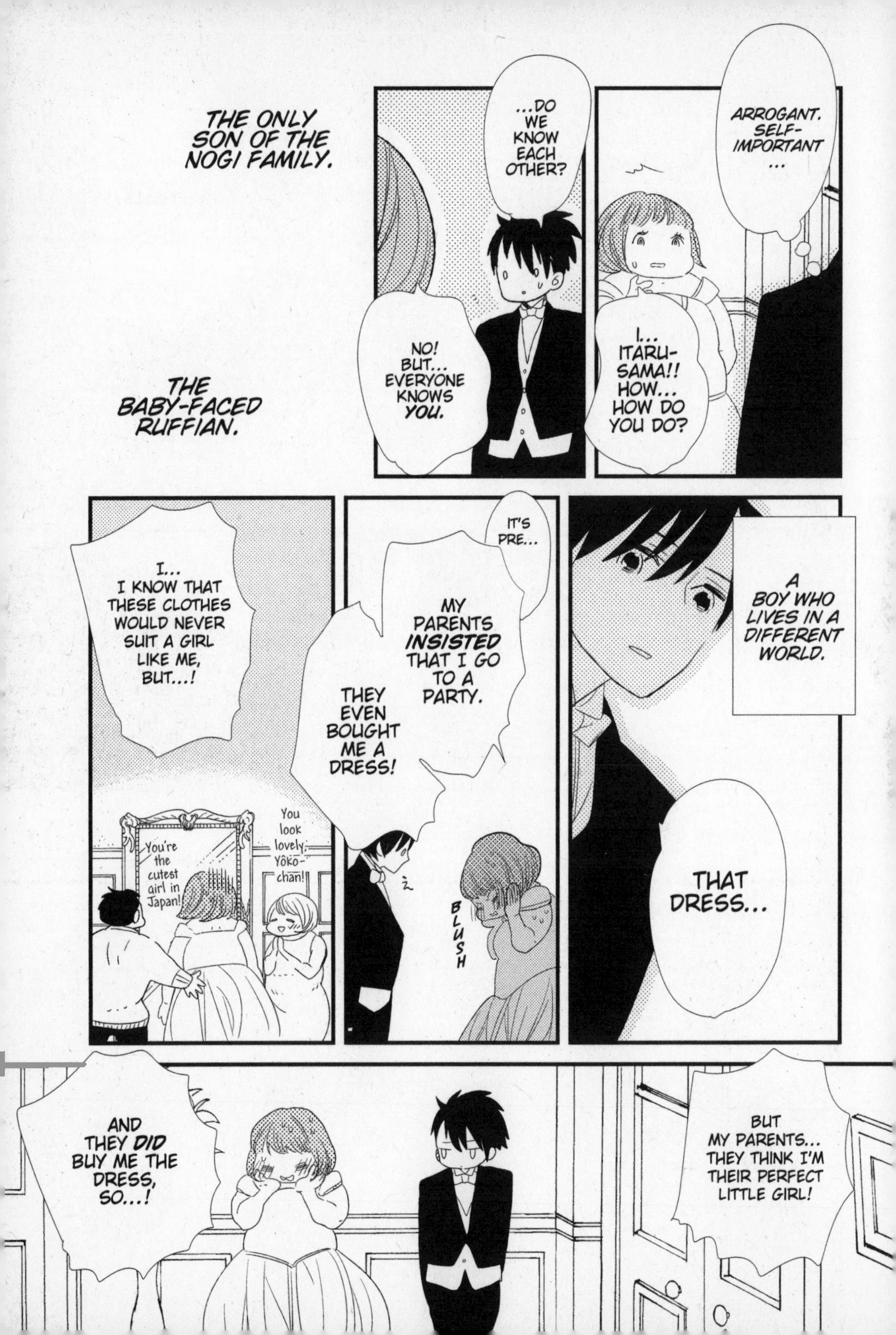

ARROGANT. SELF-IMPORTANT ...
I... ITARU-SAMA!! HOW... HOW DO YOU DO?
...DO WE KNOW EACH OTHER?
NO! BUT... EVERYONE KNOWS YOU.
THE ONLY SON OF THE NOGI FAMILY.
THE BABY-FACED RUFFIAN.
A BOY WHO LIVES IN A DIFFERENT WORLD.
THAT DRESS...
IT'S PRE...
MY PARENTS INSISTED THAT I GO TO A PARTY.
THEY EVEN BOUGHT ME A DRESS!
BLUSH
I... I KNOW THAT THESE CLOTHES WOULD NEVER SUIT A GIRL LIKE ME, BUT...!
You look lovely, Yōko-chan!
You're the cutest girl in Japan!
BUT MY PARENTS... THEY THINK I'M THEIR PERFECT LITTLE GIRL!
AND THEY DID BUY ME THE DRESS, SO...!

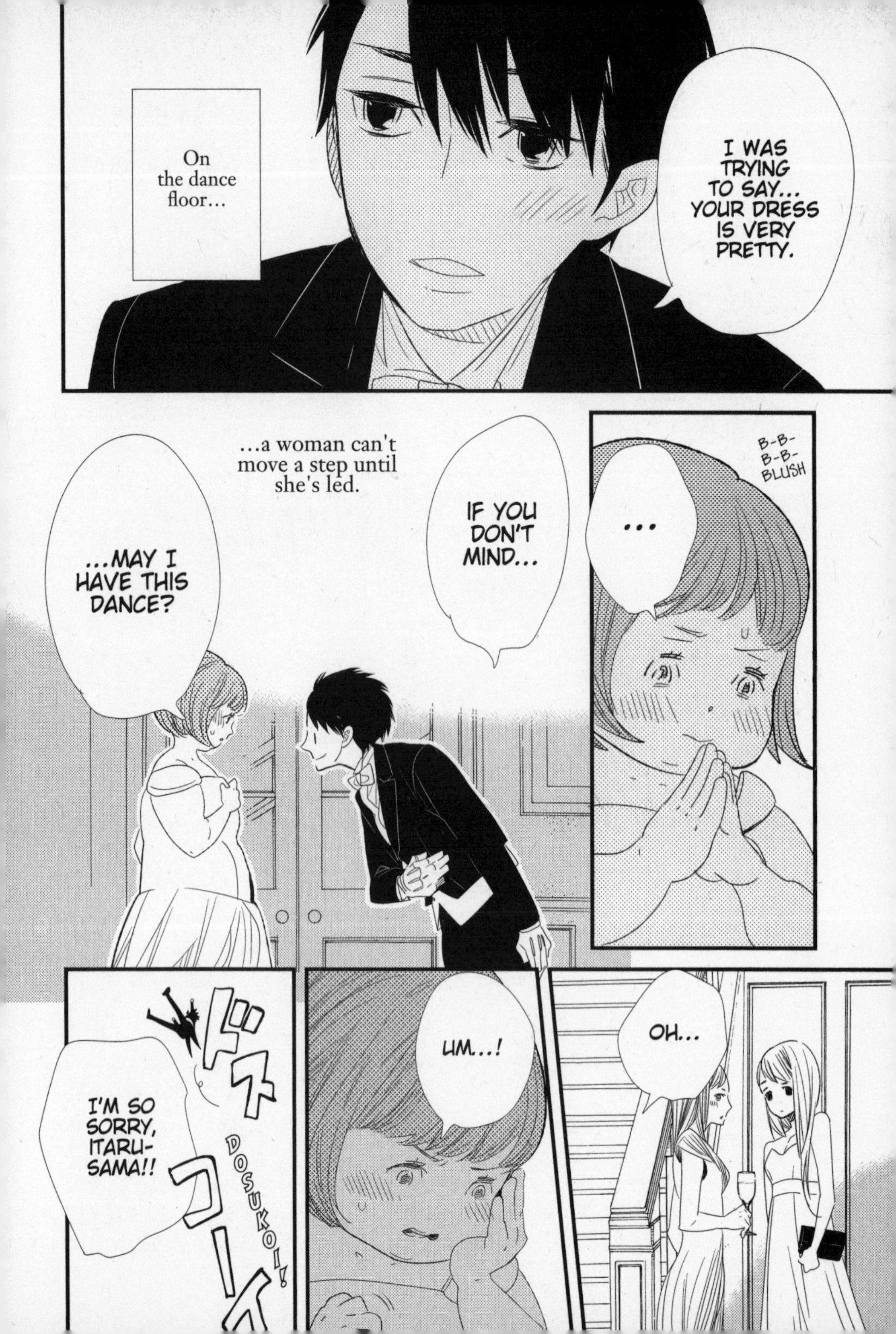
I WAS TRYING TO SAY... YOUR DRESS IS VERY PRETTY.
On the dance floor…
B-B-B-B-BLUSH
...
IF YOU DON'T MIND...
…a woman can't move a step until she's led.
...MAY I HAVE THIS DANCE?
OH...
UM...!
ドスコーイ
DOSUKOI!
I'M SO SORRY, ITARU-SAMA!!

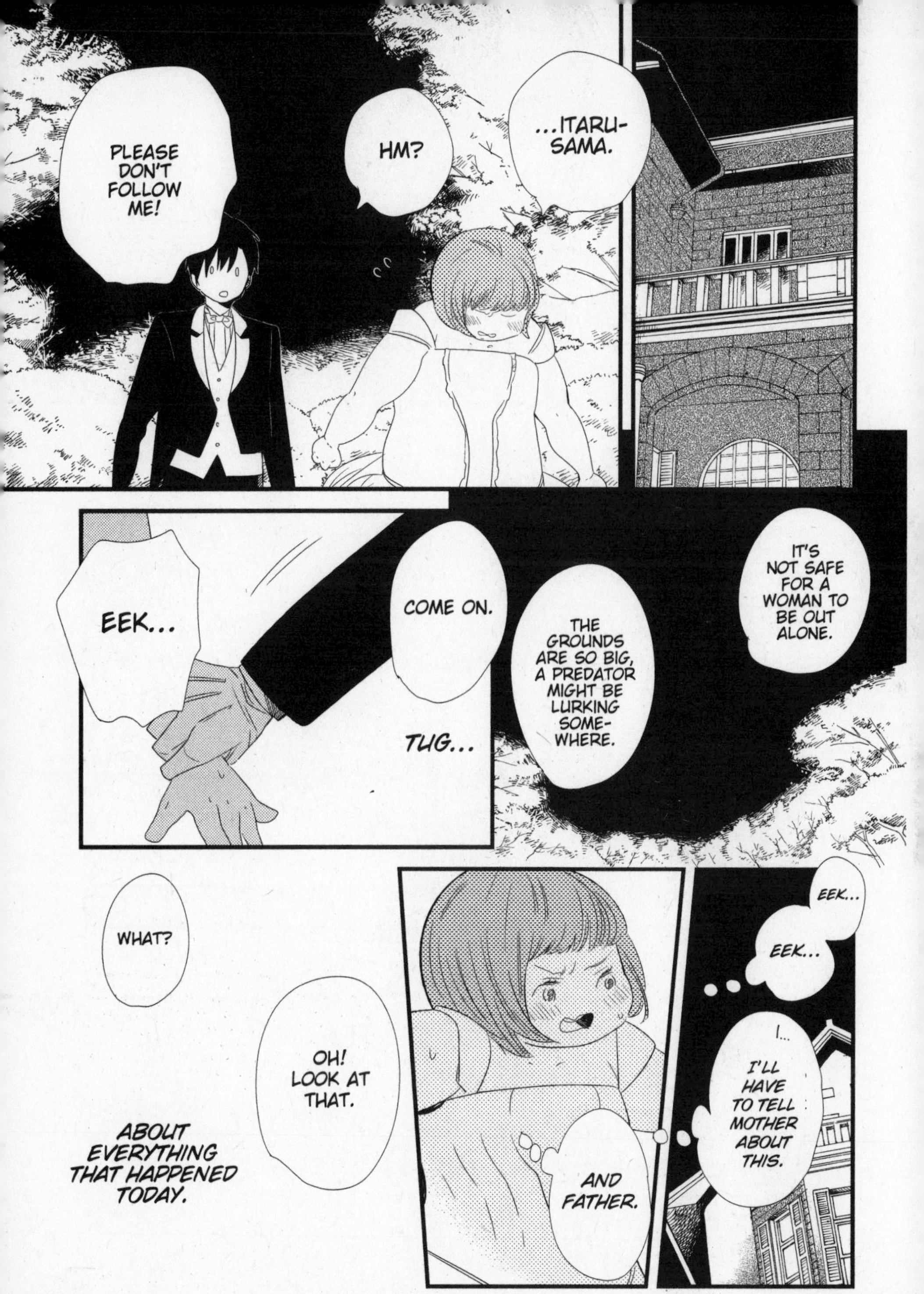
...ITARU-SAMA.
HM?
PLEASE DON'T FOLLOW ME!
IT'S NOT SAFE FOR A WOMAN TO BE OUT ALONE.
THE GROUNDS ARE SO BIG, A PREDATOR MIGHT BE LURKING SOME-WHERE.
COME ON.
EEK...
TUG...
EEK...
EEK...
I...
I'LL HAVE TO TELL MOTHER ABOUT THIS.
AND FATHER.
WHAT?
OH! LOOK AT THAT.
ABOUT EVERYTHING THAT HAPPENED TODAY.

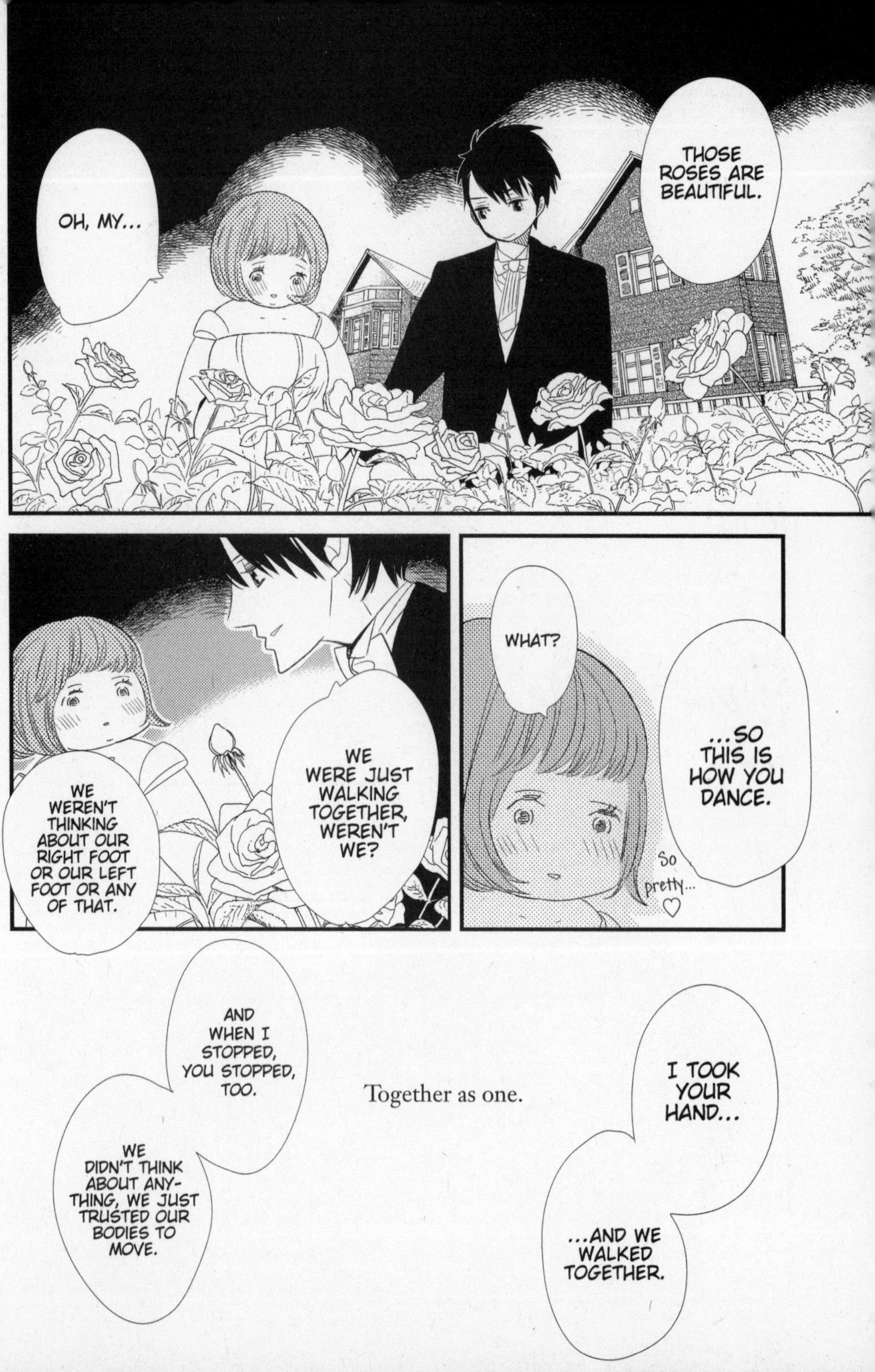
THOSE ROSES ARE BEAUTIFUL.
OH, MY...
...SO THIS IS HOW YOU DANCE.
WHAT?
So pretty... ♡
WE WERE JUST WALKING TOGETHER, WEREN'T WE?
WE WEREN'T THINKING ABOUT OUR RIGHT FOOT OR OUR LEFT FOOT OR ANY OF THAT.
I TOOK YOUR HAND...
...AND WE WALKED TOGETHER.
Together as one.
AND WHEN I STOPPED, YOU STOPPED, TOO.
WE DIDN'T THINK ABOUT ANY-THING, WE JUST TRUSTED OUR BODIES TO MOVE.

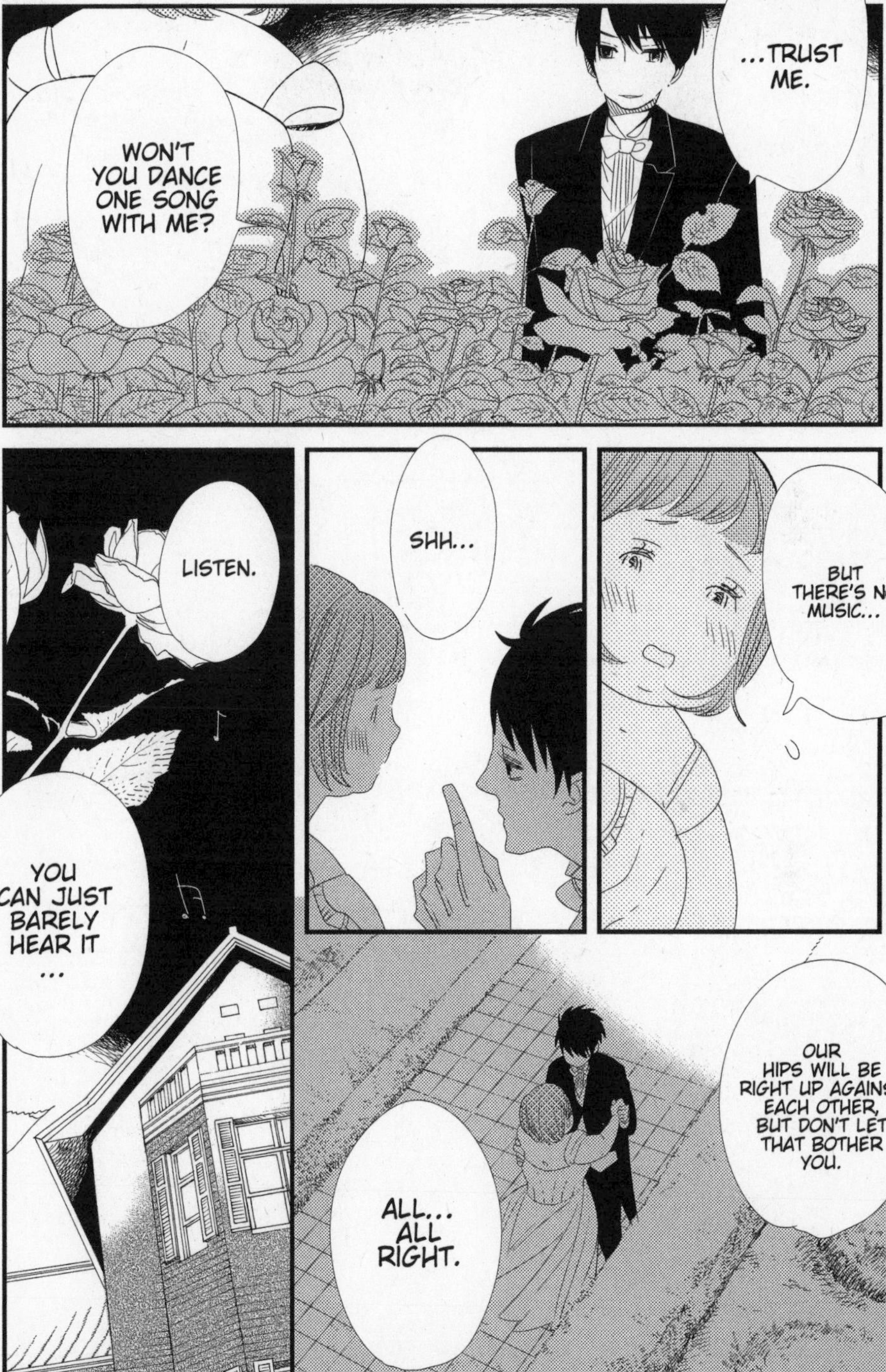
...TRUST ME.
WON'T YOU DANCE ONE SONG WITH ME?
BUT THERE'S NO MUSIC...
SHH...
OUR HIPS WILL BE RIGHT UP AGAINST EACH OTHER, BUT DON'T LET THAT BOTHER YOU.
ALL... ALL RIGHT.
LISTEN.
YOU CAN JUST BARELY HEAR IT ...

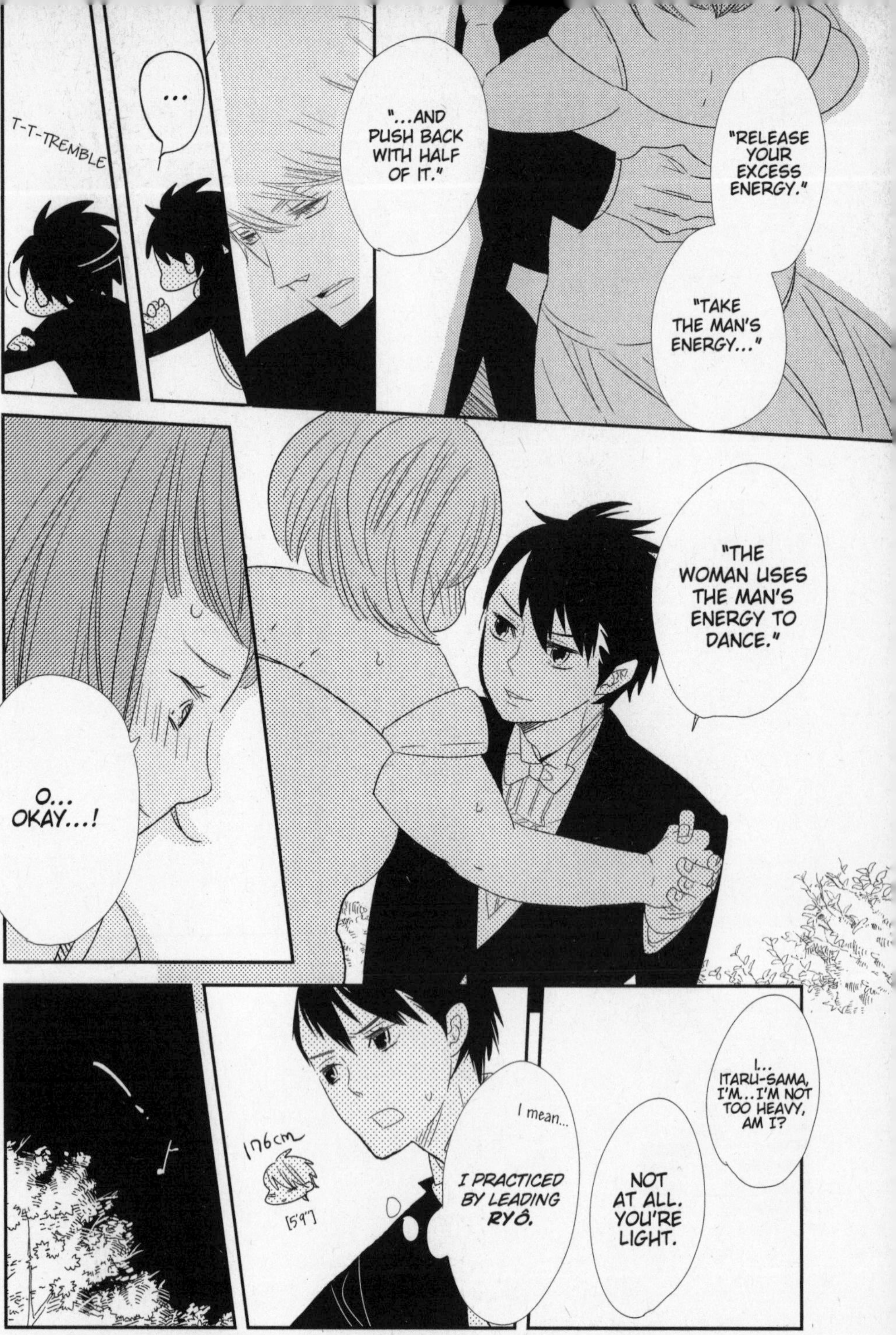
"RELEASE YOUR EXCESS ENERGY."
"TAKE THE MAN'S ENERGY..."
"...AND PUSH BACK WITH HALF OF IT."
...
T-T-TREMBLE
"THE WOMAN USES THE MAN'S ENERGY TO DANCE."
O... OKAY...!
I... ITARU-SAMA, I'M...I'M NOT TOO HEAVY, AM I?
NOT AT ALL. YOU'RE LIGHT.
I mean...
I PRACTICED BY LEADING RYÔ.
176cm
[5'9"]

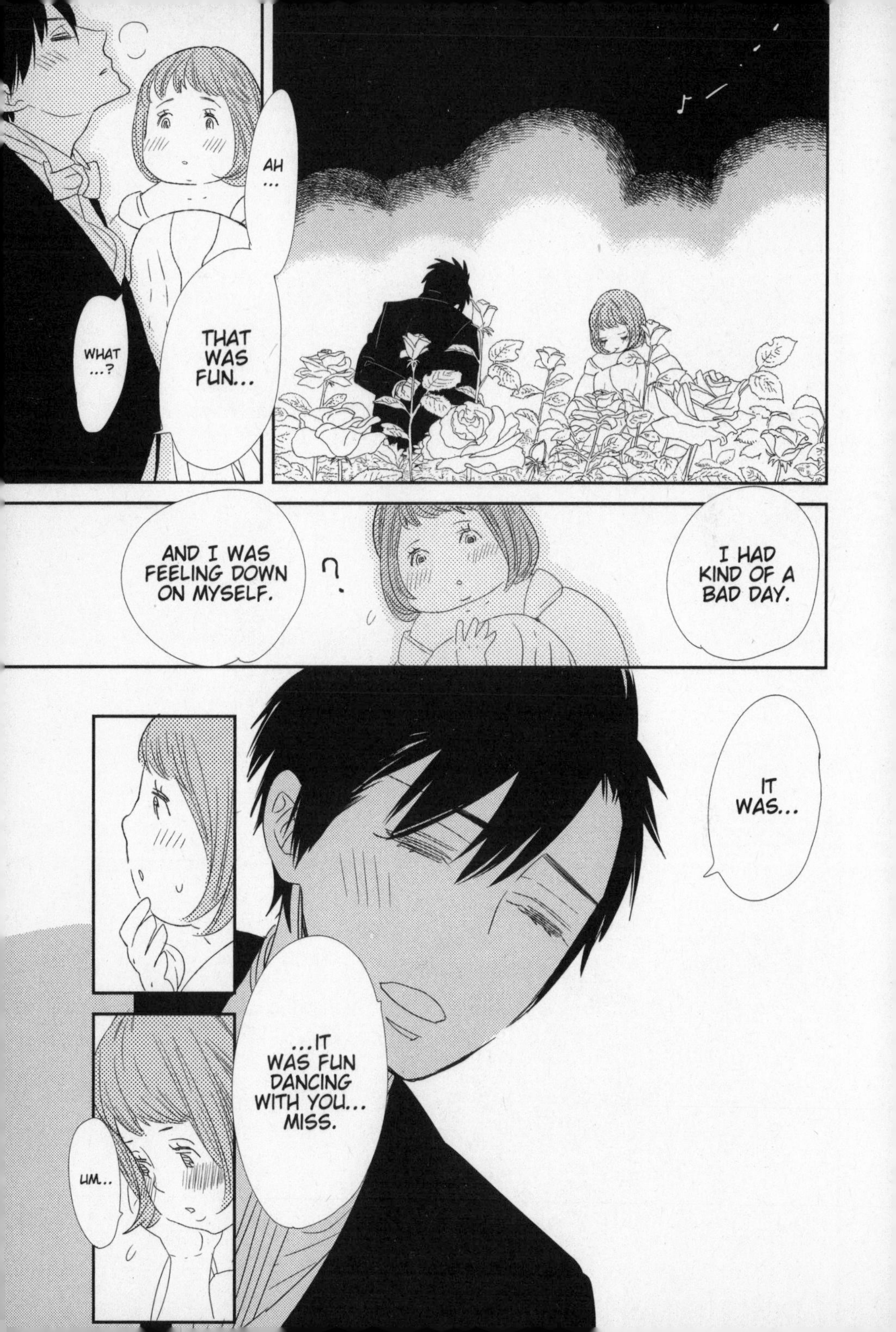
AH ...
THAT WAS FUN...
WHAT ...?
I HAD KIND OF A BAD DAY.
AND I WAS FEELING DOWN ON MYSELF.
IT WAS...
...IT WAS FUN DANCING WITH YOU... MISS.
UM...

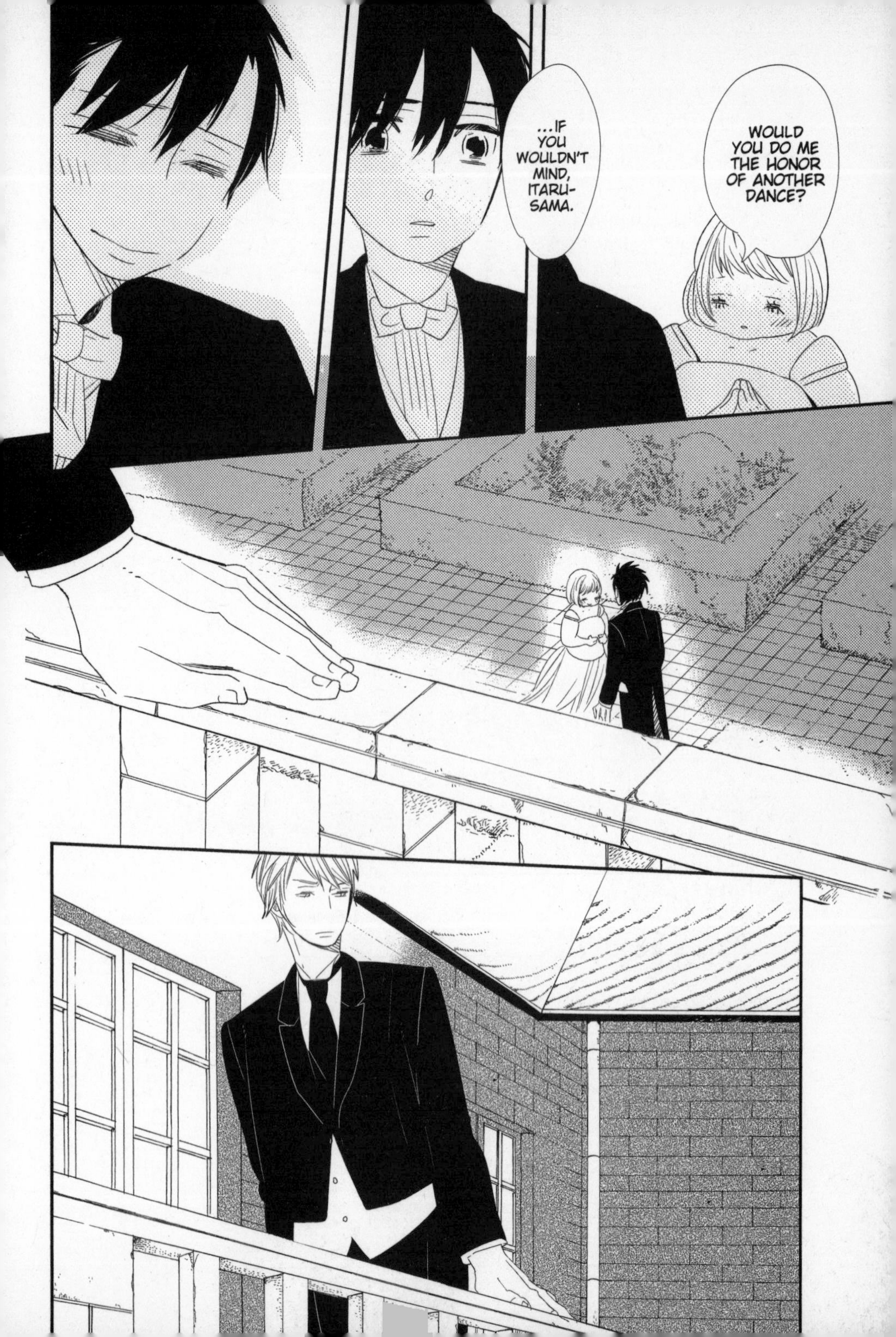
WOULD YOU DO ME THE HONOR OF ANOTHER DANCE?
...IF YOU WOULDN'T MIND, ITARU-SAMA.

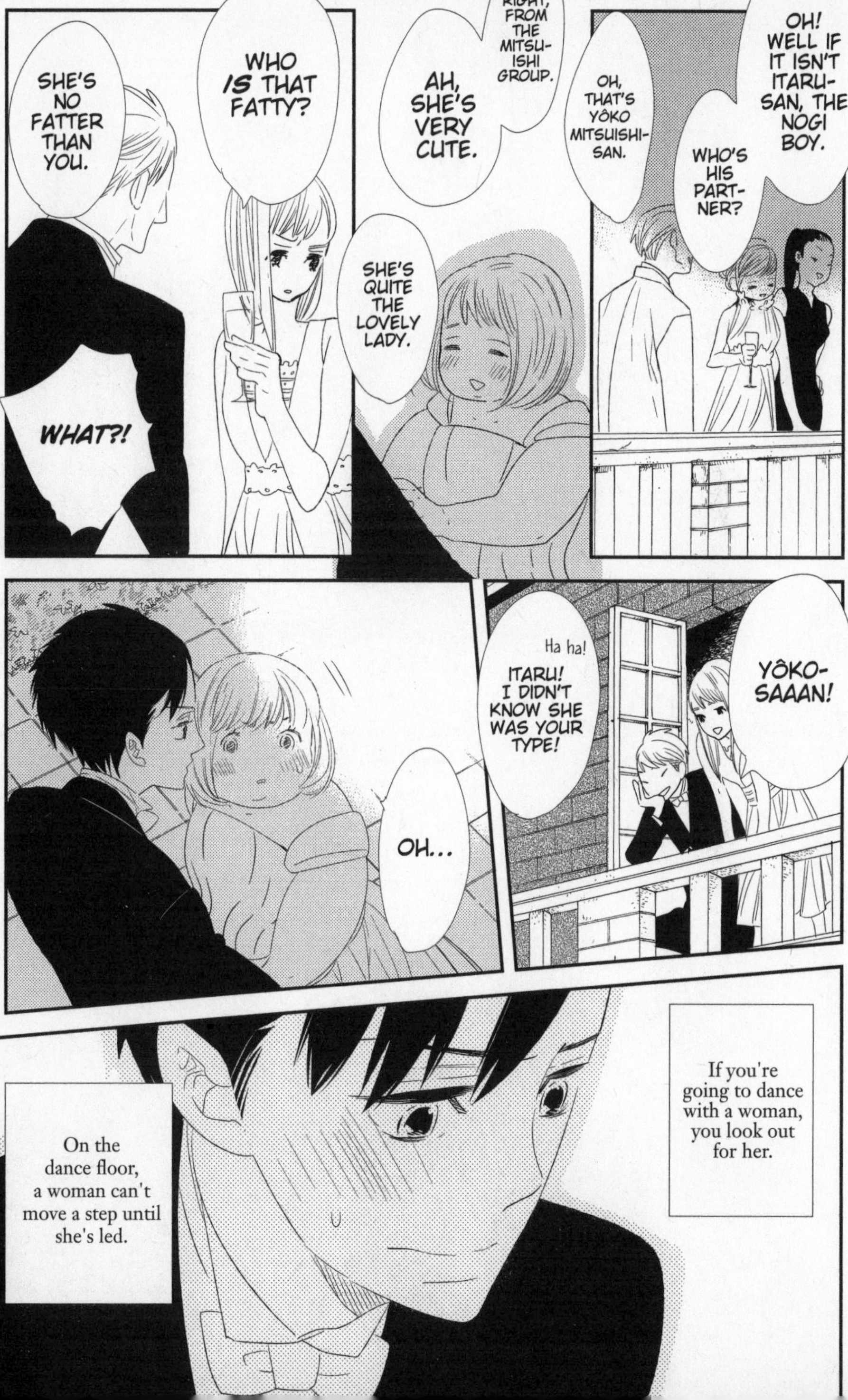
OH! WELL IF IT ISN'T ITARU-SAN, THE NOGI BOY.
WHO'S HIS PARTNER?
OH, THAT'S YÔKO MITSUISHI-SAN.
RIGHT, FROM THE MITSUISHI GROUP.
AH, SHE'S VERY CUTE.
SHE'S QUITE THE LOVELY LADY.
WHO IS THAT FATTY?
SHE'S NO FATTER THAN YOU.
WHAT?!
YÔKO-SAAAN!
Ha ha!
ITARU! I DIDN'T KNOW SHE WAS YOUR TYPE!
OH...
If you're going to dance with a woman, you look out for her.
On the dance floor, a woman can't move a step until she's led.

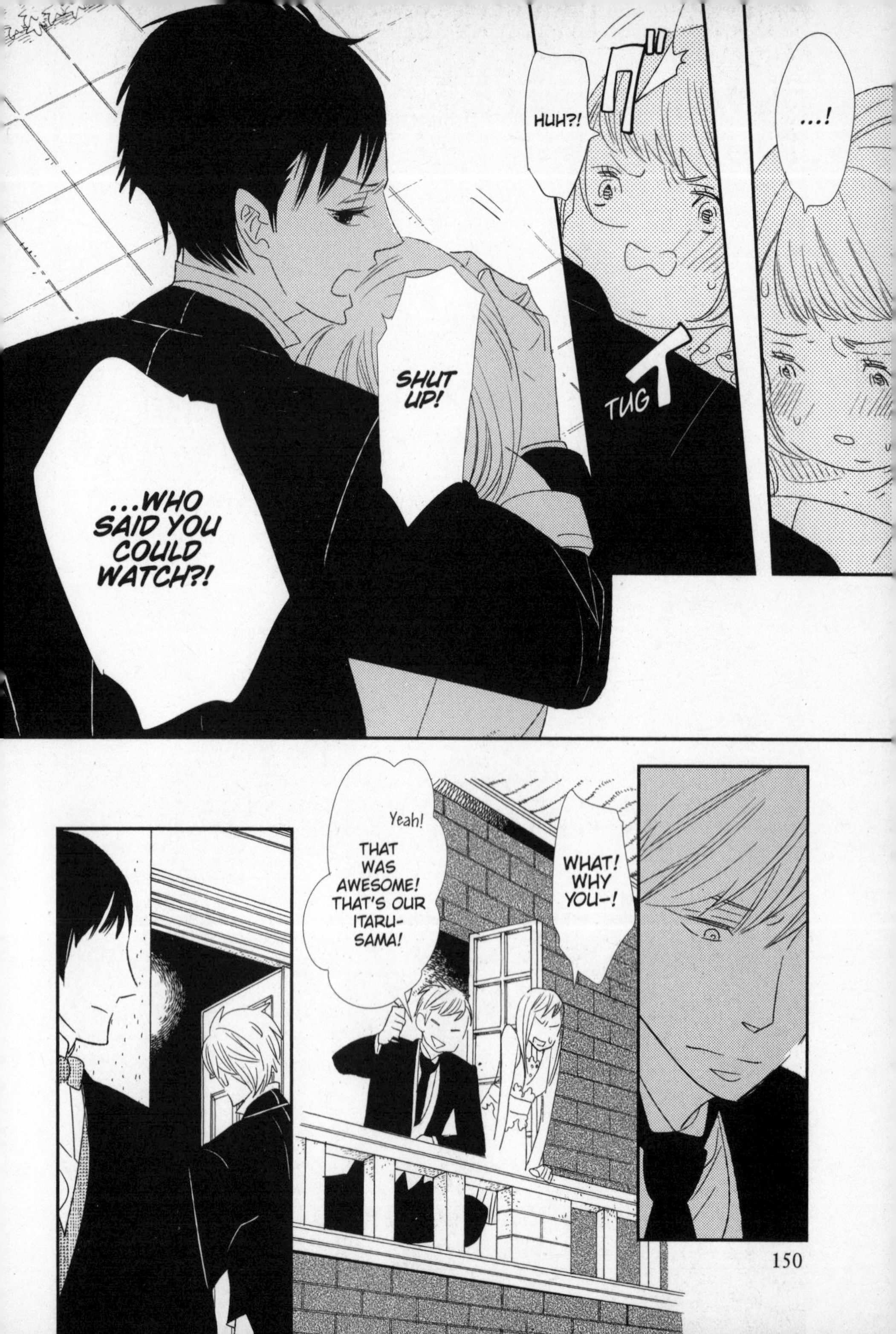
...!
HUH?!
TUG
SHUT UP!
...WHO SAID YOU COULD WATCH?!
WHAT! WHY YOU–!
Yeah!
THAT WAS AWESOME! THAT'S OUR ITARU-SAMA!

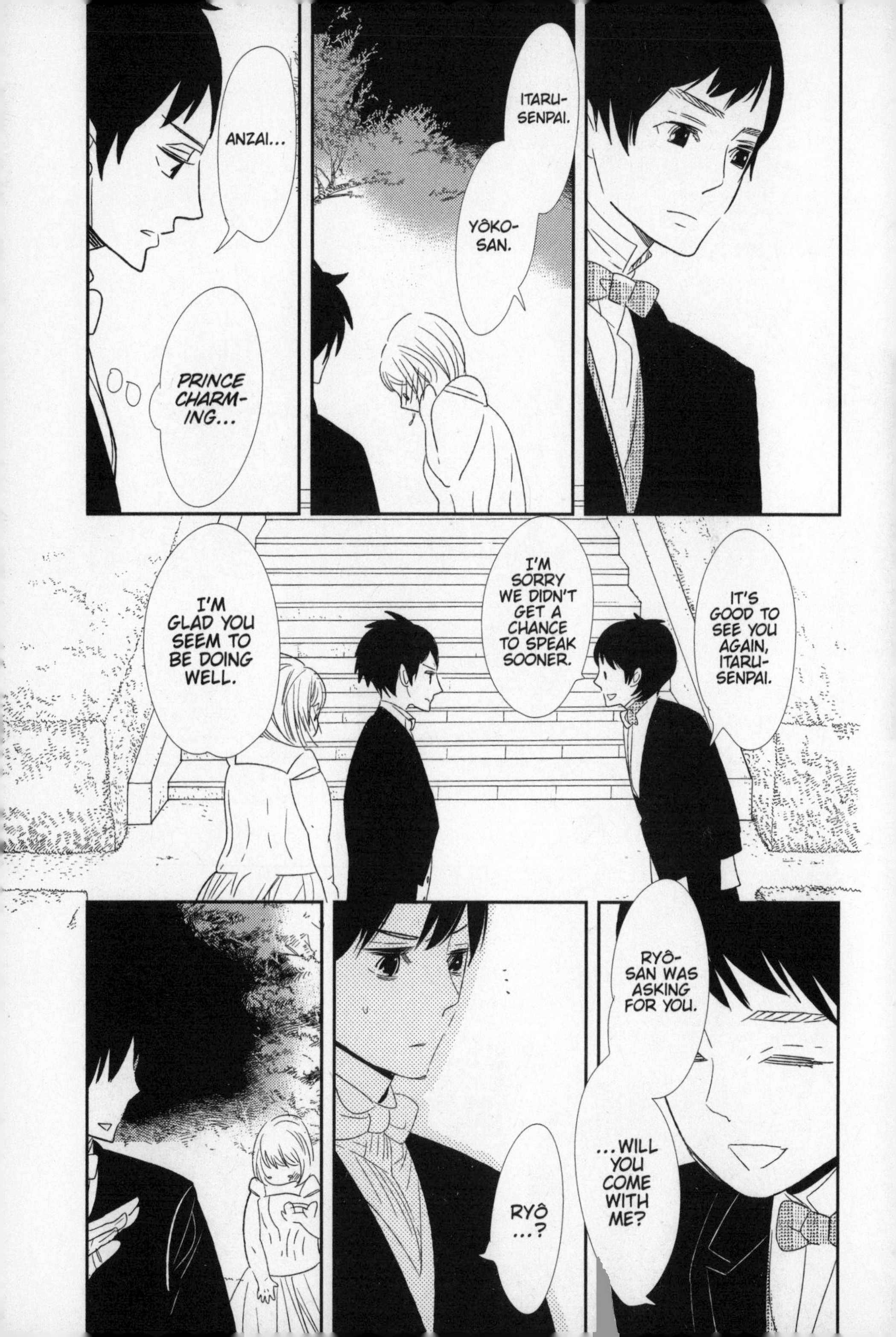
ITARU-SENPAI.
YÔKO-SAN.
ANZAI...
PRINCE CHARMING...
IT'S GOOD TO SEE YOU AGAIN, ITARU-SENPAI.
I'M SORRY WE DIDN'T GET A CHANCE TO SPEAK SOONER.
I'M GLAD YOU SEEM TO BE DOING WELL.
RYÔ-SAN WAS ASKING FOR YOU.
...WILL YOU COME WITH ME?
RYÔ...?

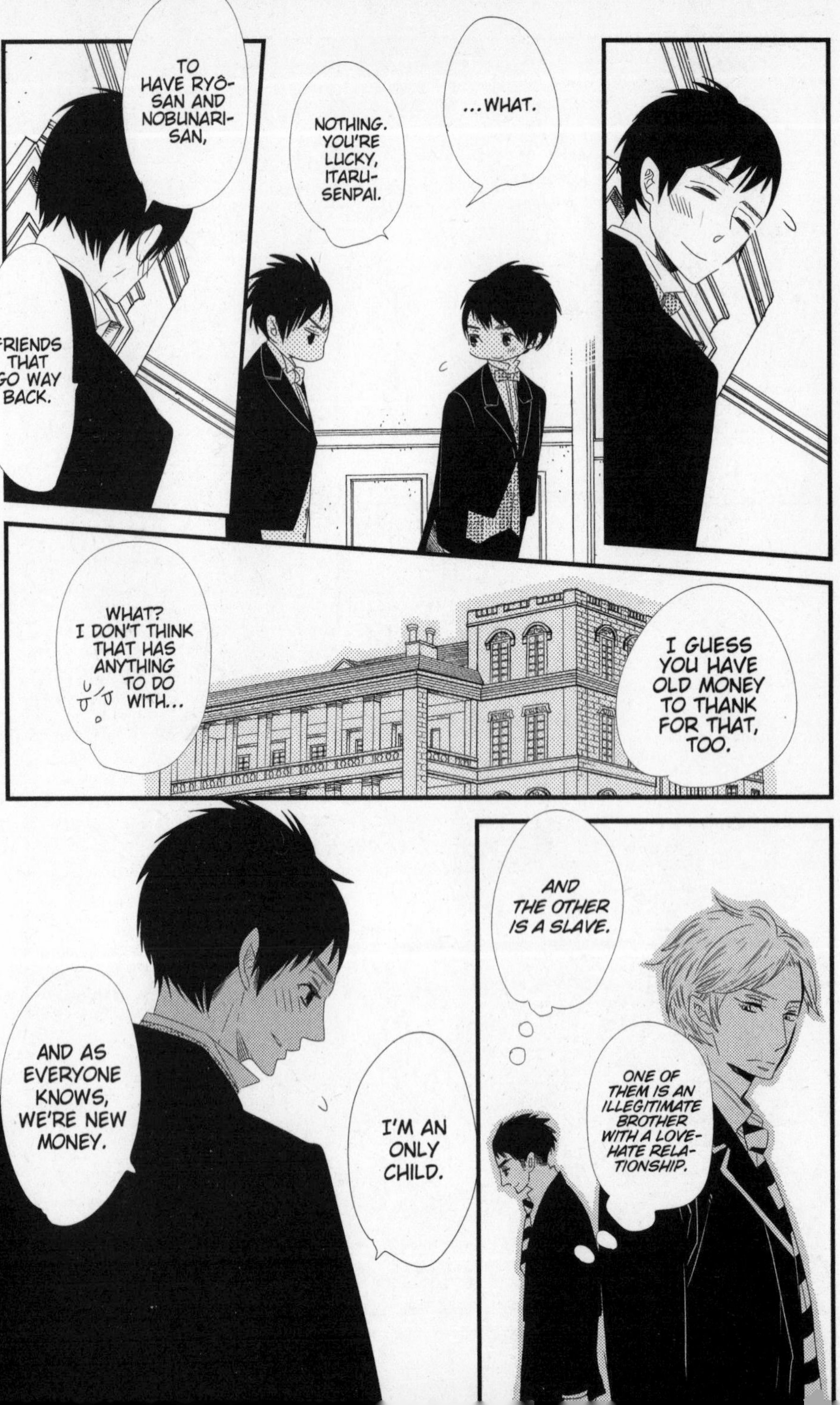
...WHAT.
NOTHING. YOU'RE LUCKY, ITARU-SENPAI.
TO HAVE RYÔ-SAN AND NOBUNARI-SAN,
FRIENDS THAT GO WAY BACK.
I GUESS YOU HAVE OLD MONEY TO THANK FOR THAT, TOO.
WHAT? I DON'T THINK THAT HAS ANYTHING TO DO WITH...
ONE OF THEM IS AN ILLEGITIMATE BROTHER WITH A LOVE-HATE RELATIONSHIP.
AND THE OTHER IS A SLAVE.
I'M AN ONLY CHILD.
AND AS EVERYONE KNOWS, WE'RE NEW MONEY.

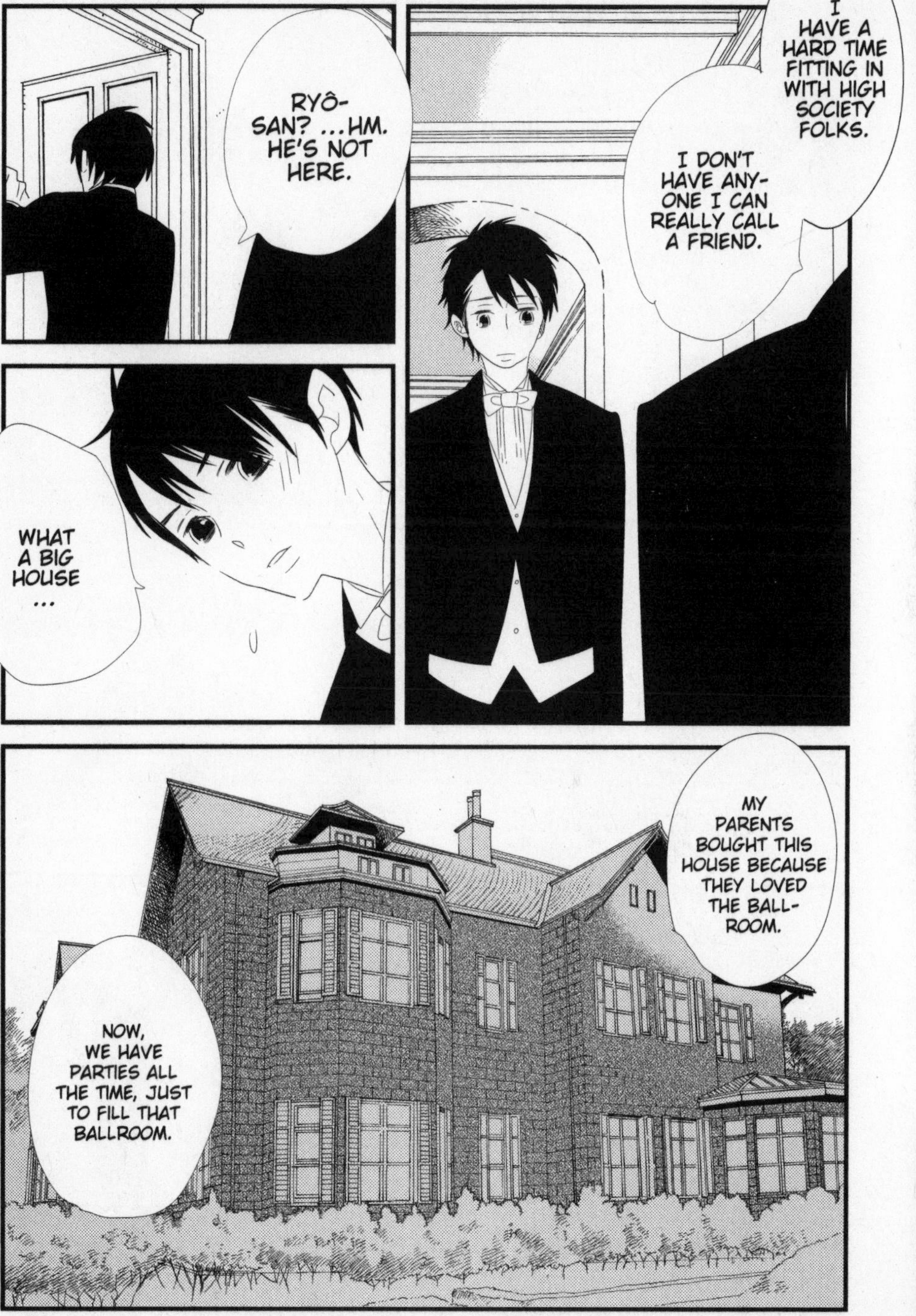
I HAVE A HARD TIME FITTING IN WITH HIGH SOCIETY FOLKS.
I DON'T HAVE ANY-ONE I CAN REALLY CALL A FRIEND.
RYÔ-SAN? ...HM. HE'S NOT HERE.
WHAT A BIG HOUSE ...
MY PARENTS BOUGHT THIS HOUSE BECAUSE THEY LOVED THE BALL-ROOM.
NOW, WE HAVE PARTIES ALL THE TIME, JUST TO FILL THAT BALLROOM.

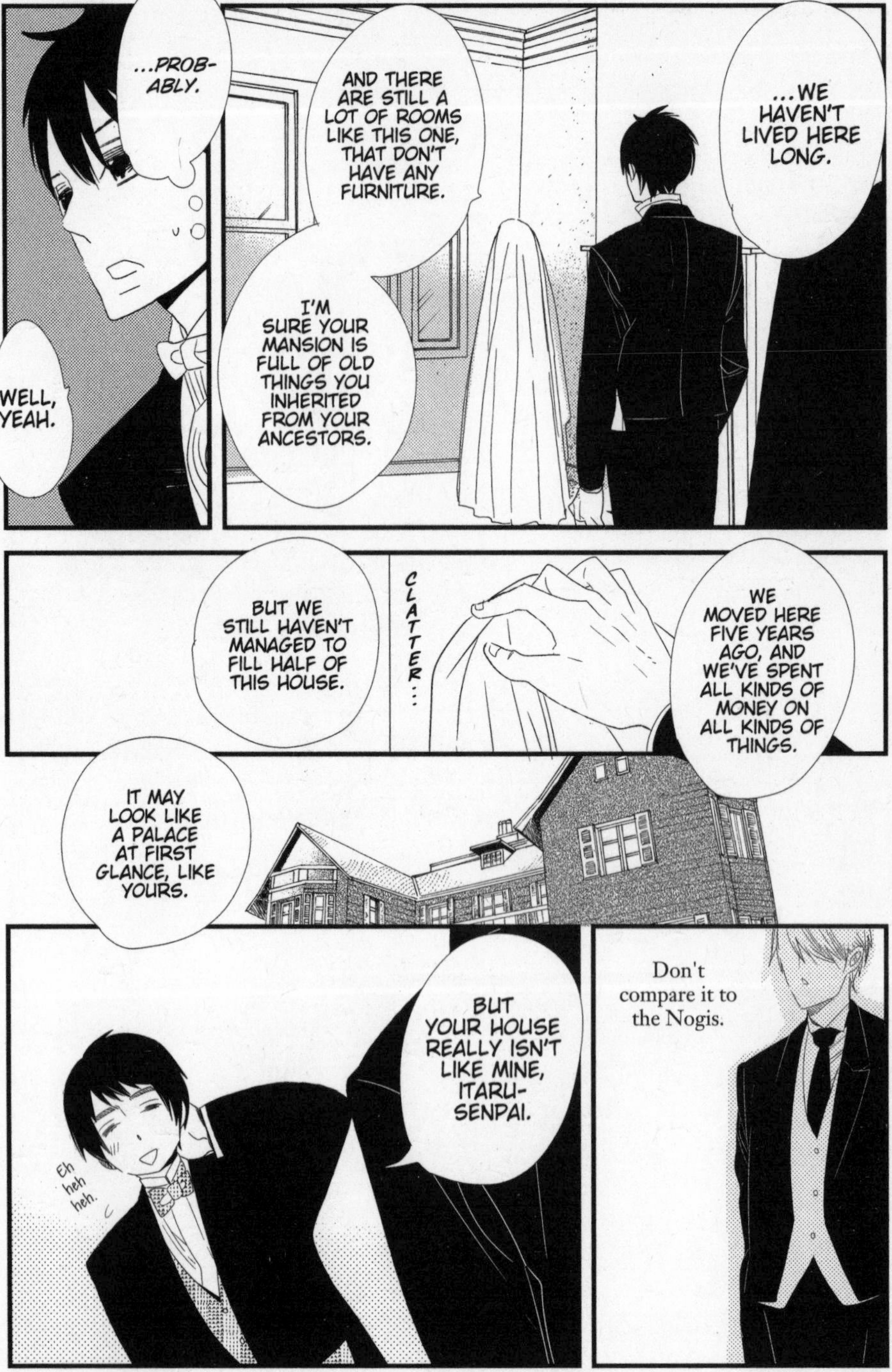

...WE HAVEN'T LIVED HERE LONG.
AND THERE ARE STILL A LOT OF ROOMS LIKE THIS ONE, THAT DON'T HAVE ANY FURNITURE.
I'M SURE YOUR MANSION IS FULL OF OLD THINGS YOU INHERITED FROM YOUR ANCESTORS.
...PROB-ABLY.
WELL, YEAH.
WE MOVED HERE FIVE YEARS AGO, AND WE'VE SPENT ALL KINDS OF MONEY ON ALL KINDS OF THINGS.
CLATTER...
BUT WE STILL HAVEN'T MANAGED TO FILL HALF OF THIS HOUSE.
IT MAY LOOK LIKE A PALACE AT FIRST GLANCE, LIKE YOURS.
Don't compare it to the Nogis.
BUT YOUR HOUSE REALLY ISN'T LIKE MINE, ITARU-SENPAI.
Eh heh heh.

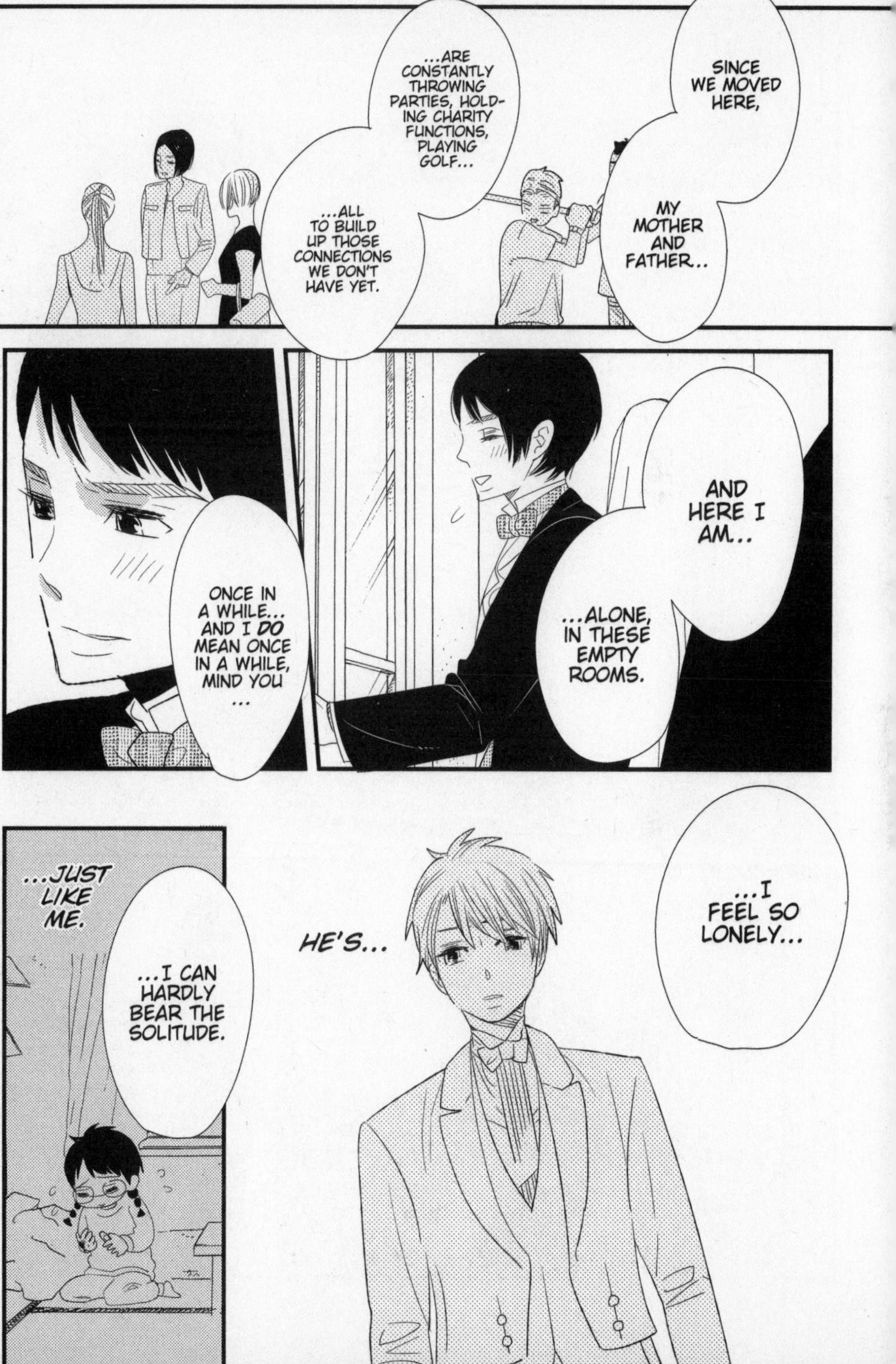
SINCE WE MOVED HERE,
MY MOTHER AND FATHER...
...ARE CONSTANTLY THROWING PARTIES, HOLD-ING CHARITY FUNCTIONS, PLAYING GOLF...
...ALL TO BUILD UP THOSE CONNECTIONS WE DON'T HAVE YET.
AND HERE I AM...
...ALONE, IN THESE EMPTY ROOMS.
ONCE IN A WHILE... AND I *DO* MEAN ONCE IN A WHILE, MIND YOU ...
...I FEEL SO LONELY...
HE'S...
...I CAN HARDLY BEAR THE SOLITUDE.
...JUST LIKE ME.

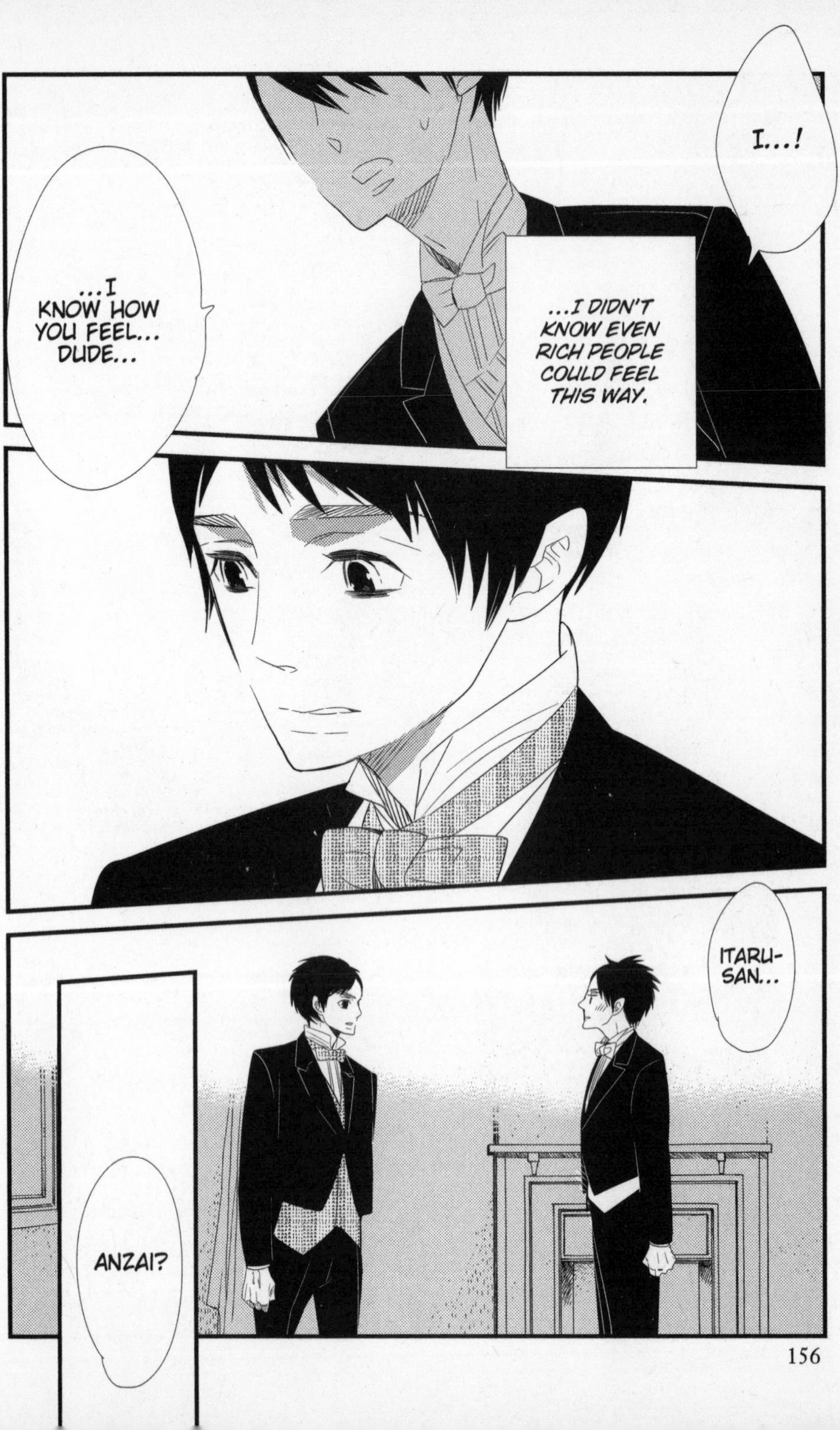
I...!
...I DIDN'T KNOW EVEN RICH PEOPLE COULD FEEL THIS WAY.
...I KNOW HOW YOU FEEL... DUDE...
ITARU-SAN...
ANZAI?

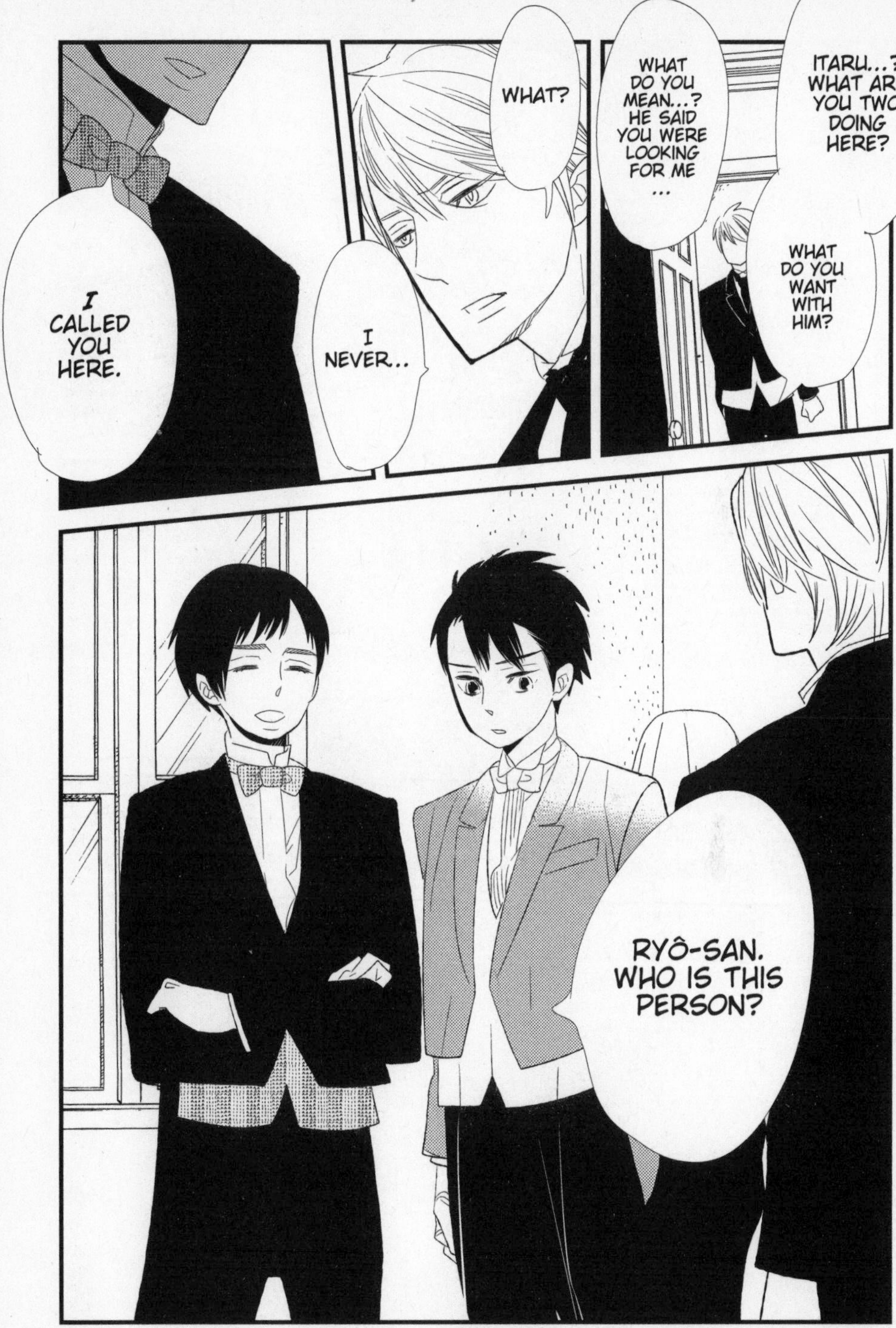
ITARU...? WHAT ARE YOU TWO DOING HERE?
WHAT DO YOU WANT WITH HIM?
WHAT DO YOU MEAN...? HE SAID YOU WERE LOOKING FOR ME ...
WHAT?
I NEVER...
I CALLED YOU HERE.
RYÔ-SAN. WHO IS THIS PERSON?

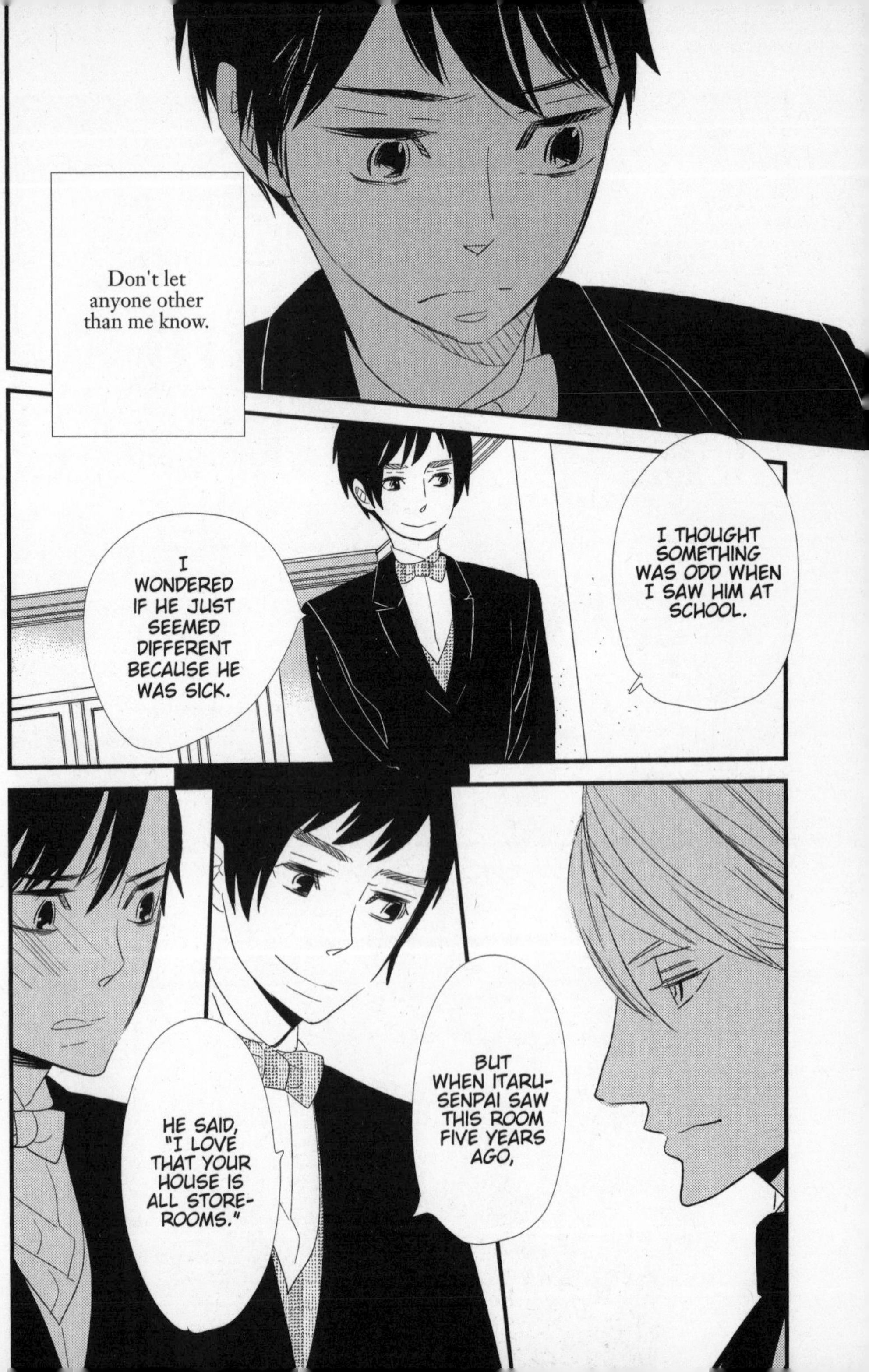
Don't let anyone other than me know.
I THOUGHT SOMETHING WAS ODD WHEN I SAW HIM AT SCHOOL.
I WONDERED IF HE JUST SEEMED DIFFERENT BECAUSE HE WAS SICK.
BUT WHEN ITARU-SENPAI SAW THIS ROOM FIVE YEARS AGO,
HE SAID, "I LOVE THAT YOUR HOUSE IS ALL STORE-ROOMS."

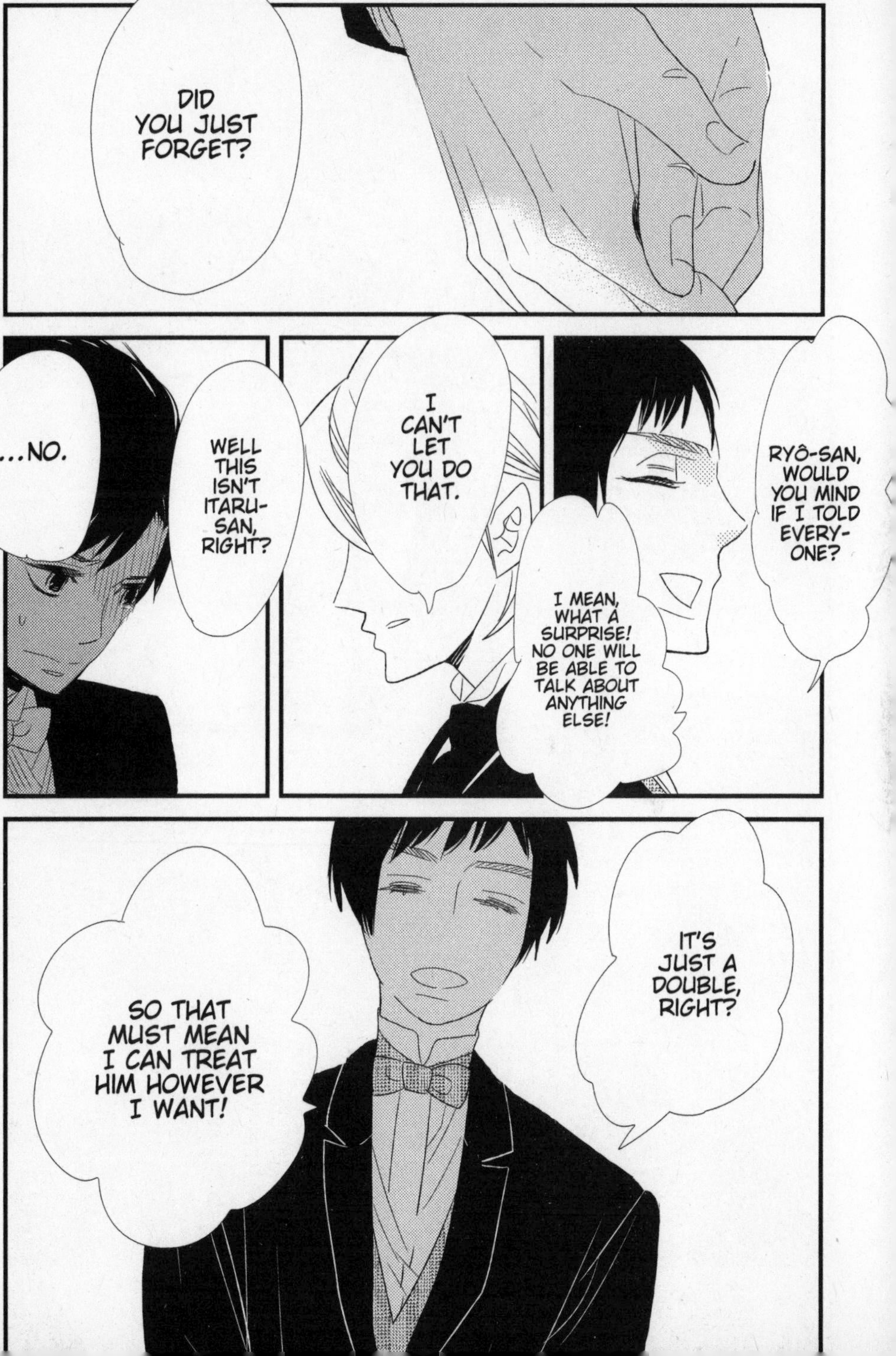
DID YOU JUST FORGET?
RYÔ-SAN, WOULD YOU MIND IF I TOLD EVERYONE?
I MEAN, WHAT A SURPRISE! NO ONE WILL BE ABLE TO TALK ABOUT ANYTHING ELSE!
I CAN'T LET YOU DO THAT.
WELL THIS ISN'T ITARU-SAN, RIGHT?
...NO.
IT'S JUST A DOUBLE, RIGHT?
SO THAT MUST MEAN I CAN TREAT HIM HOWEVER I WANT!

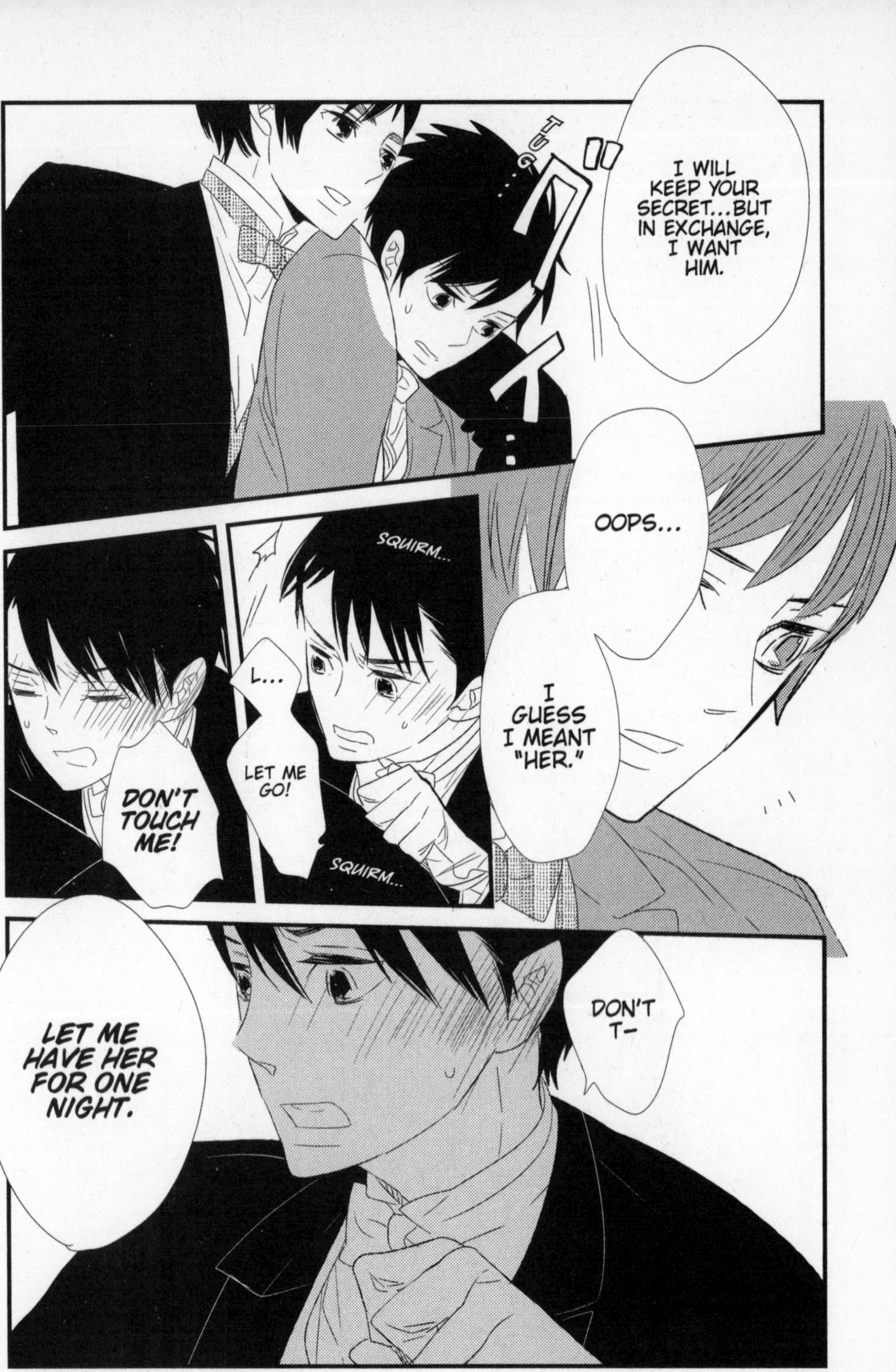
I WILL KEEP YOUR SECRET...BUT IN EXCHANGE, I WANT HIM.
TUG
OOPS...
I GUESS I MEANT "HER."
SQUIRM...
L...
LET ME GO!
SQUIRM...
DON'T TOUCH ME!
DON'T T–
LET ME HAVE HER FOR ONE NIGHT.

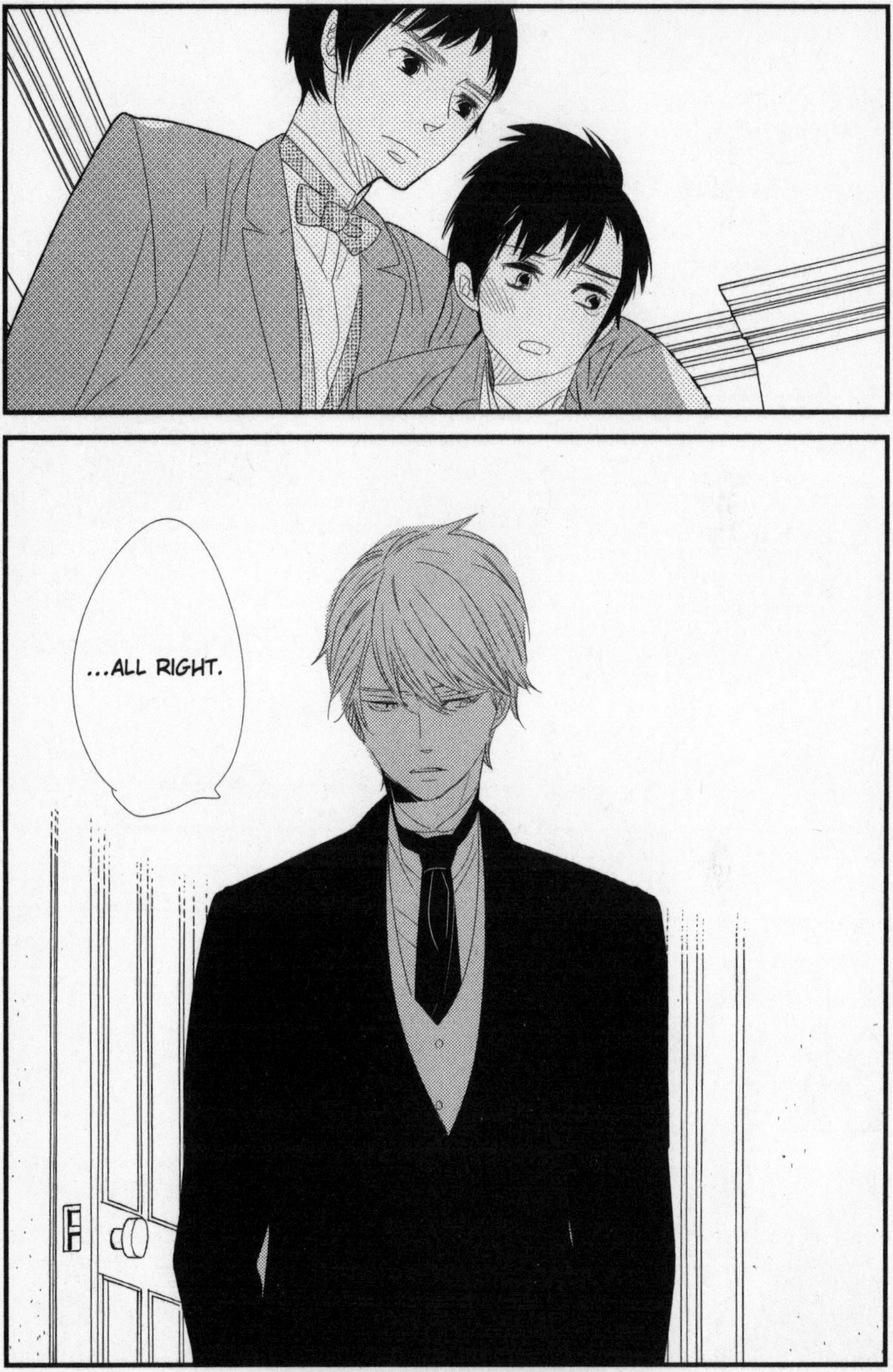
...ALL RIGHT.

to be continued in vol. 3

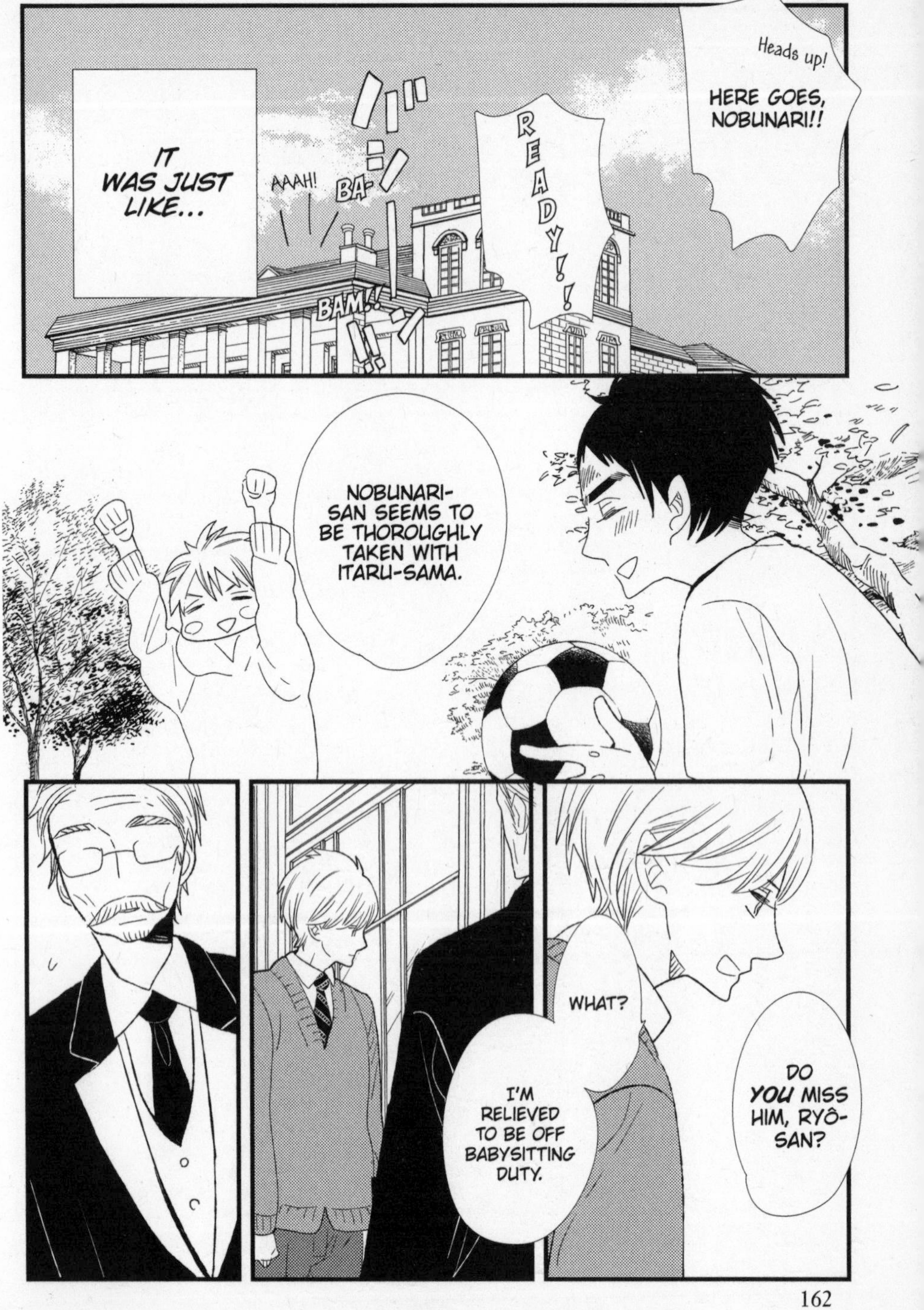
Heads up!
HERE GOES, NOBUNARI!!
READY!!
BA-
BAM!!
AAAH!
IT WAS JUST LIKE...
NOBUNARI-SAN SEEMS TO BE THOROUGHLY TAKEN WITH ITARU-SAMA.
DO *YOU* MISS HIM, RYÔ-SAN?
WHAT?
I'M RELIEVED TO BE OFF BABYSITTING DUTY.

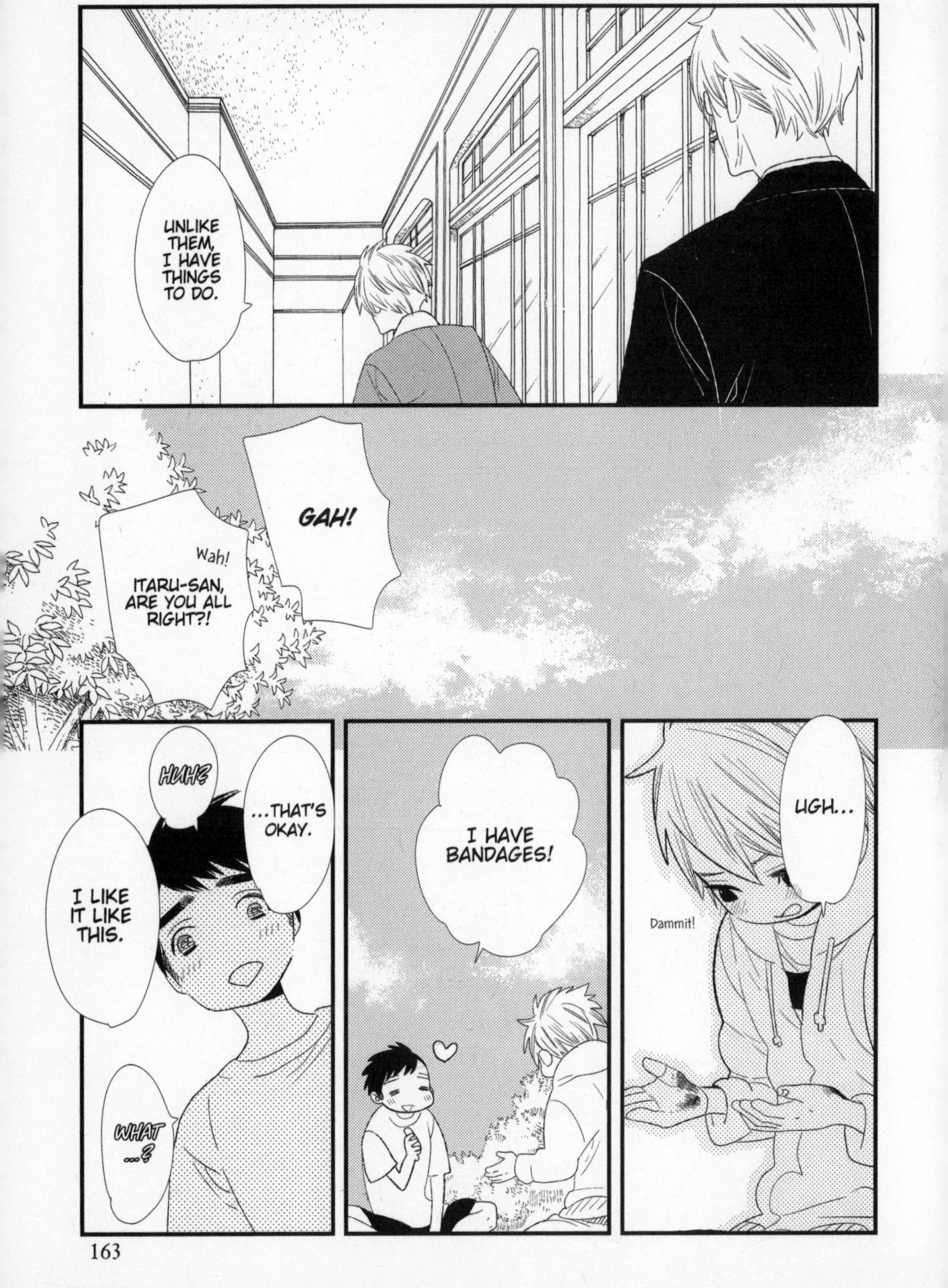
UNLIKE THEM, I HAVE THINGS TO DO.
GAH!
Wah!
ITARU-SAN, ARE YOU ALL RIGHT?!
UGH...
Dammit!
I HAVE BANDAGES!
...THAT'S OKAY.
HUH?
I LIKE IT LIKE THIS.
WHAT ...?

Whaaat!
ITARU-SAN?!
Where are you going?!
RYÔ!
RYÔ!
WHAT?
You're so annoying.
RYÔ!
I'M HURT!
LOOK!
GNN
IT WAS JUST LIKE...

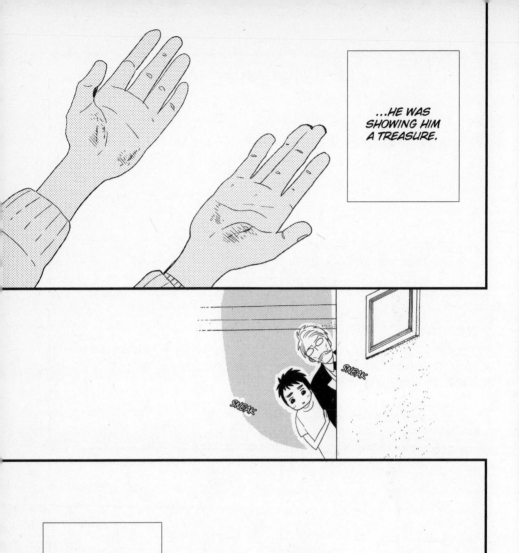

...HE WAS SHOWING HIM A TREASURE.

SNEAK

SNEAK

AND HE WOULD ACCEPT IT.

the end

Translation Notes

I'm a busy man, page 13

Here, Itaru uses the first-person pronoun *ore*, which is a typically masculine way to say "I." As a woman, it is considered rude and inappropriate to refer to the self as *ore*. A Japanese reader would have recognized the masculine speech pattern right away.

If it were a big bottle, page 28

In Japanese host bars and clubs like these, one can order a bottle that is put on hold for a specific patron. The patron can keep coming back to share a drink from the same bottle with their preferred host(s).

Nickie versus Niki, page 28

In the English pronunciation, Itaru's chosen name Nickie sounds like the shorter version, Niki. But in Japanese, the name has an extra syllable. When pronounced in Japanese, it sounds like "nick-key."

Drag princess, page 30

The term used here is *Joso-ko*. It is a made up nickname using the words *josou*, which means to "dress up as a woman" and *-ko*, which is a common ending for girl's names.

Sissy, page 40

In this panel, Itaru is called an *okama*, which is the most commonly used Japanese term referring to gay men. It is not always an insult, for many people self-identify as *okama*, too. The definition itself has changed throughout the years. For example, in the early 2000s, the term connoted more of a gendered performance, not just a specific sexuality or romantic interest. Since then, and today, *okama* has come to refer to people in male-to-male relationships more broadly. But in the context of two children fighting, calling someone an *okama* implies that they must be gay because they are males who are effeminate in personality, character, mannerisms, and speech.

Your face is small, page 73

This is commonly said in Japan of people with beautiful faces, but it doesn't necessarily have to do with the actual size of the face. Often it has more to do with proportions—either of the face itself, or of the face in relation to the body. Having a small face can be a delicate or dainty feature for a woman. It can also refer to having a cute, childlike face.

Bunmeido dorayaki, page 79

Bunmeido is a famous Japanese store that specializes in sweets. Dorayaki is a popular Japanese sweet snack made of two fluffy, circular cakes, with red bean paste in the middle.

That discount store, page 82

Although the original Japanese text erased part of the words, enough of it is left to tell Japanese readers that the thrift store in question is Don Quijote. This chain sells a variety of goods, including groceries.

Dosukoi, page 142

Dosukoi is derived from *dokkoi*, an interjection used when doing heavy labor (something like an "oof!"). This specific pronunciation of *dosukoi* is yelled by sumo wrestlers during a match.

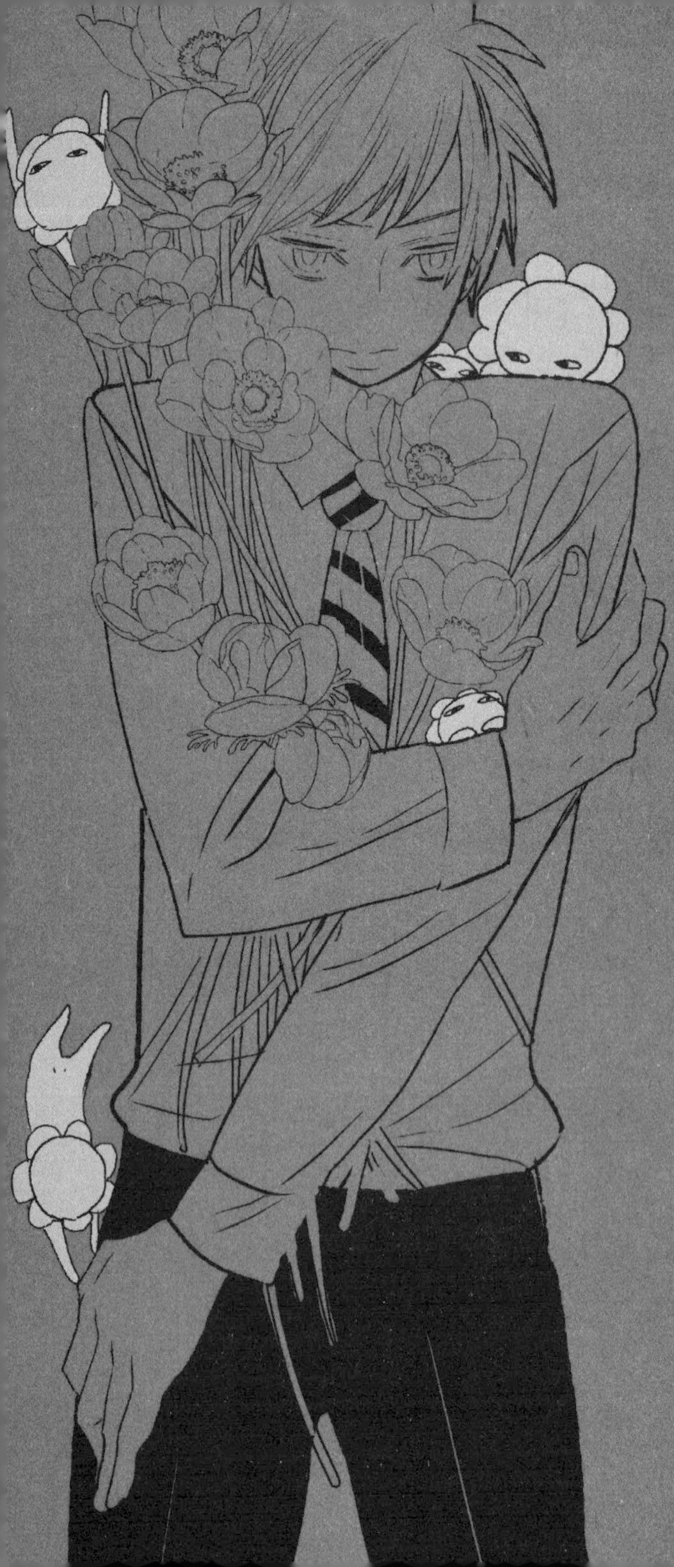

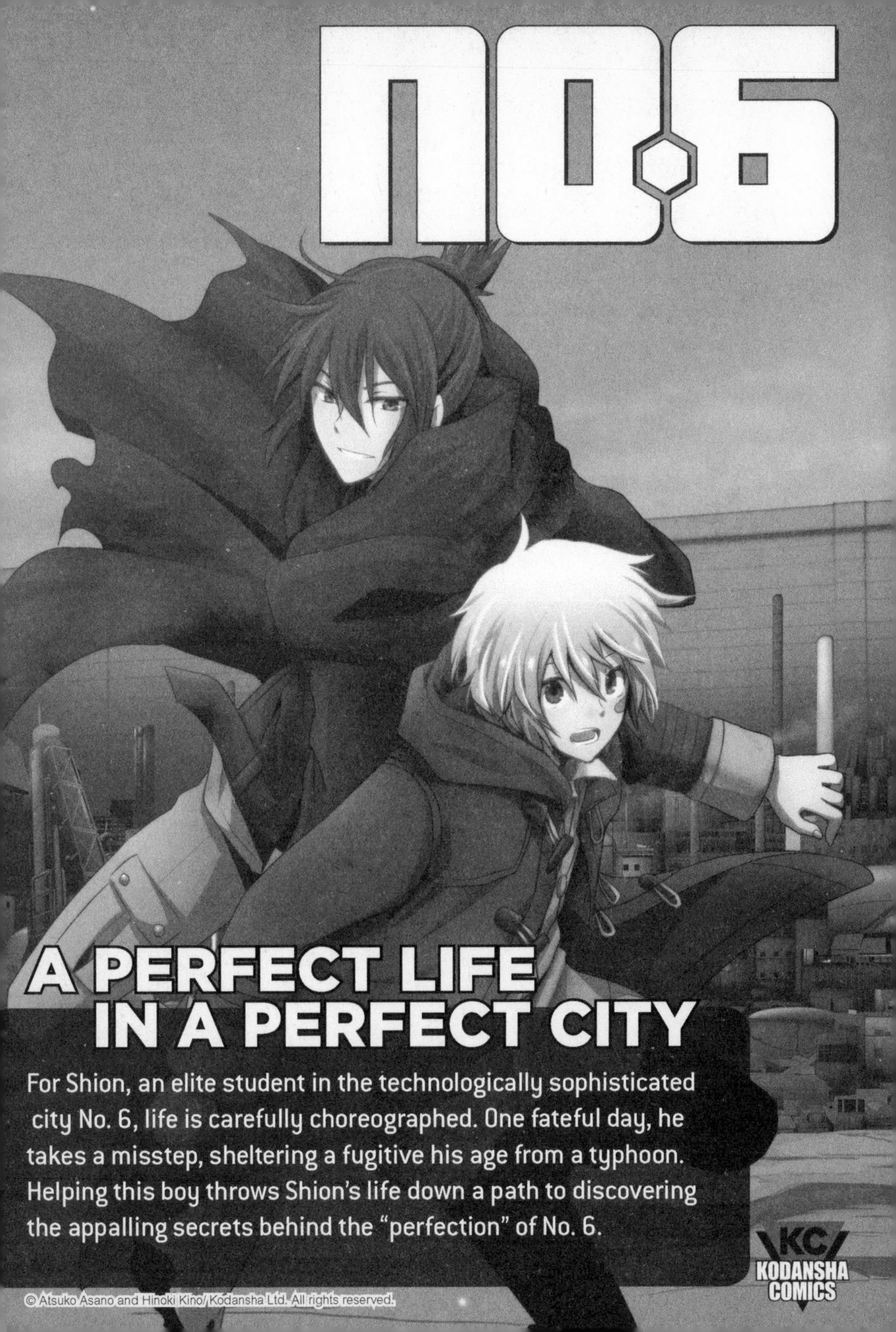
NO.6
A PERFECT LIFE IN A PERFECT CITY
For Shion, an elite student in the technologically sophisticated city No. 6, life is carefully choreographed. One fateful day, he takes a misstep, sheltering a fugitive his age from a typhoon. Helping this boy throws Shion's life down a path to discovering the appalling secrets behind the "perfection" of No. 6.
KC KODANSHA COMICS
© Atsuko Asano and Hinoki Kino/ Kodansha Ltd. All rights reserved.

KC
KODANSHA
COMICS

Mei Tachibana has no friends — and says she doesn't need them!

But everything changes when she accidentally roundhouse kicks the most popular boy in school! However, Yamato Kurosawa isn't angry in the slightest— in fact, he thinks his ordinary life could use an unusual girl like Mei. But winning Mei's trust will be a tough task. How long will she refuse to say, "I love you"?

My Little Monster

OPPOSITES ATTRACT...MAYBE?

Haru Yoshida is feared as an unstable and violent "monster." Mizutani Shizuku is a grade-obsessed student with no friends. Fate brings these two together to form the most unlikely pair. Haru firmly believes he's in love with Mizutani and she firmly believes he's insane.

KC
KODANSHA
COMICS

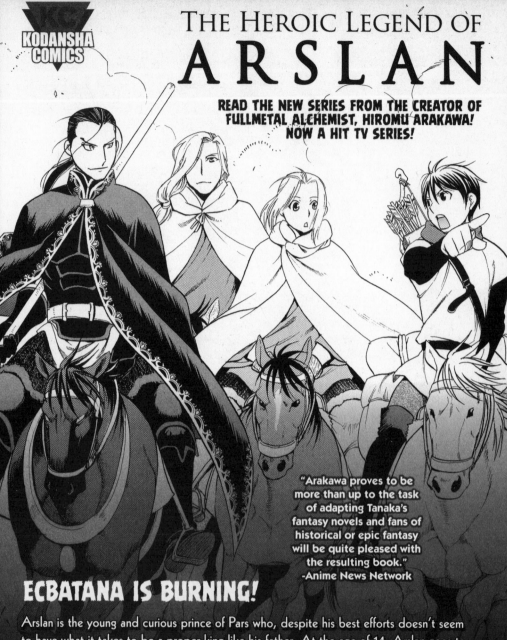

a Silent Voice

KC
KODANSHA COMICS

"The word heartwarming was made for manga like this."
–Manga Book-shelf

"A harsh and biting social commentary... delivers in its depth of character and emotional strength." -Comics Bulletin

"A very powerful story about being different and the consequences of childhood bullying... Read it." –Anime News Network

Shoya is a bully. When Shoko, a girl who can't hear, enters his elementary school class, she becomes their favorite target, and Shoya and his friends goad each other into devising new tortures for her. But the children's cruelty goes too far. Shoko is forced to leave the school, and Shoya ends up shouldering all the blame. Six years later, the two meet again. Can Shoya make up for his past mistakes, or is it too late?

Available now in print and digitally!

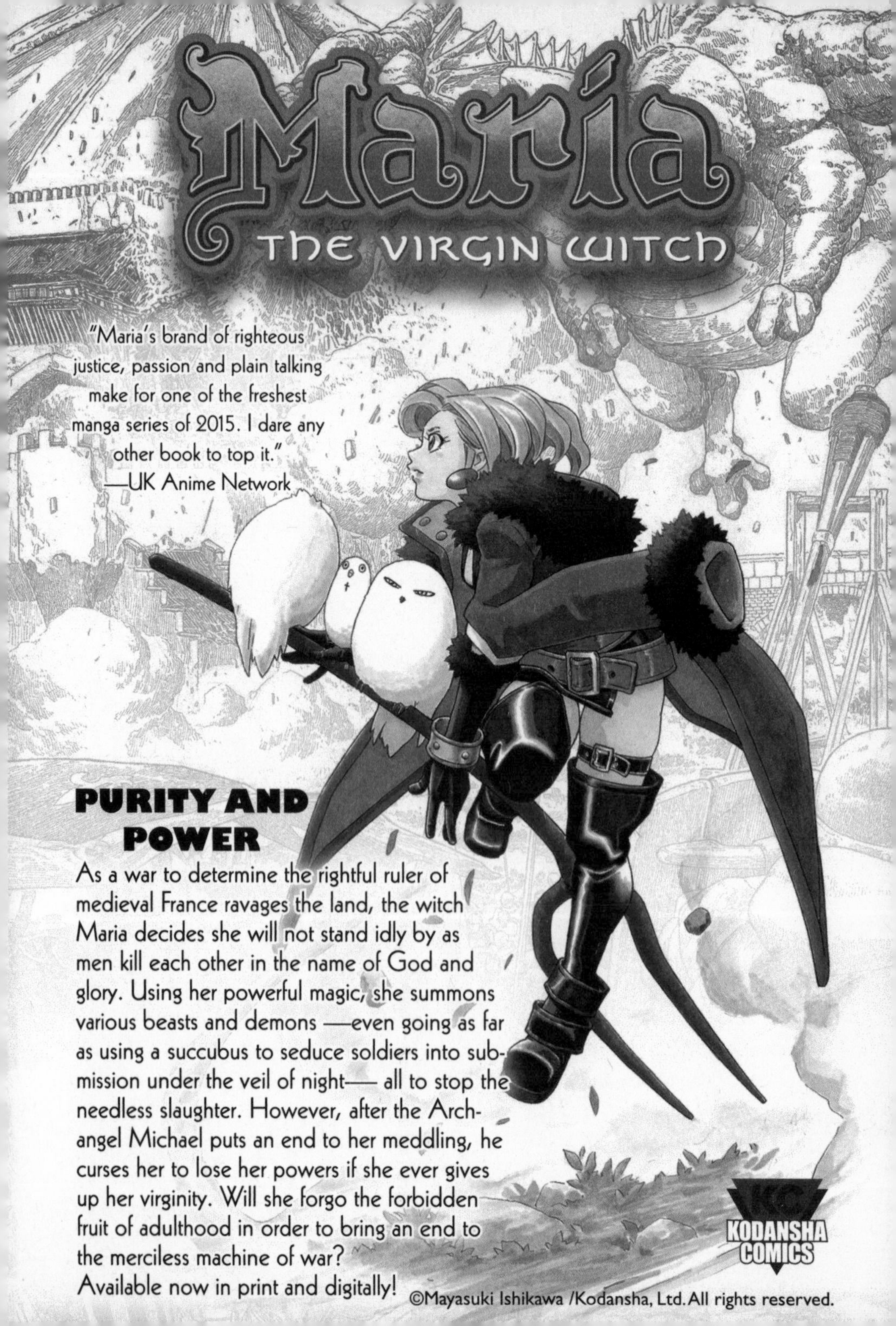
Maria
THE VIRGIN WITCH
"Maria's brand of righteous justice, passion and plain talking make for one of the freshest manga series of 2015. I dare any other book to top it."
—UK Anime Network
PURITY AND POWER
As a war to determine the rightful ruler of medieval France ravages the land, the witch Maria decides she will not stand idly by as men kill each other in the name of God and glory. Using her powerful magic, she summons various beasts and demons —even going as far as using a succubus to seduce soldiers into submission under the veil of night— all to stop the needless slaughter. However, after the Archangel Michael puts an end to her meddling, he curses her to lose her powers if she ever gives up her virginity. Will she forgo the forbidden fruit of adulthood in order to bring an end to the merciless machine of war?
Available now in print and digitally!
KC
KODANSHA COMICS
©Mayasuki Ishikawa /Kodansha, Ltd. All rights reserved.

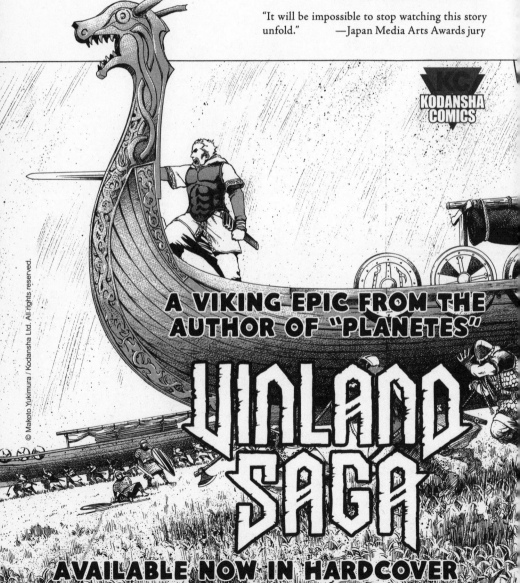

Yamada-kun AND THE Seven Witches

"A very funny manga with a lot of heart and character."
—Adventures in Poor Taste

SWAPPED WITH A KISS?!

Class troublemaker Ryu Yamada is already having a bad day when he stumbles down a staircase along with star student Urara Shiraishi. When he wakes up, he realizes they have switched bodies—and that Ryu has the power to trade places with anyone just by kissing them! Ryu and Urara take full advantage of the situation to improve their lives, but with such an oddly amazing power, just how long will they be able to keep their secret under wraps?

Available now in print and digitally!

KC KODANSHA COMICS

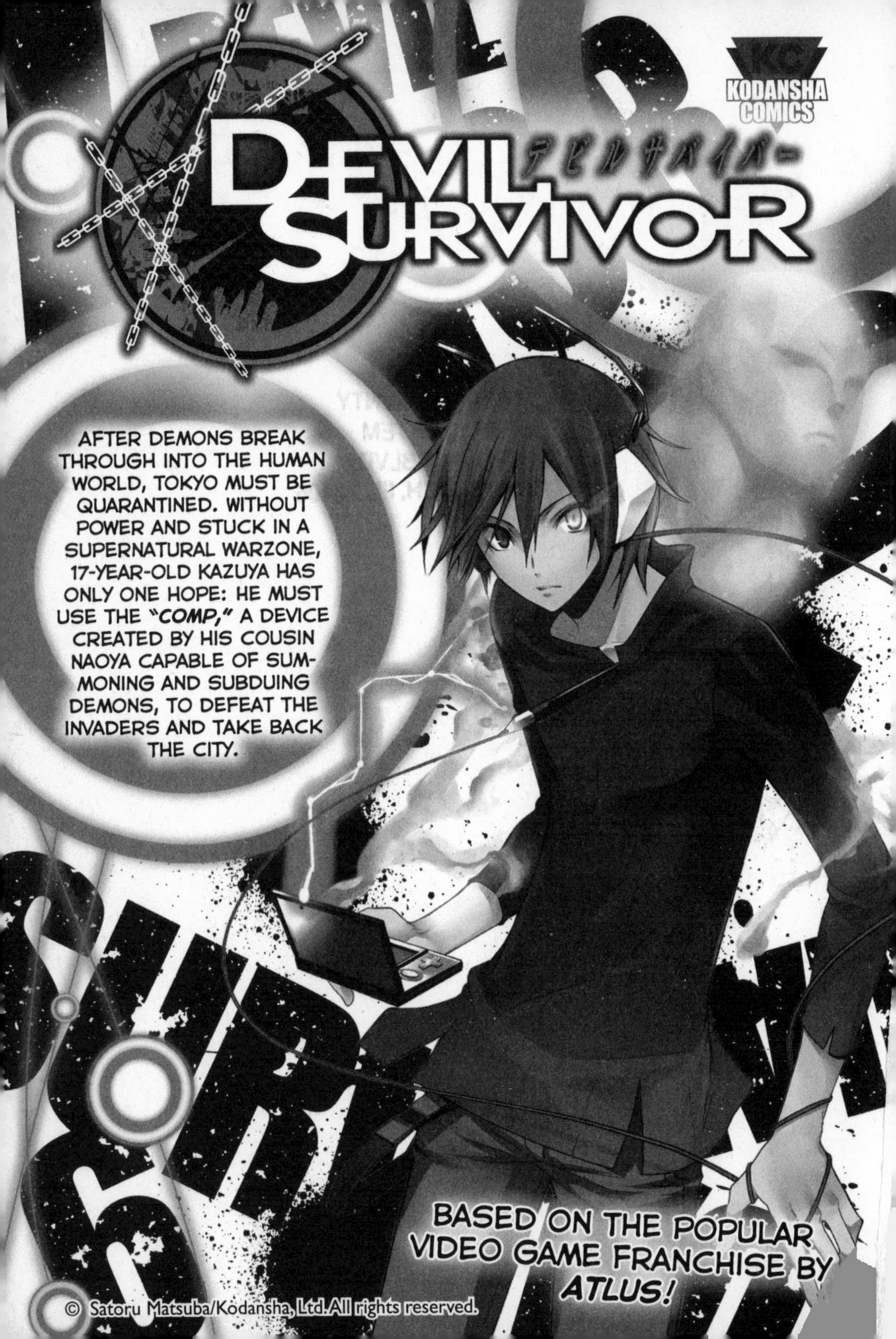
KC
KODANSHA COMICS
DEVIL SURVIVOR
デビルサバイバー
AFTER DEMONS BREAK THROUGH INTO THE HUMAN WORLD, TOKYO MUST BE QUARANTINED. WITHOUT POWER AND STUCK IN A SUPERNATURAL WARZONE, 17-YEAR-OLD KAZUYA HAS ONLY ONE HOPE: HE MUST USE THE "*COMP*," A DEVICE CREATED BY HIS COUSIN NAOYA CAPABLE OF SUMMONING AND SUBDUING DEMONS, TO DEFEAT THE INVADERS AND TAKE BACK THE CITY.
BASED ON THE POPULAR VIDEO GAME FRANCHISE BY *ATLUS!*
© Satoru Matsuba/Kodansha, Ltd. All rights reserved.

The Prince in His Dark Days volume 2 is a work of fiction. Names, characters, places, and incidents are the products of the author's imagination or are used fictitiously. Any resemblance to actual events, locales, or persons, living or dead, is entirely coincidental.

A Kodansha Comics Trade Paperback Original

Published in the United States by Kodansha Comics, an imprint of Kodansha USA Publishing, LLC, New York.

Publication rights for this English edition arranged through Kodansha Ltd, Tokyo.

ISBN 978-1-63236-368-8

Printed in the United States of America.

www.kodanshacomics.com

9 8 7 6 5 4 3 2 1
Translation: Alethea and Athena Nibley
Lettering: Maggie Vicknair
Editing: Haruko Hashimoto
Kodansha Comics edition cover design by Phil Balsman